MYSTERIES

OF THE

KABBALAH

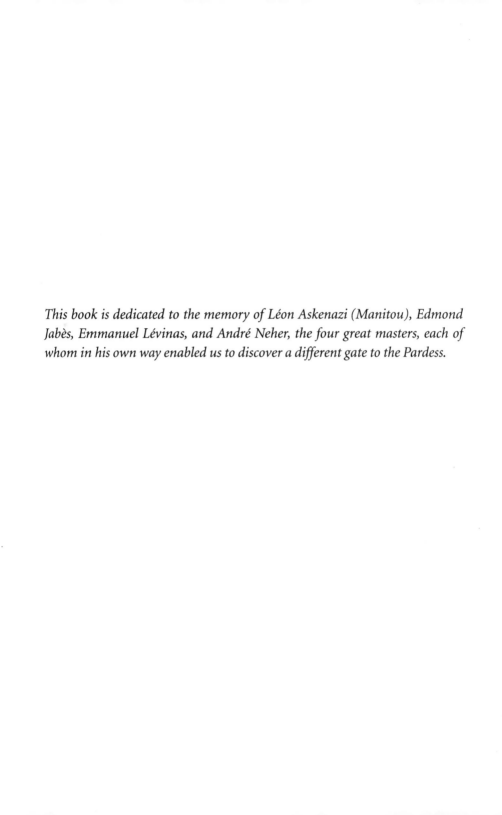

This book is dedicated to the memory of Léon Askenazi (Manitou), Edmond Jabès, Emmanuel Lévinas, and André Neher, the four great masters, each of whom in his own way enabled us to discover a different gate to the Pardess.

Mysteries of the Kabbalah

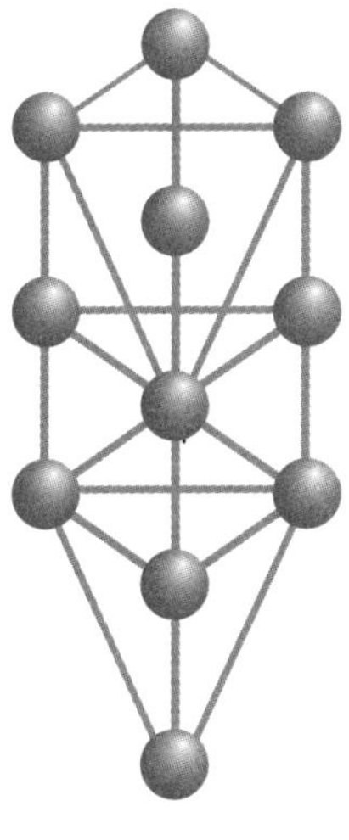

Marc-Alain Ouaknin

Translated from the French by Josephine Bacon

ABBEVILLE PRESS PUBLISHERS
New York London Paris

CONTENTS

Part Five

THE HORSES OF FIRE ה

Part Six

GEMATRIA ו

Part Seven

THE NAMES OF GOD ז

The Kabbalah is first and foremost a lesson in living.
It does not aspire to make man good.
It merely hopes that one day he will become better.

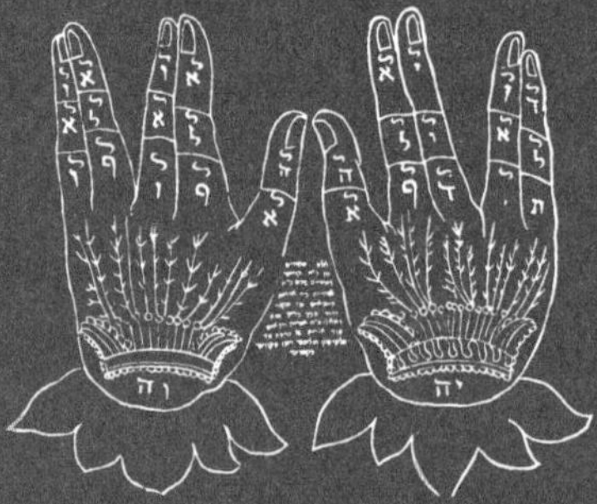

Introduction
The Tree of Light

Two eyes.
Two ears.
Two maxims.
One mouth.
One face.
Seven lights to illuminate the world.
Seven worlds to receive the light.
The Zohar

What is an angel?

What is the hidden structure of the universe?

How can the secret codes of the Bible
be deciphered?

How can one ascend by degrees
through the different levels of the soul?

Why is the number 13 a way
of expressing love?

Is there life after death?

Is the Kabbalah also a form
of healing?

Can one study the Kabbalah on one's own,
or must one meet a master?

Does one have to be a Jew to gain access to the
secrets of the Kabbalah?

What are the basic texts
of the Kabbalah?

What does the mysterious book,
entitled the *Zohar*, contain?

Rabbi Simeon began to weep, saying: "Woe is me if I reveal these mysteries and woe is me if I do not reveal them."
Zohar (III, 127b)

Definition of the Kabbalah

The word *Kabbalah* designates the mysteries of the Jewish mystic tradition.

The Kabbalah is both theoretical philosophy and a practice close to that of meditation. It is a path to spiritual elevation, a mystique.

The tradition of the Kabbalah was originally transmitted orally from master to disciples, from Adam through to Moses, by means of Abraham, Isaac, Jacob, and Joseph, and was then transcribed, codified, and commented upon in works such as the Pentateuch, the Books of the Prophets, and other texts, of which the most important were written in the Holy Land between the first and fourth centuries C.E. and in Spain between the eighth and the fifteenth centuries. (See the full history of the Kabbalah in part 1; these books are still difficult to access in the original, even though some of them have been published in good translations.)

The Kabbalah embraces an immense, detailed, and consistent vision of man's relationship with the universe. It contains metaphysical discourses of extraordinary power, combined with specific methods to help us go beyond our normal level of consciousness and discover another light, deep within ourselves, that will lead us far beyond the commonplace of our daily life. Its origins are lost in the mists of time.

It is emerging ever more clearly that since its birth about four thousand years ago, Judaism has always possessed an esoteric side. This way of approaching the divine is sometimes deeply buried, exercising a hidden, barely discernible force. In other periods of Jewish history it has blossomed and flourished and captivated almost whole generations.

The Word *Kabbalah*

The word *kabbalah* comes from the Hebrew *qabbalah*. It is derived from the verb *leqabbel*, whose root is *qbl*, "to receive or welcome." *Kabbalah* thus means "receiving" or "reception."

The most correct Hebrew transliteration of the word is *qabbalah*. Since there is no universally accepted form of Hebrew transliteration into the Latin alphabet, however, and the sound represented in the Latin alphabet as "q" has a "k" sound in Hebrew, authors and translators of kabbalistic works have used a variety of spellings, including *Qabbalah, Cabbalah, Cabalah,* and *Kabalah*. The form normally used is "Kabbalah," so this is the spelling that has been adopted.

The Kabbalah: A Way of Life

The roots of Judaism lie in the text of the Bible, whose concrete, revealed form presents the exoteric side of the religion. The secret, unrevealed tradition constitutes its esoteric side. It is the whole of this hidden, secret dimension, which can be summarized as esoteric, that constitutes the Kabbalah.

The Kabbalah contains two separate approaches: the hermeneutic approach and the mystical approach. The Kabbalah presents itself first as a mystical commentary on the text of the Bible. It is thus above all a learning tool for interpreting biblical texts and the world, the art of unraveling mysteries. This approach to the Kabbalah is termed hermeneutics; in it the Kabbalah is an art of listening to voices from elsewhere, from the great symphony of the celestial spheres to the humble prayer of wet grass and wayside trees, via the rhythm of human hearts, discreet sonatas of tenderness and love.

This music is also an inner light because in the truly mystical sense, the Kabbalah has a more specific meaning, closer to its etymological origin: it is the act of receiving or attaining the light of the infinite, and the whole range of techniques and methods that make it possible to receive it.

To summarize:

- The Kabbalah is the mystical tradition of Judaism, which is presented like a coded commentary to the text of the Bible.
- The Kabbalah thus constitutes an anthology of techniques for reading and deciphering these texts, so as to reveal and make known its secrets.
- The Kabbalah is the receipt of wisdom from on high.
- Through listening to the soundless and seeing the invisible, the Kabbalah retains the ability to receive the light of the infinite.
- The Kabbalah is a set of practices, prayers, rites, and meditations that enable man to elevate himself to a higher intellectual and spiritual plane.

The Kabbalah Is Not a Doctrine but a Power

Let me begin with a story told by Gershom Scholem at the end of his book *Major Trends in Jewish Mysticism*:

> When the Baal Shem Tov, Master of the Good Name and founder of Hassidism, had a difficult task before him or saw a misfortune about to befall the Jewish people, he went to meditate in a certain part of the forest; there, he lit a fire, lost himself in prayer and what he had decided to do became possible: the miracle was performed, the misfortune was removed.
>
> A generation later, when his disciple, the Maggid of Mezeritch, had to intervene with the Heavens for the same reason, he would go to the same place in the forest and say: "Master of the Universe, hear me. I no longer know how to light the fire, but I am still capable of saying the prayer."
>
> And the miracle was performed yet again.
>
> In the following generation, in order to save his people, Rabbi Moshe Lev of Sassov also went into the forest and said: "I do not know to light the fire, I do not know the prayer, but I remember the place and that ought to be enough."
>
> And it was enough.
>
> Then it was the turn of Rabbi Israel of Rijine to lift the threat. He sat in his gilded chair within his castle, put his head in his hands and addressed God in these terms: "Master of the World, I am incapable of lighting the fire, I do not know the prayer, I cannot even find the place in the forest. All that I know how to do is to tell this story, that ought to be enough."
>
> And yet again, the miracle was peformed.

It is now our turn to assume the infinite responsibility of continuing to transmit the spark, the fire, the history of the narrative.

The city has replaced the forest, the library has become our castle, but the Kabbalah still lives. In our turn, we want to become the children and the disciples, not only of the Baal Shem Tov but also of all the masters who since ancient times have meditated, studied, and succeeded in transmitting the light, the fire, and the brilliance of a thought and an experience that makes man feel that his life has a purpose and that living is a constant upward movement.

The Kabbalah is not a doctrine but a force, a breath of life that constantly reminds man that his perfection resides in his perfectibility. The Kabbalah is, first and foremost, a lesson in life. It does not aspire to make man good. It merely hopes that one day he will become better.

Of course, the Kabbalah has a history. It has a beginning, a development, a literature, a folklore, and a cast of legendary characters. But its strength lies in life and not in what might become of its ideology. In every age, the Kabbalah and the masters who have contributed to its creation have changed not only Jewish thought but the whole climate and quality of Jewish existence. Without the words of the Kabbalah, without its songs and its disciples, without the power of their appeal, without the dizzying dance of thought and the body, what would Judaism have become?

Strange as it may seem, the Kabbalah is not an exclusively "religious" phenomenon. It is a way of being, characterized by an excess of vitality and vivacity, by another way of existing in the world, one that is more open to and aware of the miracle of life.

The Kabbalah is the marvel of feeling the continuous vibration of the world, feeling that everything has a meaning, that there is no "area of indifference," no "dead time" or down time. It is the joy of living and enthusiasm of creating something. . . .

In a nutshell, the Kabbalah is a window on the world, on God, and on mankind. It is a magnificent universe that has its own philosophy of life. It is thus a whole range of ways in which each individual is enabled to expand, to develop his capacities and to tell of the unique vocation that it brings. The Kabbalah is thus a philosophy and practice of living. It is neither speculative nor practical, but both of these at the same time—otherwise it is not the true Kabbalah.

The practice of the Kabbalah centers around such focal points as prayer, meditation, certain breathing and chanting rituals, dancing, and a new way of experiencing and perceiving sensations. The practice of the Kabbalah is also a way of behaving toward oneself and toward other people. It involves learning calmness and serenity, the generosity of time that one can offer to another person, or merely a smile or a word. It is thus a quest for harmony and well-being, for oneself and within the human race.

Man can attain this flowering through studying the structure of what has been called "primitive man," or *adam qadmon*. The structure is that of the ten *sefirot*, the ten fundamental principles through which man can attain balance and perfection.

Within this balance, the kabbalist can embark upon the way of light and the path of rectitude.

"Love of Wisdom" and "Wisdom of Love"

> ***A kabbalist is someone whom one probably knows little about, but who tries to know as much as possible about himself.***
> —A. D. Grad, *Le Temps des kabbalistes*

Method is least of the priorities of the Kabbalah. It is not the technical aspect but the spirit that is the most important. The Kabbalah is not merely a science but an art, the art of the heart and of knowing how to love. It requires a certain skill of the heart that is difficult to acquire; a savant should also try to be one of the just. Science is not enough in the Kabbalah; love is also needed.

Where philosophy ends, Rabbi Nachman of Breslov teaches, the Kabbalah begins. This can be understood as meaning that the Kabbalah is the true balance between the love of wisdom and the wisdom of love.

A Seven-Branched Tree of Light

Before "primitive man" can be defined, the analytic tools and the ground plan around which this analysis is organized and deployed must be explained.

For the sake of clarity, the book has been divided into seven sections, represented by the symbol of the menorah ("tree of light"), the seven-branched candelabrum that stood at the center of the sanctuary in the Temple in Jerusalem. It is through this symbol that the higher and the lower, the infinite and the finite, the Creator and the creature, are able to meet.

The first part, or first light, entitled "Kabbalah and the Kabbalists," defines the Kabbalah, its history, its various approaches, its specific language, and the ways in which it is transmitted.

The second part explains "The Ground Plan of the Kabbalah," a very simple plan that organizes the universe in vertical relationships between the worlds above, the source of light and life, and the multiple worlds of creation, or worlds below, that receive this light. The whole of the Kabbalah is based on an understanding of this scheme of things and the internal dynamics at work between these two focal points, which make possible the giving and receiving of "light-life-energy."

The third part, "The Colloquy of Angels," takes us into the mystical world of the depths of the soul and of the intermediate worlds that are the angels. It is here that we will explain the five modes or conditions of the soul, the hierarchy and function of the angels, the adventures of the soul, and metempsychosis, and suggest certain meditation exercises.

The fourth part, "The Ten *Sefirot,*" presents the structure of the various worlds of which primitive man consists. Ten modalities, ten ways of being, called the *sefirot* ("spheres"), are also the steps enabling man to ascend or descend the ladder between earth and heaven. We have also devoted a chapter to the kabbalistic metaphor of the tree.

The fifth part is entitled "The Horses of Fire." For the Kabbalah, the world was created with the letters of the alphabet. These are at the center of any relationship in the world. Living is knowing how to read, decipher, and interpret the texts. To do this, we will explain the meaning of the letters of the alphabet, their power, and their role in the process of the liberation of the soul and the healing of the body. It will thus also be a question of the relationship between psychoanalysis and the Kabbalah, and between the Kabbalah and therapy in general.

Kabbalah and the Kabbalists
The Ground Plan of the Kabbalah
The Colloquy of Angels
The Ten *Sefirot*
The Horses of Fire
Gematria
The Names of God

The sixth part, "Gematria," is an extension of the fifth and deals with a particular, but fundamental, property of the Hebrew language: each letter also represents a number, a phenomenon called gematria, or the art of making numbers speak. In this part, we will explain the various methods of this strange numerology and its applications in the art of numbering and deciphering texts.

This mystical meditation on and special interest in numbers can be found in philosophers outside kabbalism, such as Pythagoras, and in other schools of thought. We shall demonstrate the reciprocal influences between these schools of thought and the Kabbalah, thus emphasizing the importance of the richness of interdisciplinary exchanges of ideas.

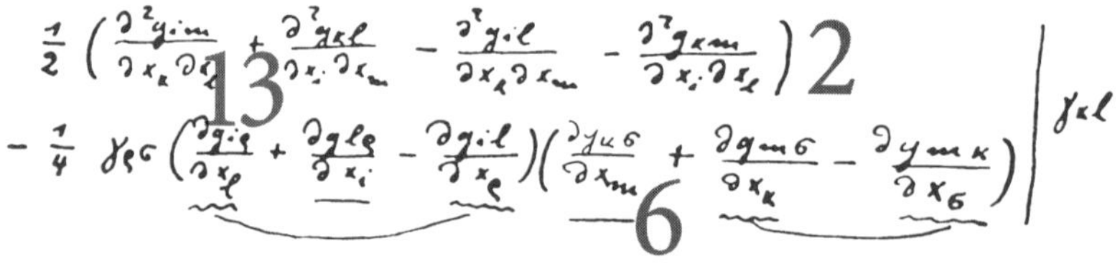

The seventh part combines, in one harmony of contemplation, the previous concerns into a meditation that becomes the absolute center of the Kabbalah: "the Names of God," and in particular the ineffable tetragrammaton YHVH. This four-letter name of God is never spoken aloud. It is a name, a number, and a "tree of light" simultaneously, through which all the energy necessary for maintaining creation is transmitted.

Thus, after explaining the ground plan and the three paths of light—spheres, letters, and numbers—we shall dedicate the last light of the tree to the secret names of God, and especially the tetragrammaton and its complex dynamics.

The book can be read from cover to cover or delved into here and there, as if on a hike or ramble of varying degrees of difficulty. Do not be afraid of failing to understand, leaving the text and thought to pass on to another chapter or section.

As in previous books by this author, references are made to texts in the Hebraic tradition as well the Eastern, Far Eastern, and Western philosophic and literary traditions, classical and contemporary. The reader should thus not be surprised to encounter in the course of the text a quotation from Gaston Bachelard, Christian Bobin, Lao-tzu, Emmanuel Lévinas, Rainer Maria Rilke, or Friedrich Nietzsche. Like the Bible, the Kabbalah is not a book but a vast library that is the fount and inspiration of the power of the word.

The following chapters contain some basic signposts that will enable the reader to explore the world of this library, to find his way on the wind-erased roads of the desert, to wander in the mountains of Galilee, to participate in an experience of meditation with some surprising masters in a remote forest in the Carpathians, to become lost on the benches of a house of study or a Talmudic academy in Babylonia, to rest in the shade of a commentary in a cool alleyway in Spain, in Safed, or in a shady street in Jerusalem. . . .

Enjoy your journey.

Part One

א

Kabbalah and the Kabbalists

1

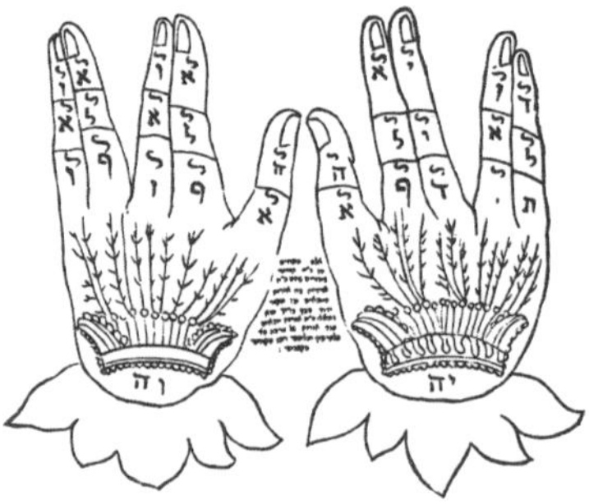
וה
יה

1

A Short History of the Kabbalah

Rabbi Hanina teaches: "I have learned much from my masters, even more from my fellow scholars, but it is from my own students that I have learned the most."
—Talmud, Taanit (7a)

The Need for an Historical Overview of the Kabbalah

The Kabbalah, like every book of knowledge, has a history, an evolution of ideas and masters that are illustrated in this knowledge. We believe that it is important to learn the history of the Kabbalah, even if it is only through a brief overview, to understand how the thoughts contained therein interlock through the dynamic of commentary.

Although this work emphasizes the existentialist aspect of the Kabbalah, we must study its history to gain an in-depth insight into the knowledge it imparts. The academic approach initiated by the major studies of Gershom Scholem and his students takes a more specific and more scholarly approach to the various currents of the Kabbalah, and it is one worth pursuing. Thanks to these researchers, the historical aspects of the Kabbalah, the multiple forces that shaped it, and the development of this branch of knowledge are now better understood. It is almost a century since

Scholem first published the writings of the great kabbalists of the past, thus granting us direct access to those sources and documents, and preventing the Kabbalah from remaining secondhand thought, a mere rumor.

There is more and more evidence for the assertion that the Kabbalah is an organic whole, its various periods merely moments when a particular aspect of the doctrine gradually revealed itself. It is not that there were different Kabbalot, but rather different moments of its revelation. That is why one can speak of periods or, more accurately, phases.

For this reason, the periods or phases will be dealt with by following the historic deployment of kabbalistic teachings from the beginning of the Talmud to the present day. For the purpose of a historic study, nothing has ever been written to outshine Gershom Scholem's *Major Trends in Jewish Mysticism,* even if one disagrees with one or two of the points it makes. Although Scholem was not the only scholar researching the history of the Kabbalah, he was the most influential; only now, and for the past twenty years or so, is a new generation of researchers emerging, though their numbers remain small, and all those who have written on the subject since Scholem have merely adopted the outlines, with various modifications, of his outstanding work. Most of the younger scholars were among Scholem's students. They have specialized in a specific trend or point of doctrine, or have concentrated on a particular author; their work is important because it builds on previous research and offers new tools and new perspectives.

One such researcher is Moshe Idel, the greatest living specialist in the work of Abraham Abulafia and the ecstatic Kabbalah, whose work is summarized in his book *The Kabbalah: New Perspectives.* Charles Mopsik, another major researcher in the science of the Kabbalah, has studied the texts of the Zohar and the works of Rabbi Moses of Leon and Rabbi Joseph Gikatillia. He has produced a brilliant new translation of the Zohar into French, published by Editions Verdier, as well as studies and publications of unknown manuscripts by the masters who lived during the Golden Age of Spain. Other researchers have concentrated on the works of Rabbi Moses Cordovero, Rabbi Isaac Luria, and others. Their publications are too numerous to list in full here, but the reader will find a comprehensive list, with most of the works translated into English, in the bibliography of this book.

Moroccan Jewish representation of Rabbi Simeon Bar Yokhai holding a scroll entitled *Sefer Zohar Ha-Qadosh* ("Holy Book of the Zohar"). Every Friday evening, Moroccan Jews sing a hymn entitled "Bar Yokhai" in honor of Rabbi Simeon.

Theurgical Kabbalah and Ecstatic Kabbalah

The distinction between the theurgical and the ecstatic Kabbalah, originally proposed by Moshe Idel, is essential for anyone who wants to learn the history and understand the meaning of the Kabbalah. Moshe Idel suggests avoiding a purely linear history; through a phenomenological description he attempts to present the essential aspects of the Kabbalah, which he has classified into these two major trends. In the introduction to his important work *The Kabbalah: New Perspectives,* he emphasizes this distinction and outlines the Kabbalah's two major trends—the "theosophical-theurgic" and the "ecstatic."

The first trend embraces two major subjects: **theosophy**, a theory of the complex structure of the world of the divine; and **theurgy**, a set of ritual or meditative rites, a set of experiences that make it possible to achieve a state of harmony with the Divinity or to affect his relationship with man. In this respect, Charles Mopsik has expanded on the Kabbalah's theurgical mysticism in *Les Grands Textes de la Kabbalah.*

The second trend is directed more toward meditative experiences to enable a human being to ascend and approach, or even join with, the Divinity. The key word of the ecstatic Kabbalah is *devekut,* meaning "cleaving" or "clinging" through ecstasy. In order to achieve this ecstasy-*devekut* or elevation of the soul, several methods of meditation can be adopted, the most frequently used being the manipulation of figures and letters, prayer, incantation, the combination of the letters of the Holy Name, the visualization of certain colors, and in certain cases, the "weeping."

In this present work, the two trends are intimately linked. We believe that the traditional kabbalist possesses attitudes that can sometimes be defined as theosophical-theurgical and at other times ecstatic, without himself really differentiating between these two attitudes. The distinction remains interesting in itself, however, for the analysis of situations and their classification.

The spice box used during the Havdalah ceremony at the end of the Sabbath, to mark the passage between the holy day and the other days of the week.

Theoretical Kabbalah and Practical Kabbalah

In *Les Etincelles du hasard,* Henri Atlan adds another distinction:

> In these present times when irrationality has reconquered lost ground and occupies the various media in one form or another, peaceful or violent—peaceful in the form of drawing-room astrology or that of the television set, violent among religious fanatics—it is not surprising that the Kabbalah is making a return in force, associated as it now is with astrology, magic, the tarot and other occult pseudosciences, as well as among certain fundamentalist and/or messianic trends in Orthodox Judaism. It is consequently all the more important to emphasize the classic distinction between the so-called speculative Kabbalah *('iyyunit)* and the philosophical Kabbalah, which is of interest to us here as a research tradition which has something in common with neoplatonism and stoicism . . . and the so-called practical Kabbalah *(ma'assit),* which today feeds superstitions and eschatological delusions. [The distinction between the ecstatic or prophetic Kabbalah and the theurgical Kabbalah] is more the result of an external comparative analysis than a genuine separation between the kabbalistic doctrines in which more often than not it is a case of nuances of emphasis. On the contrary, the distinction between the speculative Kabbalah and the practical Kabbalah has become much more profound since modern science and critical philosophy established a clean break with pre-scientific knowledge and practices of the *Magia Naturalis.* The speculative or philosophical Kabbalah is the traditional subject of research among the "students of the sages" *(talmidei khakhamim),* the talmudic academies, and the "lovers of wisdom," *philosophers* of Antiquity. The axiological vision is incapable of separation from the quest for rational intelligibility but it is cognizant of the

חוספי הרא"ש שמאי פרק ראשון נדה ב עין משפט נר מצוה

שמאי

אומר כל הנשים דיין שעתן הלל אומר מפקידה לפקידה ואפילו לימים הרבה וחכ"א לא כדברי זה ולא כדברי זה אלא מעת לעת ממעטת על יד מפקידה לפקידה ומפקידה לפקידה ממעטת על יד מעת לעת כל אשה שיש לה וסת דיה שעתה והמשמשת בעדים הרי זו כפקידה וממעטת על יד מעת לעת ועל יד מפקידה לפקידה כיצד דיה שעתה היתה יושבת במטה ועסוקה בטהרות ופרשה וראתה היא טמאה והן טהורות אע"פ שאמרו מטמאה מעת לעת אינה מונה אלא משעה שראתה: גמ' מאי טעמיה דשמאי קסבר העמד אשה על חזקתה ואשה בחזקת טהורה עומדת והלל כי אמר העמד דבר על חזקתו היכא דלית ליה ריעותא מגופיה אבל איתתא כיון

First page of the Talmudic tractate *Nidda*.

> sciences and in dialogue with them. Practical Kabbalah, on the other hand, is merely . . . an additional source of superstitious beliefs with which to fuel obscurantist and fundamentalist passions. [We] can and must stigmatize and rail against those "kabbalists" who persist in using an esoteric jargon without placing it within the context of the various reworkings of the text and the philosophical and scientific achievements of the age in which it was written. The lure of mystery and the occult make it possible to sell superstition, talismen, astrological and numerological predictions, palmistry and so on, en masse. Fake kabbalism exists in the same way as cheap Buddhism, in which the exoticism of the vocabulary attempts in vain to conceal the absence of thought behind it.

Ethical Kabbalah and Existential Kabbalah

The present work proposes a new formulation of the Kabbalah that repeats and pursues the various orientations presented previously, but continues to emphasize the existential and ethical dimension. The result is thus not a purely "*'iyyunit*-speculative" Kabbalah because it has an aspect that is "*ma'assit*-practical," namely that of the change in a person who can learn through the Kabbalah to change himself, to become different, better, to become open to creativity in study and through study, to invent new forms of existence and discover paths that lead ever onward and upward.

The Limitations of the Historical Approach

The historical approach to the texts is a method that is in danger of considering the past as belonging solely to history. The past only becomes intelligible via the learned and critical mediation of the historian.

The historian tries, for example to find, reconstitute, and understand the life led by the Hebrews in the desert, Jewish life in Talmudic times, and so forth. The historian shows how Jewish language, clothing, and living space were borrowed from the Greek or Roman world; the philologist indulges in the deciphering of words with Persian, Greek, or Latin consonances, giving him the opportunity of revealing the rapprochements or distances in customs, mentalities, and myths. As regards the Kabbalah, one can detect the influences of Neoplatonism, the Albigensians, or the Sufis on certain kabbalists, and establish a rapprochement with other mystics. But the historian remains aloof from a desire and effort to become familiar with the texts and traditions. He finds it difficult to see himself as the person to whom the text is addressed, and to submit to the demands of a text, as this might interfere with the objectivity of a researcher. He is probably right. But is it really possible to remove oneself and to be a mere machine, reading and interpreting? If any interpretation is made, this automatically implies subjectivity on the part of the interpreter!

Our own approach—which obviously does not reject the light thrown on the subject by history—chooses, where possible, genuine involvement and an attempt at an existential interpretation of the text we have read and studied.

The Eight Periods of the Kabbalah

That we have distanced ourselves from a purely historical approach does not mean that we should fail to mention the major lines of the successive stages of the Kabbalah. The historians of the Kabbalah—particularly Gershom Scholem in *Major Trends in Jewish Mysticism,* as previously discussed—define several periods, phases, or schools. These divisions clarify the teaching of the complex universe that constitutes the Kabbalah.

The history of the Kabbalah can be divided into eight basic periods.

The first period is the mysticism of the *merkava* (Kabbalah of the heavenly chariot) and of the *ma'asseh bereshit* (Kabbalah interested in the structure of the creation of the world). These two trends are still called "mysticism of the Talmud." The period extends from the second century B.C.E. to the twelfth century C.E., and encompasses the *Sifrut Ha-Hekhalot* ("Kabbalah of Palace Literature"); the *Sefer Yetsira* ("Book of Creation"); and the first commentators on the books of the Kabbalah.

The second period, which only covers one century (ca. 1200–1300 C.E.), consists of three main schools: one in Provence, in the south of France; another in Germany, or more specially at Worms; and the third in Spain. This period saw the emergence of the *Sefer Ha-Bahir* ("Book of Clar-

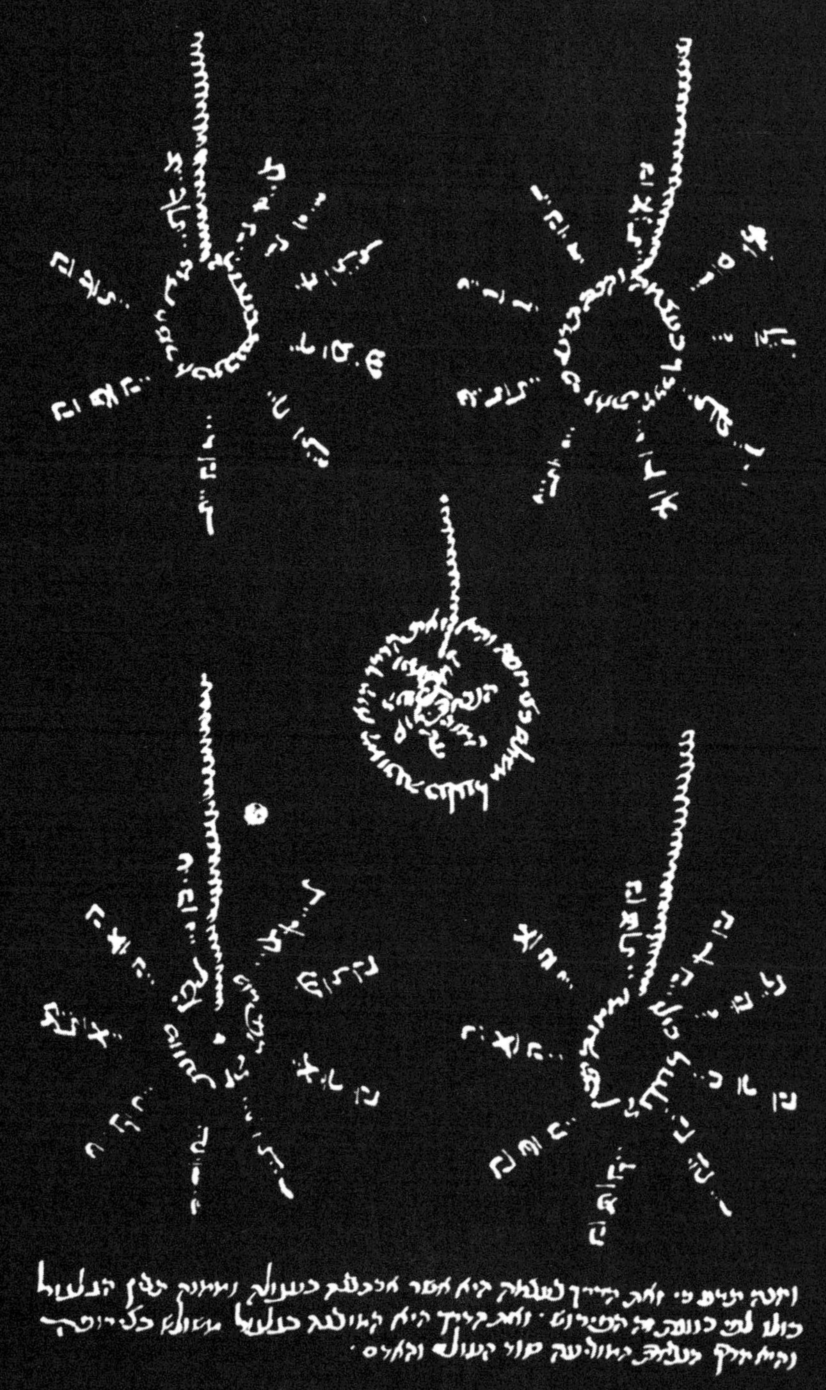

Manuscript of *Khayei Olam Ha-Ba* [Life of the World to Come] by Rabbi Abraham Abulafia (1280). The letters are arranged in circles which the kabbalist is supposed to spin in his head in order to achieve ecstasy.

ity") and the *Sefer Ha-Hasidim* ("Book of the Devout Men"), to name the best known. It was the time of such great masters as Isaac the Blind, Ezra of Gerona, the person called Azriel, Nachmanides, and several members of the Kalonymos family of Mainz, to say nothing of the first works by Rabbi Abraham Abulafia and his disciple Rabbi Joseph Gikatillia (ca. 1245–1300).

The third period, almost contemporaneous with the second, started in Spain around the compilation of one of the most important books of the Kabbalah, the *Sefer Ha-Zohar* ("The Book of Splendor"), known as the Zohar. This work, which appeared in Spain ca. 1280–1300, is one of the most remarkable in the tradition of Jewish mysticism. It was published by Moses of Leon (1250–1305) under the name of the great Rabbi Simeon Bar Yokhai, who had lived in the second century, shortly after the destruction of the Second Temple in Jerusalem. The Zohar is written in an exalted Aramaic style and contains a fascinating mixture of the metaphysical, mythical cosmogony and esoteric psychology. It immediately aroused a passionate interest in kabbalists and nonkabbalists alike.

This was also the period of the flowering of the ecstatic and prophetic Kabbalah of Rabbi Abraham Abulafia, whose subsequent influence was so powerful.

The fourth period, which extends over more than two hundred years (right up to the end of the seventeenth century), is linked to one of the greatest traumas of Jewish history, the expulsion of the Jews of Spain in 1492.

Numerous Spanish masters and those of Spanish origin had sought refuge in the Land of Israel, especially in a small town in Galilee called Safed. A school for kabbalism was founded there that took the name of "New Kabbalah" or "Kabbalah of Safed," whose most illustrious masters were Rabbi Moses Cordovero, Rabbi Solomon Alkabets, Rabbi Joseph Caro, and the most famous of all, Rabbi Isaac Luria (1534–1572) and his disciple Rabbi Hayyim Vital. This Kabbalah presented itself both as a continuation and a commentary on the Zohar, with an insistence on the meaning of the *sefirot* and the adventures of the divine presence *(shekhina),* on not only a cosmic but a historical level, in relation to the events of the expulsion from Spain. The key works of the period are *Pardess Rimonim* ("The Pomegranate Orchard") by Rabbi Moses Cordovero, Cordovero's commen-

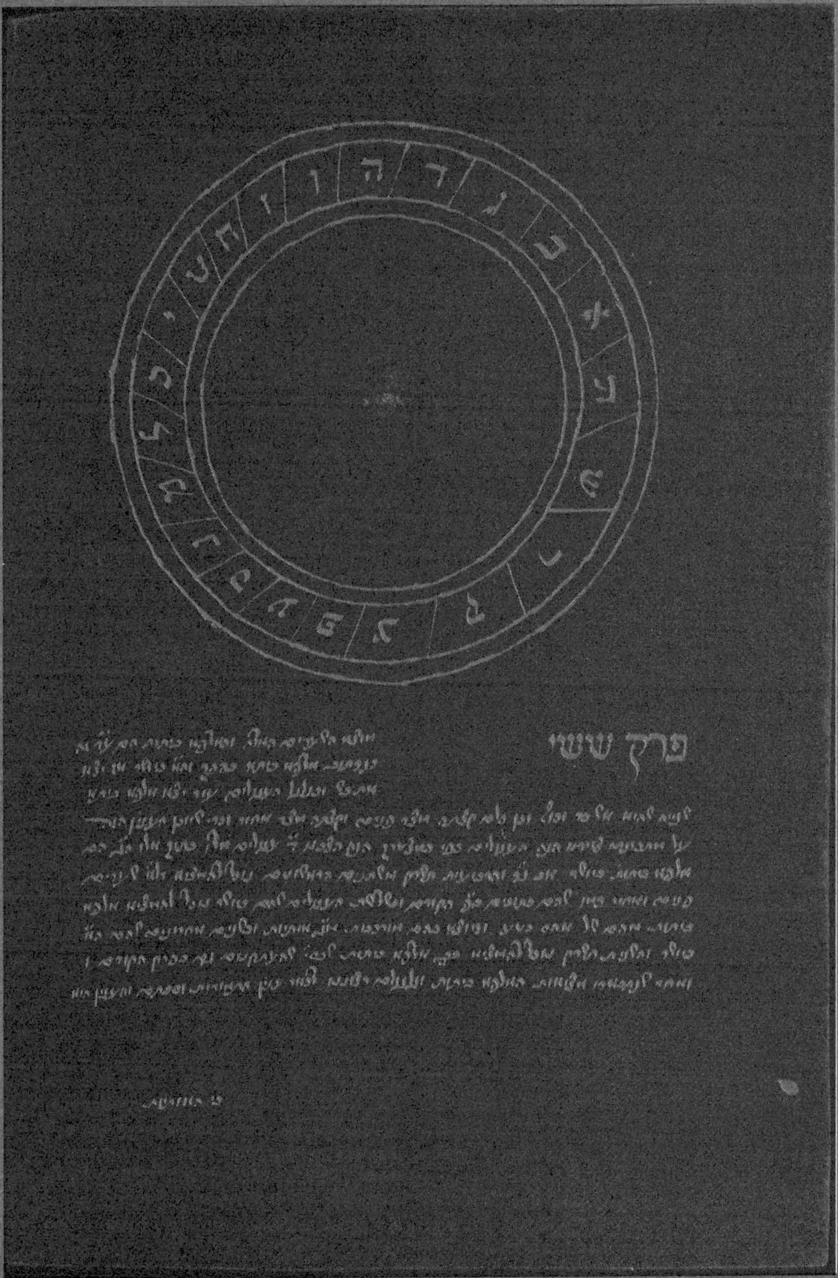

Page from the *Pardess Rimonim* ("The Pomegranate Orchard") by Rabbi Moses Cordovero. The twenty-two letters of the Hebrew alphabet are arranged in a circle. The circularity symbolizes the importance of a language in motion for man in motion.

taries on the Zohar, and *Ets Hayyim* ("The Tree of Life"), the great work by Rabbi Isaac Luria. Several chapters will be devoted later in the book to Luria's triple analysis of the history of the human race, which he summarized as *tsimtsum-shevira-tikkun*, the alternation of "reduction-breakage-repair."

The fifth period, according to Scholem—that of the mystical heresy of Shabbetai Tsvi (1625–1676)—is very important for understanding how the Kabbalah developed subsequently. This mystic oriented Luria's Kabbalah in a messianic direction, and with the help of his disciple and prophet, Nathan of Gaza, presented himself as the savior. Shabbetai Tsvi and Nathan were very serious master kabbalists who believed in their vocation and wanted to bring to the world their beliefs about redemption. They gained many followers before Shabbetai Tsvi, arrested by the Sultan and forced to choose between conversion to Islam or death, chose conversion. This brought an official end to a flame of messianism that had attained a certain measure of success.

This was an important period; it witnessed the birth, or rather rebirth, of the Jewish concept of a messiah, though one who converted to another faith and was thus, according to his own sayings and the commentaries that his disciples eventually produced, Jewish on the inside and non-Jewish on the outside. Thus Shabbetai Tsvi revalidated the practices of the Spanish Marranos or "new Christians," Jews who had been forced to convert to Christianity. This conflict is also interesting from the point of view of the Kabbalah, creating as it does a duality between two worlds, the visible and the invisible, thus opening up a secret dimension.

The sixth period is called Hasidism, and is the result of a school of thought founded by Rabbi Israel ben Eliezer, better known under the name of Baal Shem Tov, "Master of the Good Name" (1700–1760). This period saw the translation of the great themes of the Kabbalah to an existential level, a quest for the light of the infinite to discover a way to life through joy. The uniqueness of Hasidism may lie in the democratization of the concepts of the Kabbalah, as its ideas have been passed on to disciples by a master, the rabbi or *tsadiq*, who becomes the central focus of the group and its world and who brings comfort, advice, and healing to his followers. Hasidism became a way of life for a whole people who discovered its wonders and the

Portrait of Rabbi Schneur Zalman of Liadi (1747–1813), founder of Chabad Hasidism.

depth of the secrets of the hidden tradition. The great masters of this period were the Baal Shem Tov and his disciples, including Rabbi Levi Isaac of Berditchev, the "Seer of Lublin," the Maggid of Mezeritch, Rabbi Nachman of Breslov, Rabbi Schneur Zalman of Liadi, and many others. Hasidism is perhaps the greatest sociological and religious movement experienced by Jews since the emergence of Christianity. Consequently, a whole chapter will be devoted to this period, which will explain the principal teachings of Hasidism.

The seventh period, which could also be called "Period 6a" because it began at the same time as the sixth period and developed in parallel to it, is that of the Lithuanian Kabbalah. The Lithuanians continued research into the Kabbalah of Safed, but they utterly rejected Hasidism, of which they were wary since they saw it as a final resurgence of the Shabbataist heresy. This Lithuanian current took the name of *mitnaged,* "opponent." The *mitnagdim* were opposed not to the Kabbalah, as many people believe, but to Hasidism as a sociological phenomenon. The representative and founder of the Lithuanian Kabbalah is Rabbi Eliahu of Vilna (1720–1797), better known as the Vilna Gaon, "The Genius of Vilna." His disciple was the famous Rabbi Hayyim of Volozhyn (1759–1821), author of the illustrious *Ne-*

fesh Hayyim ("Soul of Life"). This type of mysticism is based on the importance of study and the application of the mitzvoth (Jewish commandments) as sources of cosmic energy and redemption of the world.

The eighth and last period of the Kabbalah, the contemporary period, has inherited all the previous trends. Many hitherto unknown manuscripts have been published, making it possible to get better acquainted with certain authors. In this respect, Gershom Scholem of the Hebrew University has done wonders, and his students have carried on his work brilliantly. A new generation has delved into the history of the Kabbalah, and explored its difficult concepts in greater depth.

The eighth period is not merely one of historical and academic research, as this would have marked the decline, and even the death, of the living Kabbalah. At the present time, almost all the trends inherent in the Kabbalah are being practiced, in some cases exclusively, though in others through a sort of creative syncretism that combines meditation (which has some aspects in common with yoga) with a study of the texts—the Zohar or the works of Rabbi Isaac Luria. There is no neglect of the Talmud and Hasidism, however, and there is even a growing desire to make contact with other mystical trends, especially those of Buddhism, and a tendency toward interdisciplinarity, in which the Kabbalah and its mysteries are confronted by the sum total of contemporary knowledge, especially those branches of science that deal with the origin of the universe.

The Kabbalah in a Christian Environment

We do not refer here to a "Christian Kabbalah"; since the Kabbalah is a secret Jewish tradition, this would be a contradiction in terms. Paul Vulliaud's book *La Kabbalah juive* devotes more than 200 pages to the influence of the Kabbalah on Christian circles, including a chapter about Jakob Boehme and Molitor, representatives of the modern German Kabbalah, and a chapter about the relationship between the Kabbalah and freemasonry.*

* See the extensive documentation in Daniel Béresniak's book *La Kabbale vivante*. For this aspect of the relationship between the Kabbalah and Christian circles, the author has used the interpretation by Gershom Scholem in *Kabbalah* (312 ff.), already discussed by Guy Casaril in *Rabbi Siméon Bar Yochaï et la Cabbale* (129–36).

> Noblemen and wealthy prelates in Italy encouraged circles of humanists, including many rabbis. [. . .] In Florence, Elia del Medigo (1460–1497), a physician of Cretan origin, and translator and commentator on Aristotle, spread Judaism and kabbalistic ideas among his Christian entourage. Pico della Mirandola and Marsile Ficin studied the parabolas of the Zohar under him. The Zohar was translated into Latin under the direction of Elia Levita (1469–1549), a Jewish grammarian who enjoyed the patronage of Cardinal Egidio de Viterbo. Christian humanists studied Jewish literature and thought as a discipline, in the same way as they studied Greek literature and thought. In Germany, Johannes Reuchlin (who had gained his knowledge of the Kabbalah from Pico) defended Talmudic literature against Johann Pfefferkorn who wanted to have the civil and religious authorities burn all Hebrew books, because they were reputed to be hostile to the Bible! An order from the Holy See (1516) granted victory to Reuchlin—or at least a few years' respite. During this truce, in Venice, Daniel Bomberg, a gentile, printed the Bible in Hebrew for the first time with its traditional commentaries and the Talmud (1517–1523). As if in exchange, a Jew, Leone Ebreo, composed neo-platonian dialogues about love in Italian (*Dialoghi d'amore,* 1502). His real name was Judah Abrabanel, and he was the son of the famous Isaac Abrabanel. Humanists studied Hebrew and Aramaic, avidly absorbing the Zohar, while, in turn, Talmudic studies became impregnated with the humanist spirit. In 1553, the truce was broken with the strictures of the Counter-Reformation. The Talmud and every other book written in Hebrew letters found in Rome were burned publicly in the Campo dei Fiori. In the second half of the 16th century, the Jews in almost every country in Europe were confined to special neighborhoods—the ghettos.

Pico della Mirandola, and Several Others

In compiling a list of the major Christian authors who were attracted to the Kabbalah—Pico della Mirandola, Johannes Reuchlin, Agrippa von Nettesheim, Paracelsus, Guillaume Postel, Robert Fludd—one cannot fail to notice that, despite their various origins and trends of thought, they all, or almost all, had one thing in common: an interest in the occult. All or almost all sought a truth beyond the rational, and for this reason they were suspected of being heretics.

In Italy, Pico della Mirandola (1463–1494) was passionate about all types of foreign knowledge. Thirteen of his 900 *Conclusiones philosophicae, cabbalisticae et theologicae* were reputed to be heretical and were condemned by Innocent VIII. Heinrich Cornelius Agrippa von Nettesheim was a German alchemist who studied magic as well as the Kabbalah; he sought correspondences between various worlds, angels, and magic names. He only escaped the vengeance of the church by seeking protection from the

Portrait of Pico della Mirandola (fifteenth-century Italy).

House of Savoy, as doctor to the royal family. Paracelsus was a nonconformist doctor of Swiss origin and a disciple of Basile Valentin, an alchemist and astrologer. He lost his patients and students and died a pauper in Germany. His English disciple, Robert Fludd, a doctor and alchemist, defender of Rosicrucianism, was bitterly attacked by the scientific authorities of his time. The Frenchman Guillaume Postel, an Arabist, prophet, and enlightened professor at the Collège de France, was prosecuted by the Inquisition in Italy and declared insane. Only Johannes Reuchlin seems to have brought to his Kabbalah studies the enlightened interest of a humanist, though this did not stop Leo X from condemning him. His writings about the Kabbalah, *De verbo mirifico* (1494) and *De arte cabalistica* (1517), although somewhat lacking in information, are more faithful to the original than those of Pico della Mirandola.

Beware of Charlatans! Alchemy and Black Magic

Christian opinion eventually concluded that the Kabbalah was an heretical doctrine associated with practices that lay somewhere between alchemy and black magic. Since it originated with the Jews, it could not be other than "sinful," and its continued attraction for occultists was that of forbidden fruit. Since that is all that was sought in the Zohar, nothing else was found.

In a desire for the picturesque, and perhaps due to traditional Jewish skills in medicine, the name of the Kabbalah was associated with a plethora of cures based on folktales and credulity. Kabbalistic amulets, parchments, or medals covered in fake Hebrew and stars of David combined with Christian crosses were very much in fashion. Jewish charlatans, or charlatans posing as Jews—such as Philoteus Montalto and Philippe d'Aquin, who attended Leonora Galigai and Maria de Medici—claimed that for sums of money they could cure any illness by using kabbalistic spells, talismen, and invocations gabbled in kitchen Hebrew. Books of magic, such as the *Keys of Solomon,* were associated with the Kabbalah. Thus the tradition of Rabbi Simeon Bar Yokhai crossed the centuries encumbered by alchemy and sorcery, only to emerge in modern times under the juicy title of occult science!

Every occultist, today as in the seventeenth century, claims to have studied the Kabbalah. Permutations of letters in the name of God reminiscent of parlor games, Cazotte's predictions of the deaths of noblemen during the Reign of Terror in the French Revolution, the wise saws in almanacs—all are attributed to the "magi" of the second half of the nineteenth century, Eliphas Levi, Stanislas de Guaïta, and Papus, whose works on the Kabbalah are all about alchemy and magic and reveal practically no understanding of its spiritual message. Antoine Fabre d'Olivet (1767–1825), the famous mystic of the French Revolution, also pretended to be a kabbalist, but his work is deplorable. His research into the origins of the Hebrew language and his attempt at a dictionary of root words are barely average in quality. All that is retained in this counterfeit Kabbalah is the name, but it has found itself incorporated into the teachings of most secret societies of occultists. Hebrew words are distorted, a tractate of the Talmud is mistaken for the name of a rabbi, and so on. A cheap novel has used the title *Zohar*. Soon fortune-tellers at country fairs will adopt the name Shekhina, and any seriously inquiring mind will find itself forced to place the Kabbalah somewhere between gypsy tarot readings, Nostradamus, and the village quack.

Derivatives and Syncretism: When Kabbalah Becomes Heresy

The positivist Jewish historians of the nineteenth century, especially in Germany with Heinrich Graetz, did not profess to hold a radically different opinion. In truth, Hasidism, which was then in deep decline, showed them what was still being called "Kabbalah" in a rather unpleasant light. There were the same superstitions and trafficking in amulets as among the Christians, as well as the same lack of spirituality. Furthermore, Christians had always held that the Kabbalah was a Jewish tendency closer to Christianity, which was enough for an accusation of heresy by ill-informed Jews.

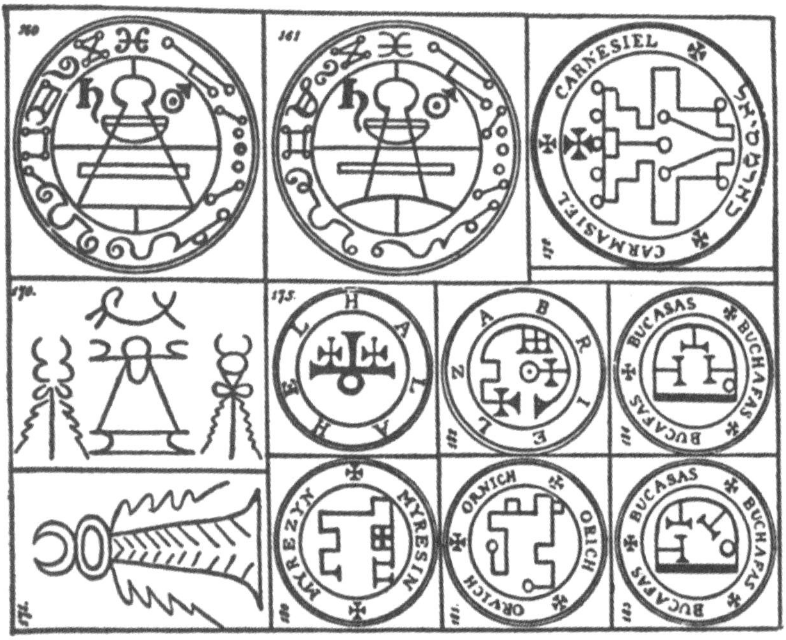

Seals used in magic ceremonies invoke the benevolent or evil powers (extract from the *Keys of Solomon*). Kabbalah and charlatanism . . .

It is a paradox, but it is also a fact that Christian kabbalists, occultists and heretics have constantly tried to prove the Christianity of the Kabbalah! According to Pico della Mirandola and Reuchlin, the Kabbalah even constituted additional proof of the truth of Christianity! Robert Fludd attempted to amalgamate Neoplatonism, Christianity, and Kabbalah, considering them to be perfectly reconcilable. In the same ecumenical spirit, Guillaume Postel and Mère Jeanne, his companion, tried to prove concordances between the Koran, the Gospels, and the Zohar, and thus reunite all peoples in a single faith.

Outside the Jewish context, kabbalistic ideas lose all meaning and cease to be kabbalistic. Thus only Hebrew words, forged in the fire of centuries of Jewish wisdom, express the fundamental tenets of the Kabbalah: *devekut, kavana, tikkun, shekhina, sefirot*, and so on. It is hardly surprising therefore that, removed from the context of Jewish piety, the Kabbalah has been mistaken for some sort of occultism; taken out of context, the words become meaningless and thus apparently mystical and "secret."

Confusion, Incomprehension, Disloyalty

Christian work on the Kabbalah would be very sparse if one omitted the secondary influences and unacknowledged borrowings, even if they are the exception. Dante—who has been dubbed an Albigensian, a revolutionary, and even a socialist—is believed to have been influenced by Jewish mystics.

Raymond Lulle (1235–1315), prior to becoming a Franciscan (the author has detected a certain Franciscan influence on kabbalistic morality), spent his youth at the court of James of Aragon, near the kabbalistic center of Gerona, and seems to have been inspired by Abulafia's methods in the definitions he uses in his *Ars Magna.* He combines nouns expressing the most abstract and general ideas along mechanical lines, in order to judge the accuracy of the contentions and discover new truths. His desire to spread Oriental languages is an indirect confirmation of this connection.

Jakob Boehme (1575–1624)

Jakob Boehme (1575–1624), a shoemaker in Görlitz, Germany, claimed his revelations were due to higher illumination, but his philosophy is too close to that of the Kabbalah for its influence to be unknown to him. Some of his closest friends, genuine scholars, were familiar with kabbalistic thought and may have explained it to him, and this may have made his intuition more specific. Boehme's metaphors were frequently compared to those of the Kabbalah by many of his commentators, such as Abraham von Franckenberg and Franz von Baader, until the mid-nineteenth century. The *mysterium magnum* is comparable to "infinity" *(en sof)*, and the wrath of God as the origin of evil corresponds to the break in the equilibrium between rigor and clemency. It is even reported that a disciple of Boehme was so struck by these resemblances that he converted to Judaism. Jewish kabbalists in the late seventeenth century, such as Koppel Hecht in Germany, also noticed the number of similarities.

Through the work of Jakob Boehme and the distortions of the first Christian kabbalists, the Kabbalah has entered the spiritual heritage of the West. Its influence on European thought has manifested itself through writers as diverse as Shelley, Spencer, Goethe, Wagner, Nietzsche, Whitman, Hugo, Baudelaire, and Rimbaud.

Robert Fludd first introduced the Kabbalah into English literature, and certain ideas in it enriched William Blake's train of thought, especially concerning the creation of man. John Milton was more clearly influenced. Although none of the mythical elements of the Kabbalah appear in his writings, he embraced its philosophical ideas. Milton read Hebrew and Aramaic; he was imbued with the spirit of Judaism, and may have read the Zohar. The concept of "God *en sof*," the unknowable and the ineffable, is found in *Paradise Lost*, which contains kabbalistic ideas as specific as those of *tsimtsum*, when he makes God say, "I uncircumscribed my self retire."

As for philosophers, the Kabbalah obviously influenced Spinoza and Gottfried Wilhelm Leibniz. The former may owe the concepts of *arish anpin* and *zeir anpin* to his distinction between *natura naturans* and *natura naturata*. Leibniz studied the Kabbalah, though not very effectively, through Knorr von Rosenroth's *Cabbala Denudata*. It might be an exaggeration to say that he owes the idea of the microcosm to Jewish mysticism, but his *Cabbalistica* (1694), a work that long remained unknown, analyzes the distinctions made by kabbalistic psychology *(ruakh, nefesh, neshama)* in relation to a pseudokabbalistic work produced by the entourage of the theosophist Van Helmont (*Seder Olam*, 1618). He also studied the division

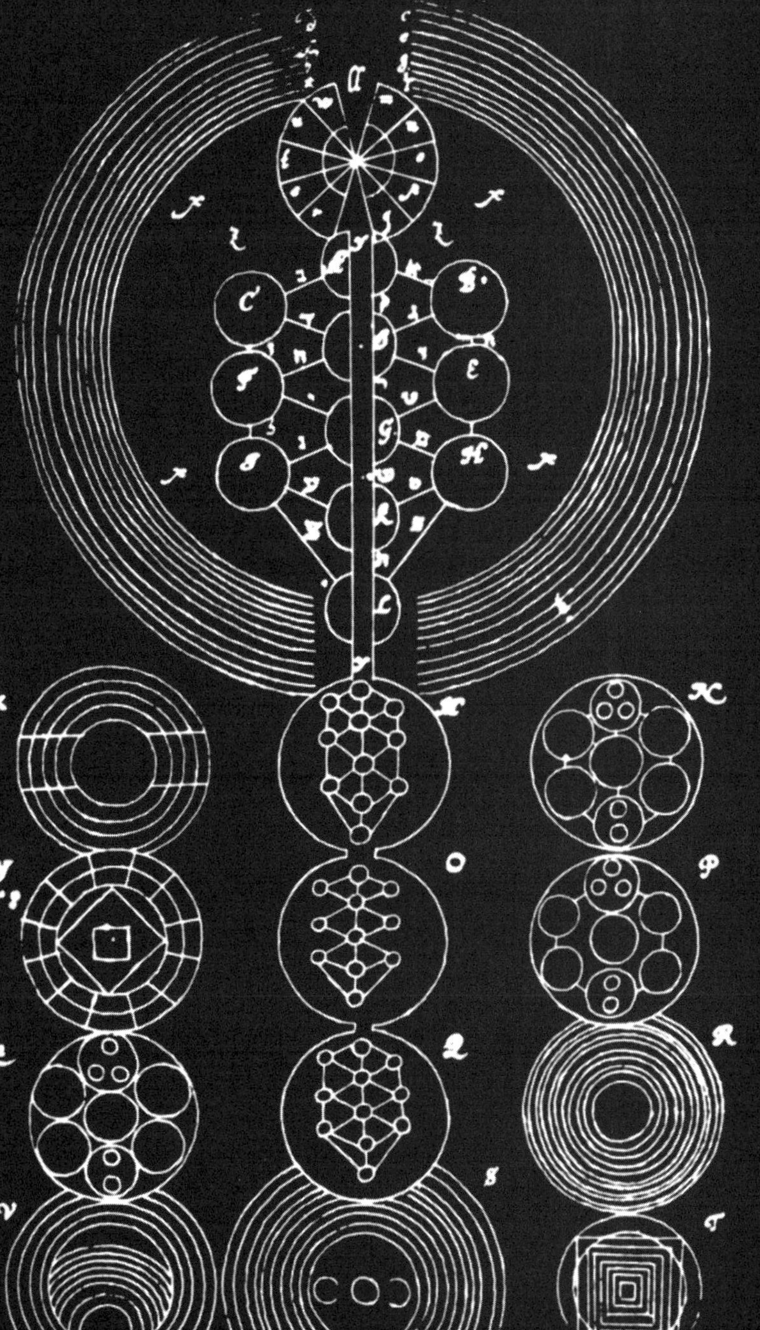

Trees of the Sefira, by Knorr von Rosenroth. The diagrams illustrate the circular and descending movement of the energies of the upper worlds to the lower worlds.

between the four worlds, those of *atsilut* (emanation, immanence), *yetsira* (formation), *beriya* (creation), and *assia* (activity) by comparing them to his own philosophy. Spinoza and Jakob Boehme may have done more than the authors of genuinely kabbalistic works to bring the concepts of the Kabbalah to Schelling's attention, and thence to German post-Kantian philosophy. Some modern researchers indicate a link with the philosophy of Martin Heidegger.*

New Perspectives on the Christian Interpretation

Christian circles are now reexamining the Kabbalah. The results of the research are uneven but often interesting. Unfortunately, much information has been gleaned at second hand, repeating the errors and misunderstandings of the past, though the work of Annick de Souzenelle is outstanding, with not only a thorough knowledge of the texts, but great feeling for kabbalistic hermeneutics. Her interpretation relates kabbalistic concepts of Judaism to Christian theology, and often to the figure of Christ himself. Though there is always a danger in using foreign conceptual tools for apologia and theological "accomplishments," further developments are awaited with interest.

* In this respect see Marlène Zarader, *La Dette impensée: Heidegger et l'héritage hébraïque.*

2

The Keys to the Kabbalah
Light and Energy

Look at the Light

To understand the Kabbalah is to enter the dynamic of the forces of life, to feel oneself penetrated by the energy that circulates in every living thing. The Kabbalah is addressed to man and whispers in his ear:

> If you wish, you can.
> Son of man, look!
> Contemplate the light of the Presence that resides in all existence!
> Contemplate the joyful life force of the worlds above!
> See how it descends and impregnates every parcel of life that you perceive with your eyes of the flesh and your eyes of the spirit.
> Contemplate the marvels of Creation and the Source of every living thing which is the rhythm by which every creature lives.
> Learn to know yourself.
> Learn to know the world, your world.
> Discover the logic in your heart and the feelings in your reason!
> Feel the vibrations of the Source of Life which is in your very depths and above you and all around you.
> The love which burns in you, let it raise its powerful root,
> extend it to the whole soul and all the worlds.
> Look at the lights . . .

Look into the lights . . .
Ascend and ascend
for you possess a powerful force.
You have the wings of the wind,
the noble wings of the eagle . . .
Do not deny them lest they deny you.
Seek them and they will find you immediately.
(Baal Ha-Orot [Master of the Lights], *Orot Ha-Qodesh*, I, 64)

Light

One of the most important words of the Kabbalah is the word *light (or):* "And God said, Let there be light, and there was light. . . ." Light is the first sign, the first word of creation, the first and highest reality of the universe, the first path to the divine. It is the highest metaphor for infinity. To understand the Kabbalah, we must constantly remember that it is a philosophy of light and, what is more, a set of behaviors, thoughts, and actions, studies, and rituals that are designed to enable man to receive the light of infinity.

light of infinity

⇩

world

This "act of receiving" is the very meaning of *qabbala* or Kabbalah. The Kabbalah means feeling the presence of the dynamic and energy that flows through every living thing. The Kabbalah is the "metaphysics of light."

The Hebrew word *or,* "light," has the same numerical value, 207, as the expression *en sof,* "infinity."

	or, "light"
is written	*aleph-vav-resh*
	אור
i.e.	1 + 6 + 200
	207
	en sof, "infinity"
is written	*aleph-yod-noun-samekh-vav-pheh,*

אין-סוף

i.e. 1 + 10 + 50 + 60 + 6 + 80

207

The masters have remarked that 207 is also the numerical value of the word *raz*, "mystery."

The Various Names for Light

A kabbalist is a person who receives the light of infinity into himself and who feels light as a vital energy, like a flow of energy that passes through him and gives him the power to exist. There are many names for this light, and it is expressed through various basic expressions that run through all the writings and stories of kabbalistic experiences:

Infinite light	Influx
Light of infinity	Infinite influx
Infinite desire	Influx of life
Divine desire	Existence of life
Cosmic divine vitality	Vitality
Cosmic divine current	Will
Energy from above	Desire to give
Cosmic energy	Positive desire
Burst of light	. . .

The Books of the Kabbalah: Books of Light

"Light," "vibration," "energy"—these are three key words in the practical Kabbalah. The triad of light-vibration-energy has a special place in the letters of the Hebrew alphabet, which thus become particles of light of tremendous force, through which it is possible to reinterpret the world, and even to re-create it. The books that contain this alphabet of the fundamental energy of life itself are the books of the Kabbalah.

It is important to stress that the Kabbalah is the "metaphysics of light," as witness the titles of the great kabbalistic works: *Sefer Ha-Bahir* ("Book of Clarity"), *Sefer Ha-Zohar* ("Book of Splendor"), *Sha'are Ora* ("Gates of Light"), *Meor Enayim* ("Light of the Eyes"), and *Orot Ha-Qodesh* ("Lights of Sanctity"), to name but a few.

The Zohar or "Book of Splendor"

Gershom Scholem explains that in circa 1275, while Abraham Abulafia was expounding his doctrine of prophetic kabbalism in Italy, a book emerged from the heart of Castille that was destined to eclipse all the other documents of kabbalistic literature in the renown and influence it gradually acquired. This was the *Sefer Ha-Zohar* ("Book of Splendor"). The importance of the book and its place in the history of kabbalism is clear from the fact that it is the only work of post-Talmudic rabbinical literature to be considered a canonical text. For many centuries it was ranked alongside the Bible and the Talmud.

However one judges the value of the Zohar, its influence has been undeniable, at first among the kabbalists and later, especially after the Exile from Spain, among the Jewish people as a whole. For centuries it was claimed to represent the deepest, most hidden expression of the intimate recesses of the Jewish soul.

Written in the form of a mystical novel, the Zohar is set in the Land of Israel of the second century C.E. and records the activities of the famous "master of the Mishna," Rabbi Simeon Bar Yokhai, his son Eleazar, and his friends and disciples as they discuss various subjects, both human and divine. As far as historians are concerned, Rabbi Simeon Bar Yokhai is the master in whose work lies the origin of the Zohar, but the book was compiled and put into its definitive form many centuries later, by a thirteenth-century Spanish kabbalist, Rabbi Moses of Leon. A distinction must therefore be made between the author who inspired the work and its compiler. Certain passages are more narrative than others, while some are dedicated exclusively to biblical exegesis and implement all the panoply of sacred hermeneutics—juggling with numbers, plays on homophones or

Title page of the "Book of Splendor," *Sefer Ha-Zohar*, Cremona edition, 1560.

words that look similar but have entirely different meanings, translations from other languages, and so on.

Extracts from the Zohar: A Lesson on the Meaning of the Word "Midnight"

Rabbi Abba set out from Tiberias to go to the house of his father-in-law. With him was his son, Rabbi Jacob. When they arrived at Kfar Tarsha, they stopped to spend the night there. Rabbi Abba inquired of his host: have you a rooster here? The host said: why? Said Rabbi Abba: I wish to rise at exactly midnight. The host replied: a rooster is not needed. By my bed there is a water-clock. The water drips out drop by drop, finishing at exactly midnight, when the wheel whirs back with such a clatter that it rouses the entire household. I made this clock for a certain old man who was in the habit of getting up each night at midnight to study Torah. To this Rabbi Abba said: Blessed be God for guiding me here!

The wheel of the clock whirred back at midnight and Rabbi Abba and Rabbi Jacob arose. They listened to the voice of their host rising from a lower floor of the house where he was sitting with his two sons, saying: It is written "Midnight will I rise to give thanks unto Thee for Thy righteous judgments" (Ps. 119:62) . The word "at" is not used, and so we assume that "Midnight" is an appellation of the Holy One, Blessed be He, whom David speaks to thus because midnight is the hour when He appears with His retinue and goes into the Garden of Eden to converse with the righteous. Rabbi Abba then said to Rabbi Jacob: Now we indeed have the luck to be with the Divine Presence.

And they went and seated themselves by their host, and said: Tell us again that which you just said, which is very good. Where did you hear it? He replied: My grandfather told it me. He said that the accuser angels below are busy all about the world during the first three hours of the night, but at exactly midnight the accusations halt, for at this moment God enters the Garden of Eden.

He continued: These ceremonies above occur nightly only at exactly midnight and this we know from what is written of Abraham that "the night was divided for them" (Gen. 14:15) and from the verse "and it came to pass at the midnight" in the story of the Exodus (Ex. 12:29) and from numerous other passages in the Scripture. David knew it, so the old man related, because upon it depended his kingship. And so he was accustomed to getting up at this hour and singing praises and on this account he addressed God as "Midnight". He said, too, "I will rise and give thanks unto Thee for Thy righteous judgments," since he knew this sphere to be the source of justice, with judgments of earthly kings deriving therefrom, and for this reason David did not ever fail to rise and sing praises at this hour.

Rabbi Abba went up to him and kissed him and said: Surely it is as you say. Blessed be God who has guided me here. In all places judgment is executed at night, and this we have certainly affirmed, discussing it before Rabbi Simeon.

At this, the young son of the innkeeper asked: Why then does it say "Midnight"?

Rabbi Abba replied: It is established that the heavenly King rises at midnight.

The boy said: I have a different explanation.

Then Rabbi Abba said: Speak, my child, for through your mouth will speak the voice of the Lamp.

He answered: "This is what I have heard. Truly, night is the time of strict judgment, a judgment which reaches out impartially everywhere. But midnight draws from two sides, from judgment and from mercy, the first half only of the night being the period of judgment, while the second half takes illumination from the side of mercy. Wherefore David said 'Midnight.'"

Upon this, Rabbi Abba stood up and put his hands on the boy's head and blessed him, and said: "I had thought that wisdom dwells only in a few privileged pious men. But I perceive that even children are gifted with heavenly wisdom in the generation of Rabbi Simeon. Happy are you, Rabbi Simeon! Woe to the generation when you will have left it." And all of them stayed until the small hours studying the Torah.
(Zohar, Genesis, 92a–92b.)

Rabbi Simeon Bar Yokhai Is Called the Holy Lamp: The Teaching on the "Face of Light"

Rabbi Simeon is the holder of several honorific titles. Some call him the Prince of Kabbalists, but he is better known in the tradition under the title of Butsina Qaddisha, "the Holy Lamp."

It is written in the Zohar (III, 132b):

Rabbi Simeon teaches:

"Listen, colleagues, he cried, all of you who are Lamps and who have come into the Circle . . . I swear by the highest heavens and by the sacred world of the Most High that I have now seen things which no man has yet seen from the day on which Moses went up on Mount Sinai for the second time; I have just seen a face as resplendent as the sun and whose luminosity is designed to cure the world, as it is written (Malachi 3:20): "But for you who revere My name, a sun of victory shall rise to bring healing."

Rabbi Simeon then reveals to his disciples the form in which he saw the "face of light" (Zohar I, 45b, and III, 291b):

Through the veils you see, said Rabbi Simeon, I perceive all the lights of the world above. The Holy One, Blessed be He, drew a veil over four pillars sur-

> rounding the four directions. Each pillar rises from the world below to the world above; the celestial chief entrusted with guarding the pillar holds a spade in his hand on which four different keys are placed; these are the keys which draw the curtain from top to bottom. The same is true of the second, third and fourth pillars which are lit by the Supreme Light which passes through the curtain. The same applies to the other pillars of the four directions of the world. I see all these worlds waiting impatiently for the words which come out of our mouths; for it is from the breath of our mouths that the curtains are formed through which we see the Supreme Light.

The source of the light resides in the seventh palace, says the Zohar. It surpasses all understanding. Men can only discover the keys that enable them to enter into the first six palaces.

> All the lamps, says Rabbi Simeon, are lit by this most mysterious Supreme Light. It is this which illuminates all the degrees. Through its light the accessible parts of each degree are revealed. All the lights are attached to one another and cannot be separated. The light of each lamp is called "the king's jewels," "the crown of the king." Everything is lit by the light which is inside but which does not flood outward. Everything is united to this light. And thus everything rises in a single degree and everything is crowed by the same word; and one is not separate from the other. He and his Name are one. The light which is revealed is called "the king's raiment." The light which is inside is mysterious and in it resides He who does not manifest or reveal Himself.

Everything is linked together in harmony and forms a whole which is inseparable from the supreme light. All light emanates from the infinite.

Energy

For the Kabbalah, true reality *(metsiut)* is the light that is found in everything. The Kabbalah speaks of sparks of light or holiness that animate each creature, from the smallest element to the largest. The reality of the world is not matter, but the vibrations of the sparks of holiness, that which today we call energy.

The Extraordinary Force of Thought: *Kavana*

In the Kabbalah, the fundamental reality is thus not matter but energy, a set of vibrations that passes through the world, making it dynamic and keeping it alive. Everything is energy, from the crudest matter to the finest, such as our thoughts and what we call the soul. As will be seen, the Kabbalah has various names for this energy, such as "light," "vitality," "infinite breath," or "rhythm."

The Kabbalah theorizes that the greatness of man lies in his ability to feel these energies, to control them, change them, and channel them in various directions. The tool for mastering this energy or life force resides mainly in our thoughts, which find their expression in certain particularly significant formulas, and especially in the names of God. A kabbalist is someone who can channel his thoughts in the right direction: this is called *kavana* (from the verb *lekaven,* which means "to direct," "to give a direction to," or "to give meaning to"; the plural of *kavana* is *kavanot*). Each person has the power within him to perceive all his own vibrations and harmonize them. Each is thus responsible for himself, his balance, and thus, above all, his thoughts. According to the Kabbalah, we are capable of changing our internal, physical, and psychological vibrations through the *kavanot.* We can change the vibrations of our bodies, our spirit, and our soul thanks to our thoughts. Prayer, for example, is a time of learning and meditation on the various *kavanot* that will help us to change our energies and personal vibrations. The great kabbalists, supremely skilled in the art of *kavana,* are capable of acting to change not only themselves but the whole world.

The Kabbalah Is Based on Optimism

A prayer that speaks of love offers us, if we succeed in integrating and internalizing the words and formulas it uses, the power to construct the vibrations of love within us and around us. The kabbalists suggest a set of *kavanot* through which to channel thought in our vision of the world, but always toward the positive and optimistic. Rabbi Nachman of Breslov teaches:

In every human being, you can find something positive.
Even those who appear to you to be the worst miscreants.
Unflinchingly, generously, seek, harvest,
Listen . . .
These are musical notes.
Dance,
Clap your hands,
Let the melody rise!
Write the joyous song of healing,
The precious song of deliverance.

Vibration and Music: The Psalms of David

The interior vibration of man has ten rhythms, or pulses, which man must try to know so as to direct them accurately. These ten rhythms are also ten different types of music, which make it possible to create music in which all the vibrations are in harmony. For the Kabbalah, man is a musical instrument, and the path of the Kabbalah consists in showing him how he can tune it to produce the most harmonious sounds.

The Psalms of David are constructed on these ten vital rhythms. Tradition teaches that a ten-stringed harp was attached to the head of David's bed, and that every evening at midnight, the wind would rise and play on the strings of the harp. At that moment, David would awake and begin to work on composing psalms. He heard the exact vibrations of the universe, of every living thing, and wrote them in words and music in this extraordinary masterpiece, which constitutes one of the essential elements of every prayer.

Rabbi Nachman of Breslov, one of the great masters of the Kabbalah and of Hasidism, lived at the beginning of the nineteenth century. He was attentive to the vibrations and energies found within each living thing, and he revealed the secret of the fundamental vibrations of the ten special psalms among the 150 which King David wrote. Rabbi Nachman called these ten psalms the *tikkun haklali,* an expression that could be translated as "the general reharmonization of all the vital vibrations." If man does not do this work of reattachment through the intermediary of his thoughts by channeling them in the right direction *(kavanot),* the resulting imbalance and unease may be translated into melancholy, depression, and illness.

The Path of Energies: The *Sefirot*, Letters, and Numbers

The purpose of the present work is to show as clearly as possible the path of energy from its source, which is called the "infinite light" and which propagates itself throughout the universe through a model of ten "transformers of energy," which the Kabbalah calls the *sefirot*. Each part of the world, from the tiniest particle to the largest, most complex matter, the structure of the spirit in its logical and rational organization or in the craziest fantasies, receives the vital energy-vibration, which has first passed through one or more transformers—the *sefirot*. We will see that these energy transformers are also deployed through the letters of the Hebrew alphabet and the figures and numbers to which they correspond.

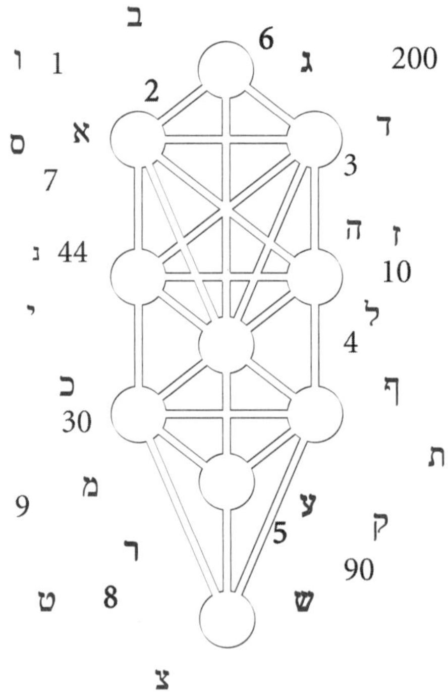

Dynamism

Movement and Change

> ***Truths made for our feet, truths that are capable of dancing.***
> —Friedrich Nietzsche

One of the basic concepts of the Kabbalah is that of movement. Light circulates through all of the worlds. It is the fundamental energy of every living thing, the flow and reflow of every organism. As soon as the world was created, it entered into a process of returning to its source and constructed itself by flowing from below to above, from the least perfect to the most perfect. There is "a striving for perfection. The world is getting better and better and is constantly acquiring new benefits, which it adds to those it already has, organizing them into units that are full of power and splendor," according to Baal Ha-Orot in the *Orot Ha-Qodesh.* Existence progresses, renews itself, moves closer to the light-without-beginning-or-end; "This process of elevation is infinite because it reveals the force of divine will in the universe, a force which aspires to absolute good. The evolution of the world is a positive process and is based on optimism in the world. For how can one despair when one sees that everything develops and everything thrusts upward?" (*Orot Ha-Qodesh,* 537, "The Law of Evolution").

The evolution of creation, with this "ever upward" movement, is the source of the fundamental optimism of kabbalistic thought. It is this optimism and joy that Rabbi Nachman of Breslov summarizes in his dictum: "It is forbidden to despair." This endless striving for a deeper, better, higher existence is the very meaning of messianism, faith in the ultimate perfection of the human being in a return to the "without-beginning," the source of all life.

The essence of being is time, which in the human being is translated as the dynamic force that constantly and infinitely renews and perfects the world.

Kabbalists and Scientists

It is understandable how fundamentally kabbalistic thought influences and provides the dynamic for philosophical, metaphysical, and scientific research. In fact, the scientific researcher seeks to unveil the secrets of the universe on a physical level, just as the researcher of the Kabbalah seeks to unveil its secrets on the metaphysical level. Both are oriented toward the construction of a more perfect world. For the Kabbalah, evolution does not end with the human race; it continues, thanks to humans, toward even higher stages. The whole "process of striving for perfection" is hope for and striving toward absolute freedom. It is then that man will attain the creative forces of which he still has no conception.

Man's present scientific achievements and his ability to change nature thereby are merely signs that are the precursors of a distant future in which "the human spirit will reveal itself freely, with force and splendor, much more than it does now" *(Orot Ha-Qodesh)*. The ultimate finality of development lies in a distant future that transcends the finitude of the human spirit. Supreme spiritual perfection cannot be achieved midway through the journey; the quest is infinite. The path with which man is confronted in the course of his development is infinite, as is his desire to "return to his infinite source, to unite with the divinity." In fact, he wants to override his human nature and rise "beyond the limits of the created being." One can no doubt envisage man at the next stage of evolution as a higher being, capable of comprehending that which transcends the narrow limits of sensory perception. The relationship between science and the Kabbalah is probably stronger than it has ever been, thanks to recent discoveries in astrophysics that, in many points, offer surprising analogies to the models proposed in the Kabbalah.

Kabbalah and "Return to Self"

Im ata ma'amin she-ata yakhol leqalqel ta'amin she-gam ata yakhol le taqen.
[If you believe that you are capable of destroying, believe that you are also capable of repairing.]
—Rabbi Nachman of Breslov

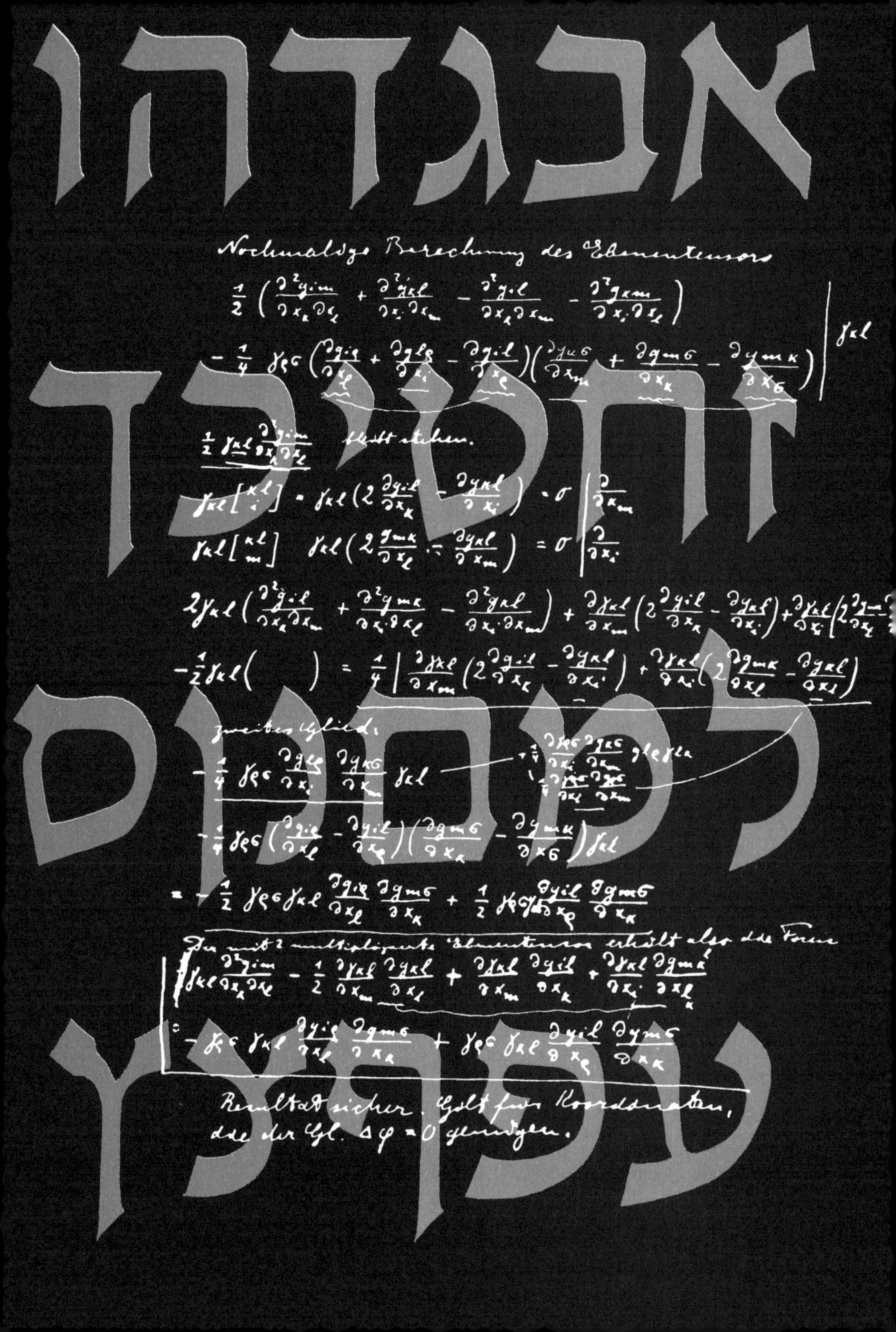

אבגדהו
זחטיכך
למםנןס
עפףצץ
Nochmalige Berechnung des Elemententensors
Resultat sicher. Gilt für Koordinaten, die der Gl. Δφ = 0 genügen.

The flow of life attracts man, moves him upward toward what constitutes both the source and the ultimate object of desire. Life remembers this primordial light, and wants to return to its days of splendor.

Natural evolution is presented as one of the manifestations of the cosmic movement of return (*teshuva*). This process of return requires the existence of the transcendence one aspires to regain. Evolution results from the power of the cosmic will, the "ardent desire" to use it in order to "return to the source of reality"—to life from life.

The Hebrew word *teshuva* has three different meanings, whose common denominator is the idea of returning. First, it means "to return to God," in the sense of repentance. Second, it means "to turn, to turn round, to turn from a particular way of life and choose another." Finally, it also means "reply" or "response." The sages of the Talmud included *teshuva* as one of the things whose creation preceded that of the world; it thus constitutes a phenomenon that is both primordial and universal, one on which the very existence of the world is based. In this perspective, *teshuva* has two meanings.

First, as it is written into the structure of the universe, *teshuva* shows that even before he was created, man was granted the ability to change the course of his life. Thus, in a certain sense, it constitutes the highest expression of human freedom, a sort of manifestation of divinity in human form. In the context of freedom, *teshuva* indicates that man is capable of releasing himself from his past and the quasi-mechanical causality that seems to lead him down a path from which there is no return, in which a sin leads to another sin, in which every action causes a reaction and every intention has unfortunate consequences. In this sense it indicates the presence of divinity in man, since God is not subject to laws nor to causality. *Teshuva* is itself a way of breaking the immutability of determinism. This concept is closely allied to the thinking presented later in the Kabbalah about astrology.

The second aspect of *teshuva*, also a universal one, is that it gives man the ability to control his movements in all the dimensions of his existence, and especially that of time. Without it, time would be linear and irreversible. Apparently there is no way of making an event that has happened "unhappen," nor can it be corrected or changed; the past is static. And yet *teshuva* implies that there is a possibility of changing the past, or at least of altering its effect upon the present and the future. It is this paradoxical capability of mastering time that explains why *teshuva* precedes the creation of the world. It has this exceptional dimension of being beyond time and the inexorable interlocking relationship between cause and effect.*

Kabbalah and Culture

The Kabbalah as a dynamic and vital force has a relationship not only to science and scientific research, but to culture in general.

What is culture? Every culture is a culture of life. It is the action that life exercises upon itself and through which it transforms itself. If "culture" means anything, it is the self-transformation of life, the process through which life constantly modifies and changes itself to attain higher forms of achievement and accomplishment, to grow, to transform itself, and to fulfill itself. A culture that does not pursue this movement of creation, elevation, and perfection, even if it considers itself to have achieved a very high level, enters the realm of barbarism. A culture that does not renew itself is a barbarian culture.

The Kabbalah represents the vigilance of the spirit as it avoids falling into the trap of cultural satisfaction, on both an individual and a collective level. The Kabbalah is a reminder of the life force that exists in every living thing, and which constantly seeks action, creation, and invention. Even when the elementary forms of the living creature seem to be transfixed and their blind transmission ends in the mere mindless, automatic repetition of infinitely repeated structures, the Kabbalah intimates that in the very deepest corners of the human being in the world, deep forces are at work that may still be allowed to emerge. Man then perceives his own strengths, hidden as though they had been asleep, "not only maintaining the state of things which permit the continuation of life, but remaining vigilant and, not content with preserving that which is, waits with a patience on a par with the millennia that it takes, for an opportunity to use the sum of knowl-

* These are the perceptions of *teshuva* that Adin Steinsaltz provides in his introduction to the Kabbalah in his magnificent work *The Thirteen Petaled Rose.* As regards the critique of determinism, see Marc-Alain Ouaknin, *Lire aux éclats* (Reading in bursts).

edge acquired in past in order, in one fell swoop, to discover hitherto unnoticed relationships, to invent a tool or an idea, to build a new world" (Michel Henry, *La Barbarie*).

Baal Ha-Orot, the Master of Lights, teaches:

> Everything moves and rises. Every step is an ascent. Even descents are ascents within themselves. Everything moves, everything flows, and everything rises. . . .
>
> Every true poet, every man who knows how to penetrate the internal nature of things, everyone who is alert to the spirit of holiness perceives all reality in his upward movement. . . .
>
> Man should perceive the world not as something complete and finished, but as something that is always in the course of moving on, of ascending, of developing, and ascending again. Everything renews itself. This is what is called "constant renewal," *khiddush hatemidi.*
>
> In each little corner of the world, at every moment, each part of the tiniest creature is in movement, attracted or repelled, ascending, descending, always on the rise even though it may look outwardly as if it is falling, constantly moving to and fro, as the prophet Ezekiel says: And the creatures came and went. *Vehahayot ratso veshov*, an expression that can also be read as *vehahayut ratso veshov*, that is to say : "And cosmic vitality is always moving to and fro." . . .
>
> Each piece of existence, however tiny, contains a spark of holiness which aspires to return to its source and it is this which produces the fundamental movement of elevation and the dynamic of existence.
>
> These rises and falls are uninterrupted in man and in the cosmos in its entirety. Every movement, even a fall, a descent or a psychological depression are an elevation. Changes of state, of mood, and even deep depressions have a positive value.
>
> It is the moon, which is almost invisible before its renewal, it is the low tide before the return of the high tide; it is sleep, which offers renewal and force for the morrow and for awakening. . . .
>
> A fall is not an accident, it is a natural movement in our participation in the world.
>
> Is the world not the result of a descent of light and of the infinite?
>
> To quote a famous expression of the Kabbalah, there is a state of *yerida letsorekh ha'aliya*, "descent for the purpose of rising," in other words, descending can have no other outcome than rising again.
>
> (*Orot Ha-Qodesh* II, fifth discourse, 511 ff.)

3

What Is a Kabbalist?

One day, a rabbi gathered all his disciples and invited them to question and even to criticize him. The disciples said to him:
– Master, your conduct surprises us, you never do what your father, your master, did, whom we knew before he chose you as his successor. How do you consider his heritage, where is your loyalty?
The rabbi looked at his disciples gravely, but he had a gleam in his eye, a spark of joy and of malice. He said to them:
– I will explain to you, it is very simple. No one is more faithful than I am! In everything, I do exactly what my father did; just as he never imitated anyone else, I do the same!
—Martin Buber, *Tales of the Hasidim*

An Initiate and a Master

The Hebrew word for a kabbalist is *mequbal.* This word poses a translation problem. The literal meaning of the word is: "he who is received." The correct term ought to be *meqabel,* meaning "he who receives" a teaching, a secret, a tradition, etc.

If being a kabbalist means "to be received," it is important to understand the meaning of such an "act of receiving."

The first interpretation teaches us that the Kabbalah is not a matter of lonely meditation, but is studied within a group of initiates. The kabbalist is indeed "one who is received, accepted into a group." The correct translation of *kabbalist* would thus be "initiate."

The second interpretation relates to the fact that man receives the title of "master" during a ceremony in which his own master recognizes his right to teach and to make legal judgments. In the second meaning, he is not received into a special group of initiates who practice meditation, but received into the chain of tradition.

The Initiation Ceremony of the Masters: *Semikha,* or the Laying On of Hands

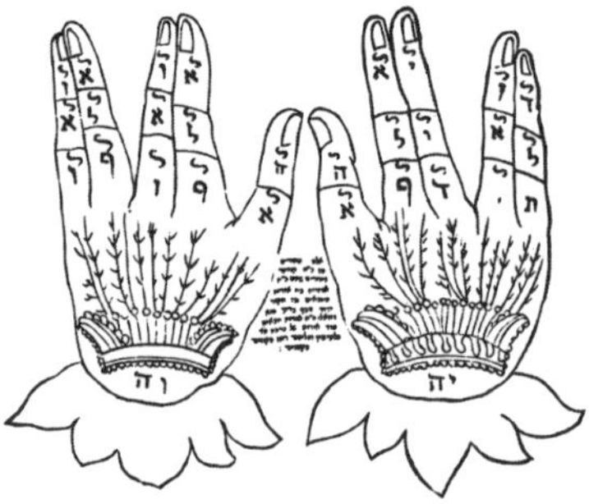

For a disciple to be promoted to the rank of master, for him to receive authorization to teach Torah, to lead the people, and to decide any judicial matter, even a criminal case, he must first provide proof of his lucidity of mind and his capacity for initiative. (We shall later define this wisdom, intelligence, and knowledge as *khokhma, bina,* and *da'at.)* Only then can the ceremony of initiation and the laying on of hands take place: "The Lord answered Moses: "Single out Joshua, son of Nun, an inspired man, and lay your hand upon him. Have him stand . . . before the whole community and ordain him in their sight. Invest him with some of your authority, so that the whole Israelite community may obey" (Numbers 27:18–20). The purpose of this ordination is clear. It is to "appoint someone over the community who shall go out before them and come in before them and who shall take them out and bring them in, so that the Lord's community may not be like sheep that have no shepherd" (Numbers 27:16–17). Although the ordination must be performed publicly, it is of a private and mystical nature. In fact, thanks to the laying on of hands, the spiritual power of the master or, at least, part of this power—Moses having received it directly from God—is secretly transmitted to the disciple (Talmud Bavli, Bava Batra, 75a).

The laying on of hands began even before Moses. It is encountered very explicitly for the first time as a ceremony of both transmission and benediction in the story of Jacob, who called all his children to him as he lay on his deathbed so he could transmit his last words to them (Genesis 48). This tradition is perpetuated to the present day in the words of the blessing that parents give their children on Friday evening or Saturday evening, at the beginning or end of Shabbat or the festivals, which are the same as those of the priestly blessing and which refer to Ephraim and Menashe, for boys and to the matriarchs, for girls:

> May God make you like Ephraim and Menashe
> [May God make you like Sarah, Rebecca, Rachel, and Leah]
> May God bless you and keep you
> May God make His face to shine upon you and be favorable unto you
> May God turn his face unto you and grant you peace : Shalom !

The Hebrew blessing consists of sixty letters that correspond to the energy of the first perfect number, 6, which runs through the ten *sefirot* (see the subject of perfect numbers below). Today, the use of the hands as a medium for the transmission of divine energy can be encountered in the ceremony of the priestly benediction (*birkat kohanim*, the plural of *kohen*).

The Laying On of Hands and the Light of Infinity

Each disciple becomes a master through the laying on of hands (*semikha*). The kabbalistic significance of this ceremony lies in the disciple's ability to receive the light of infinity into himself. He then opens himself up to a new perception of the celestial energies, which he may transmit in his turn. The prophet Habbakuk (Hab. 3:3) said:

> The majesty of the Eternal has covered the skies and the earth is full of his praise, his brilliance is like the light *(or)* the rays are emitted from his hand and this is the hidden place of his power.

Sefer Ha-Bahir (the "Book of Clarity") relates:

> The disciples asked their master:
> –What is the meaning of "the 'rays' are emitted from his hand"?
> –There are five rays, replied the master, which correspond to the five fingers of the human right hand.

The light from above is extended in the fingers of the right hand and is transmitted to the disciple. The light of infinity is also transmitted through the five fingers of the left hand, but this is not evoked explicitly in this verse. It will be seen below that all of the thought of the Kabbalah is to some extent a commentary on the ability to receive and use this light of infinity.

Tradition and Innovation

The fact that a disciple, ordained as a master, follows a long and powerful tradition in no way weakens his initiative. He must assume his own responsibilities. After having bowed his head while receiving the *semikha,* the disciple raises it again immediately. His first gesture assumes respect for the past; the second, consciousness of the present and responsibility for the future.

The Kabbalah bears witness to the Revelation. This revelation is not consumed in the mystic fire of an exceptional event; it remains inexhaustible. It offers reason infinite possibilities of research. Since not only faith, but reason itself, contains multiple virtualities, *semikha* offered to the disciple, far from hindering his intellectual development, should only serve him as a support. In the eyes of his pupil, the master merely represents the support given to him by the past.

Despite its profound respect for the past, the Kabbalah does not languish in a static attitude. It throws man into the perpetual movement of time. The past extends into the present, renews itself, and opens up to the miracle of the future (see A. Safran, *The Kabbalah,* 101–15).

The Kabbalist Is Someone Who Follows a Path

Never forget that you are a traveler in transit.
–Edmond Jabès

God always travels incognito.
–Anonymous wayfarer in Jerusalem

It is interesting to note that many of the texts of the Kabbalah, the Talmud, and the Midrash are introduced by a journey: "Rabbi Bahya and Rabbi Hiya were on their way . . . ," or "Rabbi Simeon and Rabbi Eleazar his son were taking the road to . . . ," and so on. In fact, the whole text of the Kabbalah opens with an inaugural announcement of "being on the way," on a path, even if the expression is not formulated explicitly. The Kabbalah, and Jewish philosophy in general, contains a concept of thought as a voyage, that of people who think as they walk and according to the truth of walking. This is certainly one of the meanings of the verse, "You shall speak of them . . . as you go on your way." (Deuteronomy 6:7)

Everything depends on the way. We are closer to the place we are going to when we are on our way than when we convince ourselves that we have reached our destination and merely have to establish ourselves. The word *way* or *path* does not necessarily have a spatial significance. It does not merely refer to a stroll through the fields or forests of wandering thought. It does not merely take us from one place to another. It is the passage of the actual train of thought.

The road makes things move, calls them into question, places them in the balance. It invites and disquiets, incites and solicits. The "wayfarer" is not solely the kabbalist, but mankind in general. To set out on the path, to go on one's way, is also the meaning of the words heard by Abraham: "Go forth from your native land and from your father's house."

Kabbalistic thought is not only the result of research but also the advances, the detours and dead ends, the fumblings and discoveries, that we experience through many hours of reading, learning, and writing.

דרך
path

Thinking—that is to say to truly experience the act of thinking, does not mean rehashing a set of definitive theses which we have in our possession, but rather the desire to discover and formulate that which one does not know or which one knows imperfectly, and to discover new modes of life itself. "We only live at the extremity of our knowledge, at the very tip of what separates our knowledge from our ignorance" (Gilles Deleuze, *Différence et répétition*). For the kabbalist, living is an adventure and not a nostalgia for forms that have already been lived!

To Be Open to Meeting with the Most Radical Strangeness

> ***An idea is false from the moment one is satisfied with it.***
> —Alain

During our lives we meet other people, encounter books, ideas, and images. This is a true dialogue, in which the conduct of the conversation is reversed. We no longer lead the conversation ourselves; we are led. No one can know in advance what will emerge from such a situation. Consequently, the time may come when we feel at a loss, defeated. But this defeat, this feeling of having strayed from the path of knowledge, is the very experience of study.

"The experience of study" denotes not only the sense of instruction that we may receive on one subject or another, but the act of being open to experiences. The kabbalist is an eternal student. His position is that of a "seeker after truth,"and not of a "possessor of truth." When they mention a sage, the Kabbalah and the Talmud use the term *talmid-khakham,* "disciple-sage." The sage always remains a disciple-sage, always ready to study. And to study means to be open to an encounter with the most radical strangeness.

The Kabbalah and Study

> ***Interpreting means to have an effect on the destiny of individuals and the world; it means giving this destiny a new course, taking the absolute responsibility for it and being ready to pay the price. . . . Also, interpreting the Book is firstly to rise up against God in order to deliver voice and pen to His power. We need to rid ourselves of the divine part that is within us for the purpose of rendering God to himself and delight in our freedom as human beings.***
> —Edmond Jabès, *Elya*

The kabbalist is not a scholar but a researcher. He is therefore constantly reading the texts of the tradition and all the writings that enable him to make progress in his research. He is always in the process of reading and interpreting. Interpretation is not a futile game but a fundamental attitude, perhaps even *the* fundamental attitude of the human being, implementing the emotional, spiritual, and intellectual functions of man. Through its interpretation a dynamic of the psyche is produced, and of man in his entirety, who has been given the essential task of invention and the activity of opening up.

This is a perfect summary of the epistemiological objective that the Kabbalah sets itself. Through several thousands of pages and over and above the various themes discussed, openness is *taguth*, a deployment of the creative imagination and unblocking of the channels of the spirit. Through interpretation, man becomes an "infinitive man," stretched in a transcendental movement toward the infinite. The Kabbalah teaches that a text is indefinite, always open to new interpretations that are not guaranteed in any encyclopedia. The most diverse philosophical, sociological, political, linguistic, and historic interpretations can each only exhaust a small part of the possibilities of the text and of life; life remains inexhaustible and infinitely open.

The essential question is not, What is interpretation? but, Why is there interpretation? There is interpretation in order to show that, "contrary to the aspirations of an ideology, the meaning must be constructed patiently, it is not identified with a pre-existing truth which can merely be appropriated once and for all and imposed upon others" (Catherine Chalier, *La Patience*).

Interpretation is not only commentary, the fact of saying something else and of saying it better. More essentially, it brings into play the very movement of thinking, which consists precisely in shaking the prefabricated institutions of sense to their foundations. Commentary is a long journey that is an invitation to the urgency of waiving the need, often a passionate one, to draw conclusions, forming a definitive opinion and a judgment. Interpretation is the patience of sense. One needs to know how to renounce "the intense need to want to draw conclusions."

Impatience is idolatry! The messiah will always arrive late. . . . Wanting everything, immediately, is wanting to a stultified being. "The instant God," a stultified God, a dead God: the golden calf! Patience means giving time the opportunity of being time. It is the very meaning of the possibility in time of being time. It is the very meaning of the tetragrammaton.

The Human Being: Constantly Called into Question

Being is to interrogate the labyrinths of the Question asked of God and of others to which there is no reply.
—Edmond Jabès, *Elya*

If the kabbalist is a researcher and not a possessor of truth, as has been emphasized, he must nevertheless always be questioning himself. "I question, therefore I am!" is one of the fundamental tenets of kabbalistic thought. Man is the "thrust toward," the effort, tension, and desire, always beyond identity. Man constructs himself, produces himself, in time, each time becoming a different man, a different life, a different experience.

Man does not exist but becomes; this means that he has a duty to exist through his incessant change. This also applies on a collective level. A society that does not devise new forms of organization is signing its own death warrant. Man is always already above and beyond himself.

The expression "above and beyond" is translated in the philosophical language derived from Greek by the term *meta*. Man is a "meta" animal—

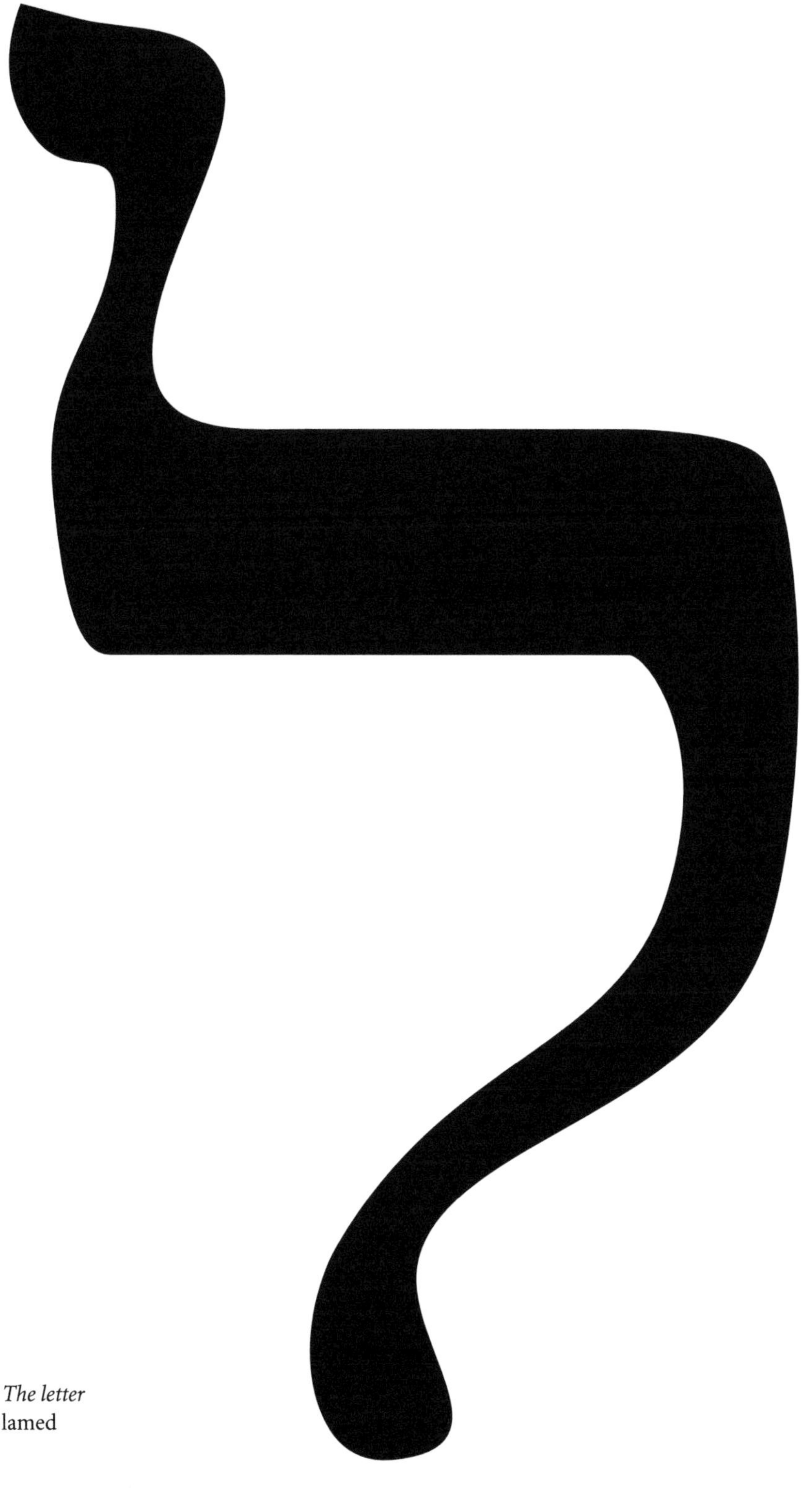

The letter
lamed

metaphysical, metaphoric, and so on. In Hebrew, this metaphoric quality of human reality is expressed as *sham,* "over there." *Sham* consists of two letters, the same letters that are used to write the word *shem,* "name," and it is the term that produced the word *shemit* or *semite.* Man is fundamentally a creature who bears a name, a name that goes before him: transcendence and "existence."

Man is an infinitive being, open to the future and the incessant possibility of calling himself into question. He himself "has become the question," according to a formulation found in the Zohar. In Hebrew, as will be discussed again later, man is called *adam,* a word with the numeric value of 45; this number can also be written in Hebrew as *ma,* "why?" Man is a Why?—his essence is the effect of dynamic questioning. Man is the sentinel of questioning. By preserving the Why? he returns the speech of which he is constituted.

The man, *adam/ma,* is an opening into the future.

4

A Revolution in Our Perception of the World

At the point where philosophy ends is the point at which the wisdom of the Kabbalah begins.
—Rabbi Nachman of Breslov

Hearing the Voices of Angels

In the kabbalistic tradition, when someone receives a message from above, that is to say, when he interprets signs as a message addressed to him from on high, he meets an angel. The word for an angel in Hebrew is *malakh*, "sent." Everything that man perceives and considers to be a message from the worlds above is an angel. All those through whom man sends a message to the world above also have the status of angels.

A Renewed Perception of the World

The Kabbalah begins with a unique way of being in the world. Although it combines an approach that is both rational and mystical, its origin lies in this unique attitude, which consists in:
– hearing the unheard;

– seeing the invisible;
– feeling the immaterial.

The Kabbalah renders man conscious of the mystery contained within him and surrounding him. To put it another way, the special attention that man can pay to the hidden and mysterious world is the key for entry into the world of the Kabbalah. "The secret is the foundation," says the Zohar. All mystical thought rests upon this principle. The entire treasury of Kabbalah is known as *khokhmat hanistar,* "the wisdom of that which is hidden." Everything has its hidden and its revealed elements. The work of the kabbalist is to penetrate deep into the inner world in order to perceive the *or haganuz,* "hidden light."

The kabbalist knows that man is essentially defined by his capacity for imagination. The word *adam,* "man," is similar to the word meaning "I shall imagine."

Seeing beyond Events

In the kabbalistic tradition, the description of the universe is that of a world that manifests an incredible richness and a stunning splendor. Using a great diversity of comparisons and metaphors, it states repeatedly that we are constantly surrounded by a grandiose cosmos.

There exist "tens of thousands of worlds with innumerable marvels, for each door contains another door, each degree precedes another degree, through which the Glory of the Infinite is manifested. . . . The marvels of creation whose dance surrounds us are continually present. A celestial flood of music and light perpetually bathes the world and all our invisible worlds. These melodious chants are said to be of such an extraordinary beauty that they may be dangerous for the unprepared mind" (Edward Hoffman, *Jewish Mysticism and Modern Psychology*).

Our conscience often seems to be engulfed in a state of exile from the *meqor ha-khayyim,* "source of life." Innumerable worlds of marvels surround us, but in characteristic fashion, we remain aware of only our most ephemeral and mundane desires. The Kabbalah is a struggle against the total oblivion of these potential kingdoms of ecstasy, which are contained within us; it is a path to enable us to find them. Any event may awaken our superior faculties, since the light of the source of life may be found "in everything and everywhere." We must learn to see beyond apparently superficial, insignificant events of everyday life.

The main task for each of us is to awaken from this internal slumber. The will to do so is of crucial importance in the process; "Through a powerful fixation of the mind and an intense concentration touching the depths of the heart, a person must force himself to perceive this song of the infinite" (Hoffman, *Jewish Mysticism*). The kabbalist feels the divine presence directly in every living thing. Each blade of grass is imbued with its own song of ecstasy, teaches Rabbi Nachman of Breslov.

The kabbalist knows that the entire universe is animated by the light of infinity, the divine vitality that is both all and one. The kabbalist is someone who is willing to listen to all the vibrations of the world and who, for this reason, is capable of hearing and understanding the language of leaves rustling in the wind, streams, and stones by the wayside.

5

The Route to Initiation

The *Ma'asseh Bereshit* and the *Ma'asseh Merkava*

The first mystics of the Second Temple period had two main preoccupations. The Talmud Hagiga (p. 28) distinguishes between the *ma'asseh bereshit* and the *ma'asseh merkava.* Groups or circles of initiates were formed around a secret, esoteric doctrine that led to a mystical interpretation of two important chapters of the Bible: the first chapter of Genesis, which develops the history of the creation of the world, and the first chapter of Ezekiel, which describes the vision of the chariot in which God rides.

The first form of this mysticism is called *ma'asseh bereshit,* "the act of beginning," which can be explained as the cosmology of the mystical masters of the Mishna, as well as exploration of the complex structure of the worlds above and of the divine in general.

The second form of Jewish mysticism is called *ma'asseh merkava,* "the act of the chariot." It consists of an exploration of the divine through multiple experiences of ecstasy and ascent.

It could be said that the *ma'asseh bereshit* represents those who analyze in these texts the way in which the light of infinity appeared and descended to our world and all the other worlds of creation. The *ma'asseh merkava* corresponds to the "ecstatic trend," attempting to discover how the initiate may attain a state of ecstasy.*

* For more about this subject, see Gershom Scholem, *Major Trends in Jewish Mysticism,* and Perle Epstein, *Kabbalah: The Way of the Jewish Mystic.*

A Talmudic Story

Our rabbis taught:

One day, Rabbi Yohanan Ben Zakkai was riding on a donkey.

As he left Jerusalem, followed by Rabbi Eleazar Ben Arakh, his disciple, the latter asked him:

—Master, teach me a chapter from the Heavenly Chariot (the *merkava*).

—Have I not taught you, my son, that the Heavenly Chariot is not taught to a person unless he is a sage who is capable of understanding it by himself?

—Permit me therefore, Master, to state certain things which I have retained from what you have taught me.

—Very well, replied Rabbi Yohanan, and he immediately dismounted from his donkey, covered himself with his robe and sat on a stone under an olive tree.

—Why have you dismounted from your donkey? Rabbi Eleazar asked him.

—Do you consider it fitting that I remain with my legs straddled over my donkey while you are commenting on the story of the Heavenly Chariot, when the *shekhina* is with us and the ministering angels accompany us?

Then Rabbi Eleazar Ben Arakh began to comment upon the story of the Heavenly Chariot.

And a fire appeared in the heavens.

All the surrounding trees, enveloped in flames, chanted a hymn of praise.

—Which one?

—"Praise the Lord, O you who are on earth, all sea monsters and ocean depths . . . all fruit trees and cedars . . . , let them praise the name of the Lord!" (*Psalms*, 148: 7)

And an angel stood in the midst of the fire and responded:

—That is indeed the true story of the Heavenly Chariot.

Then Rabbi Yohanan Ben Zakkai rose, kissed his disciple on the forehead and said:

—Blessed be the Lord, God of Israel, who gave Abraham our father a descendent such as Eleazar Ben Arakh, capable of understanding, analyzing, and explaining the Heavenly Chariot. There are those who interpret well but who perform badly [the words of the Torah]; there are others who perform it well but do not know how to interpret it. But you, Eleazar Ben Arakh, you interpret [the words of the Torah] as well as you perform them. Be glad, Abraham our father, that you have a descendent such as Eleazar Ben Arakh!

(*Hagiga*, 14b)

The *Ma'asseh Merkava;* or, The Structure of the Heavenly Chariot

The *ma'asseh merkava* is a meditation and mystical practice founded upon the vision of the "heavenly chariot" described in the first chapter of the prophet Ezekiel, a text that it is important to read at least once in order to understand the origin of many of the images found in many descriptions of mystical visions.

> In the thirtieth year, of the fifth day of the fourth month, when I was in the community of exiles by the Chebar Canal, the heavens opened and I saw visions of God. On the fifth day of the month—it was the fifth year of the exile of King Jehoiachin,—the word of the Lord came to the priest Ezekiel son of Buzi, by the Chebar Canal, in the land of the Chaldeans. And the hand of the Lord came upon him there.
>
> I looked, and lo, a stormy wind came sweeping out of the north—a huge cloud and flashing fire, surrounded by a radiance; and in the center of it, in the center of the fire, a gleam as of amber. In the center of it were also the figures of four creatures. And this was their appearance:
>
> They took the form of human beings. However, each was [fused into] a single rigid leg, and the feet of each were like a single calf's hoof; and their sparkle was like the luster of burnished bronze. They had human hands below their wings. The four of them had their faces and their wings on their four sides. Each one's wings touched those of the other. They did not turn when they moved, each could move in the direction of any of its faces.
>
> Each of them had a human face [at the front]; each of the four had the face of a lion on the right; each of the four had the face of an ox on the left; and each of the four had the face of an eagle [at the back]. Such were their faces. As for their wings, they were separated: above each had two touching those of the others, while the other two covered its body. And each could move in the direction of any of its faces; they went wherever the spirit impelled them to go, without turning when they moved.
>
> Such then was the appearance of the creatures. With them was something that looked like burning coals of fire. This fire, suggestive of torches, kept moving about among the creatures; the fire had a radiance and lightning issued from the fire. Dashing to and fro [among] the creatures was something that looked like flares.
>
> As I gazed on the creatures, I saw one wheel on the ground next to each of the four-faced creatures. As for the appearance and structure of the wheels, they gleamed like beryl. All four had the same form; the appearance and structure of each was as of two wheels cutting through each other. And when they moved, each could move in the direction of any of its four quarters; they did not veer when they moved. Their rims were tall and frightening, for the rims of all four were covered all over with eyes. And when the creatures moved forward, the wheels moved at their sides; and when the creatures were borne above the earth, the wheels were borne too. Wherever the spirit impelled them to go, they went—wherever the spirit impelled them—and the wheels were borne alongside them; for the spirit of the creatures was in the wheels. When those moved, these moved; and when those stood still, these stood still; and when those were borne above the earth, the wheels were borne alongside them—for the spirit of the creatures was in the wheels.

> Above the heads of the creatures was a form: an expanse, with an awe-inspiring gleam as of crystal, was spread out above their heads. Under the expanse, each had one pair of wings extended toward those of the others; and each had another pair covering its body. When they moved, I could hear the sound of their wings like the sound of mighty waters, like the sound of Shaddai, a tumult like the din of an army. When they stood still, they would let their wings droop.
>
> Above the expanse over their heads was the semblance of a throne, in appearance like sapphire, and on top, upon this semblance of a throne, there was a semblance of a human form. From what appeared as his loins up, I saw a gleam as of amber—what looked like a fire encased in a frame; and from what appeared as his loins down, I saw what looked like fire. There was a radiance all about him. Like the appearance of the bow which shines in the clouds on a day of rain, such was the appearance of the surrounding radiance. That was the appearance of the semblance of the presence of the Lord. When I beheld it, I flung myself down on my face. And I heard the voice of someone speaking.

The Mystical Circles of the *Merkava:* Initiation

The kabbalists of the *merkava* used to meet in small groups to meditate upon the text and experience a meeting with the divine, an ecstatic experience and one of ascending to the heavens. The *ma'asseh merkava* is a study that seeks to understand how man can relate to the infinite light of God, how man can gain access to the higher worlds. These paths remained shrouded in mystery and hidden except to the initiates.

Anyone desiring to become a member of the brotherhood of kabbalists became a postulant and had to take an examination in various subjects. The conditions of admission into the circles of mystics of the *merkava* comprised both an examination of theoretical knowledge of the doctrine and a requirement that the novice exhibit certain moral characteristics.

According to some sources, the novice is also supposed to have been accepted on physiognomical and chiromantic criteria. Other sources, such as the *Sefer Hekhalot* ("Book of Palaces") speak of eight conditions for acceptance into the circle of initiates.

If the novice passed the examination, he became *mequbal,* "received"; that is to say, he had been received into kabbalism. The word "kabbalist" thus originally meant acceptance into a circle of initiates in an attempt to reproduce mystical experiences of "ascents" and "journeys."

Vision of the heavenly chariot in the first chapter of Ezekiel.
The prophet is in a state of ecstasy beside the Chebar Canal, in Babylon, and sees the chariot or *merkava* (taken from the Christian "Bear Bible," England, seventeenth century).

The Mysteries of the Hand

In the Zohar, the bones, nerves, and the whole body of man are but signs of higher wisdom. This is what the Zohar says about it:

> Just as God sowed the sky with stars and planets in which astrologers read divine secrets, so he has heaped testimony upon testimony on the human body; and just as the positions of the stars and planets change depending on that which happens in the world, so the features and lineaments in man are subject to change from time to time, depending on his destiny. . . . Just as the expanse of the sky constitutes a map containing figures which reveal the highest truths to the initiate, so the exterior of man, the features of his face, the lineaments of his forehead, the lines on his hands constitute the mirror in which the character of the individual can be read, down to the minutest detail.
> (Zohar II:67a, 70b)

The palm of the hand is a sort of summary of the human soul; hence the importance of studying it, and studying its lines, the technique of chiromancy. Chiromancy is usually defined as a method of divination, and is thus a practice more or less related to the art of magic.

One can sometimes encounter a whole crowd of diviners, fortune-tellers, and readers of horoscopes. Chiromancy is no doubt a pretext for explaining the unpredictable and for superstitious mythomania. It should not be forgotten, however, that kabbalistic chiromancy has no other purpose than to reveal, through the lines of the hand, the character of a potential candidate for the study of sacred texts, especially those of the Kabbalah. Chiromancy is part of the entrance examination, as it were, into the circle of initiates.

In this respect, the Zohar recalls the passage in Exodus (18:21 ff.) in which Jethro, Moses' father-in-law, assists him with advice on how to govern the people during the long march through the desert. The task is a delicate one. It involves choosing collaborators, the "judges" who can settle all the affairs of the people and any disputes arising among them. "You shall seek [them] out," says Jethro to Moses; that is to say, rightly, and attribute the greatest importance to their physiognomy and ascertain everything about their deepest being to assess their reliability as well as the impartiality of their judgment. For a true kabbalist, there is no question of venturing beyond this. Divination, in all its forms, is severely prohibited by the Torah.

We read in the Zohar :

> The lines of the hand, even those of fingers, conceal great mysteries. It is the lines of the right hand which are the most important. . . .
>
> Five faint lines at the bottom of the inner surface of the little finger, and four lines above on the same surface, as well as four vertical lines on the outer surface of the same finger indicate a careless, lazy person; such a person will often suc-

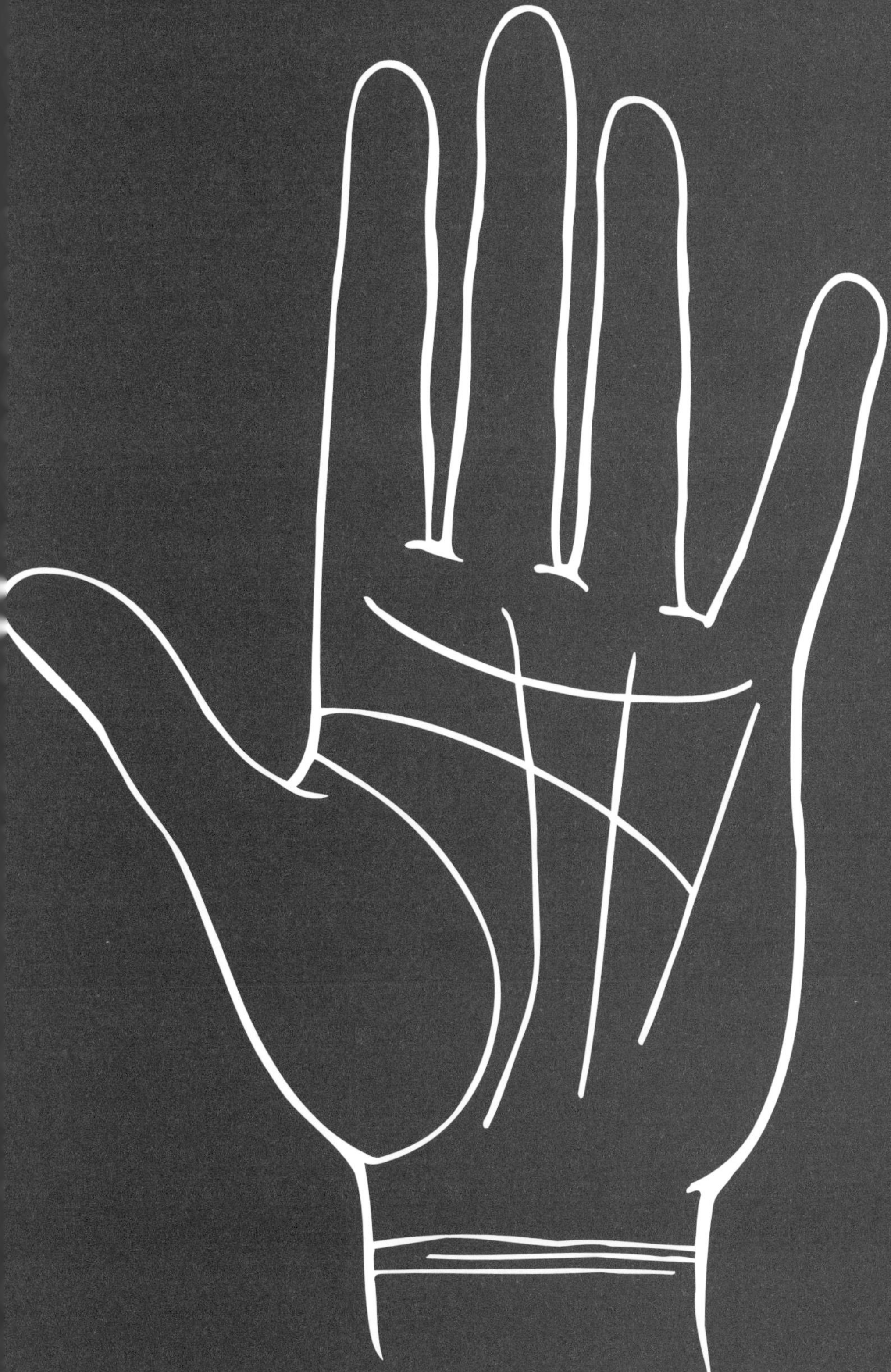

> ceed in his endeavors, if he can decide to go on a journey, but his laziness always prevents him. This mystery is also expressed in the vertical form of the Hebrew letter *zayin.*
>
> A vertical line on the inner face of the middle finger indicates a well-balanced person who thinks before acting and does not undertake anything without having first weighed up all the disadvantages that could result from his action.
>
> Two vertical lines on the same surface of the finger, which do not disappear even when the finger is extended, indicate a person who is not much given to considering a matter and all of whose actions are precipitous.
>
> There is also the "refined and reflective" person all of whose exertions are intended to enable him to walk in the ways of the Holy One, Blessed be He, without any other ambition. Let us carefully examine the palm of one such just person. Three vertical lines on the same surface of the finger, with another two or three lines on the back of the same finger, that is to say the back of the middle finger where it joins the ring finger.
>
> As for the wicked person, the lines of his hand will not fail to betray him: "Four or five lines on the outer surface, and as many lines on the inner surface of the middle finger."

Does this mean that people cannot change and that the marks on the hand are a fatality without freedom? The fatality of an inexorable destiny is unknown in the Kabbalah. The path to *teshuva,* "return to oneself," always remains open. Thus, thanks to contrition and prayer, man is capable of altering his own destiny; and in this case the number of lines also changes; three lines are sometimes reduced to two, two may be changed to four, and so on. The lines of the hand are not permanent; they change according to a person's behavior. Neither the macrocosm that is the universe nor the microcosm that is the human being are linked by laws of inexorable fatality.

> Just as a constellation is not permanent—for sometimes it is a star which appears in one direction and sometimes another star that appears in the opposite direction—so the lines traced on the human body, which corresponds to the constellation of the firmament, are not permanent, but metamorphose depending on the behavior of man.
> (Zohar II:76b)

Preparation for Ecstasy

The mystics of the *merkava* used to meet after long fasts that could last between forty and ninety days. In a state of physical and psychological exhaustion, the *mequbal* or kabbalist would take an almost fetal position, sitting on the ground with his knees bent and his head between his knees.

The body posture that is typical of these ascetics is also that of Elijah in prayer upon Mount Carmel. It is an attitude of profound forgetfulness of self that, to judge from certain ethnological parallels, is favorable for inducing prehypnotic autosuggestion. Dennys gives a very similar description of a Chinese woman who is conjuring up the spirit of a dead person: "She sits on a low chair and crouches forward so that her head rests on her knees. Then in a deep and level voice, she repeats an exorcism three times; suddenly, there seems to be a certain change in her." This posture is also found in the Talmud, as being characteristic of forgetfulness of self, in relation to a master called Hanina ben Dosa when he was deep in prayer (reported by Gershom Scholem in *Major Trends in Jewish Mysticism,* 63.) In this position, he began to recite softly long hymns and sacred chants whose words have not come down to us.

The Seven Palaces

After making these major preparations, and in a state of ecstasy, the kabbalist begins his "journey."

The texts of this tradition do not offer details of the ascent of the mystic through the seven heavens, but they describe his voyage through the seven palaces located in the highest heaven. The journey is an initiation in the course of which the *mequbal* has to discover the keys that give access to the seven palaces, at the end of which it should be possible to see the *merkava,* or Heavenly Chariot.

On his way, the kabbalist meets a multitude of "porters" posted on either side of the entrance to each celestial palace that the soul must cross in its ascent. This is where the soul needs a password to continue on its journey without danger, a magical seal consisting of a secret name that has the power to chase away demons and repel hostile angels.

Each successive stage in the ascent requires a new seal with which the traveler seals himself in order to avoid being "dragged into the fire and flames, in the whirlwind and the storm which surround God" (Scholem,

Major Trends in Jewish Mysticism). It is this need for the soul to be protected during its voyage that has created these seals with their dual function, that of a protective armor and that of a magical weapon.

The seven mystical seals that permit entry into the *merkava*, attributed by some to Nahamiel Gaon.

The magic protection of a single seal is sufficient at first, but the difficulties experienced by the devotee eventually become greater. A simple, brief formula is no longer effective. Plunged into his ecstatic trance, at the same moment the mystic has a feeling of disappointment, which he attempts to overcome by using longer, more complicated magical formulas and the symbols required for a more difficult struggle in order to pass through the gates which bar his way. As his psychic energy wanes, he makes a greater magical effort and his attempts at reciting incantations become stronger until he has managed to complete the recitation, without understanding the meaning, of all the pages of the magic words which will provide the key to opening the closed door.

Each mysterious name seems to supply a new defensive weapon against demons where, for example, there might be insufficient magic power to overcome the obstacles on the path to the *merkava*.

The *Ma'asseh Bereshit*, "Book of the Beginning"

The other major esoteric trend in Judaism in this early period of the Kabbalah is called the *ma'asseh bereshit*—literally, "the act of beginning." The word *bereshit* means "beginning," and it is the first word and the name of the first chapter of the Bible.

A much more speculative trend is mainly concerned with the structure of the cosmos and our connection therewith. Its fundamental questions are, How was the world created? What existed before? What is time? What is space?, How do the forces of on high react upon the forces of what is below? and so on.

The Mystical Writings of the Period: The Literature of the Palaces

The mystical works of the period—which could also be called the mysticism of the Talmud since many of the members of these circles of initiates were Talmudists—are collected into several treatises.

All these documents take the form of short essays, brief treatises, or scattered fragments of variable length, no doubt extracted from much more voluminous works. There are also a number of crude, almost unformed documents from a literary point of view. Most of these treatises are called the "Books of the *Hekhalot*," meaning that they are descriptions of the *hekhalot*, the heavenly halls and palaces through which the visionary must pass; the seventh and last of these halls contains the throne of divine glory. One of these treatises is called the "Book of Enoch."*

In addition to the Book of the Palaces, there are treatises called the "great *hekhalot*" and the "small *hekhalot*"—the Great and Small Palaces.

Extract from the *Sefer Hanoch* ("Book of Enoch")

Rabbi Ishmael in the seventh palace:

> Enoch walked with God. Then he was no more, for God took him. (*Genesis, 5:24*)
>
> Rabbi Ishmael said:
>
> When I rose to the heights to contemplate my vision of the chariot, I entered into six palaces, one inside the other, and when I attained the threshold of the seventh palace, I stood in prayer before the Holy One, blessed be He. I raised my eyes upward and said: "Master of the universe, may it please you, I beg of you, to enable me to benefit presently from the merit of Aaron, son of Amram, lover of peace and pursuer of peace, who received the priestly crown before your glory on

* There is a wonderful commented translation into French by Charles Mopsik, one of the greatest living experts on the Kabbalah, called *Le Livre hébreu d'Énoch* or *Livre des palais.*

Mount Sinai, so that Prince Qatspiel and the angels that are with him shall not rule over me and shall not throw me out of Heaven." Immediately, the Holy One, blessed be He, conveyed my intention to His servant, the angel Metatron, Prince of the Face.

He beat his wings and came to meet me with great joy, to save me from their hands, and he seized me in his hand beneath their gaze and said to me: "Come in peace, you have been approved before the Most High and the Exalted, to contemplate the semblance of the chariot."

At that moment, I entered the seventh palace and he led me to the camp of the *shekhina,* he presented me before the Throne of Glory so that I could contemplate the chariot. But as soon as the princes of the chariot looked at me, and the seraphim of flame cast their eyes upon me, I was seized with a fit of shaking and began to tremble. I fell prostrate and lost consciousness due to the radiance of the emanation from their eyes and the brilliance of the aspect of their faces. Thus, the Holy One, blessed be He, scolded them and said to them: "My officiants, my seraphim, my cherubim, my ophanim, close your eyes before my son, Ishmael, my beloved, my preferred and my glory, so that he does not fear nor tremble!"

Then came Metatron, Prince of the Face, who restored my soul and put me back on my feet, but I still did not have enough strength to sing a hymn to the Glorious Throne of the Glorious King, the Majesty above all kings, the splendor above all sovereigns, until an hour had passed. An hour later, the Holy One, blessed be He opened for me the portals of the *shekhina,* the portals of peace, the portals of wisdom, the portals of strength, the portals of valor, the portals of speech, the portals of song, the portals of the *qedusha,* the portals of melody, and he illuminated my eyes and my heart with words of praise, of glorification, of jubilation, of acclamation, of song, of magnificence, of beauty, of lauds, of fervor. When I opened my mouth and began to sing before the Throne of Glory, the sacred beings beneath the Throne of the Glorious King and above the Throne responded after me, crying: "Holy, holy, holy" and "blessed is the Glory of the Lord in his hall."

The *Sefer Yetsira* ("Book of Creation")

The most important text of the mystical *ma'asseh bereshit* is the *Sefer Yetsira* ("Book of Creation"), the oldest Hebrew text of systematic and speculative thought that has come down to us. It is considered to be the first written work of metaphysics, and despite its small size, it has had an enormous influence. No other work matches it in its combination of brevity—less than two thousand words, even in the longer version—with an obscure, laconic, and enigmatic style and terminology. That is why the book has been inter-

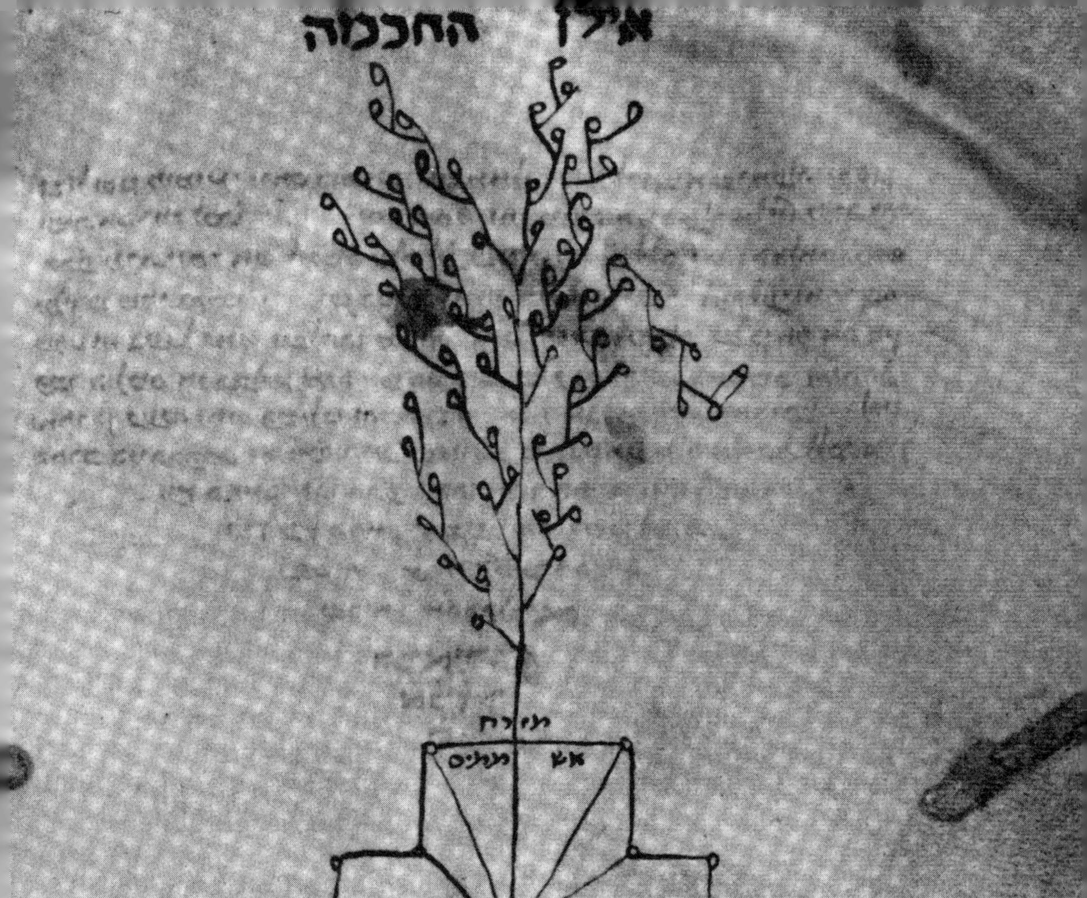

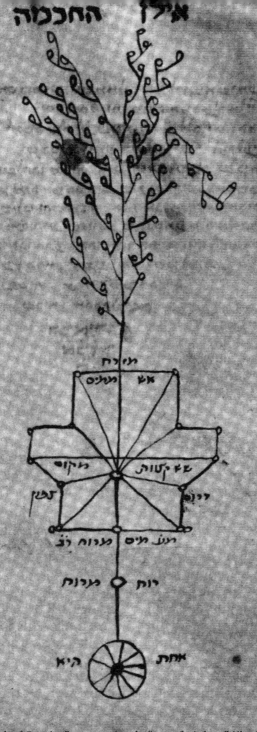

Page from the "Book of Creation" representing the "tree of wisdom," (*ilan ha-khokhma.*)

preted in so many different ways for more than a thousand years and why, even thanks to the scientific research undertaken in the nineteenth and twentieth centuries, it has not been possible to produce an unambiguous interpretation of it.

Like all the major early kabbalistic texts, the *Sefer Yetsira* is an item of pseudepigrapha (a literary genre that consists in attributing to an ancient, famous personality books actually written at a much later date.) The "Book of Creation" is attributed to the first of the biblical patriarchs, Abraham (although another version is attributed to Rabbi Akiva).

Numerous commentaries—some of which are very perceptive and have had a strong influence on the mystical literature of Judaism—have been produced on this fundamental text, which dates from the first or second centuries of the common era. The doctrine of the *Sefer Yetsira* is considered by kabbalists to be a precursor to that of the Zohar, and the thought that emerges from this doctrine—based on the symbols of decimal numbers and the division of the Hebrew letters of the alphabet—is of great interest to metaphysics. (More will be said later on this subject starting on page 293.)

The influence of the *Sefer Yetsira* upon Jewish thought has been considerable. It opened up new horizons into a mystical world, thanks mainly to the commentaries on it of great writers such as Saadya, Donolo, Barzilai, Harabad, Ibn Gabirol, Yehuda Halevi, and Ibn Ezra. Its theory of the *sefirot* was reused many times and acquired many deep insights, produced by subtle thinkers. In other words, through its symbolic formulae using numbers and letters, the "Book of Creation"* is central to metaphysical speculation in the Kabbalah.

* Translator's note: The word *yetsira*, from the root *y-ts-r*, "to produce or make," is translated into English as "formation" in every context except in the name of the "Book of Creation," whose standard English title is *Sefer Yetsira*. The Hebrew word for creation, in the sense of the creation of the world, is *beriya*.

6

Journey to Paradise
The Four Masters of the Pardess

The Talmud is an encyclopedic text that analyzes law *(halakah)* as well as legend *(aggadah)*. It is the principal judicial legal text, as well as a commentary and biblical exegesis, and was completed circa 500 B.C.E. Many of the great sages who labored to compile the Talmud were fully initiated into the secret tradition of the Kabbalah, though not all were inclined to practice it. Even then, its initiates warned that very real physical and mental danger awaited those who rushed into this garden of metaphors, however sincere their motives.

One of the most famous texts of the initiatory literature of the period, which appears in various versions, of which the Talmudic version is the best known, is a story contained in the pages of the tractate Hagiga, which the Talmud rightly associates with the mysticism of the *merkava* and the *ma'asseh bereshit.*

> Four entered Paradise, Ben Azai, Ben Zoma, "Aher," and Rabbi Akiva.
>
> Rabbi Akiva addressed them, saying
>
> —When you approach the stones of brilliant marble, do not say "Water, water," for it is writtten: "He who profers lies shall not dwell in my presence."
>
> The first one looked and died.

> The second one looked and went mad.
> The third one cut himself off from his roots and became a heretic.
> The fourth one entered in peace and went out in peace.

This archetypal story emphasizes the fact that four great Jewish sages, Ben Azai, Ben Zoma, Elisha Ben Abuya, and Rabbi Akiva, followed the secret path to the end. They entered paradise. The commentaries say that they "rose to heaven" by using holy names. They thus had a collective ecstatic experience and visited the heavenly palaces. The text is an important one, since it clearly points to the fact that the great masters of the Talmudic tradition were in the habit of resorting to mystical practices.

The Dangers of Ascent into the Palaces

As the text of the Pardess shows, great dangers are inherent in the ascent to the palaces within the sphere of the *merkava*, especially for those who undertake the voyage without the necessary preparation. The dangers increase as the journey progresses. Angels and judges leap on the traveler and try to evict him; a fire emanating from his own body threatens to devour him.

The *Hebrew Book of Enoch* contains the story of a description given by the patriarch to Rabbi Ishmael of his own metamorphosis into the angel Metatron, when his flesh was transformed into "blazing torches." According to the "great *hekhalot*," each mystic must undergo this transformation, but being less worthy than Enoch, he is in danger of being devoured by the "blazing torches." Passage through the stage of mystical transfiguration is an inevitable necessity. According to another fragment, the mystic must be able to remain upright "without hands or feet," for both have been burned. The position of being without feet in a bottomless place is always mentioned as being a characteristic experience shared by numerous ecstatics.

Those initiated into this visionary tradition were called *yordei merkava*, "those who descended in the chariot." There were two reasons for this. First, if it is easy to ascend, it is not always easy to descend; the test is thus the ability to return "to earth" after ecstasy. Second, the initiates always descended internally further than the remotest corner of their own mind. It was said that the airborne chariot, ready to carry the disciple away and raise him through all the levels of consciousness until the celestial image of Ezekiel could be contemplated, was buried deep in the profoundest spheres of meditation.

In the writings of the *hekhalot,* the masters of the system traced like expert cartographers the difficult interior terrain that a devotee who launched into the quest would have to traverse, describing what the initiate would probably see and feel. For example, the sixth celestial plane was said to resemble a brilliant and infinite reflection of the waves of the sea. At each stage that progressed into the interior self, the visions became more disturbing, even terrifying. For instance, the *Hebrew Book of Enoch* reads, "From Makhon to Aravot, the voyage lasted five hundred years. . . . What is there? Treasure chambers containing benedictions, storerooms of snow, warehouses of peace, the souls of the just and the souls still to be born, the terrible punishments reserved for the wicked."

Yet the sages intimated that these images were, in the end, subordinate to the disciple's own spirit. This same literature advised the practitioner not to become overwhelmed by the apparitions that rose before him. If he had prepared himself adequately by training in advance, he would be capable of pronouncing the appropriate words at the right moment and banishing the visions that were so destructive to his soul. Fasting, special breathing exercises, and rhythmic chants were typically used as aids to bring the initiate into a modified state of consciousness. It is interesting to note striking parallels between this approach to higher consciousness and those of several other spiritual traditions.

The Pardess and the Four Levels of Meaning

The text of the four rabbis who entered the Pardess was a very popular one in the Kabbalah and the Talmud, since it served as a starting point for a consideration of what is commonly known as the "four levels of meaning in the Scriptures." These four levels upon which the scriptures can be read have been given names:

- ***pshat***: the simple or literal meaning

- *remez*: the allusion or hint
- *drash*: the meaning solicited
- *sod*: the hidden or secret meaning

The initials of these four words form an acronym that, when vocalized, is pronounced "Pardess," meaning both "orchard" and "paradise." We progress increasingly from that which is present in the text to that which is absent as we pass from one level to another, starting from the *pshat.* The meaning is totally present in the text at the *pshat* level, the simplest. It begins to disappear at the *remez* level, that of allusion; something of the meaning is still present in the text, although it is incomplete; the *remez,* the allusion or hint, is therefore intended to bridge a gap.

At the next level, that of *drash,* we find a gap; an additional meaning is not even in the text, but added as a question in relation to the context—as it were, to cover a lack at the second degree, which concerns not the text but the unsaid context. Here, the interpretation is applied by the reader to himself. It is an existential application. The reader understands himself, but this comprehension remains at the intellectual level.

Finally, at the level of *sod,* it is no longer a matter of a gap in the text, nor a perceived gap on the basis of what is present but incomplete, as for the *remez,* nor of a gap perceived in what is already missing from the text, as in the case of *drash.* The *sod,* the hidden meaning, is totally absent from the text, even in the form of a loophole, or gap, a request of any sort. Furthermore, it constitutes a text in itself, a different reading of the text on the basis of a rearrangement of the letters of the text. Here again, the reader understands himself, but he goes beyond the purely intellectual approach. The *sod* is more of a mystical experience than a reading.

The Jewish Interpretation and the Christian Interpretation

At this stage, it is useful to consider the difference between the Jewish and the Christian exegesis.

- **Christian exegesis:** The Middle Ages saw the development of the theory of allegorism, whereby the Holy Scriptures (and later, by extension, poetry and the figurative arts) could be interpreted in four different ways—

literal, allegorical, moral, and anagogical or mystical. This is the Pardess.

The origin for this theory is to be found in Saint Paul. It was taken up by Saint Jerome, Saint Augustine, John Scot Erigenes, the Venerable Bede, Hugh and Richard de Saint-Victor, Alain de Lille, Saint Bonaventure, Thomas Aquinas, and many others, and it constitutes the key to medieval poetry. A text conceived on this principle is indisputably endowed with a certain openness; the reader knows that each sentence, each character, embraces a multitude of meanings that it is up to him to discover. Depending on his state of mind, he will choose whichever key he deems the best and will use the text in a way that may be different from that adopted during a previous reading.

Thus, in this context, openness does not mean indeterminate communication, infinite possibilities of form, liberty of interpretation. The reader merely has at his disposal a range of carefully determined possibilities that are conditional upon the interpretative reaction never escaping from the author's control. If we take a verse (of an event in biblical history) and have available the four forms of writing, we exhaust all the permissible readings of it. The reader may choose one meaning rather than another within the verse, which evolves on four separate planes, though without escaping from the preestablished and unequivocal rules. The significance of the allegorical and emblematic figures that one finds in medieval texts is determined by encyclopedias, bestiaries, and lapidaries of the period; their symbolism is objective and institutional.

- **Jewish exegesis:** On the other hand, in the Talmudic and kabbalistic concept of interpretation, the text is undefined and open to constantly changing interpretations. One finds the four meanings of the Scriptures, but these meanings remain all-purpose; they are not guaranteed by any encyclopedia. The most diverse philosophical, symbolic, psychoanalytical, psychological, sociological, political, linguistic interpretations can only exhaust, in each case, one part of the possibilities offered by the text, which remains inexhaustible and open because its structure is that of the "visible-invisible."

As far as Jewish thought is concerned, the text is complete in itself—not a letter may be missing, not a single additional letter may be inserted—and yet, despite this completeness, the text is open to infinity.

Innumerable points of view of the interpreters and innumerable aspects of the text respond to each other, meet, and mutually enlighten each other, so that to reveal the text in its entirety, the interpreter must absorb it in one of its particular aspects and, conversely, a particular aspect of the text must await the interpreter, who is capable of capturing and thus giving a renewed vision of the completeness. All these interpretations are definitive in the sense that each of them is the text itself, as far as the interpreter is concerned; but they exist in a temporary time frame because the interpreter knows that he must continue to extend his own interpretation indefinitely.

To the extent that they are definitive, these interpretations are parallel, in such a way as to exclude others while not denying them.

Thus Revelation is the gift of the keys to interpretation. Tradition is the transmission, on the one hand, of these keys, and on the other hand, of the constituted acquired meaning—the spoken word. But at the same time it is renewed by the Master, the vehicle through whom the tradition-revelation-creation is transmitted. The fact that revelation is not the effective communication of an actual given, one that has substance and can be expressed, makes it possible to understand the existence of a plurality of interpretations, of a plethora of meaning. This is taught by the prophet Jeremiah (23:29), when he says, "Behold, my word is like fire, declares the Lord, and like a hammer that shatters rocks and causes innumerable sparks to fly." Interpretation is not only perception; it is a constituent of meaning.*

All these remarks should enable us to understand the meaning of the following text in the tractate Menahot (29b), one of the most famous of the Talmud, which features Moses and Rabbi Akiva together. The tractate relates:

> Rav Yehuda said in the name of Rav:
> —At the moment when Moses ascended to the heights [to the heavens], he found God seated and attaching crowns to the letters.
> Moses asked him:
> —Master of the world, what is hindering you?

* On the question of interpretation, the reader can consult *Le Livre brûlé* and *Lire aux éclats, éloge de la caresse,* by the author of this book, as well as David Banon's *Lecture infinie.*

—There will be a man in the future, after several generations, whose name is Akiva ben Yossef, who will interpret thousands of Laws on the point of these crowns.
—Master of the world, show him to me.
—Go back.

Moses went back and sat at the end of the eighth row [in the house of study] and did not know what they [the master and his disciples] were saying.

He began to lose his strength.

When Akiva reached a certain point in his teaching, his students said to him:
—Master, what is the source of your teaching?

He replied to them:
—*Halakha le-Moshé mi-Sinai.* [The law that was given to Moses on Mount Sinai.]

Moses spirit was calmed.

He returned to stand before God and said to him:
—Master of the world, you had a man like that at your disposal and yet you gave the Torah through an intermediary like me?
—Be quiet, that is how I decided to do it.

7

How to Transmit the Secret

The philosophers aspired to "explain" the world, in such a way that everything would become clear and transparent that life would no longer hold any problems or mysteries (or as few as possible).
But should one not, on the contrary, insist on showing that the very thing which seems to be clear and comprehensive to men is strangely enigmatic and mysterious?
Should one not try to deliver oneself and deliver others from the power of concepts whose clarity kills mystery?
The sources of being are actually in that which is hidden and not in that which is exposed.
—Léon Chestov, *Athènes et Jérusalem*

The Importance of Poetry

For the Kabbalah, the essence of the world is poetic. When speaking of the Kabbalah, one needs to find a language that offers an opening onto infinity. The great texts of the Kabbalah, especially the texts of the literature of the Palaces and later the Zohar, used poetic language.

Could any reading of the earliest meanings be other than poetic? The perception of the invisible and the unheard is not always conceptually justifiable nor philosophically convincing. It is poetically certain! The original images, metaphors, and symbols constitute the first terms, even before there was any logical discourse.

Language and our understanding of the world begin in this preliminary region in which a set of complex correspondances echo each other and succeed in enabling us to experience the most infinite subtleties of our presence in the world. Before philosophy and that important tool, the concept, time passed in silence, the silent procession of the rhythm of the seasons, things, beings, leaves, flowers, fruits, colors, and the sounds of life. Poetry is that which seeks to restore all the richness and all the details of the world and make all of the deepest light vibrate within us.

One of the last great kabbalists, Rabbi Abraham Itshaq Kook (1865–1935), also called the Baal Ha-Orot or Master of the Lights, as well as the Baal Or Tov, Master of the Good Light, wrote, "It is very difficult to express the depth of thought of the Kabbalah in simple language, because, despite all the enlightenment, the essential meaning is beyond comprehension and above all remains close to poetry. [Poetry constitutes] the most accurate mode of comprehension, it succeeds in penetrating the depths of the essence of the concept. This is something that prose is unable to do."

The ability of poetry to convey the deepest essence of things is powerful, though reality is not "prosaic" but is poetic in itself: "May misfortune fall," said the Baal Or Tov, "on he who wants to remove the poetic aspect of life, he loses the very savor of this life and all its truth."

Reality is not static and does not consist of eternal essences that can be understood by means of fixed concepts; it is the constantly unfolding future of life which bursts forth and renews itself. One cannot thus perceive reality unless it is by using a language and images that are constantly in motion.

Of course, the Kabbalah cannot be reduced merely to a piece of poetry, but its first language is that of poetry.*

Intuition and Illumination

Understanding the Kabbalah is firstly an illumination or an intuition that transcends the signs by virtue of which thought is transmitted.

* For further commentary on this theme see d'Elaine Amado-Lévy-Valensi's *La Poétique du Zohar.*

By its nature, this illumination rebels against the signs or concepts that form the warp and weft of an analysis. When it is a question of expressing the essence, "the signs must be illuminated by a higher light" (Zohar). Yet signs, letters, words and phrases, images and symbols, are necessary; without them no expression exists, and yet they constitute no less of an obstacle to the comprehension of reality as it is, since they can only reduce it to their own size.

How to Offer the Secret

The Kabbalah therefore begins with a contradiction and a paradox. We are required to understand the infinite, although our own means of doing so are finite. The Kabbalah sets a challenge, that of uniting two opposing fundamentals: on the one hand, that of spiritual enlightenment, which rejects all limitations, and on the other hand, the signs of a language or the symbols needed for perception and for thought, which themselves require frontiers and simplification. We will see later on that numerous kabbalistic techniques were devised to help resolve this problem of the contradiction between the finite and the infinite, such as that which we shall see of the dynamic and the static.

In order to express through language the living essence of the deepest reality, forms that are appropriate for this essence must be found, but such forms cannot be perfectly clear or precise.

These are matters for consideration of such exaltation that it is not possible to express them clearly without damaging them. When we penetrate the intimacy of the soul of something and perceive it in all the grandeur of its essence, we are quite incapable of expressing it. And yet—what shall we do if we want to find words to express the intimacy that is felt? And what if we want to transmit it to others? How, if only silence is adequate, is it possible to create a tradition? How can the secret be offered?

Light and Shade: The Chiaroscuro of Secrecy

> ***Just as a phosphorescent stone which emits light when placed in the dark but when exposed to the light of day loses the fascination it had as a precious jewel, so beauty loses its existence if the effects of shade are removed.***
> —Tanizaki, *In Praise of Shade.*

The glory of infinity must be encapsulated in a single word in order to exist there, but it must immediately be unraveled, recanting without disappearing into the void. Infinity must be both said and unsaid.

Thus the higher metaphysical truth can only be transmitted esoterically, through a secret, encoded language, and not through clear and unequivocal concepts. Over and above the essence of being-in-the-world, there is a need for ambiguity: a flashing of meaning. Contrary to the truth and unequivocal speeches of the theologians, the words of the Kabbalah are revealed in a flashing light.

The word of the Kabbalah is visible and invisible, enigmatic. The light of revelation of the infinite also requires shade.

Writings That Exist at the Same Rhythm as Life

The kabbalist does not necessarily seek to make his thought obscure, and the veiled style of his writings does not signify a desire to complicate the task of the reader. Naturally, there is a desire to permit access to this wisdom only to those who are suitable for receiving it, but the difficulty of kabbalistic phraseology lies elsewhere, in the need to find a language whose rhythm most closely expresses the fundamental vibrations of life.

The kabbalist seeks to discover a language that is descriptive and poetic, one that is very vivid, that harmonizes with nature, which is itself vivid, and with reality. Such language should gradually enable the reader to achieve personal and living, not merely intellectual, comprehension.

This is a means of uniting creation and life, requiring the kabbalist-writer and the kabbalist-reader to unburden themselves of simple, immobile concepts, of worn-out images and words. The soul of the kabbalist must be completely free in relation to those logical methods that lock reflection into a pattern and destroy poetry.

The kabbalist has the soul of a poet. Even abstract subjects speak more clearly to such a soul. Many of the ideas are incomprehensible at first sight. They must also be approached with the sensitivity of great finesse. This is no doubt why the Torah is also called *shira*, "song" or "poetry."*

May God Magnify My Soul . . .

The Baal Or Tov, the Master of the Good Light, wrote:

> To the open sea, to the open sea.
> May God magnify my soul . . .
> That it may never be enclosed in a prison,
> Neither material nor spiritual.
> My soul is like a ship,
> under the expanse of the heavens.
> The walls of my heart cannot contain it.
> Nor can those which are made
> Those of morality, of politeness
> The soul surpasses all this and flies away . . .
> It is above everything that one can name
> Above all pleasure
> Everything that is pleasant and beautiful
> It transcends that which is exalted.
> O my God, may your help come to me in my pain
> Give me the ability to speak
> Give me a tongue and an expression
> Together I shall speak my truth and your own.

* The reader is referred to the book about Rav Kook by Yossef Ben Shlomo, *La Poésie de la Vie.*

Part Two

The Ground plan of the Kabbalah

2

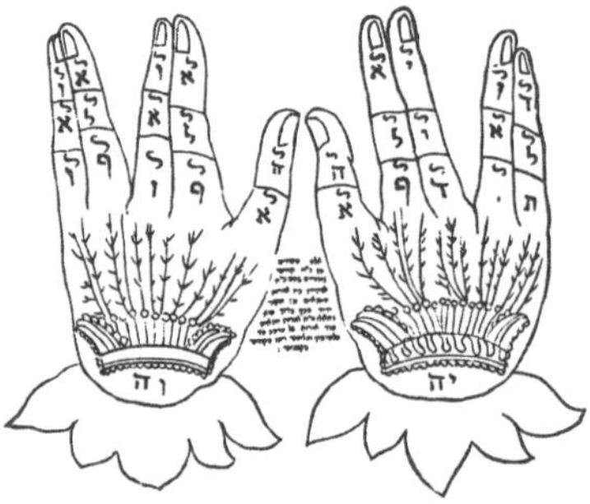
וה
יה

8

A Dialectic of Light
The Ground Plan of the Kabbalah

The Kabbalah has a very simple, basic plan that is easy to comprehend; thus we can move on from simple things to more complex thoughts. A reader who wishes to follow us into the extraordinary universe of the secret tradition first needs to memorize the ground plan.

The plan has a vertical structure that illustrates the tension existing between the "light from above" or "light of infinity" and the receipt of that light in the "worlds below." All the rest is merely commentary. . . .

As has been shown, the Hebrew word for "light" is *or,* and the act of receiving the light is called *qabbalat ha-or* or simply *qabbala;* in other words, Kabbalah.

the light of infinity *(or en-sof)*

⇩

act of receiving the light *(qabbala)*

The Three Worlds

If the ground plan of the Kabbalah is so simple, why are there so many trends, commentaries, and disparities between kabbalists, and between schools of mystics?

The reason is simple. If, as has already been stated, the purpose of the Kabbalah is to enable man to receive the light of infinity, nevertheless different paths and means can be adopted to achieve the descent and passage of the light. Between the light source and its receipt are multiple intermediaries. Some speak of *sefirot* (spheres), others of angels or trees, still others of ladders, yet others of holy names, and others again of a "just man" *(tsadiq)*. The study of the Kabbalah is the study of these various paths. In the Kabbalah, especially as interpreted by the Maharal of Prague, there are three worlds:

– *olam ha-eliyon,* the "world on high": the source of the light
– *olam ha-takhton,* the "world below": the place of receipt of the light
– *olam ha-emtsa'i,* the "intermediate world": where all the different but possible ways for the light to filter down from on high to below are assembled.

The most accurate image for representing this intermediate world, the world of *emtsa,* is probably Jacob's ladder, on which the angels go up and down:

world on high

⇩

intermediate world

⇩

world below

Jacob's Ladder, school of Avignon. Jacob rests his head on a stone that, like the cane received from his father, symbolizes transmission between the generations.

The Traditional Ground Plan

According to *Sefer Yetsira,* the "Book of Creation," there are only three intermediaries:

– the letters of the alphabet or "book": *sefer*
– figures and the world of mathematics and geometry: *sefar*
– the ten fundamental elements: the ten *sefirot*

The ground plan thus emerges as:

world on high

⇩

letters
figures
sefirot

⇩

world below

The following could be added:

- the many names of God (especially the ineffable tetragrammaton YHVH)
- the text of the Torah
- the study of the sacred texts: Torah, Talmud, and Kabbalah
- prayer
- the mitzvoth
- the master or rabbi or *tsadiq*
- Jacob's ladder
- the tabernacle in the desert
- the Temple and its symbolism

Thus, all of the teachings of the Kabbalah can be seen to be very simple. After we have laid out the basic ground plan and explained how it is built on, we will discuss the world of letters, figures, and the *sefirot.*

9

Offering and Accepting
The Figure 2 as the Foundation of the World

The Secret: Tension, Chasm, Void, between the Two . . .

The Kabbalah is the history of the relationship between the world on high and the world below, the history of the reciprocal nostalgia between the creator and the creature he created. God is on one side, and man on the other. God and man are separated, and it is within this separation, this "middle world," this *emtsa* in which neither dwells, that their relationship is cemented.

The Kabbalah is, on the one hand, the challenge launched by God to the unbridgeable chasm that separates the Creator and the created, and on the other, the challenge launched by man to the very gap that separates the finite from the infinite, the offerer and the accepter. The relationship with the Other, with God, Source of all life, Light of all lights, is a transcendent relationship; that is, there is an infinite and, in one sense, unbridgeable distance between them. A deep, hidden, insurmountable tension sets them against each other, separates them from each other, places them in positions of mutual competition—a tragic relationship.

An unbridgeable chasm, and yet . . .

The Kabbalah finds a resting place in this: "and yet . . ."

Separation engenders a deep desire for the other person, an exacerbated nostalgia that is translated by a set of words and actions that constitute the very heart of kabbalistic practice.

The Kabbalah Is a Love Story

The great mystics translated this mad nostalgia for the Creator into prayers and love poems comparable to the most inflamed speech of passionate individuals set alight by the burning and sometimes devastating flame of desire. It can then be understood why it sometimes becomes difficult, or even impossible, to distinguish an erotic love poem, which tells the story of two individuals who love each other, from a mystical poem that describes the relationship of man to God and vice versa.

The *Song of Songs* is no doubt one of the best examples of this ambiguity. The text is magnificently, and for some scandalously, erotic, yet it is included in the Bible not only as a sacred text *(qodesh)*, but as a text that is considered holiest of all *(qodesh qodashim)*. "I am sick with love. . . ." That is the rending cry that pervades the universe of the mystic.

It can be said with certainty that to be a kabbalist, one must at least know what it is to be in love; that is an essential condition. This does not mean that it is enough to be in love in order to be a kabbalist.

The Love of Wisdom and the Wisdom of Love: A Path through Life

As was stressed in the introduction, the Kabbalah is not only a science but an art, **an art of the heart and of knowing how to love.**

The Kabbalah requires a certain skill of the heart, which is difficult to acquire. That is to say, a scholar should also tend to be one of the just. Knowledge is not enough, love is needed as well. The Kabbalah is the true balance between the love of wisdom and the wisdom of love. In this balance, the kabbalist can only take the path of light. . . . As was stated at the beginning of this book, the Kabbalah is first and foremost a lesson in life. It does not aim for man to be good; it merely hopes that one day he may become better.

Although certain kabbalistic practices are close to magic, it is because the words of the book itself are magic; the kabbalist uses language as a way of acting upon matter, and first upon himself, so that he may attain a life that is richer and more luminous.

Prayer: A Vital Dialogue

> ***Seeing that the Rabbi of Zans went to the synagogue well before the service began, his disciples asked him:***
> ***—Master, what do you do before prayer?***
> ***—I pray, he replied, to be able to pray better!***
> —Martin Buber, *Tales of the Hasidim*

Prayer is the most perfect expression of the desire to enter into a relationship with the "source of light."

"The man at prayer," wrote André Neher in *Le Puits de l'exil,*

> is a man who is extended, a man who takes to the road, a man who is thus projected from the depths to the heights. He is a nostalgic man who harbors an unquenchable desire, who is harassed by a throbbing need. Of all the ways of approaching God, prayer is the most typical of the essence of man since it guarantees the purity of that which can never be anything but an approach. . . .
>
> In praying, man adopts the only dignity which responds to his created nature, that of the poor man who is always outside, in front of the gate through which he can never go and who, deprived of the basic necessities of life and of warmth, begs for them in a position of acceptance. For man, to pray is to don the garments of humility, whose only weapons are those of waiting with outstretched arms in the void of the universe.

The Zohar (I:6a–8a) tells the story of the village of Tarsa, which had been visited by the plague:

> The inhabitants, learning that Rabbi Aha was on his way from the inn, rushed over to him in order to beg him: "For seven days, the plague has decimated us. Come to our aid!" Rabbi Aha immediately made his way to the prayer-house, fol-

> lowed by a weeping throng. They were joined by more people on the way, who brought dramatic news of one death and another person near death. "There is not a moment to lose," cried Rabbi Aha. "So I am going to choose from among you the forty most just men and separate them into four groups of ten." As soon as said, it was done. He then arranged the four groups on the four sides of the town, enjoining them to recite with faith and devotion a chapter from the Book of Numbers. He himself went to minister to the dying and ordered all the villagers to return home and begin to pray. What happened? The plague ended, as if by magic spell, but the following laments were heard in the village: "lord of plague, lord of the plague, do not ever return to this village, because there is someone here who will prevent the pain of suffering!"

The performance of a sacred service has itself produced a veritable liturgy that is expressed on earth and rises to the "celestial palaces."

Prayer rises to the upper spheres, passing through a number of paths, which may differ markedly from each other, since the supplicant may choose one *sefira* or another, depending on the teachings of the esoteric traditions. Prayers that rise from the earth are echoed by the angels.

Each of the gates to the celestial palaces is guarded by a gatekeeper. There are "gatekeepers of the day" and "gatekeepers of the night." They find themselves assigned to the four directions of the world. The prayers of the unhappy and the persecuted rise from the north and south. The gates of the dawn open in the west. In the east, prayers are collected from human lips, and these words from the earth are combined and fused with the twelve letters of the Holy Name, which dance in the ether.

As for more informal prayer, which rises amid weeping and wailing, its value is no less great, and it is particularly likely to be granted.

The proclamation of the Holy Name is heard in the *shema,* which constitutes the zenith and apogee of prayer. The head angel picks roses and weaves them into a sacred wreath, assembling the garlands in the shape of all of the sacred names. Finally, the roses are woven into a sacred crown, which is offered to the Holy One, blessed be He (Zohar II:20 a).

It is appropriate here to emphasize the huge contribution made by Hasidism, the existential kabbalism that first emerged in the seventeenth century. This trend is opposed to stereotypical prayer and the mere recitation of set formulas. Naturally the Hasidic masters accepted traditional ritual, but they transformed it from within, while deepening its meaning. There is no point in reciting a prayer unless it truly comes from the heart. Merely reusing or imitating formulas created by others cannot satisfy religious aspirations. If traditional prayer is to be used authentically, it must therefore be constantly renewed and reinvented for the benefit of the person who expresses the need to resort to it, as a speech repeated to translate the authentic expression of his feelings.

Consequently, the kabbalist prefers individual, private prayer that comes from the heart, independent of the liturgical forms, of study, and of knowledge. The legends associated with the Baal Shem Tov—the Master of the Good Name, founder of Hasidism—are full of praise for simple and spontaneous prayer, as it may pour forth from the depths of the poorest and most ignorant of men.

The Gates of Tears Are Never Shut

This is a story told by a Hasidic master:

> One evening, at the end of the Day of Atonement, when the prayers had ended, the Baal Shem Tov was sitting at a table with his disciples. Suddenly, he cried out: "Tell Alexei (the name of his coachman) to harness the horses!" He took his favorite disciple, Rabbi Nachman of Kossov, with him, entered his coach, and gave the order to ride to a distant village.
>
> As soon as he reached his destination, the Baal Shem Tov went to the inn, and when the innkeeper arrived and asked his prestigious but unexpected guests what

they would like, the Baal Shem Tov asked him: "How did you pray on the holy Day of Atonement, the Yom Kippur?"

The innkeeper suddenly panicked. It was some time before he could answer, stammering: "Holy Rabbi! It's true, I committed a terrible sin, I did not pray with the congregation. Unfortunate man that I am!"

Then the Rabbi said to him: "Tell me what happened."

"Yesterday," began the innkeeper, "I went with my wife and children with me and we took to the road so as to celebrate the holy day in town and pray with the congregation there. Suddenly, I remembered that I had forgotten to lock my cellar. Fearing that some passerby would take advantage of the fact in order to plunder me, I turned back, while my family continued on their journey.

"I had barely entered the house when a messenger from the nearby castle arrived and asked me for a few bottles that were needed, according to him, for a small celebration. So I gave him what he needed.

"In the meantime, more customers had arrived. I ought to have refused to serve them and left immediately to join my family so as to spend the festival among the sages and pious men of the community.

"It was still daylight, and I thought I could reach town before nightfall. But the customers kept coming without a pause. Finally, when no one was left at the inn and I went to lock the cellar, I realized to my horror that night had fallen and it was thus no longer possible for me to leave. What should I do, I asked myself. So I went into a small room in the house in order to pour out my heart. Nor could I find a prayerbook. My wife and children had taken them all with them.

"I do not know why but I then began to weep hot tears before the Lord, saying: 'Master of the Universe, You see how heavy my heart is because on this holiest of days I am unable to join the congregation in order to pray with it. I do not even have an order of service that I can use! Nor do I know any of the prayers by heart! But now I know what I shall do, the only thing that it is in my power to do. I shall recite the alphabet, with all my heart, like a child who does not yet know how to read. And you, O Lord! It will be your task to put the letters in the right order and use them to compose the words of my prayers.'

"I ask you, Holy Rabbi, what else could I have done?"

Then the Baal Shem Tov rose and placed his hand on the innkeeper's shoulder and said to him:

"Rest assured, God was delighted with your prayer! It is a long time since such a holy and fervent prayer has risen to heaven!"

The Prayer of God: God in Search of Man

Man is not alone, since, according to the Kabbalah, "from the other side of the void of the universe, God himself is also praying." There is a surprising text in a Talmudic tractate (Berakhot, 7a) that teaches that God also prays:

Rabbi Yohanan said in the name of Rabbi Yossi Ben Zimra:
—How do we know that God also prays?
—Because it is said: "I will bring them to My sacred mount and let them rejoice in My house of prayer." (Isaiah, 56: 7); it is written, in "My" house of prayer and not in "their" house of prayer; so the Holy One, blessed be He, also prays.
—What does he pray?
Rav Zutra Bar Tuvya said in the name of Rav:
—The prayer goes as follows: "May it be My will that My compassion overcomes My anger, that My compassion surpasses My other attributes. May I deal with My children according to my attributes of loving-kindness *(khessed)* and remain in their favor beyond the strict limits of justice."

The World of Two: The Benediction

In a very beautiful midrash, Resh Lakish teaches, "God needs men." This enigmatic formula is designed to stress that the relationship of man to God, which is one of tension and desire, is reciprocated. It is the meaning behind the text of the prayer attributed to God himself.

Prayer is not the juxtaposition of two monologues, there is a true dialogue of benediction. Benediction is the meeting between God and man "through" as well as "over and above" each other's solitude. The Hebrew word for benediction is *berakha;* its root, *b-r-kh,* is also the root of the word *berekh* ("knee," the organ of articulation). Benediction, André Neher writes, is "the articulation of dialogue." In praying, man does not merely ask; he shows that he is open to someone other than himself, that his person is always and already constituted "for the other."

Existence is ontologically ethical. "Existing," writes André Neher in *Le Puits de l'exil,* "already means being there for someone else. There is no such thing as egoist existence. Existence is that which reveals itself, manifests itself, gives itself. For he who is for himself cannot be said to exist. Existence is that which exists for.... Duality is thus not a symbol of being torn apart; it is the sign of existence."

It can thus be understood why the first word of creation, *bereshit,* like the word *berakha,* "benediction," begins with the letter *bet,* the second letter of the Hebrew alphabet, which also represents the figure 2. The Kabbalah develops within the order of *bet,* in a permanent tension between distance and proximity, the unstable middle ground *(emtsa)*, which is simultaneously a chasm and a bridge, a wound and a benediction.

ב

10

The Kabbalah and Love
Minor Metaphysics of the Smile

Male and Female
Two Focal Points of the Ground Plan of the Kabbalah

The ground plan consists of:

light of infinity *(or en-sof)*

⇩

receiving the light *(qabbala)*

The masters of the Kabbalah noted that the tension-link that exists between "light" *(or)* and the "act of receiving" *(qabbala)* is of the same type as that which exists between male and female.

The proof of this phenomenon is based, as in so many cases in the Kabbalah, on faith in the power of figures and numbers to reveal certain secrets. For instance, the numerical value of the word *or*, "light," is 207, which is written:

aleph-vav-resh
אור
1 + 6 + 200
207

The numerical value of *qabbala* is 137:

qof-bet-lamed-heh
קבלה
100 + 2 + 30 + 5
137

The numerical value that represents the kabbalistic link is that which results from receipt of the light, i.e.: 207 – 137 = 70. The number 70 is a key number in the Kabbalah because it is the numerical value of the word "secret" *(sod).*

This is an example of gematria; the meaning of secret derives from the distance of the light from the possibility of its being received.

light of the infinite *(or en sof)* = 207
⇩
secret *(sod)* = 70
⇩
receiving the light *(qabbala)* = 137

The analysis of gematria (numerical value) shows that the word *male, zekhar* in Hebrew, has the numerical value of 227 (207 + 20), which in Hebrew is written as "like the light": *keh-or.* The word *like* is written *keh* and corresponds to the letter *kaf* (= 20). The word *female, neqeva* in Hebrew, has the numerical value of 157 (137 + 20), a number that corresponds to the expression "like receiving (the light)": *keh-qabbala.*

Thus, the distance and link between male and female, 227 and 157, is also 70 and constitutes the fundamental secret of the Kabbalah.

male/"like the light" = 227

⇩

sod = 70

⇩

female/"like receiving the light" = 157

An Observation on the Meaning of the Words *Male* and *Female*

Just as the male dialectic is central to the Kabbalah, it is important to specify what is meant by the words *male* and *female*. It should be stated from the outset that the terms do not merely apply to men and women but to the whole structure of the universe.

For the Kabbalah, the whole world is divided into male and female. Man is both male and female. Woman is also similarly male and female. These are two aspects of creatures in general. All life is based in this intimate duality.

The male is that which gives, *noten* in Hebrew. The female is that which accepts, *meqabel* in Hebrew.

The outpouring of light, the offering of light, is male. The "residence" of light is female: it is then known as *shekhina*. Thus a man who receives and accepts is "female"; a woman who offers is in the dimension of the source of light and in "male" mode.

Why the Number 13 Is Lucky

On this level, kabbalistic reasoning is associative rather than logical. One idea gives rise to another through the use of identical or similar words and ideas or through numerical equivalents.

The "secret" of the Kabbalah is its ground plan, whose numerical symbol is 70. It also lies in the tension between "male" and "female," which is given another name in the Kabbalah: love! Love is the "secret of secrets," and it is from love that the tetragrammaton YHVH, is revealed as the fundamental "middle" *(emtsa)*.

The word for "love" in Hebrew is *ahava*, a word that is written *aleph-heh-bet-heh* and whose numerical value is 13.

love
ahava
aleph-heh-bet-heh
אהבה
1 + 5 + 2 + 5
13

It is thus understandable that, for Jews, the number 13 was and remains a good luck symbol.

13: the number of love!

According to the complete ground plan, there is a reciprocal relationship between the person offering and the person receiving; this is the intermediate world or *emtsa*, which consists of the love that passes from the source of light to the world and love of the world that passes to the source of light:

male

13 ⇩ ⇧ 13

female

Love: The Foundation of Existence

This plan can also be read as the numerical addition of the two loves, which results in the number 26.

male
⇩
13 + 13 = 26
⇧
female

The number 26, to which an entire chapter will be devoted on the subject of the names of God, is the exact numerical value of the word *havaya*, which means "existence."

Havaya is written *heh-vav-yod-heh*

הו"יה

5 + 6 + 10 + 5

26

The importance of these observations will be realized when it is understood that the word *havaya* is an anagram of the tetragrammaton YHVH, a word that also has the numerical value of 26.

male

⇩

havaya = existence = 26

⇧

female

Important remark:

It is most surprising to note that if one seeks to find a numerical link between 70 (secret) and 26 (existence, the result of the meeting of love) the result is 44, another of the numbers that is central to the Kabbalah (among other things, it is the numerical value of the word *yeled*, "child."

The Art of Loving: Loving Is Giving

For the Kabbalah, the world rests upon this fundamental relationship between female and male, which is translated by love.

What is love?

Love is first and foremost an art. *The Art of Loving*, a wonderful book by Erich Fromm, consciously links Talmudic and kabbalistic thought. Loving is the art of knowing how to give and share. Love consists basically of giving and receiving. For the kabbalist, giving is the source of more joy than receiving, not only because it contains an element of privation but because, as Erich Fromm so aptly puts it, "it is a matter of privation, because my vitality is expressed through the gift. It constitutes the highest expression of power. In the very act of giving, I provide evidence of my strength, my richness, my power. This experience of accrued vitality and power fills me with joy. I feel myself to be overflowing, expending, living henceforth as joyful."

"The simplest example," adds Fromm,

> is to be found in the secular sphere. Male sexuality attains its culmination in the act of giving, the man makes a gift of himself, of his sexual organ to the woman. At the moment of orgasm, he donates his semen to her. He cannot avoid giving it if he is potent. The process differs little for the woman although it is a little more complex. She also gives of herself, granting access to the center of her femininity; in the act of receiving, she is giving. If she is incapable of giving, if she can only receive, she will be frigid. In her, the gift manifests itself again, and what is more not merely as a lover, but as a mother. She gives of herself to the infant that grows within her, she gives her milk to the suckling, she gives the warmth of her body. Not to give would be painful.
>
> In the sphere of material realities, giving means being rich. It is not the person who owns much who is rich but the person who gives much. The hoarder who worries anxiously at the thought of losing something is a good example, psychologically speaking, of a poor, impoverished man, however wealthy he may be. Anyone capable of giving of themselves is rich. He proves himself capable of conferring of himself to others.

The Joy of Sharing: True Love Is Reciprocal

A person who gives does so not with the intention of receiving but because the act of giving is a great joy in itself. But when giving, a person cannot help that which has engendered life in another from rebounding upon himself; in truly giving, he cannot avoid receiving that which is given back to him. As soon as one person gives, the other also becomes a donor, and both participate in the joy of what they have caused to come to life. Something takes shape in the giving, and the two people involved are grateful for the life that is born for them. In the specific case of love, this means: love is a power that produces love, powerlessness is the inability to produce love. If we love without arousing love, that is to say that our love, such as it is, does not produce love, if through the expression of our life as a loving person, we do not make of ourselves a person who is loved, then our love is powerless and unhappy.

To be precise, it is not only in giving that love manifests its active nature, but also in the fact that it always implies certain fundamental elements, whatever forms it takes. In this case, these are solicitude, responsibility, respect, and recognition.

Offering a Smile

On the other hand, adds Erich Fromm, the most important sphere of the gift is not in material things but in the specifically human kingdom.

What does one human being give to another?

He gives of himself, of the most precious thing he has: he gives his life. This does not necessarily mean that he sacrifices his life for another; but he gives that which is living within him, he gives his joy, his interest, his understanding, his knowledge, his mood, his sadness. In short, he gives everything that expresses and manifests what is living within him.

By thus giving of his life, he enriches the life of the other person, he enhances its sense of vitality, while enhancing his own sense thereof. In this respect, the Talmud (Ketubot, 111b) has a very beautiful teaching. In the text of the blessing that Jacob bestows on Yehuda, it is written:

> The searching taste of your eyes is better than wine and the white of your teeth is better than milk.

Many commentators labored to find a satisfactory interpretation of this verse, until the advent of Rav Dimi, who taught:

> The assembly of Israel says to God:
> —Master of the world, gives us a sign with your eyes, for this is better than wine, and show us your teeth, for this is better than milk.

The teaching can be understood thanks to the formulation provided by Rabbi Yohanan:

> The whiteness of the teeth offered to a friend is better than a nice glass of milk.

Rashi completes the thought in his commentary by saying that in the human face there is the smile of the eyes and the smile of the mouth, the smile of above and the smile of below. It is in this sense that the blessing given by Jacob to Yehuda should be understood:

> Never forget that the smile of the eyes is preferable to the best of wines and the smile of the mouth to the most comforting glass of milk.

11

Hasidism: An Existential View of the Kabbalah
The *Tsadiq*

Goodness consists only of gestures
These gestures do not lead to great victories
no legend contains them.
These gestures are the gestures of every day
far more heroic
than any heroism.
Goodness consists only of gestures
These gestures do not lead to great victories
no legend contains them.
These gestures are the gestures of every day
far more heroic
than any heroism.
—Christian Bobin, *La Vie passante*

The *Tsadiq*: The Just Man and the New *Emtsa*

With the Hasidic movement of the eighteenth and nineteenth century, kabbalism moved in a new direction. It is the master or who, physically and spiritually, by his presence as one of the "just" (*tsadiq* in Hebrew), unites sky and earth; he is thus at the center of the ground plan of the Kabbalah. To explain this phenomenon, it is important to present a brief history of the Hasidic movement.

Hasidism

The word *Hasidism* is derived from a Hebrew word that means "pious." Piety is, first and foremost, loving-kindness *(khessed)* toward others, even before it becomes a relationship with the divine. The *Hasid* is the person who is capable of kindness, which is located on a higher plane than goodness.

There are two particularly important periods in Hasidism. The first is that of the Ashkenazi Hasidim in twelfth-century Germany; the second is that of Polish Hasidism, which emerged in the eighteenth century and continues to the present day. For the picture of the Kabbalah to be complete, both periods will be explained here, although only the second is relevant for the theory of the *emtsa* in the ground plan of the Kabbalah. In the history of the Kabbalah, this initial period of Hasidism dates back to the twelfth century.

The *hasid,* or "pious man," is someone who has *khessed.* The biblical term *khessed,* which is usually clumsily translated into English as "loving-kindness," contains the sense of a legal or moral tie between associates. Hasidism, in its purest meaning, is a spontaneously evinced empathy between two individuals without any prior association that might have rendered it natural or necessary. In the modern sense, as presented here, it is the final phase in the development of the Kabbalah.

In Jewish tradition, the word *hasid* (of which the plural is *hasidim*) produced two movements called Hasidism. The first emerged in medieval Germany, while the second was a folk movement that emerged in the eighteenth and nineteenth centuries in that part of Eastern Europe that is now Russia, Poland, the Ukraine, and Belarus. There is no actual link between the two movements, apart from the name. There are many histories of the Hasidic movement; those that despise it, those that celebrate it, and those that understand nothing about it. Some consider it to be an essentially social revolution, others the rehabilitation of imagination and fantasy, still others as a mutation and popularization of Rabbi Isaac Luria's Safed Kabbalah. In fact, it is all of these; Hasidism is not a single system nor a single doctrine, but a religious current that has had numerous expressions, each giving priorities to one or more aspects.

Hasidism marked a time of renewal. Its founders and followers exploded the medieval inertia of the ghetto, putting an end to a static Judaism that merely expressed opinions and was incapable of any initiative. In the revolution of mentalities, Hasidism was a master stroke. In contrast to the "emancipation" through which Jews left the ghetto through the disintegration and dissolution of Judaism, Hasidism accomplished emancipation, not through flight from oneself but through powerful and sincere Jewish integration. In this sense, Hasidism is the precursor to all successive Jewish trends of renewal, stimulated by the spirit of the age but focusing on a desire to remain Jewish. Hasidism emerges whenever a society remembers that it is not enough to exist, that in order to truly love one has to continue to invent and find new ways of existence constantly.

The Baal Shem Tov, Founder of Hasidism

"At the moment when the Jewish imagination was almost exhausted, writes Elie Wiesel in *Célébration hassidique,* "when the spirit reaches an impasse in its researches into the impossible possibilities of talmudic law, at the time when bodies and minds were still reeling from the horrific persecutions of 1648 and the winds of messianic and Frankist folly were still blowing, a miracle occurred. 'Let there be light' and there was light. Rabbi Israel, son of Eliezer, known as the Baal Shem Tov, the 'Master of the Good Name,' came on the scene of history. Modern Hasidism began its long march."

In historic terms, the Baal Shem Tov (Besht for short) remains a vague and nebulous figure. Little can be said about him with certainty. Those who claim to have known him, approached him, or loved him are incapable of speaking of him except as poets. They describe him as they would a dream.

The Baal Shem Tov is something between myth and reality, between fiction, invention, and fact. He left no valid autobiography. "Obsessed by eternity, he neglected history and allowed himself to be borne along by legend," wrote Elie Wiesel. Apart from the legend, there are a few dates and events that have a historic ring, but nothing more. Some say he was born in 1690, others in 1700. All are agreed on the year of his death—1760. Rabbi Israel ben Eliezer was born of elderly, impoverished parents in Okop, a small town in Podolia. Orphaned at a young age, he earned a meager existence as an assistant teacher. According to Hasidic tradition, at the age of twenty he retired to the solitude of the Carpathian Mountains to devote himself to spiritual exercises and preparation for his vocation. Thus he lived there for several years, digging in the ground for clay that his wife sold in the town.

Despite what the legend supposes, it should not be believed that the Besht (abbreviation for Baal Shem Tov) came out of nowhere. At the time, Eastern Europe was overrun with individuals who were part hobos, part sages, miracle workers, bone setters, and fortunetellers. This "wandering intelligentsia" played a decisive role in the propagation of the Shabbataist movement. Its members performed the function of relayers and transmitters, and circulated ideas more quickly than any publication. They had stopping places in every location. They were particularly well disposed to receiving and spreading news of a revolutionary nature that could reverse the established order.

The Baal Shem Tov was a member of this subterranean intelligentsia, an expression which covers the physicians and folk magicians who went from village to village selling remedies and amulets. The medications were based mainly on medicinal plants, but we should remember that even within this bohemian brotherhood, the term *baal shem* was derogatory; it was one of the lowest levels, but had no relationship with the importance of a soothsayer, for example.

The figure of the *tsadiq noded,* the "wandering just man," predominates in the period. The Besht was one such a man, always on the move, always the bearer of news and a good word. These travelers would partly excuse the need for their journeys by explaining that they needed to gather the sparks of holiness that had been scattered throughout the world.

According to the tradition, in 1734, at the age of thirty-six, Israel had a revelation of all the Besht's spiritual mastery. It is said that the first person in whom he confided was his brother-in-law, who immediately became one of his most fervent defenders. As a very respected rabbi and kabbalist, he was to become an important link between the religious authorities and the humble villagers in the emerging movement whose spark had been lit by Rabbi Israel ben Eliezer.

The Democratization of the Kabbalah

The Besht's teachings spread rapidly among the majority of Jews who were unlearned, but soon attracted some of the most remarkable scholars of the time. Many of them were far better versed than the Besht in the subtleties of the Talmud, but they found his charismatic personality irresistible.

The multitude of legends that began to spread soon after the death of Israel ben Eliezer claim that the Besht had an incomparable mastery of the Kabbalah and convinced his more learned contemporaries that he was really in contact with higher powers. Like Isaac Luria two centuries previously, the Besht transmitted his teaching strictly by word of mouth. Of the hundreds of aphorisms, homilies, and interpretations by him that have come down to us, not one word issued from his pen. Although he never wrote a book, he maintained an active correspondence (four letters attributed to the Baal Shem Tov still exist today).

The Besht took the abstruse concepts of the Kabbalah and, by the simple power of his presence—according to stories and legends—made them accessible to the impoverished Jews of Eastern Europe. His message of hope and passion was like a purifying breath of air to tens of thousands of Jews who had come to feel that the insistency of orthodoxy on Talmudic erudition was painful and oppressive. The Baal Shem Tov emphasized that book learning is an excellent thing, but in the last resort useless unless it is part of deep-seated and sincere belief: "A child can only be born through pleasure and joy," he would say. "Similarly, he who wants his prayers to be granted must offer them up with pleasure and joy."

Fervor and Joy

The Besht instructed his disciples to pray with such fervor that the walls and doors of the synagogue itself would seem to melt away. He also urged them to accept the delights of the physical world. Life on earth is made to be enjoyed and praised, not despised, he insisted, declaring, "Without a feeling of love, stimulated by pleasure, it is difficult to feel a genuine love of God."

Furthermore, Israel ben Eliezer advocated specific meditation techniques, compatible with those of Isaac Luria, in order to attain higher states of consciousness. As an echo of the teachings of the sixteenth-century sage, the Baal Shem Tov preached that it is our mission to release the innumerable sparks that have fallen into the material world. Each act—if performed with sincerity or *kavana*—helps to redeem the cosmos from confusion and obscurity. Despite any feeling of helplessness we may display, all the routes leading to the presence of God are open to us.

There Is a Unique Path for Everyone

The Baal Shem Tov observed, "No two people are gifted with the same abilities. Each person must work in the service of God according to his own talents. If one man tries to imitate another, he may well lose an opportunity to do good through his own merits." This idea was of great importance in his teaching.

"Each person born into this world," writes Martin Buber in *The Way of Man,* commenting on the teachings of the Baal Shem Tov,

> represents something new, something which did not exist before, something original and unique. It is the duty of every Jew to appreciate that he is unique in the world through his own character and that there has never been anyone like him, since if there were someone like him, there would be no reason for him to be in the world. The very first task of every man is the fulfillment of his unique opportunities, which are without precedent and never repeated, and not the repetition of something that someone else, even if he were the greatest of them all, has already done. It is this idea which Rabbi Zusya expressed shortly before his death: "In the next world, no one will ask me: 'Why were you not Moses?' I shall be asked: 'Why were you not Zusya?' "

You May Also Have Your Say!

Rabbi Nachman, the Baal Shem Tov's great-grandson, taught that each of us can attain a higher degree of spiritual consciousness through individual effort. The evidence is this important text, which is considered Rabbi Nachman's manifesto:

> There are rabbinical masters who are famous for their knowledge of the Torah. They have an extensive knowledge of the texts and the interpretations of their predecessors. But, for this very reason, they are incapable of innovating *(lekhadesh)* in the Torah, for they are too learned.
>
> When any of these masters wants to introduce something new, his massive learning troubles him and shuts him in; he begins to formulate numerous preliminaries and summarize the sum total of his knowledge on the subject and for this reason his own speech is muddled and he has nothing new to say that is of interest.
>
> When someone wants to innovate through new speech [new meaning], he must reduce his knowledge [literally: make a *tsimtsum* in his mind], that is to say, create a void, not to precipitate himself into his known original considerations which embroil his spirit and are unnecessary for innovation. He must act like someone who does not know and, only then, can he innovate through the new meanings put progressively into the right order.
>
> Anyone who wishes to innovate in the Torah is permitted to innovate and interpret everything he wishes, everything that he is lucky enough to innovate through his mind, as long as he does not innovate new laws.
>
> It is even permitted to innovate in the Kabbalah of Rabbi Isaac Luria, according to its possibilities, as long as no new laws are innovated.

Thus, Rabbi Nachman was in the habit of saying, "Never ask the way of someone who knows it, because you will not be able to get lost!"

The Rabbi and the Just

Hasidism proposes very high spiritual values, which are sometimes hard for the majority of people to live up to. Only those who are above average for their generation, who are distinguished by the heights of their spirituality, by the special soul that they possess and by their pure and saintly behavior, are assured of attaining them. Yet Hasidism does not address itself only to the elite of the disciples.

Hasidic texts plead the cause for a spiritual renewal through a fervent and holy man, a *tsadiq*, one of the just devoted exclusively to God, but who is also required to be His envoy to the people. The spiritual imperative that motivates him prevents him from separating from the community and avoiding the task of saving, elevating, and sanctifying. He must therefore stay among simple people and even those with a wicked heart. But if the *tsadiq* can recognize evil in man, he never considers man as inherently bad.

The *tsadiq's* relationship to people is first one of love and comprehension. He does not judge but understands. Martin Buber reports a famous story about Rabbi Levi Isaac of Berditchev in *Tales of the Hasidim:*

> One day, he saw a coachman who was wearing his prayer shawl and phylacteries while greasing the wheels of his carriage. The Rabbi lifted his eyes to heaven and exclaimed:
> —Master of the world, look at this man! See the piety of your people! Even when he is greasing the wheels of his carriage, he cannot prevent himself from praying.

Contact with everyday reality and "impurity" thus takes on an unexpected social significance, which is played out in highly complex ties that bind the *tsadiq* to his community. For its benefit, he is forced to leave the heights of his *devekut,* his attachment to God, and require his community of disciples and faithful, the Hasidim, to follow him in their turn in his ascension to even more intense holiness and spirituality.

The master, rabbi, or *tsadiq* and his faithful, the Hasidim, constitute an inseparable couple. The *tsadiq* experiences the difficult test of trying to improve the spiritual life of his whole community, which consists not of exceptional people or sublime mystics but, more mundanely, of people with honest hearts and a naive faith, individuals who commit transgressions, secretly or publicly.

One of the most fundamental innovations of this latter Hasidic movement is the decisive change it produced in the way of life of Jewish communities. Holiness was no longer the prerogative of a few elite enclosed within the narrow confines of their faith; it lives in the very midst of social life. The charismatic must be oriented toward his community, and the community must trust him and, through reciprocal contact, eventually be elevated with him to a higher plane.

The *tsadiq,* the guide of the Hasidic community, is subjected to tension between the mystic way of the individual and the intermediary role in the community whose spiritual forces he must identify. He thus plays the role of a pillar or column, linking the higher with the lower—divine existence with the concrete reality of the world, in the form of its community, whose material needs are very great. His feet touch the ground, but his head reaches to the heavens. He is ceaselessly ascending and descending. The dialectic of "going and coming," from greatness to smallness, leaves him no respite. Sometimes he enjoys higher *devekut* and the light of the infinite fills his soul; sometimes he descends from these sublime heights to the lower realities of the world, where he perceives the light through the *qlipot* ("husks")—a world that, from the psychological and sociological point of view, is that of the mass of people who are concerned first and foremost with material things. It is here that he must assume his mission of sanctification and purification. Contact between this man of God and evil is played out here, on the lower plane, and the *tsadiq* then reveals his charismatic personality, gifted with the ability to awaken spirituality and produce a divine dynamism of all the fields of reality.

The *tsadiq* is like a soul who puts life into the limbs of a body. He animates the community spiritually, he gives it its breath of life, and in return the community offers him its body. It is also said that his soul contains all those of his generation: "If this is a generation of wicked men and he is so high up that he can only elevate them, he must then descend toward them because of the constancy of their sinning . . . and then, when he has joined them, he can enable them to ascend with him" (Yoram Jacobson). Through the strength of the link that binds him to the community, the *tsadiq* knows the needs of his heart, his aspirations, and he himself demonstrates his propensities. The *tsadiq*'s empathy with his community is a recurring theme in Hasidic texts, which insist on the friendship that must unite them and the comprehension of the one of the needs of the other.

But for the *tsadiq*'s work of mending to be effective, the link must be reciprocal. The spiritual guide cannot content himself with remonstrance and moralizing, pronounced in the name of Heaven. He must truly share the trials and tribulations of his people to fulfill his mission to repair and mend, and he also needs the community to become attached to him so that they may eventually ascend with him.

Solely through the power of his contact with the world, with its desires and pleasures, the *tsadiq* becomes a cornerstone, accepting influence from above to bring to the world below, to "all the worlds and all the creatures," even those who, by their attitude, hardly deserve to receive it. The *tsadiq* receives this divine emanation purely for the purpose of playing the role of mediator because "the strength of the Creator, blessed be His name, is so immense that one cannot receive it without an intermediary" (Yoram Jacobson).

As the incarnation of generosity *(khessed)* and mercy *(rakhamim)*, the *tsadiq* must also relate to the most simple people, listening to their futile conversations and the stories of those who hang around on street corners. He must debase himself, in fact, in order to rise again and ascend, to assemble in a holy manner the letters that have fallen into the degradation of profane and impure reality, and produce a shape from the material with which he has to work.

The *tsadiq* incarnates the incessantly dynamic process of rising and falling. He leads what makes the world live back to its divine source by converting evil, and in affirming the trappings of holiness, he awakens the hidden source to make it provide an overabundance of dynamism, goodness, and benediction, in the spiritual as well as the material world. That is the destiny of the *tsadiq* and of every man. He oscillates between heaven and earth, he distances himself from the sky, which he never ultimately attains. He wanders over infinite distances that separate his heart from the eternal source that is within him, the source of holiness and renewal. He ascends and descends, and his ascension is never-ending.*

The Importance of Storytelling in the Teachings of the Besht

There is a tradition among the Hasidim—and this is one of the basic forms of the whole movement—to tell stories of their *tsadiqim,* their masters.

The Hasid is proud to be able to say that he was present when a particular great event happened. He must therefore tell of it and bear witness to it. The words of the story are more than mere words, for they transmit a real experience to future generations, a story of something that actually happened, whose telling becomes a deed in itself, a holy deed. It is said that one day the "Seer of Lublin," saw a great light spreading around a hasidic academy; he entered and found a group of *hasidim* who were telling stories about their *tsadiqim.*

* See Yoram Jacobson, *La Pensée hassidique.*

The Hasidic tradition inaugurated with the Baal Shem Tov introduced a form of teaching that is handed down not only through commentaries on the traditional texts of the Torah, the Talmud, or the mystical texts, but also through the telling of stories or anecdotes about the masters of Hasidism themselves. Everything is told as if the master were a substitute for text, and instead of commenting on the words of a text, the commentary takes the form of a story about the actions and gestures of the master.

The Power of the Story

According to the hasidic credo, wrote Martin Buber in his *Tales of the Hasidim,* the primordial divine light is infused in the *tsadiq;* from whose person it passes into his works; and from his works it also passes into the story which relates them. It also enlightens the words of the *hasidim* who turn it into a story. The Baal Shem Tov, founder of Hasidism, is credited with claiming that he who praises the *tsadiqim* in some way evokes the mystery of the "celestial chariot" seen by Ezekiel. A *hasid* of the fourth generation, Rabbi Mendel of Rymanov, a friend of the "Seer of Lublin," provided an additional explanation when he claimed, "For the *tsadiqim* are themselves the Chariot of God."

But the story is quite different from a mere reflection. The sacred essence from which it emanates is perpetuated through storytelling, and is maintained in the tale itself. The mere fact of relating the miracle reproduces and revives its strength. It is through living speech that the virtue that was once so active is perpetuated, and it will continue to be, even after generations have passed.

One day a rabbi whose grandfather had a been a disciple of the Baal Shem Tov was asked to tell a story, and he replied:

> "A story must be told in such a way that it acts and is a help in itself." Then he told this story: "My grandfather was paralyzed. Since his master had asked him to tell him something, he began to tell how, when the Baal Shem Tov prayed, he would hop and dance about on the spot. And to demonstrate how the Master did it, my grandfather, while telling the story, stood up and himself began to hop about and dance. From that moment on, he was cured. Well, that is the way in which a story should be told."

I Offer My Stories to You

The story of the death of the Baal Shem Tov (reported through the oral tradition here) takes all its meaning from the context of the narrative identity that we are trying to convey here.

Feeling that death was approaching, the Baal Shem Tov, Master of the Good Name (1700–1760), the founder of Hassidism, decided that while he was still alive, he would distribute the few worldly goods that he possessed.

He gave one disciple his prayer-shawl, to another he offered his book of psalms, a third received a silver tobacco-box. . . . His most faithful servant, Reb Shmuel, waited for his turn to come, but by the time the Master had handed out everything he had still been given nothing.

Then the Baal Shem Tov turned to Reb Shmuel with a smile and said to him: "To you, I offer my stories. You will travel throughout the world in order that they may be heard." Surprised, Reb Shmuel thanked the Master, in whom he always had absolute trust, without really understanding the significance of this inheritance.

The Master died. Reb Shmuel was alone. He said to himself: "Is that an inheritance? Stories that no one will hear?" Poor he was and poor he would remain. . . .

But one day, a rumor began to circulate whereby there was a man who was willing to pay large sums of money just to hear stories of the doings of the Baal Shem Tov. Reb Shmuel asked around and let it be known that he was the person who could help. He was sent an invitation and, after a long journey, he arrived one Friday morning in a big city in Russia. He was greeted by the man who had brought him there, who was none other than the president of the local community.

That very evening, on the occasion of the Shabbat, the whole community gathered at a magnificent feast prepared in honor of the important guest. In the middle of the meal, the president rose and took the floor: "We have the honor to receive in our midst the disciple and secretary of the Baal Shem Tov, who has come especially to tell us stories about the life of his master. Reb Shmuel, over to you."

Reb Shmuel arose, happy at finally being able to talk about his Master. He looked over the assembly with a warm smile and was about to begin to tell a story. But he opened his mouth and—nothing came out. He remembered nothing! His head was empty, he was unable to recount the most insignificant anecdote, the slightest little memory. The president, perceiving his predicament, began speaking again and told the assembly: "Reb Shmuel is certainly very tired after his long journey. After a good night's rest, he will recover his strength and his memory and will tell us a beautiful story."

The following day, in the middle of the Sabbath midday meal, Reb Shmuel rose to speak and, once again—nothing, nothing but blankness. He could not remember a single story. He sat down again in confusion. Once again, the president was understanding and promised those present that everything would be fine at the third Sabbath meal, the *Seuda shelishit.* But unfortunately, the scenario was played out once again and, on the following day, Reb Shmuel, covered in shame, was discreetly and coolly accompanied to the departure point by his host.

Very few people turned out to wish a safe journey to the man whom the whole town had already nicknamed "the man without a story" . . . The horses were just about to move off when Reb Shmuel stood on the running-board of the carriage and shouted : "Stop, stop, I have a story. . . ." The horses were reined in and from the open carriage, Reb Shmuel addressed the president, who looked at him with a gleam of hope: "It is just one anecdote, I do not know if it will interest you, but anyway. . . ." The president encouraged him with a slight nod.

"One winter's night, the Baal Shem Tov wakened me and said: "Reb Shmuel, quick, harness the horses, we must leave." We traveled through deep forests, in the cold and snow, and after a few hours had passed, we arrived at a great and handsome residence. The Master entered but emerged after only half an hour and said: "Let's go home!"

Upon hearing this whole story, the president began to weep, sobbing bitterly, with all the tears in his body…

Reb Shmuel looked at him in stupefaction.

Through his tears, the president read the astonishment written on the face of all those present and said to them:

"Let me explain. The person whom the Baal Shem Tov was visiting, was me! At the time, I was a very important person in the ecclesiastical hierarchy. It was my task to organize forced conversions, which were always accompanied by violence and persecution of the Jews. When the Baal Shem Tov marched into my house on that memorable night, I was in the middle of preparing one of the cruelest decrees of my career. As soon as he entered, the Master said to me in a voice that became louder and louder: "How long? How long? How long will you make your own brethren suffer like this? Did you not know that you are a Jewish child who survived a pogrom, who was rescued and raised by a Polish family who has always hidden your origins from you? The moment has come to return to your brothers and to your tradition." I was utterly overcome, and immediately decided to abandon everything I was doing and start my life over again and I asked the Master: "But how will I know that I have been pardoned for all my terrible crimes?" The Baal Shem Tov then told me: "The day when someone comes and tells you this story, you will know that you have been pardoned. . . ."

This extraordinary story is an exemplary illustration of the need to hear one's story told to be able to continue to exist. It is to this very story that the *mamzer* (bastard) has little chance of access. And it is to prevent the suffering caused by not hearing such a story that the Torah is so harsh on the child who is the product of adultery. It is not a matter of punishment, but of alerting, and teaching the infinite sense of responsibility.

The Heirs of the Baal Shem Tov

Several years before his death, the Besht chose and carefully trained the disciples who would succeed him in expanding the Hasidic movement. Within the space of fifty years after the demise of the Besht, in 1760, Hasidism had spread with such astonishing rapidity—although strongly opposed by certain Jews—that it had won over half the Jewish population of Poland and Russia, the two great centers of Jewish life in the eighteenth and nineteenth centuries. The message of the Baal Shem Tov had clearly touched a deep chord throughout the Jewish world.

Knowing How to Get Up

> One day, a *hassid* slipped and fell into a patch of mud. An unpleasant passerby went up to him and said:
> —You slipped in the mud because you are a *hassid !*
> —It was my own fault that I fell into the puddle, replied the man humbly, but if I manage to get up, it is because I am a *hassid!*
> (Martin Buber, *Tales of the Hasidim*)

Part Three

The Colloquy of Angels

Angels and the Modes of the soul

3

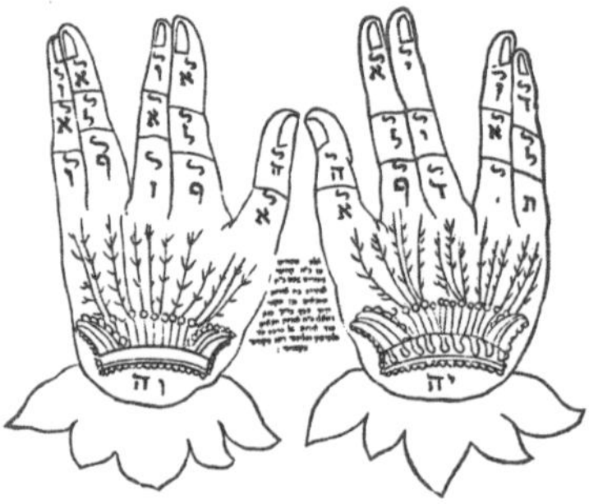
ו ה
י ה

12

The Four Worlds

The Kabbalah basically distinguishes four different worlds, which are organized into a hierarchy. Certain worlds are closer to the source of energy—or light of the infinite—and for this reason are called "the worlds above," in relation to those that are more distant from it, and are thus called "the worlds below." These four worlds are deployed from top to bottom and bear the following names:

- *Olam ha-atsilut,* the world of emanation
- *Olam ha-beriya,* the world of creation
- *Olam ha-yetsira,* the world of formation
- *Olam ha-assia,* the world of action

When light descends to the physical cosmos and to man as a physical creature, it has to pass through the Four Worlds, stage by stage, from top to bottom. Certain rites or actions by man are designed to act in different ways upon a particular world.

The World of Action (*Olam ha-Assia)*

The world in which we normally live, with all that it contains, is called the world of action; it includes both the world of our sensory perception and that of our extrasensory perception. This world of action consists of two dimensions. The lower part, which is called "the world of material acts," consists of the physical world, characterized by processes that are more or less mechanical; it is a world in which natural laws predominate, especially the principle of causality. The upper part of this same world, however, has a dimension that could be called "the world of spiritual action."

Man participates in both worlds simultaneously. As a being belonging to the physical system of the universe, man is subject to the physical, chemical, and biological laws of nature. However, as regards his knowledge, man belongs to a higher world, the world of ideas, and this is the case even where his knowledge is applied to the realm of everyday life. Each aspect of human existence thus consists of both matter and spirit. But the world of action, the spiritual world, remains subject to the material world, in which the laws of nature determine the aspect and form of all things and serve as the focus for all the processes.

In other words, as abstract as it may be, as distant as what is normally called reality, thought nevertheless continues to belong to the "world of action."*

The World of Formation (*Olam ha-Yetsira*)

The second world, which is above the world of action, is the world of formation (*olam ha-yetsira*). The world of formation is basically that of feelings. It is a world whose substance consists mainly of the various emotions that people display. It is here that feelings are experienced, and they constitute the elements from which this world is created. The living existences found in it are either conscious manifestations of particular impulses—destined to act or react—or manifestations of the energy needed to satisfy a particular inclination or inspiration through a certain stimulus.

* The present chapter is based on the commentaries of Rav Adin Steinsaltz in *The Thirteen Petalled Rose.*

The World of Creation *(Olam ha-Beriya)*

Just as the world of formation consists of spiritual existences whose essence is pure sentiment and emotion, so the world of creation is a world of pure spirit.

"Pure spirit" does not mean an exclusively intellectual faculty. This world further represents the ability to comprehend the authentic and intimate essence of things; in other words, it is the spirit in its creative capacity as well as in its ability to conceive and incorporate knowledge. The world of creation is the central point at which the flow that rises from the lower world encounters that which descends from the upper world, and where a sort of relationship is established between them.

The World of Emanation *(Olam ha-Atsilut)*

The fourth, and highest, world is the world of emanation. When the light of the infinite enters the empty space resulting from *tsimtsum,* this constitutes the first world. It is not yet completely matter, nor is it only light any longer, but a tangent of both. On the level of human indicators, it represents the highest world of the spirit in which man can enter into contact with the *en sof.*

After the world of action, that of feelings, and that of intellectual thought, the world of spirituality embraces action, feelings, and thoughts, all of which are oriented toward spiritual elevation and the will to make contact with the light of the infinite.

The Palace of the King

According to the Kabbalah, three basic elements must be taken into account—space, time, and the soul. These three terms are expressed in Hebrew as *olam,* "world," *shana,* "year," and *nefesh,* "soul," and are found in each of the worlds, but with different names and meanings.

That which corresponds to space in the material world is called "palace" in the world of spiritual action and in the three other, higher worlds.

Time or the Year: The Purest Essence of Change

Time also has a different meaning in the higher worlds. In our area of experience, time is measured on the basis of the movement of physical objects in space.

The year *(shana)*, as it is called in the abstract, constitutes the very process of change; it is the passage from one thing to another, from one form to another. In fact, the higher one goes in the order of the worlds, the more this temporal system becomes abstract, bearing less and less resemblance to time as we comprehend it in the material world. Eventually time comes to represent nothing more than the purest essence of change, and even the mere possibility of change.

Souls

That which we call the soul corresponds, in the physical universe, to an array of living creatures who play a role in the dimensions of space and time in our world. Although souls constitute an essential part of creation, they are different from the rest of it because of their consciousness of themselves and the knowledge they have of this world. Similarly, in the higher worlds souls are beings that are conscious of themselves and act within the context of the "palace" and the "year" of their world.

The Names of the Angels

The angels live among the souls of the various worlds and play a very important part therein.

The names of the angels depend on their mission or their origin, and these are reflected in their Hebrew names. The best-known angels are those

whose names have been adopted as human first names:
- Uriel, the angel of light
- Raphael, the angel of healing
- Gabriel, the angel of power or virility
- Mikhael, the angel who is close to God
- Nuriel, the angel of fire

The Hebrew initials of these angels, arranged in this order, form the word *argaman*, which means "purple."

A noun or a word merely needs the suffix *el* added to it to make it the name of an angel (*el* means both "God" and the direction "toward"). Names that end in *el* are said to be "theophorous;" that is, containing the name of God. Another series of angels bears theophorous names with the ending *yah*, which is another way of saying God. In fact, *yah* is the first two letters of the tetragrammaton, just as *el* consists of the first two letters of Elohim, another of God's names. Examples of such names are Gabiryah, a variation of Gabriel, or Zerahyah.

Several angels have names that end in the suffix *ron* or *on*, which is sometimes distorted into *an* or *phon*. In such a case, the name is either of entirely Greek or Latin origin, or a Hebrew name with a suffix that sounds Greek. This is the case, for example, with Metatron,* the best known, as well as with Sanegoron, Adiriron, Sandalphon, Na'alphon, and so on.

Angels who belong to the same "camp" have the same generic name. Examples are the names of the groups of angels ending in *im* or *in*—for example, the seraphim, *ophanim*, or *irin*.

Remark:

There are different categories of angels in the four worlds. As will be shown, angels are creatures who constitute the link between the various worlds. Yet the works of the Kabbalah do not all use the same terminology to designate the angels of a particular world. The word *malakh* is a general term for an angel, based on a root meaning "having a function," "doing a job of work." Thus the word for work, in the sense of a craft, is *melakha*, the feminine form of the word *malakh*.

* The name of Metatron is discussed by Charles Mopsik in his book about angels, *Le livre hébreu d'Enoch*, 49 ff.

The correspondence between the worlds and the angels is as follows:

- in the world of action, the *ophanim,* one particular angel whose name is Sandalphon, "the angel of the sandal"
- in the world of formation, the *malakhim* and the *hayot haqodesh*
- in the world of creation, the seraphim

The Angel or *Malakh*

In the world of formation, beings that have life, the "souls," who function therein just as we function in the world of action, are called *malakhim*—a word generally translated as "angels." (There are various approaches to the question of angels. The interpretation given here is basically the same as that used by Adin Steinsaltz in his magnificent book *The Thirteen Petalled Rose.*)

That which is called *malakh* is a spiritual reality with characteristic and unique attributes.

What makes one *malakh* different from another is nothing to do with physical separation in space. What differentiates them is a difference of level—one being "above" or "below" another—in the order of a fundamental causality that determines the differentiation of their essence. Since the *malakhim* belong to a world that prioritizes emotions and feelings, the essence of a *malakh* is to be an impetus or impulse—a penchant or tendency —toward love, fear, compassion, or their equivalents.

When one seeks to define an even wider range of emotions or impulses, one speaks of a "camp of *malakhim.*" If one takes the camp of love, in general, it contains a number of subdivisions. These are "nuances," in which the various degrees of tenderness are virtually innumerable.

No two loves are alike, just as no two ideas are identical. Thus every tendency, every impulse that is general, represents an entire camp. But while the emotions felt by human beings are liable to change with circumstance, time, and place, a *malakh*, on the other hand, is exclusively the manifestation of a single emotional essence.

The essence of a *malakh* is consequently defined by the limits of a particular emotion, just as it is depth of personality and intimacy that define the ego of each human being in our world.

Angels are often represented by birds or winged creatures.
Here, an eagle is drawn in micrography by the scribe Levi Rabinovitz. It consists of minute representations of the five scrolls or *megillot.*

Thus, the true difference between man and a *malakh* lies not in the fact that man has a body, but in that which distinguishes the human soul from that of the *malakh.* The human soul covers a vast and complex world of existential elements of all kinds. The *malakh,* however, possesses a single essence; in a certain sense, it is a unidimensional being. Each *malakh* has a well-defined character, which manifests itself in the role it will play in our world. That is why it is said that a *malakh* can only undertake a single mission, because the nature of a *malakh* is not as complex as that of a human being.

This does not prevent a *malakh* from manifesting in a great variety of actions and forms, but as with natural forces, it always continues to look like itself. Even if a *malakh* has a divine conscience, its specific essence and its function remain unaltered, just like those of the physical forces in our world, which have a specific method of functioning that is special and invariable.

The human soul is capable of differentiating between various values, especially between right and wrong. It is this ability that enables it to ascend to the greatest heights as well as falling into evil ways. Neither of these two options can be found in the *malakh.* From the point of view of its essence, the *malakh* is eternally the same; it is static. The angel is said to be *omed,* "standing with feet together."

That is why the most important prayer of the synagogue service is said silently, standing with feet together, in the same position as the angels. This prayer is called the *amida* ("standing").

The Angel Is a Messenger of the Influx of Energy

A *malakh* is not merely a fragment of existence that does nothing more than manifest an emotion; it is a complete being, conscious of itself and its environment; it is capable of acting, creating, and accomplishing certain things as part of the "world of formation." To a certain degree, as its Hebrew name indicates, a *malakh* is a messenger and constitutes a permanent link between our "world of action" and the higher worlds. It is the *malakh* who assures the transmission of the vital flow between the worlds. It may be called upon to play this role in either direction, from top to bottom; it may be sent by God to other *malakhim* or to worlds and creatures situated below the "world of formation." When it operates from bottom to top, it is transmitting things from our world to the higher worlds.

Man Is Capable of Creating Angels

Not all angels have the same life span. Some *malakhim* are ephemeral, others eternal.

Among the numerous *malakhim* that can be found in diverse worlds, there are those who have existed since the dawn of time. They are part of the infinite source of the *en sof* and of the fixed order of the universe. In a certain sense, these *malakhim* constitute *tsinorot* (channels) through which the divine energy flows up and down between the worlds. But there are also *malakhim* who are constantly being re-created, in all the worlds. That is particularly true of the world of action, in which thoughts, acts, and experiences give rise to all kinds of *malakhim*. In fact, each mitzvah that we perform is not merely an act of transformation of the material world but also a spiritual and intrinsically holy deed.

This aspect of holiness and spirituality, concentrated on the mitzvah, is the fundamental component in what will become a *malakh*. In other words, emotion, intention, and holiness, which are the very essence of the holy deed, combine to become the essence of the mitzvah. Henceforth, it has its own existence, which contains a genuinely objective reality. And this separate existence of the mitzvah—unique and holy—creates the *malakh*, a new spiritual reality who belongs to the world of formation.

The performance of a mitzvah extends beyond its immediate effect in the material world. Through the force of spiritual holiness that it possesses—a holiness that communicates directly with the higher worlds—this deed produces significant and fundamental changes. Consequently, any person who performs a mitzvah, prays, or directs his spirit toward the divine creates a *malakh*, which is like a part of man that extends into higher worlds. Such a *malakh* is linked, in its essence, to the man who created it; yet it continues to live, overall, in a different dimension of existence, the world of formation. It is here that the mitzvah takes on substance.

As it ascends, the content that is specific and intrinsic to the mitzvah introduces various changes in the system of higher worlds. This process is created first and foremost in the world of formation, but such an event will also affect the other, higher worlds. This is what makes it possible to measure the entire importance of a deed performed down here when it is detached from its place of origin, from its time, and from its author and becomes a *malakh*.

world of formation
(world of *malakhim*)
⇩
malakh
(messenger)
⇧
world of action
(world of men)

Modern historians of the Kabbalah use the phrase "theurgic actions" to describe this phenomenon, meaning the set of human actions that have an effect in the higher worlds.

This theory of angels is very important because it emphasizes man's infinite responsibility: he is first responsible for himself and then for the whole of the universe.

Guardian Angels

The approach that we have just described also makes it possible to understand what could be called a "guardian angel." This is an angel created by a deed of great value—whether it is a mitzvah (ritual deed) or not—which a person is in the habit of performing consciously or unconsciously and which comes into existence in the world of formation.

This angel protects its "creator," that is to say, the person who performs the deed and who is thus at the origin of its creation. If a person believes that he has a guardian angel and for one reason or another has given it a name, according to the Kabbalah, it is possible to find out by analyzing the meaning of the name how the angel originated.

The Various Categories of Angel

If the generic term for all the angels is *malakhim* (the Hebrew plural), the term also designates one category among ten others.

The *malakhim* are subdivided into ten categories:

- the *hayot*, "living creatures"
- the *ophanim*, "wheels"
- the seraphim, "those that burn"
- the *keruvim*, "cherubim"
- the *arelim*, "creatures of divine light"
- the *tarshishim*, "messengers from afar"
- the *khashmalim* (the translation for these angels is difficult, but the word *khashmal* is used in modern Hebrew to mean "electricity")
- the *elim*, "divine creatures"
- the *malakhim*, "angels"
- the *ishim*, "creatures of fire"

The Seven Palaces of the World of Creation

Immediately above the world of formation, there is the world of creation *(olam ha-beriya)*. Like the other worlds, it contains various domains, levels, and numerous and varied palaces. However, from bottom to top, seven palaces have been distinguished, whose names are:

- Palace of the Whiteness of Sapphire *(livnat ha-sapir)*, or Palace of Joseph
- Palace of the Profound Essence of the Heavens *(etsem ha-shamayim)*, or Palace of the Prophets I
- Palace of Clarity *(noga)*, or Palace of the Prophets II
- Palace of Transparency *(zakhut)*, or Palace of Isaac
- Palace of Love *(ahava)*, or Palace of Abraham
- Palace of Will *(ratson)*, or Palace of Jacob
- Holy of Holies *(qodesh qodashim)*, or Throne of Glory

The Six Gates and the Six Angels of the Sixth Palace

The texts of the Kabbalah state that in the sixth palace there are six gates, and at each of these gates there is an angel.

Mikhael is in the south on the right, Gabriel in the north on the left,

Raphael is in the east, and Uriel is in the west. In certain situations, Uriel is in the east and Raphael is in the west. Sometimes Uriel adopts the name of Nuriel. An angel named Raziel is responsible for all of these palaces.

The four angels Mikhael, Gabriel, Raphael, and Uriel are called the "four faces" and correspond to the celestial chariot *(merkava)* in Ezekiel's vision.

The Seraphim

The living souls who exist in the world of creation are "superior" *malakhim* called seraphim. Just like the *malakhim* of the world of formation, the seraphim are unique abstract essences, which do not have the power to change. But whereas the *malakhim* of the world of formation are created of pure emotions and sentiments, those of the world of creation are the essences of pure intelligence. The seraphim are *malakhim* that manifest the highest levels of the spirit. They also reflect the diversity of the levels of conscience and comprehension, which in itself constitutes a particular aspect of the life of the spirit. Finally, each of the creatures of this world of creation also serves as a messenger. It receives the flow of souls from the world of formation and sends them on to the world of creation and, even higher, to the infinite heights.

world of creation
(world of the *seraphim*)
⇩
messenger
(saraph)
⇧
world of formation
(world of the *malakhim*)

Angels of the Study of the Torah

One of the essential moments of Jewish ritual and kabbalistic meditation is the study of the text of the Torah. During study, each letter and each word that is pronounced gives birth to angels of the seraphim category, for this is the world of study and the spirit, the world of the essences of the intelligence.

It is for this reason that when studying, it is not enough to read and understand but to say aloud in a clear voice each letter, whose role as a messenger enables man, the student, to be connected to higher worlds and to permit the divine influx to descent, carried by the seraphim, who, like *malakhim*, are constantly ascending and descending Jacob's ladder.

When a letter of the alphabet is spoken aloud during study with a holy intent, that is to say when the link is created between the lower worlds and the higher worlds, it takes the name of an angel, by the addition of an "angelic" suffix to its name, and thus ascends to higher spheres. Thus, for example, Aleph becomes Alephiel and Bet, Betiel.

When the letters of study are transformed into seraphim, they, like the actions of the mitzvoth, become guardian angels. The angels of study are thus seraphim. Nowadays a great many kabbalists, especially the Lithuanian kabbalists of the school of the Vilna Gaon and of Rabbi Hayyim of Volozhyn, are strongly insistent on the mystical function of study, which has become the main activity in the majority of the talmudic academies, the *yeshivot.*

The word *seraphim* comes from the root *saraph,* "to burn." According to *The Hebrew Book of Enoch,*

> the seraphim bear this name because they burn the registers of Satan. Every day, Satan sits down with Samael, the Prince of Rome and Dubiel, the Prince of Persia. He inscribes the sins of Israel into the registers and commissions the seraphim to take them to the Holy One, blessed be He, for him to judge according to these records. What do the seraphim do? Every day, they take these registers from the hands of Satan and burn them in the fiery brazier that stands facing the elevated and exhalted Throne so that they cannot reach the Holy One, blessed be He, when he happens to be sitting on his Throne of Judgment and judges the whole world according to the truth.

One Day, My Master Appeared to Me in a Dream . . .

Then he said to me: "I am going to tell you of an important moment in my existence. One day, I was invited to a colloquy organized by the angels. I believe that I was the only human being there. The colloquy lasted for several days. These are the memories of it that I have retained. When I entered the large conference room, I saw strange creatures who looked like long silk cocoons. I waited to see the chrysalises emerge from them. An imperceptible movement seemed to pass through these creatures, which made their wings open and close.

"Each angel had six wings. Two covered its feet. Two covered its face. Two enabled it to fly. Their wings opened again and I saw their faces. There were well-known angels, others that were less well-known:

"Nuriel, the angel of fire;

"Uriel, the angel of light;

"Tahariel, the angel of purity;

"Padael, the angel of deliverance;

"Raziel, the angel of secrets;

"Zekheriel, the angel of memory;

"Ts'khokiel, the angel of mirth.

"There were happy angels who had known the olden days, as well as angels from more recent times who had known days of sadness when man lost the face of man. Each angel spoke in turn. Some of them sang, others bore witness as to what they had seen as they traveled the world. There was one who made everyone laugh by telling funny stories, another who told stories that were much less funny in an extraordinary voice that made the air and the souls vibrate . . .

"I have not remembered everything, for the time that has since passed has clouded my memory. I remember a sad angel who recited a poem. The angels of the colloquy turned to me and said: 'Teach us the secrets of human existence!'

" 'I smiled at them and said: 'The road is a risk . . .'

"A deep silence descended upon the hall. The angels looked at me in astonishment. I realized that they had not understood.

"So I added a quote from Rabbi Nachman of Breslov:

" 'Never ask the way of someone who knows it because this means that you cannot get lost.

" 'Learn to ascend to the heavens.

" 'But learn also how to descend to the bottom of the chasm.

" 'Ascent is deployment of the future.

" 'And descent is also a construct of time.

" 'Learn one and the other.

" 'Together they will tell you the way.'

"The angels rose, came to me and embraced me.

"They unhooked their wings and threw them out of the large windows of the conference hall. Feathers fell and fell . . . it was raining feathers . . .

"My master then said to me: 'If one day by chance, while you are on your way, you find one of these feathers, bend down and pick it up. You will become a writer . . .'

"I found one of these feathers. I picked it up. Then I felt the magic of the signs, the drunkenness of the bird, the taste of the volcano, the strength of new audacity . . ."

13

The Five Modes of the Soul

The Bible texts, and later those of the Midrash and the Kabbalah, contain five expressions that are used to designate the soul—that is, that which enables man to live a harmonious life on the physical, psychic, and spiritual planes. The five expressions are:

- *nefesh*
- *ruakh*
- *nekhama*
- *khaya*
- *yekhida*

All these terms can be found in the Bible and can be given definitions with multiple shades of meaning. Some commentators see these expressions as containing five degrees organized hierarchically, *nefesh* being the lowest and *yekhida* being the highest.

These modes of the soul should be equated with the four worlds that have been discussed:

- *nefesh*—the world of action
- *ruakh*—the world of formation
- *nekhama*—the world of creation
- *khaya*—the world of emanation
- *yekhida*—tangential with the *en sof* (a situation of *devekut*)

Remark about this representation:

It seems right to us to speak of the different modes of the human being, which enable the structure of the individual to work properly.

Here again, various approaches to understanding exist. Here we present this question at a more concrete and practical level, so as to enable readers to perform the work of meditation and spiritual progression. Certain complex notions have been formulated using terminology borrowed from psychoanalysis. The reader should not be surprised at these analogies. The richness of a thought lies in its abilities to dialogue with other thoughts. As will be said later, on the subject of mathematics, mathematicians love bridges, and so do kabbalists.

The exercises and techniques presented in this chapter, which in this respect is unlike any of the others, are reminiscent of some of the techniques of yoga. These exercises are inspired by the Kabbalah of Rabbi Abraham Abulafia (1240–1291).

Nefesh

The first dimension of the person is his *nefesh.*

The *nefesh* is first and foremost the body and all of its opportunities for action. For this reason, it corresponds to the world of action *(olam ha-assia).*

To fully understand the various modes of the soul of a human being, it is important to make a distinction between what the Bible calls *dmut* and what it calls *tselem.* In the first chapter of Genesis, the creation of man is described as follows:

> And God said, "Let us make man in our image , after our likeness." . . . And God created man in His image, in the image of God He created him; male and female He created them.

This verse, which has been translated a thousand times and commented upon ten thousand times, uses an interesting and important terminology that sheds light on the question of the human body.

In addition to the surprising plural "let us," the reinforcement of "image" with the word "likeness" poses a fundamental problem. The verse introduces a fundamental distinction between the image *(tselem)* and "likeness" *(dmut)*.

What precisely do the terms *tselem* and *dmut* cover?

The meaning of *dmut* is interpreted in the commentaries as being the "visible and exterior" aspect; that of *tselem* as the "invisible and interior" aspect. Thus Rabbi Itshaq ben Hayyim, son of Rabbi Hayyim of Volozhyn, wrote,"The Zohar and the writings of the Ari [Isaac Luria] affirm that the *tselem* refers to the hidden world, whereas the *dmut* refers to the revealed world."

Physical Diagram and Body Image: The Contribution of Analytical Terminology

One of the best explanations of these kabbalistic concepts can be achieved by taking a detour through the conceptualization and terminology used in psychoanalysis, especially in the writings of Françoise Dolto. "A young girl," writes Dolto in *L'Image inconsciente du corps*, "in her first session alone with me, drew a very beautiful vase of flowers which were fully opened, indicating the level of the water in which the stems stood."

"Subsequently, I had a meeting with the mother in the presence of the young girl. While we were talking, the young girl produced a second drawing, that of a tiny bouquet of drooping flowers."

Commentary:

Here we have a young girl whose body, whose material, anatomical body, her body-as-thing, is defined by a set of objective data. It is a concrete reality, a matter of fact. It is a body that makes possible "a carnal life in contact with the physical world."

This body-as-thing constitutes the "body diagram." The body diagram is basically the same for every member of the human race (of approximately the same age living in the same climate). Between the moment in which the young girl is alone and the moment she finds herself in the presence of her mother, her physical, anatomical body, her body-as-thing, as an object, in other words, her "body diagram" remains unchanged. She is the same young girl. And yet . . . and yet there is a fundamental difference in the drawing, in the way in which she symbolizes, externalizes, demonstrates her "interior grammar." This is a grammar whose syntax and vocabulary change as a result of emotional experiences, to produce a "body image." This image is unique to each person. It is part of the subject and his or her history. The image of the body is the unconscious symbolic incarnation of the desiring subject.

In the example of the little girl with the flowers, the distinction between the body diagram and the image of the body is easy to understand: "One sees here the difference in the young girl's body image, as she perceives it unconsciously, depending upon whether or not she is in the presence of her mother. In relation to her mother, she feels herself to be miserable and drooping, whereas when she is alone with the analyst and is getting his/her entire attention, she feels she has the right to blossom into her full narcissistic, seductive beauty."

Dolto expands upon the distinction between diagram and image: "The material body, the site of the conscious subject, makes him or her constantly conscious of its position in space and time. The body image, on the other hand, is outside place and time, it is a pure creation of the imagination and an expression of the effort put into it by the libido."

The body image is not the body diagram, although the body diagram contributes to its creation. "The unconscious body image is a living synthesis, which is constantly updated, of the emotional experiences which we repeatedly experience through elective erogenous sensations, whether previously felt or being felt currently by our bodies. An actual evocative turbulence guides the unconscious choice of those underlying emotional associations which it allows to come to the surface."

The body image is a carrier of the temporal dynamic, the dynamic of desire and its dynamic record in time; it records the passing of the time of desire, its peregrinations, halts, and the possibility of pursuing a harmonious, balanced, and oriented temporality.

Spatiality also has its place in the body image, but much less fundamentally than temporality. The body diagram refers the actual body, the material body in space, to the experience that is actually taking place. To return to the example of the little girl and the flowers: "The body diagram of this little girl remained unchanged by the presence of her mother. On the other hand, her presence produced a change in the body image and consequently in the way in which she projected her presence. This change makes it possible to understand how the current relationship between mother and daughter is disrupted. Thanks to the two drawings she made, the little girl expressed her wounded narcissism in her relationship with her mother."

Fundamental remark:

Drawings, model making, and other creations produced by a child (or an adult) may give the illusion of direct access to the body image. They may be drooping, as opposed to flourishing; in a vase containing water, or waterless; with a complete stem, a cut stem, and so on. However, it is only through dialogue with the child or with the adult that one can draw and sketch the contours of the body image. "The body image is not the image of what is drawn here or what is represented in a model; it must be revealed through analytical dialogue with the child or patient."

Nefesh: A Living, Breathing Human Being

The author believes that the concept of *nefesh* can be compared, though not exclusively, with the "body diagram," while the "body image" corresponds to the higher modes, especially that of the *ruakh.* On a semantic level, the word *nefesh,* used as a verb, means "to rest, to relax," as well as to "animate, revive."

In its substantive form, *nefesh* means "soul, life, respiration" and again, in the current meaning of the term, "person, living being." Other meanings are "will, desire," or "sentiment, feeling," or "breast, throat" and even "memorial."

The *nefesh* is the living being that can rest after exertion and is thus in dialectic and alternate movement with "work-rest," "tension-relaxation," an alternation that makes it possible to rest, to "breathe," to prevent effort from being taken to its ultimate impossibility, death.

Nefesh: a living being that breathes. In this case it is not the breath that is being referred to, but the movement of life in the infrastructure of the body, the organ and cells that are constantly changing, taking the substances needed for their energy and rejecting the substances and waste that block their vital energy and prevent them from working properly.

The *Nefesh* and Blood

A Short Physiology of the Blood Circulation

There is a Bible reference that presents a definition of the *nefesh.* Verse 14 of chapter 17 of Leviticus reads, "ki nefesh kol bassar damo hee," which translates as, "For the *nefesh* is all flesh, it is his blood." And Rashito, to dispel any confusion, specifies in his commentary, "*ha-nefesh hee ha-dam*" ("The *nefesh* is the blood"). Blood, *dam* in Hebrew, literally constitutes one-third of man, for which the Hebrew word is *adam (aleph-dalet-mem).*

The *nefesh,* like the blood, is that which makes possible cellular and organic respiration; it is the circulation of vital substances that vitalize the whole of the human body in its most physical dimension. The other meanings of *nefesh* are analagous and metaphorical. Thus will, desire, feeling, and passion are all moods in a being whose whole body is energized physiologically.

The blood circulates not only oxygen, but also the whole range of vital substances that are ingested through eating and passing into the blood as they are digested. Thus, thanks to blood, the various cells of the various organs receiving oxygen, water, proteins, fats, and salts can live, grow, and reproduce.

Waste from the cells is also captured by the blood before being filtered through the kidneys and other organs and eliminated.

The Body and Lettering: The Relationship between the Body and Letters

Kabbalistic meditation on the *nefesh* tries to make consciousness of the dynamic of the body possible by means of exercises in which lettering and the body enter into a resonance. According to the *Sefer Yetsira* ("Book of Creation"), there is a relationship between the letters of the Hebrew alphabet and the organs and limbs of the body. The Tikkunei Zohar, a book of themes and variations on the first word in the Bible—*bereshit*—emphasizes this analogy between "body and lettering." The structure of these relationships is complex. Sometimes it is direct, sometimes associative—through homophonies or homomorphisms, or even though the appropriateness of a structure to a word.

The word *hand*, for example, is *yad* in Hebrew: two letters, *yod* and *dalet*, whose semantic energy is 14

yod-dalet

יד

10 + 4

14

And in fact, anatomically, the hand consists of fourteen phalanges!

The relationship between figures and letters is rarely as obvious.

One aspect of meditation involves trying to construct relationships between bodies and letters. Reference will be made to the interpretation of the "Book of Creation," which dwells on the Hebrew term used to designate the organ or limb, a term that it is important to know in order to practice the meditation techniques.

Certain kabbalists have tried to build a relationship between the letters of the Hebrew alphabet and body postures. These postures can be performed alone or in a group, depending upon the complexity of the letter. Jewish meditation has not definitively codified the positions of the body corresponding to the letters, leaving it up to the individual to invent his own bodily relationship with lettering.

However, the following orientations can be given in reference to the three elementary forms—dot, line, plane—corresponding to *yod-vav-dalet*.

- Each posture in which the body is folded over itself, hunched up, curled up, assuming the fetal position, etc., represents the letter *yod*: י.

- Each posture in which the body is vertical represents the *vav:* ו.
- Each posture in which the body forms a right angle makes it possible to express the letter *dalet:* ד.

Nefesh and Meditation

The gematria of the word *dam,* "blood," is important. It is 44.

dalet-mem
דם
4 + 40
44

The number 44 is one of the central numbers in the Kabbalah because, through the set of numeric equivalents it relates to the word *yeled,* "child," the *ribooa* ("square root") of *ehyeh,* "I shall be,"and the number of lights lit on the festival of Hanukkah.

The kabbalist's action in relation to the *nefesh* is to meditate on the number 44 and the possibility of making the body move. The *nefesh* is the consciousness that the body is not an object but an essential dimension of life. The *nefesh* is saying to oneself, "I am my body" and not "I have a body." I am in the process of being, I am reaching toward life, toward movement. It is feeling the internal dynamic that inhabits our bodies and runs through us, but here it is essentially on the physical level. The emotions involve the *ruakh,* the next mode.

In order to feel this interior movement of the *nefesh,* the meditative Kabbalah suggests certain exercises. The example given here is for the foot, but the same exercise can be performed with other body parts.

Exercise: The Example of the Foot

The foot is visualized in the mind along with the Hebrew word *regel,* "foot" *(resh-gimmel-lamed).* When breathing in, one must imagine that one is making the blood *(nefesh)* and vital energy *(khaya)* flow from the foot and the word *regel* to the heart.

When breathing out, attention is directed to sending energy back to the foot and to the three letters *resh-gimmel-lamed,* which correspond to that part.

There are variations of this exercise; it can be made slightly more complex by devoting an in-breath to one letter and mentally specifying whether you are concentrating on the right or the left foot (in Hebrew, *yamin* and *smol*). Certain kabbalists do not visualize the word for foot, but the letter attributed to it in the *Sefer Yetsira,* as has already been explained—for example, the letter *tsadeh* for the right foot and the letter *qof* for the left foot. Apart from a feeling of warmth in each part of the body thus concentrated upon, one needs to focus on the energetic aspect of the process. As has been stressed several times, the energy that runs through the body uses language as a support: a static body language will tend to create a static body, and vice versa. The essential aim of meditation is to produce a language in movement for a human being in movement.

Ruakh

Ruakh is first and foremost the set of emotions, impulses, and other internal forces that drive us forward and make us exist; it is the emotional engine of the *nefesh.* Based on the terminology we employed above, it is the spiritual image that we have of our own bodies. It is not only the physical but also the interior way we have of feeling ourselves within our bodies.

The *ruakh* corresponds to the world of formation *(olam ha-yetsira).*

Breathing and Speech

From the semantic point of view, the word *ruakh* signifies "wind, air, breath, breathing, spirit." It is one aspect of the respiratory system from the mouth and nose to the lungs. The lungs are oxygen's "interface" between the interior and the exterior. The circulation of air, entering the nose and mouth on the one hand and the lungs on the other, is the *ruakh.*

The word has undergone two changes. It originally meant "spirit" as well as "speech." Similarly, speech is another modulation of the breath on the vocal cords. In the Zohar and the Tikkunei Zohar, the organs of *ruakh* are found in the tetragrammaton in the form of the letter *vav* (the trachea or windpipe) and the two *hehs* (the lungs).

The physiology of breathing, although very complex, can nevertheless be represented diagramatically as a place of change in the lungs, which capture the oxygen that passes into the bloodstream, fixed in the red corpuscles, and eject the carbon dioxide that is carried in the bloodstream from the cells. When we breathe, we very often think of "air-oxygen" (entering and leaving), forgetting the link between the circulatory and the respiratory systems.

The living *ruakh* is the result of a rich emotional life. It can be achieved by becoming aware of the exchanges between our body and our emotions and the outside world.

Breathing and Vowels

The existence of different vowels not only produces sounds and information with different meanings but also permits varieties of vibrations that have important effects on the whole of the human organism. The emission of vowels during exhaling produces a vibratory self-massage of the organs, and these vibrations reach the deepest tissues and the nerve cells; blood circulation increases in the tissues and organs affected. The glands of internal secretion—the pituitary, pineal, thyroid, thymus, and adrenal glands, and the gonads—which secrete their hormones directly into the blood and lymph, are stimulated.

The sympathetic nerve and the vagal nerve are not immune to the beneficial effects of vocal vibrations. The muscles of the respiratory tract are both relaxed and fortified thereby. Breathing becomes deeper, thus increasing the flow of oxygen throughout the body. Electromagnetic waves emitted by these vibrations are also produced and propagated throughout the body, increasing dynamism and joie de vivre. Concentration improves. The whole body relaxes under the effect of this internal vibromassage, which psychologically releases inhibitions, through harmonizing the whole psyche.

The following chapters will show how these vibratory considerations are applied.

Furthermore, the function of the ear does not lie solely in its ability to hear information, messages, or other sounds. It is also, and foremost, the principal generator of nervous energy. It behaves like a dynamo, and most of the energy needed by the brain comes from the power generated by the auditory system. The ear is responsible for loading the cortex; it generates energy. It has dynamic power.

The effects of energization include those that are linked to sounds of charging and sounds of discharging. Low notes are more easily integrated into the discharge zones; high notes are real generators of energy.

Breathing and Vibration

According to Rabbi Abraham Abulafia, meditative breathing consists of three stages:

- inhaling
- retaining breath in the lungs
- exhaling.

As Moshe Idel emphasizes in *The Mystical Experience in Abraham Abulafia*, this is the same three-phase breathing used in yoga. In Abulafia's technique, as in yoga, exhaling should last at least twice as long as inhaling. Exhaling is performed after holding the breath and should be accompanied by a vocalization the purpose of which is to regulate the breath and produce various vibrations.

Abulafia's technique uses only the five Hebrew vowels: *holam* ("o"), *qamats* ("a"), *hiriq* ("i"), *tsereh* ("e"), and *quboots* ("oo").

Exercises :

The first exercise consists in performing five three-stage breaths, emitting a different sound each time ("o," "a," "i," "e," "oo") during a slow exhalation, after retention of the breath. From the therapeutic point of view, this combination of breathing and sounds produces specific vibrations that cause better blood circulation and vital energy and have a positive effect on the nervous system.

Each sound has its own sphere of influence:

- **"o"** *(holam)* **acts upon the center of the thorax and the diaphragm, and tones the heart;**
- **"a"** *(qamats)* **acts upon the esophagus, the upper three ribs, and the upper pulmonary lobes;**
- **"e"** *(tsereh)* **acts upon the throat, the vocal cords, the larynx, and the thyroid;**
- **"i"** *(hiriq)* **vibrates upward, toward the larynx, the nose, and the head, and dispels migraines;**
- **"oo"** *(quboots)* **acts upon all the abdominal viscera, including the stomach, the liver, the intestines. and the gonads.**

When contemplating, one must concentrate on the emotion that the vowel arouses. One inhales through the nose, holds on to the breath, and slowly exhales the vocalized sound while humming and concentrating on the spot in which the vibration is occurring, emptying the lungs as slowly and completely as possible, but without straining. Vibratory massage dispels and eliminates the tensions that have accumulated in the tissues, while the increased flow of well-oxygenated blood nourishes and revitalizes the cells.

The second exercise puts the same process into effect, but adds variations of consonants to the modulations of the vowel.

There are 22 consonant pairs that include the letter *aleph.* The 5 vowels and 22 letters that can be combined with *aleph* produce a total of 11,100 possible combinations.

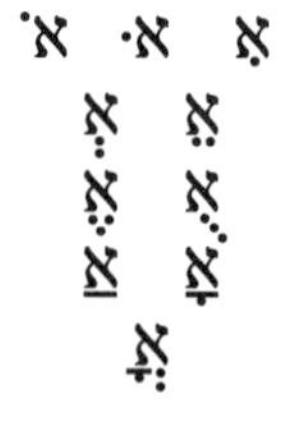

Example of *aleph* combined with the five vowel sounds and their derivatives.

The third exercise involves visualizing the letters pronounced and moving the head to reproduce the shape of the letter. This movement may accompany an actual vocalization or an internal mental and silent sounding of the letter.

The Body and the Name of God

There is another approach in the Kabbalah, by virtue of which man draws his energy from the name of God, the tetragrammaton YHVH, which passes through him. Each organ represents a different vocalization of the tetragrammaton, the Holy Name of God.

Thus, Rabbi Isaac Luria writes in the *Shaar Ha-Yikhudim* (1:3):

- the skull corresponds to the vocalized *qamats,* that is to say the vowel "a," tending to sound like an "o" (short "a");
- the brain corresponds to the vocalized *patakh,* that is, the long "a";
- the heart corresponds to the vocalized *tsereh,* the short "e";
- the right arm corresponds to the vocalized *segol,* the long "e";
- the left arm corresponds to the vocalized *sheva,* the truncated "e";
- the trunk corresponds to the vocalized *holam,* the "o";
- the right lower limb corresponds to the vocalized *hiriq,* the "i";
- the left lower limb corresponds to the vocalized *quboots,* the open "oo";
- the penis corresponds to the vocalized *shurooq,* the closed "oh" tending toward the "o";
- the tip of the penis corresponds to an unvocalized noun, for it receives all the vocalizations at the same time.

Water and the Breath

We try to understand and approach this strange creature called man. In Hebrew he is called *adam,* and the word *adama* means "the earth"—just as in Latin *homo* is related to *humus,* "the earth, the soil, the topsoil." "Earthy" would be a good translation if man were merely dust, but he is also breath and speech. He is a speaking breath: *ruakh melalela.*

To understand man is to return to the subject of breath. It is the first breath that turns into a cry when on the very day of our birth we are in the place and time of separation and cutting, separation of the body tearing it from its previous attachments. Understanding man is thus returning to the aquatic dimension of man, the primordial place of birth.

Man is earth, water, and breath. . . .

Water and breath have a very important relationship at the moment of birth. We have barely been torn from our mother and the protective amniotic ocean in her belly when a fountain of air takes its place within us; thus we emit our first cry. How enigmatic is this first cry launched into space! Is it a cry of despair at having abandoned the amniotic paradise?

Is it a cry of pain caused by having to pass through the narrow passage?

Is it a cry of fright before the vastness surrounding us?

Is it a glorious cry, "an auroral hallelujah" that young lungs try to trumpet from the laryngeal tubes to cause a few walls to tumble that still manage to resist?

Perhaps it is a simple reflex of a sphincter that is blocked against the expiration of a brand-new organ, the lung, which is being used for the first time?

May each dream and recreate the memory of the moment of his birth!

The inaugural breath is a cry of silent breathing, and the discreet letter *heh* is the only one in the Hebrew alphabet that does not require any part of the mouth in order to pronounce it. It is pure breath. Each exhalation is a *heh,* a breath, a prayer. Already, breathing is praying!

ה

The Talmud teaches in the name of Rav Yehuda, son of Rabbi Ilayeh: the world was written with the letter *heh,* as it is written:

> Here is the story of the heaven and earth on the day on which they were created *(behibar'am);* do not read it as *behibar'am* ("where they were created"), but as *beh heh bar'am* ("with a *heh* he created them").

Each breath is a *heh,* and each *heh* is the site of a creative power.

These poetic remarks that the masters of mysticism made have had ethical repercussions of considerable importance. What should one do when faced with a human being who has lost all his faculties, who no longer speaks, who no longer moves, who is unable to eat, and who is often referred to by the devaluing term of "vegetable"?

Is he not still a breathing human being—someone whose every breath is a prayer and silent speech, the speech of the creation of multiple worlds?

Neshama

Neshama is the third mode of the soul and corresponds to the world of creation *(olam ha-beriya).* For this reason, it is the most intellectual dimension of the soul. It is interesting to note, however, that this term has become more closely identified than the previous two terms with the soul, in the vague and populist meaning of the word. In fact, originally *neshama* came from the root *nasham,* which means "to breathe." The word *neshima* means "breathing." It would thus appear to be very difficult to make a distinction between *ruakh* and *neshama.*

However, it could be said that the *neshama* is the spiritual dimension of man.

As soon as he has a healthy body *(nefesh),* through which energy circulates in the right way, and he is capable through his breathing and speech to energize his body and to do so in a way that he experiences profoundly by balancing his emotions *(ruakh),* man can organize his spiritual life by delving into the texts of the tradition and their commentaries. It is now that meditation becomes the primary preoccupation.

Reading and interpretation:

The first level concerns the body; the second, the voice and the emotions; the third, the text and the spirit. The *neshama* is thus an intellectual and spiritual respiration that passes through a relationship with the text. Man is no longer what he was in the second level of *ruakh,* a "sentient speaking animal," but a "reading thinking commentating animal."

Apart from studying the texts of the tradition, it is possible to perform meditation exercises linked to writing and visualization.

Study as Intellectual Respiration

Study is one of the highest levels of meditation. The *Mishna* says, "Talmud Torah keneged kulam" ("The study of the Torah is as important as all the other rituals combined").

The masters of the Kabbalah remarked that the verb "to study" is symbolized by the letter *lamed* ("learn"), the only one of the twenty-two letters of the Hebrew alphabet that crosses the line of writing because it is taller. To study is to become taller, to become greater, to open the gates of infinity.

One of the most important places in the life of the kabbalist is the house of study, or *bet-ha-midrash.* It is also known as the yeshiva (plural, yeshivot). Both Talmudists and kabbalists can be found in the house of study. There are no prior qualifications for entry—all that is required is the desire to learn. Nor is there an age limit. It is a world out of time in which one meets children and sages. It would be worthwhile to pay a visit to the kabbalists' "dojo."

Let us push open the door.

The study room has changed little over time. The same atmosphere reigns now as it did in the yeshivot of Poland, Russia, and Morocco, in the previous centuries. The stories and testimony confirm this impression of timelessness and sometimes give us the feeling that we are somehow closer to the dimension that the poets have called "eternity."

Disorder, brouhaha, vehement gesticulation, constant comings and goings—that is the atmosphere of the *bet-ha-midrash.* The house of study is a place that is bubbling with life, that also serves as a synagogue and even, on many occasions, as a dining room. Students of the Talmud and the Kabbalah are not silent like monks, nor is silence the rule at the tables, which are rarely aligned in rows, and which are piled high with a mass of books lying higgledy-piggledy on top of each other.

The students—whether sitting, standing, or kneeling on benches and chairs—are bent over the pages. They sit next to each other, or more generally facing each other, and they read out loud, swaying to and fro, left and right, punctuating difficult articulations in reasoning with broad gestures of the thumb, sometimes frenziedly hitting the books or the table, or even the shoulder of a fellow student, leafing feverishly through the pages of the commentaries, removed from the shelves of the huge library, which runs right round the room, and replaced in quick succession. The protagonists in this "war of the senses" try to understand, interpret, and explain.

Before a lesson is given by the master, there is *hakhana*, "preparation." After the lesson there is *khazara*, "repetition." There is only one lesson a day, and in large classes there may be no more than a single lesson a week!

Perhaps most surprisingly, the study pairings do not necessarily consist of people of the same age. A young man of twenty may be paired with a man of forty, or even sixty or older. Here, learning does not depend on age!

Students consult the master—though fortunately, they do so rarely—as to the meaning of a passage studied, and he explains, takes a stance in relation to the theories presented, and for a moment calms the passionate debate between the consultants.

Two elderly men with white beards approach a young man to ask him to arbitrate in a disagreement on the interpretation of a text. The young man must be an *ilui* (a particularly gifted student). Some are more like geniuses than merely possessing wisdom. Since study is mainly oral, little is written down in the house of study. The Talmudists and kabbalists develop an extraordinary visual memory for the text, to such an extent that certain *iluyim* are capable not only of reciting thousands of pages of the Talmud with its commentaries but also of remembering where a passage is located on the page of the Talmud. In Eastern Europe and North Africa in the past, and in Israel and the United States today, there were men who could recite all the words touched by a pin plunged into a tractate of the Talmud at random.

At another table, farther away, a student has fallen asleep, his arms folded over a text of the Talmud; next to him, another student sips coffee and smokes a cigarette with a pensive air, the form of concentration he needs in order to pursue his studies.

Suddenly, the bodies rise, and one has the impression of waves surging in a troubled sea. The students have risen and sat down, moved by an invisible force that has touched them—the master has passed by! The respect due to the master is translated into this dance of the body, which is performed in harmony with the thought process.

Study is not only a science or an art but the very possibility of the existence of the cosmic force that maintains the world. For the mystics who devoted their lives to study, it is necessary to patrol constantly, in order to ensure that study does not stop for a single moment; if it did, the world might be in danger of disappearing.

Everything is moving! The *bet-ha-midrash* is in a constant state of turmoil, day and night, with loud voices and the infinite rustling of study—the song of study.

Jewish study involves the spirit. It is a spiritual act of great significance as soon as it is understood that studying is bonding with the light of infinity, which reaches this world by being borne on the letters of the Hebrew alphabet or, as it says in the text of the Tikkunei Zohar, carried by "horses of fire."

The *Neshama,* or Soul-Breath

One of the most singular aspects of study is that it is not spoken but chanted. This song of study is called *nigun* and takes on a special importance in kabbalistic meditation. Study is chanting, chanting is prayer, prayer is meditation. . . .

Rabbi Nachman of Breslov taught: "Make prayers of my studies and studies of my prayers." The exercises recommended for the benefit of the *neshama* are linked to chanting, which will bring out the vibrations necessary for the body, the spirit, and the soul.

What should be chanted? The first exercise consists of chanting the names of the letters of the Hebrew alphabet, clearly enunciating the sounds made by each letter.

Most of the Hebrew letters have names based on the various sounds they make. What in English is called "a" is called *aleph* in Hebrew; what in English is called "l," is called *lamed* in Hebrew, and so on.

Example of the letter *aleph*:

א

The "a" is vocalized, then the "l," varying the places at which the tongue touches the palate so as to be clearly aware of the space inside the mouth and the elevation of the tongue needed to pronounce the "l." The "e" is then vocalized, and one finally exhales on the "ph." And it continues thus for all the letters.

Although there are traditional melodies, any tune is fine for such exercises.

Time should be taken to develop all the harmonics of each part of the letter.

The rhythms and tonalities can be varied, one can go from flat to sharp and vice versa. One can sing alone or in a group, choir, or canon, in harmony or as a solo—every variation is acceptable. The main thing is to feel the vibrations, to experience them, and to perceive the joy of pure sound of a song of jubilation.

The Intentions of *Nigun:* The *Kavanot*

An important aspect of *nigun,* "melody," is the emotional state it produces or that one produces through chanting it. Each vowel and each consonant are full of meaning. At the moment of meditation on the *nigun,* it is important to meditate on the meaning of the letters that one is chanting and become imbued with the emotion that they can produce. The "a" represents strength and energy; the "i," gift, opening up, and availability to others; the "m," the flowing of water; the "d," the door open to the world or closed on our intimacy; and so on.

A link has also been shown between letters and the body, a relationship that we have called "body and writing." When we sing or chant a letter, another method is to also concentrate on the corresponding organ or part of the body.* It is possible to make the letters dance, depending on their vari-

* All these techniques can be found in certain forms of yoga; authors interested in a Christian version can consult the book by Hélène Foglio, *Yoga, son et prière.*

ous shapes, or at least to draw the letters with hands and arms. One can choose between the various Hebrew alphabets, but for the purpose of this exercise, the Protosinaitic form of the Hebrew letter is recommended, for it is the most evocative and the easiest to memorize.

Visualization and Writing

After exercises concerning respiration and the "circulatory breath," the energization of the letter-body and vibratory "vocalizations," Jewish meditation devotes itself to a series of meditations through visualization. According to the technique suggested by Abulafia (and reported by E. Hoffman), it requires using the shape of Hebrew letters as a medium for meditation: "In tranquillity and in semi-darkness, take a pen, ink, and a board."

So all we need is to take unlined white paper, black ink, and a writing instrument that can make thick and thin strokes.

Exercises:

In the first exercise, after a session of breathing and vocalization, one traces a complete set of the letters of the Hebrew alphabet, which should take the ritual form of the letters shown opposite. This is not a mere exercise in writing technique, but the interiorization of these forms so we can subsequently try to understand their impact upon us.

At first, we need to let ourselves be impregnated intuitively by these forms. Subsequently, each letter should be repeated one at a time while meditating and visualizing with closed eyes everything that the letter evokes, on an individual and collective level. We must place ourselves literally in the mental position of *aleph, bet,* and so on.

This exercise can be practiced alone or in a group. If alone, after meditating, all the evocations should be written in a notebook dedicated for the purpose.

When the exercise is performed in a group, individual meditation should be followed by a collective discussion about the meaning and the evocation of each letter. Remember that everything that is said is only an individual interpretation and not a dogma to be imposed on ourselves or

dalet	*gimel*	*bet*	*aleph*
ד	ג	ב	א
ket	*zayin*	*vav*	*heh*
ח	ז	ו	ה
final kaf	*kaf*	*yod*	*tet*
ך	כ	י	ט
noon	*final mem*	*mem*	*lamed*
נ	ם	מ	ל
peh	*'ayin*	*samekh*	*final noon*
פ	ע	ס	ן
qof	*final tsadeh*	*tsadeh*	*final peh*
ק	ץ	צ	ף
	tav	*shin*	*resh*
	ת	ש	ר

The traditional Hebrew alphabet (read from right to left) used for writing the Torah.

others—proposition, not imposition! After this collective discussion, each person should go back to his exercise books to note the salient points or details of the session.

It is important to study the dynamic of the formation of the letters and to be capable of subsequently memorizing them and visualizing them in the mind.

The second exercise consists in meditating on the letters of one's Hebrew first name or name of habitual use. One proceeds in the same way as before: first, write down the letters until they can be seen in the mind's eye; second, consider everything that these letters bring to mind, note them down, and discuss them in a dialogue with another person.

In this exercise, a combination of letters *(tseruf)* must be used; that is to say, one must try to write the maximum number of words using the letters of the first names. For those who do not have a Hebrew first name, it is possible to choose one and discover the correct way to write it in Hebrew.*

Note that it is also possible to do the work of meditation using the Protosinaitic script and the archaeographical method, which will be described in the fifth part of this book.

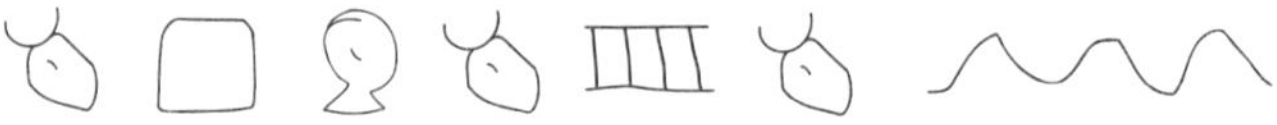

The next step consists in repeating the breathing exercises in which the sounds emitted are the vowels or consonants (first the vowels on their own, then the vowels in association with consonants) of the name.

Example: Abraham

in vowels:	A – A – A
in vowels with consonants :	AB – BA
	RA – AR
	HAM – MAH

etc.

אברהם

* One can be helped in the task by consulting the book written by this author, *Le Livre des prénoms bibliques et hébraïques.*

The third exercise is an extension of the previous one. It means doing the same thing using the first names of parents, grandparents, and so on. The purpose of this task is to place oneself in a living time frame that includes the past and the future. In Jewish tradition, there is no future without a past.

The fourth exercise is the logical progression from the previous step. It consists of a meditation on the first names of one's children or first names that one might wish to give one's children.

All these meditations thus bring into play contemplation, visualization, writing, breathing, and the movement of the head or body in order to "dance" the shape of the letters. Thus a word becomes a set of interrelated movements. The exercises should be performed slowly and rhythmically.

Fundamental remark:

The exercises involving names are merely preliminaries to those that use the holy names, which are too complex to be explained in this introduction. There is enough information in the preceding chapters, however, to make it possible to begin interesting and productive meditation.

Many sessions could be devoted to the tetragrammaton YHVH, and the other divine names explained in the sixth section, by applying all the breathing exercises already explained. In such meditations, however, mental visualization must be dissociated from vocalization. In any case, since the tetragrammaton is unpronounceable, it cannot be vocalized. The exercises explained here only concern the consonant letters, which can be visualized dynamically. Later, there will be an explanation of the graphic structure of the tetragrammaton based on the combination of the three elements of point-line-plane. It is a case of covering the ground between nothingness and the writing of the tetragrammaton and from the tetragrammaton back to nothingness.

This is how it is done: nothingness must be visualized by representing a white expanse on which one suddenly produces a point *(yod)*, then a line *(vav)*, and finally a plane *(dalet)*. Then one mentally writes the tetragrammaton by following the movement of its graphic construction. The second step is to take the opposite path in order to return to nothingness.

Khaya

This is the fourth level of the soul, which corresponds to the world of emanation *(atsilut)*. It is a degree of spirituality that also embraces the consciousness of the body as well as intellectual feelings and thought.

Khaya is a word that also appears in the book of Genesis during the "formation" of man and is associated with the words *nefesh* and *neshama*: "Vayitsereh hashem Elohim et ha-adam afar min ha-adama, vayipah beapav nishmat hayyim, vayehi ha-adam lenefesh khaya" ("And YHVH-Elohim created man: the dust of the earth. He breathed into his nostrils the breath of life [*nishmat hayyim*] and man became a living soul [*nefesh haya*]").

The word *haya* or *khaya*, from the verb *hayo*, means "living"; *hayyim* means "life." According to the biblical text, *nefesh khaya* designates every living creature, whether man or animal. This breath of life is not only the fact that man breathes and speaks but that he is also capable of prayer.

The level of *khaya* is translated by prayer: *tefila*. Prayer is one of the highest levels of meditation. *Khaya* is the state in which man feels the possibility of dialogue with infinity and perceives himself as being in receipt of the light of the *en sof*.

Although prayer possesses a complex structure, it can be said to be constructed essentially upon the psalms of David.

The Psalms

Art is like prayer, a hand extended in the darkness that attempts to seize a piece of grace in order to be transmuted into a hand that gives.
—Franz Kafka, "Preparations for a Country Wedding"

The greatest number of terms in the Bible concerned with prayer, meditation, and contemplation are to be found in Psalms. From biblical times down to the present day, psalms have played a central role among the disciples of kabbalism and meditation.

The Hebrew word for the psalms is *tehilim.* The word derives from the root *halal (heh-lamed-lamed),* which is usually translated as "to glorify." The psalms are thus usually considered as a simple set of praises addressed to God. Yet the root *halal* has two other meanings, which are more evocative from our point of view. The first involves the concept of brilliance and splendor, a perception of spiritual light. The second refers to moving beyond normal consciousness.

It is noticeable upon reading the psalms that several of them begin with a specific formula: "Of David, a psalm" *(Le-David mizmor)* or "A psalm of David" *(Mizmor le-David).* According to the Talmud, when a song begins with the first variation, it indicates that David recited the psalm after having attained the *ruakh haqodesh,* the "holy spirit." On the other hand, when the poem begins with the second phrase, it means that David used the psalm to attain spiritual elevation.

This means that eighteen of the psalms at least were composed for the sole purpose of bringing the faithful to the highest states of consciousness.

But the Midrash goes even further, suggesting a peculiar analysis of Psalms 90 to 100, which according to tradition, were written by Moses (in any case, Psalm 90 is entitled "Moses' Prayer"). The Midrash notes that "Moses composed these eleven psalms through prophecy." According to the Talmud, Psalm 91, which is one of the eleven, is called the "Psalm of the Oppressed." If the Midrash is to be believed, Moses recited this psalm on Mount Sinai in order to preserve himself from the forces of evil. According to Rabbi Joseph Gikatallia (circa 1245–1300), the psalms were composed for this very purpose.

Psalm 119 is one of the most important of all the psalms. Its very structure makes it different from all the other passages. In fact, it is written in the form of a poem, divided into twenty-two parts of eight verses, each of which corresponds to a letter of the Hebrew alphabet. Each letter of the alphabet is repeated eight times here. This becomes highly significant when one realizes the significance of the figure 8. According to the Maharal, the figure 7 refers to the seven days of Creation (six days and a day of rest), and consequently to the perfection of the physical world. The figure 8 represents the next stage, meaning that which follows on from the world that we are familiar with. In other words, it designates the spiritual kingdom.

Exercises:

At this level, the meditation exercises are both simpler and more complex. It is a matter of reading the psalms. There are several ways in which they can be read, but in every case they must be read aloud, chanted in a way that is suited to the rhythm of the text. They can be read in a group, each person reading a verse, thus producing a fundamental circulation of energy. They can be read in Hebrew or in translation. They can be read alone, preferably outdoors in nature, but this is better suited to the next level of the soul *(yekhida),* as will be shown.

Tikkun Hatsot

The kabbalists suggest reading certain specific psalms, which they group in various categories. These different groupings include mystical poetry and lamentations recited in the middle of the night during a ceremony of which kabbalists are particularly fond and which is called *tikkun hatsot,* that is to say "the redress or redemption recited around midnight."

Tikkun hatsot consists of two *tikkunim, tikkun Rakhel* and *tikkun Leah. Tikkun Rakhel,* the first group of psalms, means "the redress or redemption of Rachel." This group includes Psalms 137 and 79. *Tikkun Leah,* or "the redress or redemption of Leah," contains Psalms 24, 42, 43, 20, 67, 111, 51, and 126.

Tikkun Kelali

After several years of investigation and meditation, Rabbi Nachman of Breslov perfected a *tikkun* that combines the power of all the other *tikkunim* and is called the "general *tikkun*" or "*tikkun kelali.*" A collection of ten psalms, it should be recited in the following order: 16, 32, 41, 42, 59, 77, 90, 105, 137, 150.

Yekhida

Yekhida is the highest level of the soul. Very few can ever attain it. It is a state of being beyond the world of emanation, in which the mystic enters into tangential contact with the divine. Certain masters believe that there is a

קלז

א עַל־נַהֲרוֹת ׀ בָּבֶל שָׁם יָשַׁבְנוּ גַּם־בָּכִינוּ בְּזָכְרֵנוּ אֶת־צִיּוֹן׃
2 3 עַל־עֲרָבִים בְּתוֹכָהּ תָּלִינוּ כִּנֹּרוֹתֵינוּ׃ כִּי שָׁם ׀ שְׁאֵלוּנוּ
שׁוֹבֵינוּ דִּבְרֵי־שִׁיר וְתוֹלָלֵינוּ שִׂמְחָה שִׁירוּ לָנוּ מִשִּׁיר צִיּוֹן׃
4 ה אֵיךְ נָשִׁיר אֶת־שִׁיר־יְהוָה עַל אַדְמַת נֵכָר׃ אִם־אֶשְׁכָּחֵךְ
6 יְרוּשָׁלָ͏ִם תִּשְׁכַּח יְמִינִי׃ תִּדְבַּק לְשׁוֹנִי ׀ לְחִכִּי אִם־לֹא
אֶזְכְּרֵכִי אִם־לֹא אַעֲלֶה אֶת־יְרוּשָׁלַ͏ִם עַל רֹאשׁ שִׂמְחָתִי׃
7 זְכֹר יְהוָה ׀ לִבְנֵי אֱדוֹם אֵת יוֹם יְרוּשָׁלָ͏ִם הָאֹמְרִים עָרוּ ׀
8 עָרוּ עַד הַיְסוֹד בָּהּ׃ בַּת־בָּבֶל הַשְּׁדוּדָה אַשְׁרֵי שֶׁיְשַׁלֶּם־
9 לָךְ אֶת־גְּמוּלֵךְ שֶׁגָּמַלְתְּ לָנוּ׃ אַשְׁרֵי ׀ שֶׁיֹּאחֵז וְנִפֵּץ אֶת־
עֹלָלַיִךְ אֶל־הַסָּלַע׃

137 By the rivers of Babylon,
There we sat, sat and wept, as we thought of Zion.
2 There on the poplars we hung up our lyres, for our capturers
asked us there for songs, our tormentors,
3 for amusement, "Sing us one of the songs of Zion."
4 How can we sing a song of the Lord on alien soil?
5 If I forget you, O Jerusalem,
6 let my right hand wither; let my tongue stick to my palate,
if I cease to think of you, if I do not keep Jerusalem in memory
even at my happiest hour!
7 Remember, O Lord, against the Edomites, the day of Jerusalem's fall;
How they cried: "Strip her, strip her, to her very foundations!"
8 Fair Babylon, you predator,
9 a blessing on him who repays you in kind what you have inflicted upon us!
A blessing on him who seizes your babies
and dashes them against the rocks!

Psalm 137.

genuine *devekut, unio mystica;* others think that one approaches a true communion with the light of the infinite, but that the kabbalist never loses consciousness of his own ego.

Etymologically speaking, the word *yekhida* means "singularity," "uniqueness." In an initial approach to the subject, it deals with the ethical level, that is to say the way in which each individual is unique. This fundamental uniqueness is the basis for the idea of responsibility. According to Jewish tradition, each human being has a unique vocation to be fulfilled and only he or she can fulfill it. The human being must respond to this vocation, this unique project. This is the person's responsibility.

As regards meditation, this is the stage that is above that of prayer. Words spoken here are not those which use the common language of prayer uttered by everyone, as was the case with the psalms. Here the kabbalist invents his own prayers in the course of a solitary retreat into the forest or into nature. This is called *hitbodedut,* "isolation." This meditation is still practiced today in the mystical group of Breslov Hasidim. Extensive literature is devoted to this subject.

The solitary mystic meditates in silence on his life and his behavior. He is in the process of returning to himself *(teshuva)* and often dissolves in tears. The Kabbalah contains many stories in which the kabbalist enters into a state of mystical "sobbing" and various lamentations.

Rabbi Nathan of Nemirov, a disciple of Rabbi Nachman of Breslov, wrote down his own prayers that he recited during his period of *hitbodedut.*

Here is one example, spoken on the occasion of the midnight ceremony *(tikkun hatsot),* in which the mystic blames himself for the loss of the Temple in Jerusalem and for his becoming distanced from the divine presence.

Prayer of Rabbi Nathan of Nemirov

I shall rise at midnight to praise Thee and praise Thy just judgments. God of goodness, who awakens the sleeping and the slumbering! Have pity upon me! Help me to rise every night, every day of my life at the exact hour of midnight *(hatsot).* May I awaken from my sleep at *hatsot* and rise fresh and ready, feeling neither heaviness nor fatigue. Do not let me relapse into sleep. May nothing prevent me from rising for *hatsot.* And You, God of goodness and mercy, ensure that the north wind that blew at midnight upon King David's harp gives me the strength to rise from my sleep at *hatsot.* "Awaken, my glory, awaken, harp and stringed instrument à corde: I shall awaken the dawn."

Master of the universe, You have often shown us the importance of rising at *hatsot,* as is indicated in the holy Zohar. But You are aware of the number of obstacles that stand in our way when we try to do so and which spoil all of our nights. God of all things! You have the power to help. That is why I permit myself to ask You how to succeed in rising every night at the exact hour of *hatsot,* six hours after the start of nightfall, in winter as in summer.

Help me to wake up and arise with all haste, full of energy, in order to recite the *tikkun hatsot,* to lament at the destruction of the Holy Temple, the exile of the Torah, whose secrets were delivered into the hands of the profane forces, to lament over my numerous sins which caused all this and so greatly prolonged this exile. Creator of the world, You know full well to what extent my sins have prolonged the exile.

What can I say? How can I justify myself? I present myself before You, bowed beneath the weight of my sins.

But the past is dead. Help me to return from now on to the right path. May another night never pass without my rising for *hatsot.* Be always with me. Help me and protect me from any migraine and any other ills in the course of my *tikkun hatsot.*

Our Father who is in heaven, raise me up and give me life! So that henceforward I may always rise at the exact hour of *tikkun hatsot,* every night, on weekdays, on the sabbath (*shabbat*) and on festivals (*yom tov*), whether I am at home or on a journey. May I recite *tikkun hatsot* and then devote myself to the study of the Torah. And thus attenuate all the harsh sentences pronounced against me, against my family, and all the people of Israel, and quash them.

Allow me to raise my eyes each morning to the Heavens in order to impregnate myself with clear, pure, true and holy knowledge, to repent and turn to You with all my heart, and henceforward lead a life which complies with Your will. Extend a thread of grace over the me each morning, the thread of Abraham who rose early in the morning. "During the day, the Eternal surrounded me with His grace; at night, I addressed my chanting and my prayers to Him, the God of my life. Eternal, Your goodness is found in the Heavens and Your fidelity reaches to the celestial heights. Your goodness renews itself each morning; Your fidelity is infinite. May the words of my mouth and the thoughts of my heart be acceptable unto You, my Protector and Redeemer."

Amen. Amen.

Part Four

The Ten Sefirot

4

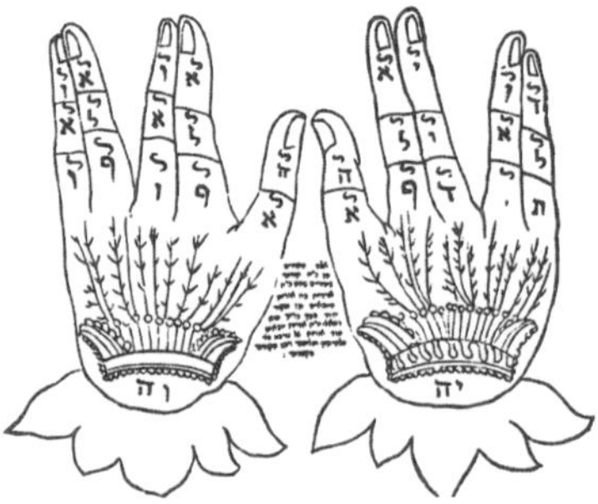
וה
יה

14

Travels of a Spark
The Kabbalah of Rabbi Isaac Luria

Rabbi Isaac Luria is no doubt one of the greatest kabbalists all time, the leading light of what historians call the New Kabbalah or the School of Safed. His personality and the themes of his philosophical works have entered in some measure into the official thought of the Kabbalah, and it is essential that we present and comment upon his key concepts.

Rabbi Isaac Luria

Rabbi Luria (1534–1572), the leader of the Safed kabbalists, is usually mentioned in kabbalistic literature as the Ari or Ari-Zal, "the [sacred] lion" (a play on the initials Ha-Elohi Rabbi Yizhak, "the divine Rabbi Isaac"). This acronym came into use in the late sixteenth century, and appears to have been first employed by kabbalistic circles in Italy. Rabbi Isaac Luria's contemporaries in Safed called him Rabbi Isaac Ashkenazi, Rabbi Isaac Ashkenazi Luria, or De Luria. The Sephardic community spelled his family name "Loria." His father was a member of the Ashkenazic family of Luria, which had emigrated to Jerusalem from Germany or Poland, where he appears to have married into the Sephardic family of Frances.

Rabbi Luria was born in 1534 in Jerusalem into a German family and showed an astonishing intellect from an early age. His father died while he was still a child, and the widow took the boy to Egypt, where he was brought up in the family of his uncle, Mordecai Frances, a wealthy tax collector. The traditions about Luria's childhood, the time he spent in Egypt, and his initiation into the Kabbalah are surrounded by legend, making it hard to establish the facts with precision. Contrary to the widely held belief that he arrived in Egypt at the age of seven, he himself stated, while recalling a kabbalistic tradition, that he studied in Jerusalem under a Polish kabbalist named Kalonymos.

In Egypt, Luria studied under David B. Solomon ibn Abi Zimra and his successor, Bezalel Ashkenazi. Even during his lifetime he became an almost mythic figure, if only for the power of his ideas, and he helped to raise the Kabbalah to an eminent position in certain aspects of Jewish thought. Even though his life was short and he lived in the backwater of Safed, he had an enormous impact on Judaism, and still continues to do so.*

At the age of seventeen, two years after his marriage, Luria devoted himself to a serious study of the Kabbalah, concentrating mainly on the Zohar and the short works of Moses Cordovero. In his quest for higher knowledge, he opted for a monastic life. Finally, by sustained practice of kabbalistic techniques, he began to experience visions.

Around the beginning of the year 1570 (there is no information about Luria's adult life before this date), Luria felt an inner call to settle in Safed. He believed these divine exhortations were hinting that he should remove himself from his family by hundreds of miles. Listening to this internal voice, he was immediately welcomed by the kabbalists of the little town and studied briefly under Moses Cordovero himself, who died in the same year.

Rabbi Luria helped to build living accommodation especially designed for his disciples and their families. Early every Sabbath morning, he and his disciples formed a procession and marched to the neighboring fields. Dressed in long white robes, they waited to receive the spirit of the "Queen of the Sabbath," a presence that they felt as a personification of the holy day of rest. They welcomed this ethereal being, who was presumed to be real,

* For more information about the great figures of the Kabbalah, the reader is advised to consult Gershom Scholem's *Kabbalah.*

with the song "Lekha Dodi" ("Come, My Beloved"). Generally on these occasions, Rabbi Luria would preach, teaching about the secret functioning of the human conscience and the cosmos.

As in the case of so many other kabbalists, Rabbi Luria's declarations were almost exclusively verbal. He readily admitted his inability to put his teachings in writing, as the Baal Ha-Orot, the Master of Light, had: "It is impossible, because everything is interlinked. I can hardly open my mouth without feeling as if the sea were breaking through the sea-wall and washing over me. So how can I express what my soul has received, how can I write a book?"

The Work and Doctrine of Rabbi Isaac Luria

Rabbi Isaac Luria's greatest disciple, who was also his biographer and scribe, was Hayyim Vital (1543–1620), who edited most of his works. The works of Vital, in the current edition, consist of about ten weighty tomes, especially the *Sefer Ets Hayyim* ("Book of the Tree of Life"), the *Sefer Ha-Hezionoth* ("Book of Visions") and the *Sefer Ha-Gilgulim* ("Book of Transformations"). These works show how interested the Safed kabbalists were in such subjects as dreams, meditation, altered states of consciousness, and parapsychology. Luria's concept of the world, with its daring images of exile and return, death and rebirth, spread like wildfire throughout the Jewish world. His teachings gave thousands of people a specific response to such events as the Expulsion from Spain and the Inquisition. Physical death was no longer the end of a person's existence, and each individual was here on Earth for a specific purpose.

Rabbi Luria's vigorous ideas gave the Jews, then living in an extremely hostile world, renewed hope and a feeling of finality. His message was first brought to Turkey and the Near East; then it reached Italy, the Low Countries, Germany, and finally Poland and Eastern Europe. With their undeniable poetical power and their respect for the Jewish legal tradition, the discourses of Isaac Luria were popularized in numerous printed versions in the late sixteenth and seventeenth centuries. In particular, they constituted the basis for books designed to induce ethical conduct from the esoteric point of view. New prayer books, whose contents were based on the practices of the Safed community, circulated freely. The ideas of Luria and his disciples also inspired new generations of poets. Great religious writers such as Rabbi Moses Zacuto (ca. 1620–1697) and Rabbi Moses Hayyim Luzzatto (1707–1746) directly drew their kabbalistic images from the Ari. Rabbi Moses Hayyim Luzzatto was himself a fervent kabbalist who wrote several kabbalistic works that are still considered authoritative.

The Basic Concepts: *Tsimtsum, Shevira,* and *Tikkun*

As has been said, the Kabbalah of Rabbi Isaac Luria was an immediate success, since it answered the existential questions of the period.

The only way these ideas can be explained here is to simplify them enormously, since they cover thousands of pages in the original. The ideas developed by Rabbi Isaac Luria are, in fact, stages in a history of philosophy which can be read on a cosmic level as well as an individual level. Hassidic doctrine was to emphasize the same themes and highlight the significance they had for human existence.

There are three basic concepts in the thinking of the Ari: *tsimtsum* ("reduction"), *shevira* ("breakage"), and *tikkun* ("repair").

Tsimtsum, or Reduction

This theme will be explained in detail at a later stage, but a brief overview now will make it easier to understand the historical development of the Kabbalah. The theory of *tsimtsum* represents one of the most surprising and daring concepts in the history of the Kabbalah. *Tsimtsum* originally meant "concentration" or "contraction." In kabbalistic language, the word would be better translated as "withdrawal" or "retraction." Rabbi Isaac Luria asked himself the following questions:

- How can there be a world if God is everywhere?
- If God is "all in everything," how can anything exist that is not God?
- How can God have created the world ex nihilo, if there is no nothingness?

Rabbi Isaac Luria replied by formulating the theory of *tsimtsum* ("reduction"). According to this theory, the first act of the Creator was not to reveal himself to something on the outside. Far from being a movement toward the outside or a sort of hidden identity, the first stage was a folding in, a withdrawal; God withdrew "from himself into himself" and in doing so left a void within his bosom, thus creating a space for the world to come.

At a certain point, within the light of *en-sof*, "infinity," the divine essence or light was eclipsed; a space was left empty in the center. In relation to the infinite, this space was nothing more than an infinitesimal point, but in relation to creation, it was all the spaces of the cosmos. God could not manifest himself because he had previously withdrawn.

This empty space left by God is called *hallal hapanooi.*

In this space, from this space, God the infinite had disappeared. The Hebrew root of the verb "to disappear" is *elem.* The place of disappearance is called *olam. Olam* is the space of the absence and withdrawal, in which there is room for the whole of creation. *Olam* is not the world, but the actual possibility of the world, of all worlds. (Over time, the word *olam* has become the standard term for "world," but we should remember that this is only its secondary meaning; *olam* is not actually the world, but the space that is occupied by the world.)

There is a philosophical and theological tradition whereby it is generally said that God created the world from nothing, ex nihilo—in Hebrew, *yesh me'ayin.* God said, "Let there be light!" and there was light. The same applies to the rest of creation. The Kabbalah, however, says the exact opposite, namely that the world was created as nothing from something, *ayin meyesh.* Instead of saying, as did the seventeenth-century philosopher Karl Leibniz, "Why is there something rather than nothing?" the Kabbalah says, "Why is there nothing, rather than something?"

For the Kabbalah, in the beginning was a single, absolute, infinite reality that filled everything from top to bottom and from side to side. It was the being of God. It is therefore not nothing that exists, but "the total absolute." And this "higher infinite light," to use the Hebrew expression, occupies the whole of existing space. There is no room for anything else. And thus, logically, the world is not possible. Yet we are here, and the world exists, apart from the absolute essence of God.

What has happened?

The infinite light has retracted, withdrawn, from the center of the infinite. This contraction-withdrawal is the *tsimtsum.* God has thus left this space empty of God, an atheistic, nontheological space. For the Kabbalah, the universe was born not because the Creator created a being, something, from nothing, but because God, the Infinite, left room from the void from which creation was rendered possible.

In the beginning, there was the void. . . . Rabbi Isaac Luria is not content with describing this withdrawal of the infinite. He goes further and asks, What are the forces at work in creation that have caused infinity to retract, to rest on the edge of the vacated space and not invade it again? In other words, What are the forces that maintain the void?

A kabbalist is not only someone who looks at the world but someone who asks, What has the world done to be the way it is? The kabbalistic way of learning to look at the world teaches that the world is not a petrified object but one of perpetual motion and change.

A comparison with the work of a painter may be helpful in understanding the thinking of the kabbalist. Wassily Kandinsky, for example, is well known for his paintings of angles, broken lines, and semicircles. If someone looking at such a painting were asked what he saw in a Kandinsky painting, he would reply, "a straight line, a broken angle, a curve," and so on. But Kandinsky would no doubt reply that the painting represents forces at work that cause the line or circle to break. In other words, he sees the world not as a discontinuous succession of scattered objects but as the very movement of the genesis of the world, in which conflicting forces are at work.

The Kabbalah does not say anything different. It questions the world in its genesis, in the course of its creation, and not the world that is placed there, with its disparate elements. Faced with the infinite, which retracted in order to make way for the world, Rabbi Isaac Luria poses the question: What forces are at work that forbid infinity from reoccupying the space and thus deleting it, and that instead permitted the world to exist and subsist? Rabbi Isaac Luria imagined a force that came from the void itself, as if the cosmic void had a voice that would say and repeat to infinity: "That is enough! Do not return!"

In Hebrew, this force has the name of Shaddai, which means "enough, that is sufficient," an abbreviation of "he who has told the world that that is sufficient." It is also the name of God, in the sense of the force that prohibits infinity to reoccupy the void that it has left. The universe is based on this void; it cannot exist without it. To summarize the theory of *tsimtsum,* creation occurred through an evacuation or withdrawal of infinity and through a force that maintained the infinite on the edge, a force that is called Shaddai.

שדי

The Second *Tsimtsum*: The Ray of Light

What happens after the *tsimtsum* ? On the one hand, infinity could not reincorporate the space because this would remove the possibility of creation, but on the other hand, if nothing happened, the world could not have been created! The kabbalists suggest a second phase of *tsimtsum* in which infinity reincorporates the empty space, but in the contracted form of a ray of light-energy from which the world would be created. This ray is called the *qav.*

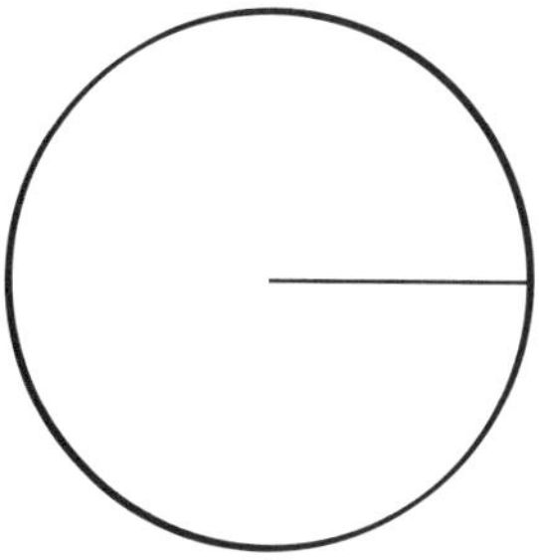

Light penetrates the empty space in the form of energy-light and becomes matter in the form of ten receptacles, to which the Kabbalah has given the name of *sefirot,* which are designed to receive and contain light. The light that created these *sefirot* fills them successively. It reaches the first *sefira,* which, once filled, transmits the excess light to the next *sefira.* The light that thus enters in the form of a ray will be at the origin of the creation of the worlds and the forces that are at work in it.

Shevira or the Breaking of the Vessels

The second stage in the process of Creation in Luria's Kabbalah is called the *shevirat kelim* or "breaking of the vessels."

After the *tsimtsum*, the divine light emerges in the empty space in the form of a straight line of light. This light is called *adam qadmon*, meaning "the primordial man." The *adam qadmon* is none other than the first face of the divine light which comes from the essence of the *en-sof* ("infinity") within the space of the *tsimtsum*, not from all sides but as a ray from a single direction.

At first, the lights emanating were balanced, that is to say homogeneous *(or yashar, veor khozer);* then the lights that sprang from the eyes of the "primordial man" emanated on a principle of separation, as atomized or punctiform lights *(olam ha-nequdot).*

These lights were contained in solid vessels, but the lights emanating from these vessels had too strong an impact for the containers, which were thus unable to hold them and burst open. Most of the light thus released returned to the higher source, but a certain number of sparks remained attached to the shards of the broken vessels. These fragments, like the divine sparks which stuck to them, fell into the empty space. At a given moment, they gave rise to the domain of the *qlipa*, the "husk" or "shell," which kabbalistic terminology also calls the "other side."

The Exile

The "breaking of the vessels" introduced movement into the Creation. Before the breakage, each element of the world occupied an adequate and reserved place. With the breakage, everything became disjointed. From now on, everything was imperfect and deficient, in a sense "fallen" or "broken." Everything was "elsewhere," remote from its proper place, in exile. This is a fundamental aspect of Luria's explanation. The basic terms here are the words *exile* and *spark*. The sparks of holiness fell into the world but were surrounded by the husks, which meant that they could not be reached; it was man's work to break the husks. The exile is not only that of the Children of Israel, but primarily the exile of the divine presence from the time of the origin of the universe.

That which happens in the world can only be the expression of this original and essential exile (one might be tempted to call it "ontological"). That the divine presence, the *shekhina,* might be ontologically in exile is a daring and revolutionary idea. All the imperfections of the world can be explained by such an exile.

The historical importance of these ideas is obvious. They provided an immediate reply to the most important problem of the era, namely, the existence of Israel in exile. Luria's system gave the Jews the reassurance that they were not alone in being preoccupied by their sufferings; their very persecution contained a deep mystery. The bitter experience of Israel is merely a symbol, however painful and concrete, of a conflict at the heart of Creation.

This kabbalistic explanation is of striking originality in that it does not consider exile to be uniquely as a proof of faith, nor as a punishment for sins but, above all, as a mission.

As will now be shown in detail, the aim of this mission is to cause the holy sparks that had been dispersed to ascend again and release the divine light and holy souls from the domain of the *qlipa,* which represents tyranny and oppression on the terrestrial and historical plane.

The *Tikkun,* or Repair

Tikkun, which means "repair," "restoration," or "reintegration," is the process whereby the ideal order is established; it is the third fundamental phase of the great cycle proposed by Luria.

The "breaking of the vessels" is a deficiency that must be remedied or repaired. Creation, from the divine point of view as on the human level, must enter into a process of *tikkun.* Everything must be set in order and find its proper nature. Repair cannot take place by itself; man is responsible for it. Man thus becomes responsible for the history of the world. The philosophy of the history of Rabbi Isaac Luria becomes an engaged philosophy in which man acquires a central place.

Man and God are associated in Creation. It is true that after the "breaking of the vessels," God revealed new lights and had already begun to repair the world, but this repair is not complete. The divine action has not repaired it entirely; the decisive act has been left to man. It could be said that the history of man is the history of *tikkun,* that is to say the history of the failure of *tikkun.* Without this failure, history itself would not exist, and man would be a complete being, that is to say, dead. The impossibility of succeeding in making the *tikkun,* this attempt at repair, defines man as a being "about to become" whose ethic is no longer that of perfection but of perfectibility.

The Second Breakage

In Rabbi Isaac Luria's texts, one encounters the idea of an initial attempt at *tikkun* with the *adam harishon,* "Adam the first man." Adam should have repaired the world, but he did not accomplish his task. If he had done so, Genesis would have led immediately to the messianic age, which means that there would have been no historical development. The cosmic exile would have ended; Adam would have been the agent of redemption, reestablishing the world in its unity. The historic process would have been completed even before it had begun. Unfortunately, or perhaps fortunately, Adam failed. Instead of uniting that which had to be united and separating that which had to be separated, he separated that which had been united: "He separated the fruit from the tree."

The failure of the first man brought the world, which had almost been repaired, back to its previous state. That which had happened when the "breaking of the vessels" occurred took place again. The upheavals caused by this breakage on the ontological level were repeated and reproduced anthropologically and psychologically.

The entry of man into the Garden of Eden corresponds to the moment when the breakage was almost repaired. The episode with the fruit and the expulsion from the Garden marks the second breakage.

Voyage of the Sparks

Adam's mission to repair and restore the world now fell to his descendants, but in an incomparably more difficult and more complex way. Before the failure, Adam contained within him all of the other human souls to come. With the second breakage, the "sparks" of the human souls now had to share the fate of the divine *shekhina* closed inside the dispersed fragments of the broken containers, meaning that they were imprisoned in the "husks" *(qlipot).* Thus the *tsimtsum,* the *shevira,* and the *tikkun* are not merely cosmological dimensions to be relegated to a mythical past. They concern man, humanity, and the human race.

Rabbi Isaac Luria taught that the soul consists of 613 parts. Each of these parts is in turn subdivided into another 613 parts or "roots" *(shorashim);* each of these so-called major roots is itself subdivided into a certain number of minor "roots" or "sparks" *(nitsotsot).* Each of these "sparks" is an individual holy soul. If Adam had accomplished his mission, all these souls and sparks would have remained within him, together bringing about the restoration, the great *tikkun.* Adam's fall totally ruined the possibility of this great *tikkun.* The souls returned on high, to their roots, and would not come back until the *tikkun* had been successfully performed. The majority of the "soul-roots" and the "soul-sparks" abandoned Adam and fell into the area of the *qlipa,* the "husk," becoming part of the domain of the "other side," an anti-Adam, the negative of the primordial man, *adam qadmon,* who is encountered in the domain of holiness.

This is how man entered the scene of history, participating in the Adam and the anti-Adam, on the side of holiness and of the "other side."

The Elevation of the Sparks

Under Luria's system, the *tikkun* implies two operations: on the one hand, the ingathering of the divine sparks that had fallen at the same time as the fragments of broken vessels in the domain of the "husks" *(qlipot);* on the other hand, the ingathering of the holy souls imprisoned in the husks and subject to the anti-Adam.

These two operations of *tikkun* are included in the symbol of the "elevation of the sparks." This symbol expresses the true meaning and mystery of the history of humanity and of Israel in particular. Certain souls are the sparks of the "area of holiness"; others have emerged from the *qlipa* of the "other side." The *qlipa* also contains holy sparks that are awaiting their *tikkun*, the breaking of the husk that will result in their release. Since Adam was ejected from the Garden of Eden, each important moment in history has been the occasion of a *tikkun*, but none of them has been radically productive. A kabbalistic rereading of the traditional texts, the Bible and the Talmud, highlights these significant moments, the attempts and failures. The revelation of the Torah on Mount Sinai, for example, was a time of *tikkun*. The world was on the point of being totally restored, but the sin of the Golden Calf brought everything back to a certain level of chaos.

Important remark:

The Law was given as a result of this latest breakage in order to perform a subsequent *tikkun* by means of the commandments. Remember that there are 613 commandments, each of which is designed to produce the possibility of restoring the 613 parts of the primordial Adam.

The Individual Sparks

The preceding paragraphs have discussed the sparks in general and collectively. Here one must emphasize the existence of individual sparks, which constitute the specificity and the unicity of each human being. The human soul consists of various lights or aspects, which as a whole produce the individual spark of each human being.

Each individual spark is divided into three levels *(nefesh, ruakh, neshama)*, and each level is divided into 613 parts. The three types of soul are classified into an ascending hierarchy in such a manner that a man cannot attain one until he has perfected the previous one. The two upper degrees, *khaya* and *yekhida*, can only be attained by a few elect souls who have been illuminated by the greatest of lights.

The task of man is to attain the perfection of his individual spark at every level. It is possible that a single life is not enough in which to complete the work; it may be that the *tikkun* must be performed laboriously and in stages in the course of various lives and transmigrations *(gilgulim)*. The idea of transmigration *(gilgul)* is a corollary of the theory of the individual spark and has penetrated the consciousness or rather the unconscious of Judaism, though strangely the idea subsequently was suppressed.

It is important for kabbalists of the Luria school to discover the root of their soul; it is as if only this knowledge makes it possible for man to restore his soul to its celestial root: "It is up to each individual to seek with application and to know the root of his soul in order to be able to perfect it and restore it to its original state which is the essence of his being. The more a man perfects himself, the closer he gets to his own being" (Rabbi Isaac Luria, reported by E. Hoffman).

Important remark:

There is an internal link, a sort of sympathy between souls, that links all the sparks originating from the same root, and these—and only these—can assist each other and influence each other, thanks to their shared *tikkun*.

Exile and Sparks

It has been shown that exile is the result of the breakage. The question of the "why" of the exile haunted those generations that witnessed the expulsion of the Jews from Spain and from other countries. The success of Luria's system stems largely—as Scholem pointed out—from the fact that it constituted a response to the historic upheavals of his time. Luria was in fact offering a system of explanation—a philosophical and mystical explanation of the historic process—that takes man to task and makes him responsible for the destinies of the world and the possibility of redemption. If man is responsible for history, he still awaits to be heard in his collective meaning. The entire nation of Israel has a special function, namely to prepare the world for *tikkun,* bringing each thing to its rightful place; it has a duty to recover and assemble the sparks dispersed to the four corners of the earth. Consequently, the Jewish people must be exiled to the four corners of the earth. Exile is not mere chance, but a mission whose aim is repair and "sorting." In fact, repair is accomplished in the form of sorting—of separating good from evil, with the aim of the total separation of the domains of the holy and the impure, which became mixed together at the original breakage and the episode of the fruit in the Garden of Eden.

The children of Israel are completely preoccupied with the process of the "elevation of the sparks," not only in the places where their feet touch the ground during their exile, but also within the cosmic exile into which they have been thrown internally and which they gradually bring to an end through their actions. It is on the basis of this concept, which will be returned to again later in this book, that the Hasidic masters created the theory and practice of journeys, not of initiation but in relation to the "elevation of the sparks."

Creating the Messiah

The ideas of Rabbi Isaac Luria soon caught the public's imagination. As has been explained, this is mainly due to the way they took into account the historical situation of the Jews of the period. Another important factor emphasized was the concrete nature of the images proposed by Luria. The images themselves are simple, even if the commentaries made in respect of them may be subtle and profound.

During the period under review, the seventeenth century, Jews, both rich and poor, lived in a state of constant uncertainty. None were safe from economic vicissitudes and the dire consequences of political upheavals. For this reason, there was little difference on the sociological and psychological level between the various communities of the Diaspora. In this context, the religious renaissance in Safed and the Lurianic Kabbalah fulfilled an ideological function that extended considerably beyond the religious perspective of its initiators. The concrete images of *tsimtsum*, *shevira*, and *tikkun* quickly acquired a national dimension and great dynamic power. The *tikkun*, when removed from its purely mystical setting, and not considered in its cosmic and ontological aspect, took on a largely political nature, which at first translated itself into the creation of a tension that was of a messianic nature. The repair of the *tikkun* soon transformed itself into the redemption of souls and bodies, and *tikkun* was understood as redemption of the individual and the collective.

The Role of the Messiah

When man and the community have completed their active role, symbolized by the "elevation of the sparks," the *tikkun* will have been completed, and everything will return to the place it occupied in the primordial time of the world. This moment will be that of redemption.

"Redemption comes from itself for it is none other than Repair" (Rabbi Luria, reported by G. Scholem in *Jewish Messianism*). The two concepts are identical. If the world is repaired, it is impossible for "redemption" not to occur, because it is merely the expression of the perfect and impeccable state of the world, a harmonious world in which each thing has its place. This is the same thing as saying that working on "repairing" the world consists in practice in working for its redemption. For Rabbi Isaac Luria, our role is to repair the internal and external world through our actions. This idea is one of the most fundamental ones because it also confers on the mitzvoth (the precepts of the law, *halakha*) a cosmic meaning and dimension. Consequently, there is a link between traditional Judaism, its precepts and ideas, and the fundamental, mysterious forces at work in the world.

When man obeys a precept, he makes it part of a universal deed. He has repaired something. Man's action itself becomes a driving force of history. Through our deeds, we are all engaged in a unique messianic adventure in which we are all required to participate. In this context, the Messiah is not he who produces redemption, but only the manifestation of his success. One can no longer await the Messiah; one must create him. As a symbol of the completion of the *tikkun*, the Messiah loses his personal value, and we can understand why he is of so little importance in the Lurianic Kabbalah.

These concepts are revolutionary, in that they are a total reversal of received ideas. The concept of the man-messiah disappears; there is no longer one redeemer who will save humanity by his mere existence and his mere suffering.

After Luria, the expectation of a predetermined messianic movement, linked to a named messiah, disappeared; the Messiah became the Jewish people as a whole. And it is the people of Israel as a whole who are preparing to repair the original breakage. In this context, it can be understood that the redemption of Israel, in the national and political meaning of the term, has been a very real and significant prospect.

To complete this summary of the key concepts of the new Kabbalah, it should be said that its revolution consists precisely in restoring to the Jew, and to man in general, the concept of his own responsibility and dignity in making him realize that history is not predetermined, that the Jew is not predestined to be unhappy and unlucky, but that it is through him, collectively and individually, that the fight for happiness and the forces of his freedom can be won.

15

The Harmony and Balance of the World
The Three Columns

Our journey of initiation continues as we follow the logic that we explained earlier. After having explained the basic ground plan that puts light *(or)* and and the receipt of light (*qabbala*) into the scheme of things, the "just" person of Hasidism, and the main concepts of the Lurianic Kabbalah, we will now tackle the infrastructure of all those worlds that link the world of above and below; that is to say, the range of intermediaries that carry and channel light and energy.

The World Rests on Three Columns

The Zohar tells this story of the death of Rabbi Simeon Bar Yokhai:

> Rabbi Simeon said: "The hour is now propitious, and I want to enter the next world without shame. So I shall reveal in the presence of the *shekhina* sacred things that have not yet been revealed, so that it cannot be said that I left the world without having fully fulfilled my mission on earth, having kept the mysteries in my heart in order to take them with me to the next world. While I am talking to you, Rabbi Abba will write down what I say. My son, Rabbi Eleazar, will repeat them and the other colleagues will meditate in silence."
>
> Rabbi Abba said: "The Holy Lamp had barely pronounced the word 'life'

when he ceased to speak. As for me, I was still writing and I thought I would have a lot more to write, but I could not hear anything more. I could not raise my head because the light was so bright and I could not look into it. Suddenly, I was seized with fear and I heard a voice saying: '. . . the length of days, years of life . . .' (Prov. 3:2) I then heard another voice saying: 'He asked you for life . . .' (Ps. 21:5)

"Throughout the whole day, the fire never left the house and no one could approach it because of the light and the fire which surrounded it. I was there lying on the ground and I cried out. But when the fire left I saw that the Holy Lamp, the Holy of Holies, had been taken from this world.

"Wrapped [in his cloak] he leaned on his right side and there was a smile on his face. But his son, Eleazar, rose, took his hands, and covered them with kisses; as for me, I licked the dust beneath his feet. His disciples wanted to lament but they were unable to utter a word. In the end they were able to shed tears and his son, Eleazar, fell down three times without being able to open his mouth.

"Finally he said: 'Father, father, we were three and one of us has gone. Now the animals will weep for him, the birds will fly away and hide in holes in the rocks of the vast sea.' "

What is the meaning in this very beautiful text of the surprising words, "Father, father, we were three and one of us has gone"?

The commentaries explain that the three are the three columns on which the world rests. The basic ground plan of the Kabbalah is slightly more complex than the simple verticality that links the world of above and below. It is deployed in three parallel vertical columns. The central column is the combination of the two lateral columns, the column of love (loving-kindness) on the right and of justice on the left. The column of love is called *khessed;* the column of justice is called *din* or *gevura.* The central column is called the column of harmony, or *tiferet.*

The Right-hand Column, or Column of Generosity

Khessed is translated as "love" or "loving-kindness." This is the correct interpretation in a general context, but within the Kabbalah, the word has a different meaning. To show how difficult it is to interpret this word, it also means incest between brother and sister. Yet this meaning gives us an indication. Incest contains an inherent refusal to see the difference. This is a world of sameness, of nondifferentiation. It is this particular meaning of *khessed* in the ontological sense, the sense of the general economics of the human being, that is used here.

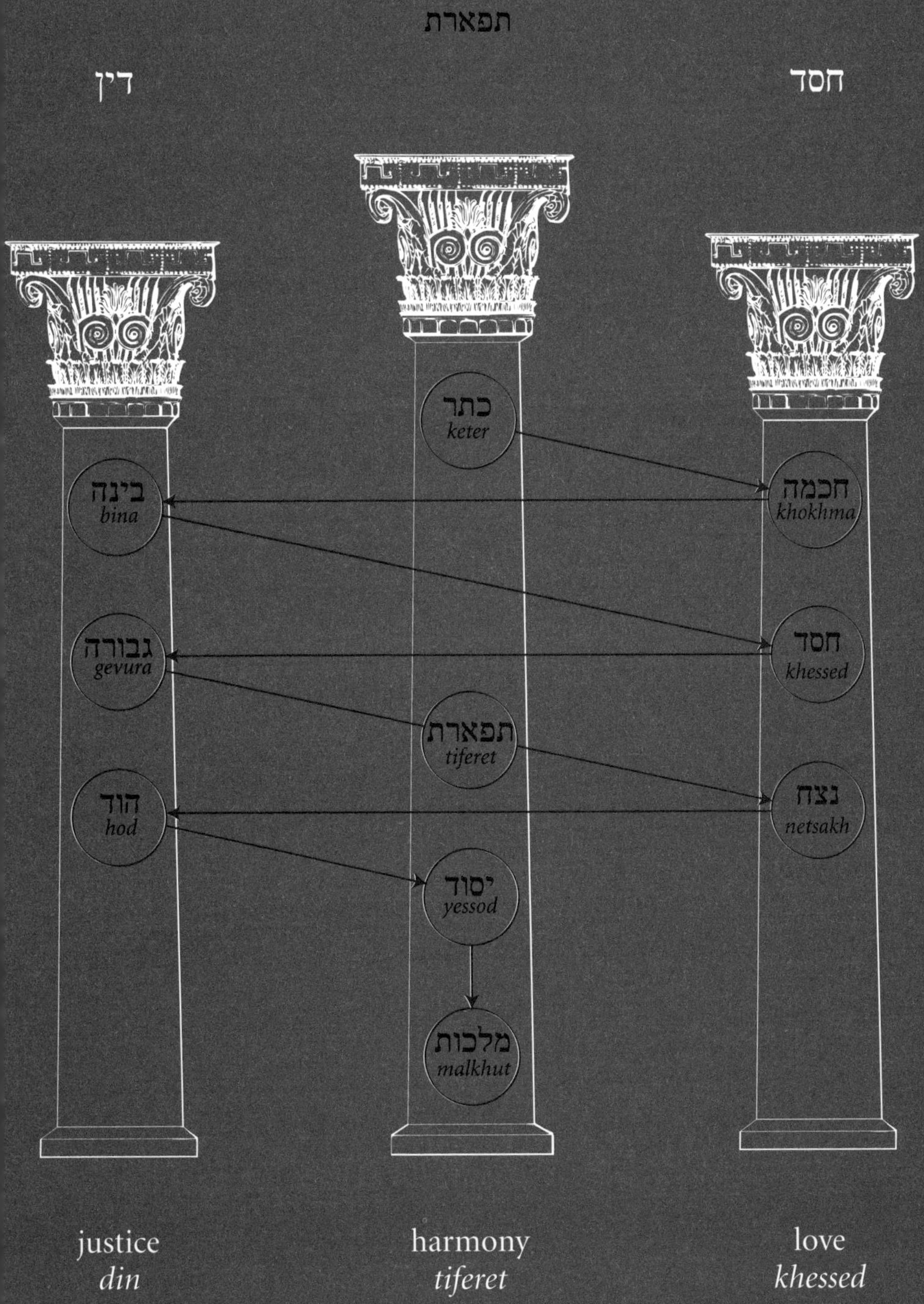

תפארת
דין
חסד
כתר
keter
בינה
bina
חכמה
khokhma
גבורה
gevura
חסד
khessed
תפארת
tiferet
הוד
hod
נצח
netsakh
יסוד
yessod
מלכות
malkhut
justice
din
harmony
tiferet
love
khessed

Khessed is "the power of expansion and extension which lends itself to nature, expansively, generously, and spontaneously. It is a moving force, the force of a being who is what he is and who operates by identification, union, communion, proximity, intimacy and resemblance. It is the totality. It is the universe of 'sameness,' of the being who is what he is" (Armand Abécassis, *Les Temps du partage*). So the meaning of *khessed* is by no means a uniquely positive one. *Khessed* is also the world that tends toward its maximum disorganization, that which in physics is called "entropy."

Probably the image best adapted to *khessed* is that of water. Water takes on every form in an undifferentiated way. If it is not controlled, it overflows and spreads everywhere, and is capable of causing loss and destruction; in the same way, a child who is allowed to do exactly as he pleases will definitely be led into situations in which he is uncontrollable and which are dangerous for himself and his surroundings.

The Left-hand Column, or Column of Justice

On the other hand, "rigor," *gevura* or *din*, is the left-hand column. This is the power of limitation, determination, and definition. It represents the universe of mastery and power, of definition and justice, the sphere of the law and difference, of otherness and radical externalization. It is the separation and distinction between terms that are related. It is the force of retention and suspension, the discovery in the very heart of the force of expansion in order to prevent its overflowing. It can thus be understood that the world cannot rest on love alone, which would be destructive, nor on justice alone, which would be unbearable. The child needs boundaries within which to develop, just as the river needs a bed in order not to overflow into the surrounding fields—just as a musical partition has rules, just as a Beethoven sonata is often richer, and even more brilliant, than free improvisation, and just as the millions of possible moves in the game of chess are the result of rules that the players know and obey.

The Middle Column, or Column of Harmony

The true reality is in the balance between these two forces, produced in the sphere of *rakhamim* ("compassion," which is also called *tiferet,* "harmony"); the effort of being oneself with one's neighbor, respected in his uniqueness.

It is a matter of reaching out with all the generous side of one's nature to one's neighbor and allowing oneself to "be" at the same time, according to what he is and what he wants to be: *khessed* and *din.* It is a matter of authorizing and, at the same time, laying down the ground rules.

To give vent to one's feelings and to respect, to help without humiliating, to understand without reducing, to collaborate without manipulating, to reign while serving, to devote oneself without denying oneself; this is the harmony designated by the third *sefira* and the axis that passes through the middle of the *sefirot.*

These axes meet up at the tenth *sefira,* which is called the "kingdom" *(malkhut).* It is here that three add up to one. Peace reigns throughout the world and in the earthly human city, here and now, when the three forces join up and each individual remains what he is; when a being enters into a relationship with another being, without reducing him, without absorbing him, without assimilating him. The relationship both separates and unites; unites because it separates, and cannot unite unless it makes a distinction.

Love needs a distinction. The love object is a particular person and no other. It is a particular face and a particular perfume. To be able to love everyone, one must first be capable of loving a single individual.

Loving is addressing oneself to someone who exists through reality, who is unique and irreplaceable. It is in the recognized and beloved difference that each of the terms in relation emerges from confusion, disorder, and anonymity. A *khessed* without *din* would lead to the radical confusion that is incest. Love balanced by rigor is thus produced through lucidity and maturity and their meeting within the reciprocal bounds.

There is no true meeting except at the frontier of beings: this is where each person fulfills himself by discovering that the other is always interpolating from another place of speech. The difference from another is necessary as an appeal to enrichment and openness.

Rakhamim ("compassion") or *tiferet* ("splendor") is the relationship of equal distance between domination and submission, fusion and otherness, continuity and separation. It is this which is deployed in the kingdom *(malkhut)*.

The disinterest of *khessed* is inherent in the spontaneity of human nature, its tendencies, its immediate orientations, its intuitions, its emotions, its sentiments, and its instincts, just as Pascal, for example, defines them and just as later Freud would summarize them in the the short and rather vague word, the "id," the urge to a state of purity.

Force, *gevura* or *din*, would thus be reason, the logos, definition, category. Compassion *(rakhamim)* or harmony *(tiferet)* are thus the total existence that, in the absence of reason, becomes madness, and in the presence of reason alone, also becomes totalitarianism. The subject is the person who gives meaning to his existence by being in perpetual dialogue with the entropy of *khessed* and its limitation through *din*.

The Kabbalah and Other Religions

To fully understand the importance of this idea of balance and harmony as love and justice meted out in fair measures, it is interesting to compare the attitude of the three great religions in relation to the theory of the three columns.

We are aware that any schematic is an oversimplification but it has the merit of giving rise to contemplation, even if it implements critical reactions and counterreactions on the part of the reader, who will have his or her own opinion on the subject. Rabbi Elie Munk, in his book *Vers l'harmonie*, writes:

> The civilization that covers the surface of the globe is based on the three great religions, Christianity, Islam and Buddhism, with their variations.... All three religions have drawn their inspiration from the sources of Judaism. But each of them has only borrowed a particular aspect on which to base its doctrine. By thus creating a single aspect of an indivisible whole which is supreme in principle and thus neglecting the rest, or by considering the rest as being subordinate, these religions have acquired the character of an incomplete, imperfect edifice, and the civilizations that they have created contain gaping holes which are hard to fill.

Christianity has opted for the cult of love. It has hypertrophied the biblical concept by teaching that divine love fills man with its grace and that relationships between human beings must be based solely on love and charity. It thus makes love the central focus of the religion, while in the Kabbalah and its complete master plan, love is merely the "right-hand column."

This key term in the Kabbalah makes it clear that the edifice of the universe contains another column opposite this one, the left-hand column. This is the column of justice. By almost totally ignoring the second pillar, Christianity has caused a weakening of the moral conscience and opened the door to serious social crises in the milieu in which humanity seeks to combine love with social justice.

If God had nothing but mercy, humanity would perish, for there would be nothing to stop crime from triumphing; there must also be justice. In terms of the *sefirot,* this is the fundamental dialectic of rigor/justice *(din)* and love/generosity *(khessed).*

Islam, on the other hand, has embraced *din* carried to extremes, the idea of the law being absolute. It has erected it as an exclusive belief, and by applying it to the universal principal, it proclaims man's dependence upon an omnipotent law, both in his will as in his actions and destiny. Man is submissive, impotent, subject to the absolute decrees of God, to the predestination of good and evil, to fatalism. This is known as *mektoub* ("it is written").

This rigid system, which contains a strong element of pessimism, adopts the left side of the ground plan of the Kabbalah, in which the factors of justice and law are merged. But it takes no account of the right-hand column, from which love and liberty radiate.

Muslim civilization has thus given rise to populations in which certain fringe elements can easily fall into the trap of fanaticism. Since the exalting power of love is lacking, Islam is incapable of tracing the route to salvation for humanity.

Buddhism has embraced the middle axis. These peoples of the "middle kingdom" had the most direct and ancient contacts with the huge Jewish communities who were exiled to Asia in the seventh century B.C.E. The great sages and legislators of the seventh century–Confucius, Buddha, and

Lao-tzu—preached, like the Judaism of their day, the middle way, that of wisdom and virtue. But they abandoned another aspect of Judaism, for the three columns of which the Kabbalah consists—love, justice, and the harmonious center—only exist to uphold the edifice itself.

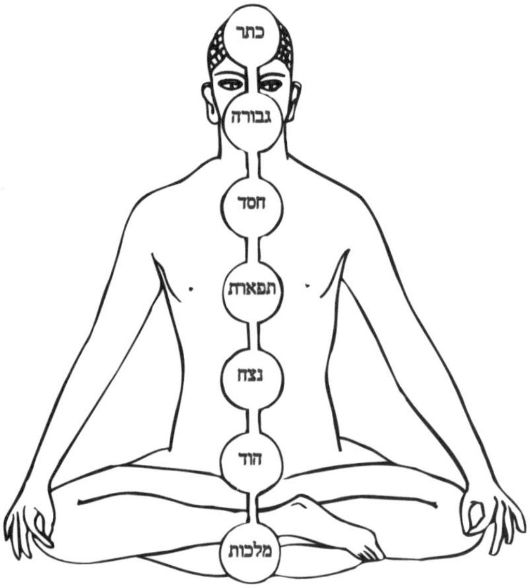

The edifice consists of three horizontal planes. At the highest level are the spiritual forces whose peaks attain the metaphysical spheres. The second level contains the moral forces, and the lowest level, which includes the material forces, serves as a foundation for the construction of the earthly city. The salvation of the world depends on maintaining a preconceived harmony between all of these diverse elements. But although it seeks the middle way, Buddhism remains fixed in the higher spheres, where it loses itself in mystical contemplation. In parallel, it demands an ascetic life, believing that suffering, which is the content of human life, is the result of passion, and that self-denial is the only way to overcome it. By thus turning aside from the lower sphere, from material life in all its forms, instead of taking account of reality, Buddhism creates a mystical, spiritualist civilization of an impassive and static nature, which may lack the impetus to change the human condition. Even if Buddha, through his position, seems to be firmly anchored on the ground, he is entirely meditation. He is thus incapable of fulfilling the kingdom of God on Earth.

Of course, each of these three religions constitutes a route whereby man can accede to exaltation and may reach the divinity. He can move closer to his God through the cult of love, as well as through absolute obedience to the law and through mystical contemplation. But, at every turn, social and spiritual imbalance dogs his footsteps.

Judaism is by no means immune to the risk of imbalance. But if such an imbalance arises, it is due to lack of understanding.

The following anecdote, heard from a Hasidic master, perfectly illustrates this situation:

> One day a master said to his disciples:
> —What do you consider to be the greatest catastrophe that has befallen the Jewish people in its history?
> —The four hundred years of slavery in Egypt, said the first disciple.
> —No! replied the master.
> —The destruction of the Temple, suggested another.
> —No! replied the master.
> —The Exile, offered a third disciple.
> —No! replied the master.
> —The Shoah [Holocaust], said a fourth.
> —No! replied the master, it is neither the Shoah, nor the Exile, nor the destruction of the Temple, nor slavery.
> —We don't see it, admitted his disciples in unison.
> —The greatest catastrophe that has befallen the Jewish people, instructed the master, was when the Torah became a religion!

This story recalls the phrase of Franz Rosenzweig *(The Star of Redemption)* who said, "God created the world, but he did not create religion."

When the laws of the Torah, the mitzvoth, become an end in themselves, forgetting all of the spiritual dimension to which these commandments could lead if we were to apply them, this is "religion." We therefore have an orthodoxy or an orthopraxy that, within the diagram of the three columns, may well position Judaism on the middle column, but toward the spheres below, disconnected from the spheres of spirituality.

Contrary to all these imperfect forms of religiosity, the Kabbalah has chosen the route of harmony. Far from restricting itself to a particular sphere, it attempts to embrace within its action all of the human functions and relationships—love and justice, liberty and law, mystical contemplation and creative action—to fulfill its universal purpose.

Clearly, this presentation is a cursory one, and those who are well versed in the great religions will certainly provide more profound, and even contradictory, comments. The discussion remains open.

The Three Columns and the Three Patriarchs

The figure 3 is the symbol of harmony, of the three columns, and the Kabbalah emphasizes that these three directions are, in fact, represented by the three patriarchs, Abraham, Isaac, and Jacob.

Abraham symbolizes *khessed*—generosity, hospitality, and love. The biblical text describes him waiting at the opening of his tent to welcome any travelers passing through the desert. The story is told of how he prepared with zeal the meal he served his guests, and he did all this only three days after he had been circumcised, the most difficult day in a man's life, according to the commentators. The word *love* is used for the first time in connection with Abraham. The Bible does not use it before that.

Isaac, the son of Abraham, represents the world of rigor, or *din,* in kabbalistic typology. He was much more introverted, and to the burning love that his father had, he added the necessary complement of absolute obedience to divine orders, manifested in his allowing himself to be bound to the altar to be sacrificed to God.

Jacob, Isaac's son, combined love and obedience in his personality. He represents harmony *(tiferet).*

An observation about the columns in Solomon's temple:

The theme of the columns is ever-present in biblical literature, from the moment of the Exodus from Egypt, when a pillar of cloud and smoke preceded the Children of Israel during their wanderings through the desert.

As it is said:

> The Lord went before them in a pillar of cloud by day, to guide them along the way, and in a pillar of fire by night, to give them light, that they might travel day and night. The pillar of cloud by day and the pillar of fire by night did not depart from before the people.
> (Exodus 13:21–22)

Similarly, in the construction of the Sanctuary, which is where the divine presence dwelt, the courtyard is surrounded by columns *('amudim)*, columns that are also to be found in the Temple of Solomon:

> And it took Solomon thirteen years to build his palace, until his whole palace was completed. . . .
> He built the Lebanon forest house. . . . Its length was 100 cubits, its breadth 50 cubits, and its height 30 cubits. It was paneled above with cedar, with the planks that were above on the 45 columns. . . .
> King Solomon sent for Hirâm and brought him down from Tyre.
> He was the son of a widow of the tribe of Naphtali,
> and his father had been a Tyrian, a coppersmith.
> He was endowed with skill, ability, and talent for executing all the work in bronze. He came to King Solomon and executed all his work.
> He cast two columns in bronze; one column was 18 cubits high and measured 12 cubits in circumference. It was hollow and its thickness was four digits.
> And similarly the other column.
> He set up the columns in the portico of the Great Hall *(Heikhal).*
> He set up one column on the right and named it Yakhin.
> and he set up the other column on the left and name it Boaz.
> Upon the top of the columns, there was a lily design.
> Thus the work of the columns was completed.
> (Book of Kings I, 7:1, 2, 13–15, 21–22)

The two hollow columns play a symbolic role. They permit the light of the infinite to descend and circulate inside. The first column, Yakhin, signifies: "He makes real, he gives a meaning to existence, he founds the positive aspect of the world." The second column, Boaz, signifies: "The power is within him." The Yakhin column is *khessed.* The Boaz column is *din.*

Thus there are three columns in the Kabbalah. In fact, man himself creates the third column, by placing himself between the other two columns; he combines *khessed* and *din* within himself. It is man himself who stands in the Great Hall, the *heikhal,* between the two columns, thus constituting the hollow column through which the energy of infinity, the *en-sof,* can circulate.

16

The Decade of Fundamental Elements

The Ten *Sefirot*

The basic ground plan has taught us that the light of infinity may be understood according to three essential intermediate worlds, namely:
- the world of the ten spheres *(sefirot)*
- the world of letters, of the book, and of the word *(sefer)*
- the world of figures, numbers, and geometric shapes *(sefar)*

The tree of the *sefirot* is the structure of creation. It is the diagram of the principles on which the world was created and whereby it continues to exist. There are ten such principles. They are called the Decade of Fundamental Elements, or the ten *sefirot:* "Ten like the ten fingers of the hand, five on the right and five on the left, the balancing the world. Ten *sefirot* and not eleven, ten and not nine, ten *sefirot,* say *belima,*" according to the enigmatic phraseology of the "Book of Creation."

The Tree of the *Sefirot*

When the primordial light of infinity descends upon the world to give the breath of life into all the world and all the creatures, it is diversified and refracted in the form of ten lights, each of which contains one aspect of the

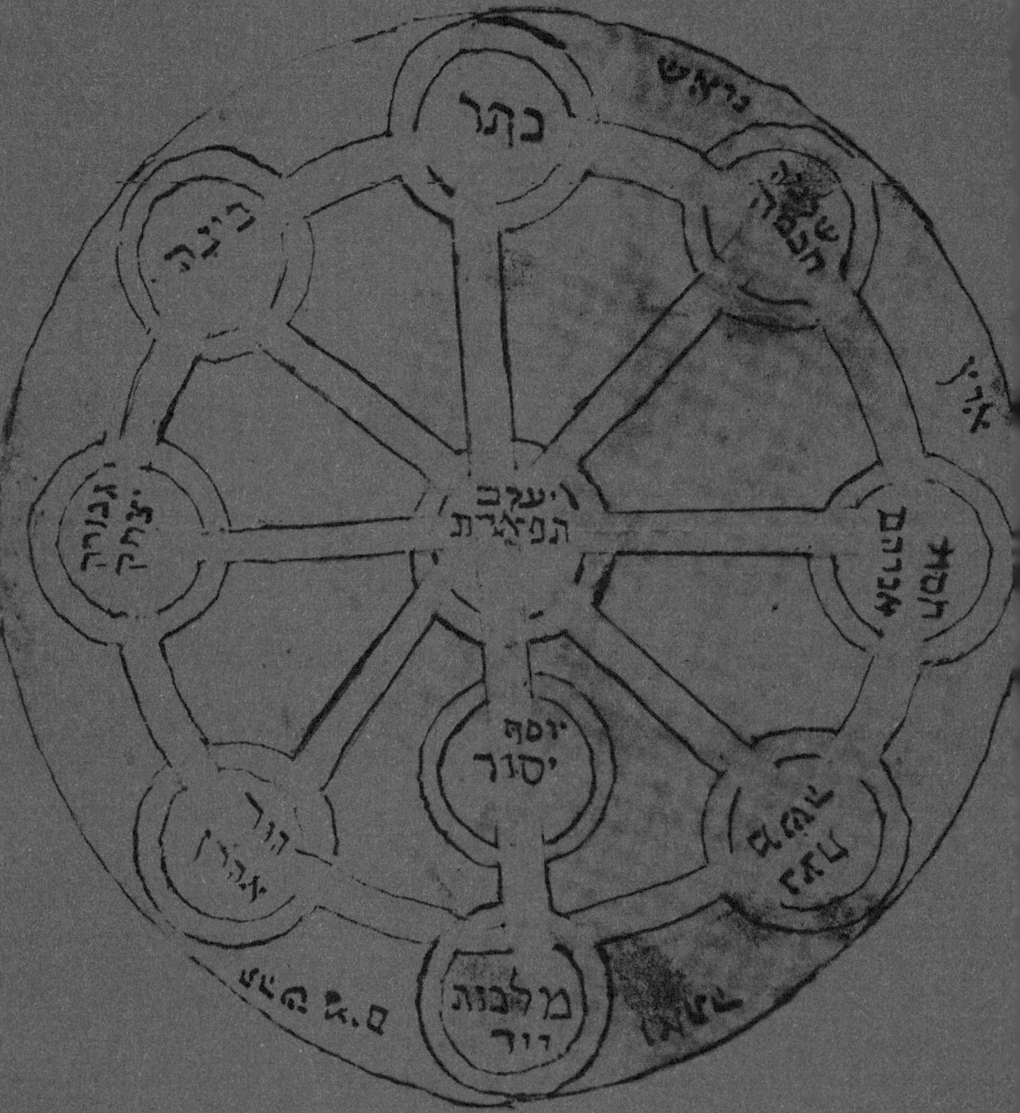

A page from the "Book of Creation" representing the ten *sefirot* arranged in a circle, in the center of which is the *sefira* of *tiferet*. In this diagram, the *sefirot* are also associated with important characters from the story of the Bible.

power of light needed for existence. Divinity in action appears as the dynamic unity of the *sefirot,* which constitutes the tree of the *sefira.* Life expands outward and vivifies creation, while at the same time remaining deeply internal. The secret rhythm of its movement, its pulse, is the dynamic law of nature.

To the extent that the divine life manifests itself in various forms at different levels of the divine emanation, that is to say when it shows itself to be effective, it takes a different form on each occasion. Thus from one point of view of the light from on high, it manifests itself under a different attribute, a different *sefira.* In fact, the word *sefira* covers a number of concepts and images according to the authorities.

For example, to quote Abraham Herrera, a seventeenth-century writer, who produced a kabbalistic work entitled *Puerta del Cielo* ("The Gates of Heaven," or *Shaar Hashamayim*):

> The sefirot are the mirror of its truth and the analogies of its being are the most sublime; the ideas of its wisdom and concepts of its will; the reservoirs of its strength and the instruments of its activity; the coffers of its felicity and the distributors of its grace; the judges of its empire who deliver their verdict; they are also the definitions, the attributes, and the name of he who is most high and the cause of all things; these are the ten inextinguishable; ten attributes of His exalted majesty; the ten fingers of the hand; the ten lights by which he reflects himself and the ten garments with which he covers himself; ten visions in which he appears; ten forms thanks to which he has shaped everything; ten sanctuaries in which he is magnified; ten degrees of prophecy through which he manifests himself; ten celestial cathedra from which he dispenses his teaching; ten thrones on which he judges the nations; ten halls in paradise for those who are worthy; ten levels which he gravitates downward and through which one can gravitate upward toward him; ten areas producing all the influxes and all the benedictions; ten aims desired of all but which only the just can achieve; ten lights which illuminate all the intelligence; ten sorts of fire which assuage all desires; ten categories of glory which animate all reasonable souls; ten words through which the world was created; ten spirits which animate the world and maintain it in life; ten numbers, weights and measures which number, weigh, and measure everything. (quoted by *G. Scholem* in *La Mystique juive,* 60)

The Light of Infinity Takes a Form: The Face

The face of man is proof of the existence of God.

—Max Picard, quoted in Emmanuel Levinas, *Proper Names*

All the forces that fill the universe derive, directly or indirectly, from the ten *sefirot.* According to Scholem, in accordance with the *Sefer Yetsira* ("Book of Creation"), these represent the ten primordial numbers on which everything concrete is based. The infinite light of God, when it becomes visible and active for creation and man, receives the name of "face."

The *sefirot* are powers of which the active divinity is composed, those through which it receives a face. "Face" is a kabbalistic way of saying that the infinite is revealed to man and acquires a certain visibility.

The hidden face of God is a factor of life that is turned toward us and which takes form, despite all its concealment. Life is manifested on ten levels, each of which both hides and reveals it at the same time. The divine light, or source of all life, manifests itself on ten levels, each of which is both manifestation and concealment of the light.

"In the face of man," comments Levinas, "a trace of God manifests itself and the light of this revelation floods the universe."

Commenting upon Levinas, Jacques Derrida writes, "The expression of the infinite is the face. The face is not only the aspect which may be on the surface of things, the animal features, the aspect or species. Nor is it purely, as the origin of the word implies, that which is seen, seen because it is naked. It is also that which sees. Not so much as a person seeing things but as an exchange of glances. The face only faces in face-to-face. As Scheler said: I do not only see the eyes of another person, I also see him looking at me."

Subsequently, the author was fortunate enough to chance upon the following text by Christian Bobin *(L'Homme qui marche):* "The gateway to what is human is the face, seeing face to face, one on one, one to one. In the concentration camps, the Nazis forbade the deportees from looking them in the eyes on pain of immediate death. He whose face I do not accept—and to accept it, I must wash my face of any element of power—is he whom I empty of his humanity and I empty my own into him."

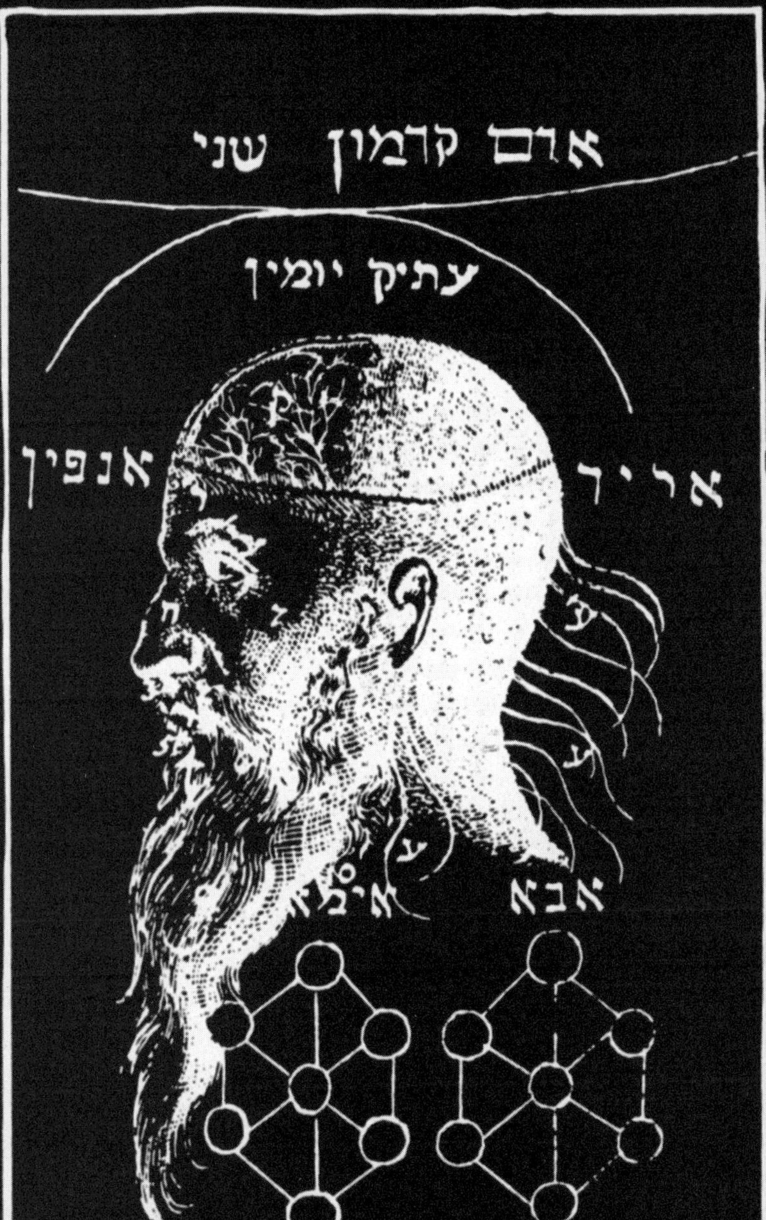

Organisation of the *sefirot* according to Knorr von Rosenroth:
zeir anpin, "little face," and *arikh anpin*, "great face."

The Grammar of the *Sefirot*

The *sefirot* are an alphabet of ten elements or ten forces that can be conjugated among themselves to form multiple combinations through which the light of infinity is reflected and, in various ways, reaches the lower worlds.

To begin with, here is the list of the ten *sefirot*, each of which will be discussed in turn:

- *keter*: the crown
- *khokhma*: wisdom
- *bina*: intelligence
- *khessed*: love and generosity (loving-kindness)
- *gevura* or *din*: force, strength, judgment, or rigor
- *tiferet* or *rahamim*: the harmony between the two previous *sefirot* (and the harmony between the right-hand and the left-hand columns on which the world rests)
- *netsakh*: victory (or triumph) and the patience of God, the master and the control of the world
- *hod*: splendor or glory, the aesthetic dimension of the world
- *yessod* or *tsadiq*: the foundation, the ability to retransmit everything that has been received
- *malkhut*: royalty and the kingdom, the ability to receive and organize oneself on the basis of the energies from the previous *sefirot*

The organization of these *sefirot* is deployed, as explained above, along three axes: a central axis, a left-hand axis, and a right-hand axis. It is very important to fully acquaint oneself with and memorize the diagram of the *sefirot*, for it is through them that all the energies descend and rise that permit all living things to exist.

Important remark:

There are always ten *sefirot*, but there are several standard ways used to count them. These different methods have given rise to various currents in the study of Kabbalah. Some kabbalists consider *keter* to be outside the system because it is an exalted state which cannot be obtained by man, and, thus do not include it among the *sefirot*. In this manner, *keter* belongs to the *en-sof*, or infinity, and it is replaced in the *sefirot* by *da'at*: knowledge. All eleven elements will be discussed in the following pages.

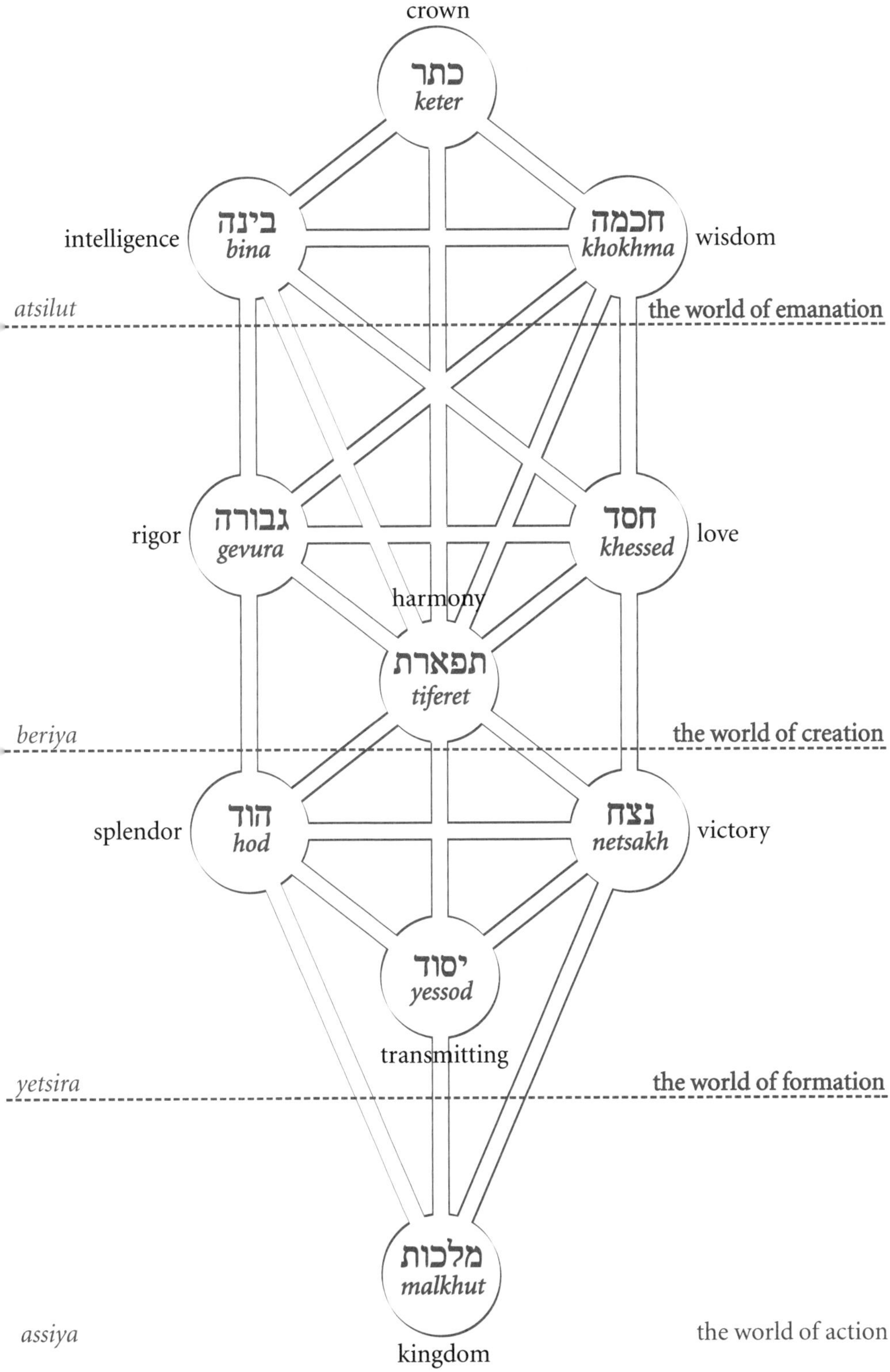
crown
כתר
keter
בינה
bina
intelligence
חכמה
khokhma
wisdom
atsilut
the world of emanation
גבורה
gevura
rigor
חסד
khessed
love
harmony
תפארת
tiferet
beriya
the world of creation
הוד
hod
splendor
נצח
netsakh
victory
יסוד
yessod
transmitting
yetsira
the world of formation
מלכות
malkhut
assiya
the world of action
kingdom

17

The Art of Being Present for Oneself
Keter, or Crown

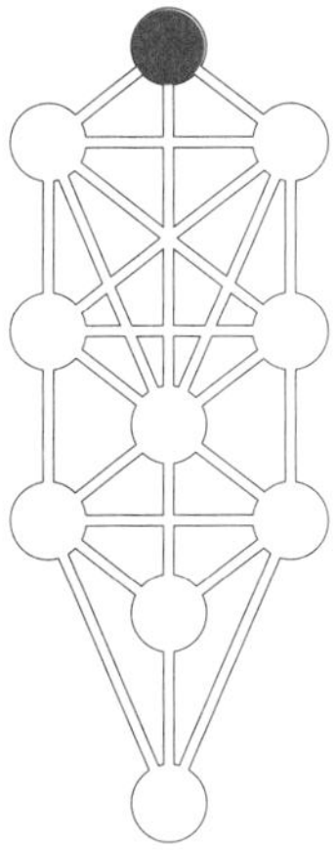

Rabbi Nachman one day encountered one of his disciples who was hurrying home. He asked him:
—Have you looked at the sky this morning?
—No, Rabbi, I did not have time.
—Believe me, in fifty years, everything that is here will have disappeared. There will be another fair, other horses, other carriages, different people. I shall no longer be here and neither will you. So what is it that is so important that you do not have time to look at the sky?
—Teaching of Rabbi Nachman, in *The Empty Chair*

The *Sefira* of *Keter:* The Here and Now

The first *sefira* designates the primordial divine will, the supreme will, the source of all will, the first awakening of the divine momentum. This mysterious will, which is devoid of restrictive plans, is pure will that acts within the being and pushes him outward. Hence the first *sefira* is also called *ehyeh*, "I shall be."

The commentaries attribute considerable importance to this *sefira* due to its ability to receive the light of infinity. It is the first or highest opening to the transcendence.

Rabbi Nachman of Breslov translates *keter* as: "Be ready!"

Be ready to receive the divine energy by being entirely present in what you are doing!

Here we encounter an idea that is present in the work of other mystics and in other spiritualities, which is often formulated in the expression "the here and now."

The Kabbalah stresses the importance of the past and the future, the need to know one's roots and to constantly be borne by hope and the ability to make plans for the future. However, the past must not consist of nostalgia for a situation that holds us back and impedes our progress, nor must the future be a flight into what lies ahead.

The Present Moment: The *Rega*

The strength of a plan must not be a flight into the future, since one risks bypassing an essential element, namely, the joy and beauty of the present moment.

In Hebrew, the word "present" is *rega,* which has the same root as the word *ragua,* which means "becalmed" and "tranquil." The *keter,* the first *sefira* and the first condition for receiving the light of the infinite, is the capacity to entirely assume the instant in which we are without saying to ourselves that we could be elsewhere or doing something else. Rabbi Nachman says that the *keter,* is "being ready to be," in the moment. Now!

Being incapable of living in the "here and now" is failing to accept that which is, but living constantly in the past or the future. Blockage! The Kabbalah stresses that despite the importance of faithfulness to the tradition and to memory, despite the need to constantly project oneself into the future in order to be able to construct and progress, life does not happen in the past nor in the future. Life is now.

There is nothing else in each moment than the now. The best thing that a person in a situation of *keter* can do is to accept this. Man is thus in harmony with life, not in conflict with it.

Hebrew considers the notion of present as being related to that of serenity *(rega/ragua)*. The English language adds the dimension of a gift. The present is a present! Let us learn how to accept it!

For the Kabbalah, it is through man that the current of cosmic energy passes *(hayut elohit)*. If he creates knots and blockages for himself, the current cannot flow, and man cannot receive the energy he needs to continue to exist harmoniously. In contemporary parlance, the idea could be expressed as follows: human beings are comparable to resistors. Where does the current pass through most quickly? Logically, it is through the place of least resistance.

And where is the least resistance to be found? In the person who lives in the here and now. As soon as we leave the here and now, we create a knot, a node, a resistance, and a conflict.

The *keter* is the crown, a shape that surrounds the place and time in which we exist and which must be donned with serenity.

Other terms are used to describe the same state of mind. Zen Buddhism, for instance, uses the terms "unintentionally," "acting without acting." Zen Buddhists express this state by saying:

When I eat, I eat;
When I drink, I drink;
When I read, I read.

In our case, the Kabbalah speaks of "intention" *(kavana)*. Before undertaking each action, one must channel one's intention.

The student kabbalist is surprised to find that he is not expected to indulge in metaphysical meditation, nor in arduous intellectual toil. He is simply asked to really say and live these words before each action: "Hineni mukhan oomezuman lekayem" ("I am entirely ready and willing to give totally of myself in what I am about to do").

Concentration on gesture and thought, so that there is no interference from extraneous thoughts or gestures: *keter!*

Keter is the secret of calm and serenity of life. When one acts, one is no longer telling oneself at the same time that one might be doing something else. That is the secret of the *rega/ragua:* the moment is serenity.*

* Apart from the Kabbalah, this question is dealt with, among others, by a populist but interesting presentation by René Egli in *Le Principe LoL²A.*

18

Learning to Be Astonished and Amazed
Khokhma, or Wisdom

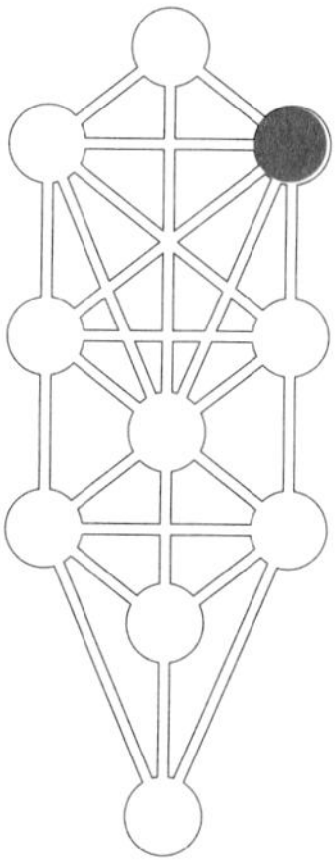

One day, a non-Jew asked a Rabbi:
—Master, why do the Jews always answer questions with another question?
—And why not? replied the Rabbi!
—Jewish folk humor

As soon as a person has adopted the habit of being entirely present *(keter)* in everything he does, each of his actions will be more complete and he can begin to explore other fundamental procedures and other *sefirot.*

As has been said above, the Kabbalah is an attitude in relation to the world. It is learning:

- to hear the silent
- to see the invisible
- to feel the immaterial

To begin to perceive these new dimensions of a world containing all those things that we may have neglected up to now, we must change our way of looking at things and abandon old habits. The awakening of consciousness begins when one is capable of questioning oneself and calling oneself into question.

The wisdom of astonishment and questioning constitutes *khokhma,* a word that the masters of the Kabbalah analyzed by cutting it in half and inverting the first two letters, yielding *koakh-ma,* "The power of what ?" (*ma* meaning "what?").

The masters noted that the numeric value of the word "man" *(adam)* is 45, the same number as produced by the word *ma.* Is not man that unique creature who defies every possible definition? Is not man an existence whose definition is to have no definition? Is not the essence of man that of having no essence? This is a paradox which Hebrew is perfectly capable of dealing with. Essence is *mahut,* the root of *ma,* meaning "what."

Surprise is the source of amazement, which itself is the possibility of seeing the world in the miracle of its eternal creations and re-creations.

Looking All Around

The Kabbalah, like philosophy, begins with wonderment.

This wonderment should encompass everything around us: time, space, things, other people, animals, plants, tools—and ourselves. Paradoxically, the question does not cover the unknown, the mysterious and invisible worlds that are remote and hard to access, the "nether-worlds," but that which is "close" and "next," everything that is nearby and that we will encounter "first of all."

Why?

"Because that which we encounter 'first of all,' is not that which is near, but always that which is habitual. Yet the habitual contains within itself the frightening power of dishabituating inhabitation of the essential, and often so decisively that it never again lets us succeed in inhabiting it" (Martin Heidegger, *What Is Meant by to Think?*).

A Revolution in the Way of Looking at Things: *Hitkhadeshut*

This is where the question, the astonishment arises. A hidebound, entrenched tradition must be reanimated, the baggage that it has accumulated over time eliminated, and the deposits it has left scraped away. This means a revolutionary way of looking at things, new perceptions, a totally positive revolution that should enable man to open up again to the world, and to do so with originality, to find himself at the dawn of a new day in the world, in which he himself and everything there is begins to appear in a new light, in which the world offers itself to him in a new way. This idea of novelty of perception, in his understanding of the world and of things, is a constant in kabbalistic thought.

This is the concept of *hitkhadeshut,* to which the principal reference is found in Deuteronomy (commentaries on chapter 26, verse 16): "Hayom hazeh Hashem Eloqekha metsavekha laassot" ("On this day, the Lord thy God commands you to do").

The Midrash Tanhuma asks:

> What is the meaning of "on this day' *[Hayom hazeh]*? Had the Holy one, blessed be He, not commanded anything until now? Yet the "today" in question happens to be in the fortieth year after the Revelation. This is what should be understood by it: Moses says to Israel: "The Torah must be so dear to you that every day must be for you the very day of the Revelation, as if you had received it on this day from Mount Sinai" *[Ke'ilu hayom hazeh qibaltem ota mehar Sinai].*
>
> "Today, may they (the commandments) be considered in your eyes as if they were new" *[Yiyou be'enekha kekhadashim].*

Through amazement and questioning, man can finally liberate himself from the restraints of certain habits of thought, convictions, theories received without verification, opinions, prejudices, foregone conclusions, which decree the nature of the world, things, people, knowledge, and so on. Each time, man is another person, another life, another experience. Man is not, but becomes; that means that he ought to exist as the emergence of new, other faces, of the thinkable and the action; that he exists through constantly changing.

This also applies to the collective. A society that does not adopt new forms of organization is signing its own death warrant.

The Holy Ark Is Always Moving

Khokhma, according to Rashi's commentary, is the ability to be willing to listen to what other people have to say. It is the dimension of listening and openness. It is the humility of a spirit that still wants to learn, a rejection of dogmatism. *Khokhma* opens instead of closing, questions instead of proving, expresses a question instead of wanting to possess an answer. It never stops. It is impossible to immobilize it, it never fixes upon anything, not even upon itself....

It is an infinite metaphor, represented by the Holy Ark that contained the Tables of the Law. The sides of the Ark had carrying poles attached to it that were forbidden to be removed. This was a symbolic interdiction: the Ark and its contents, the light of infinity, must never settle in a definitive place, must never be still; it must always be moving, moving along the way.

Kabbalistic thought is a way of calling consciousness into question, not merely a consciousness of calling into question. This experience constantly changes the being of the kabbalist, who becomes a questioning human being—"the man-question"—and no longer merely the man who asks questions.

By refusing to fall into a "definitive" time and by preserving the grandeur of "infinitive" time, the Kabbalah stresses the words of questioning, the momentum of reasoning against the dogmatism of truth.

19

Wisdom, Intelligence, and Knowledge
Khokhma, *Bina*, and *Da'at*

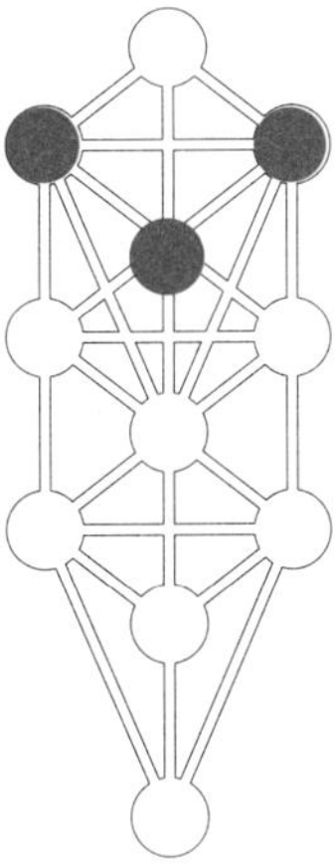

The Diagram of *Segol*

After the *sefira* of *khokhma,* there is the *sefira* of *bina* and that of *da'at.* We will show the connection between them.

The shape in which these three *sefirot* are organized is that of a *segol.* The *segol* is a Hebrew vowel that consists of three points or periods, which form an equilateral triangle, with the base at the top—the symbol of balance and harmony, as well as that of peace.

In Hebrew writing, the *segol* is the vowel that is pronounced "eh."

The word *segol* has produced the word *segula,* which is often translated as "elect or "chosen," as in the expression *am segula,* translated as "the chosen people," but which really means "a people in balance and harmony like the shape of the *segol*."

Being the elect is no doubt an essential form of responsibility, which means ensuring that the world itself is in equilibrium.

A Fine Balance between the Rational and the Emotional

The explanations of a *sefira* are cumulative. An initial approach to *khokhma* has been provided, but this approach can be completed by positioning *khokhma* within the *segol* diagram along with *bina* and *da'at.*

The Kabbalah might be thought to be antirationalist or purely emotional. That would be a mistake; for the Kabbalah, the real opposition is not between reason and irrationality (or between intelligence and emotion), but between a dessicated, dogmatic, narrow intellectualism and a liberated and open intellectualism concerning everything that transcends the boundaries of logical thought.

Furthermore, it is just as important to challenge an irrationality that rebels against all logic or sensitivity deprived of thought, to enhance a sensitivity that enriches the soul, brings the mind to life, and reinforces the quality of thought.

The text of Exodus states that Betsalel, who had been commanded by God to build the Tabernacle, was invested through the spirit of Elohim with *khokhma, tevuna,* and *da'at.* Betsalel was the archetypal artist. In order to enter into the art of life, one must be equipped with three qualities—*bina, khokhma,* and *da'at.*

Bina

Each person within the depths of his being speaks two languages. One of them is that of logic and technology, which makes it possible to deal with the realities of the world. Logic is based on the principle of causality, the relationship between cause and effect.The link that exists between cause and effect would in this case be *bina,* "between two." *Bina* is the mind's ability to deduce one thing from another or to induce it. This is the daily, prosaic state of the world.

Khokhma

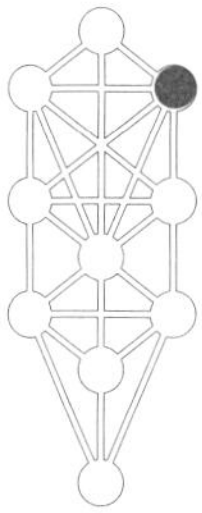

The other human language is that of smashing this logic, fracturing causality, opening the way toward something beyond this world, towards the dream and the imagination, poetry and the poetic state. This is *khokhma.*

Khokhma, according to Rashi, is also the ability to be open to the words of another person—the dimension of listening and opening. It is the humility of a mind that still wants to learn, that rejects dogmatism.

Dogmatism is nothing more than an opinion, according to which truth consists of a proposition that is a fixed result or a proposition that is immediately known.

Khokhma opens rather than closes, questions rather than tries to prove, expresses a question rather than wanting to possess an answer. It should be remembered that the masters of the Kabbalah analyzed the word *khokhma* as *koakh-ma,* "the force of What?"

Da'at

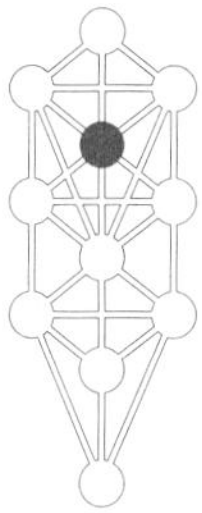

Da'at is not positive and static knowledge but that which is felt, what is today called emotional intelligence, the result of existential experience—the joy or sadness that we feel, for example, at meeting someone, something we read, or some other event.*

Logic and Poetry

In the language of the Kabbalah, *khokhma* is called *aba,* "father," and *bina* or *ima,* "mother." Thus the so-called maternal language would be the language

* Concerning this interpretation, the reader can consult Nehama Leibovitz, *Commentaries on the Book of Exodus,* which quotes the thinking of Rabbi Isaac Horowitz.

of logic, causality, and philosophy. The father, on the other hand, is the poetic aspect. A role reversal!

Is there not some inherent desire here to make us rethink the fifth of the Ten Commandments? "Honor your father and your mother. . . ."

Respect the father and mother in yourself, the two fundamental languages that constitute the essence of man, the language of logic and the language of poetry.

"Be a poet!" is what the Fifth Commandment is saying. We can thus formulate this strange conclusion: "Do not forget to be a poet!" ought actually to be part of the Ten Commandments.

Notelet: Kabbalah, Epistemiology, and Biology

This meditation on wisdom and the various ways in which it is formulated in Hebrew leads to postulating existence in these three terms—*khokhma, bina,* and *da'at*—which are three different modes of approaching the world: the poetic, the logical, and the emotional. It has been explained that according to the Kabbalah, *khokhma* is connected with paternal language, and *bina* with maternal language. A study of the texts of the Kabbalah also reveals that in the space occupied by the human being, *khokhma* is situated on the right and *bina* on the left.

What use is this information? Lucien Israël has written on the subject in his *Cerveau droit, cerveau gauche: Cultures and civilisations,* an explanation of the left brain, right brain theories of Roger Sperry, winner of the Nobel Prize for Medicine in 1981. Scientific publications and explanations of the relationship between the right and the left brain "are about to revolutionize neuro-psychology and psychiatry, but also esthetics, ethnology, sociology, theories of education, and even politics. . . . 'Know thyself!' These were the words the those consulting the oracle at Delphi would receive from Apollo, son of Leto. This fascinating injunction was made to man at the dawn of civilizations by the Sun god, the divine player of the lyre, and by that nation that would also say: 'Man is capable of anything,' the race that gave us logic, science, democracy, liberty, and at the same time, tragedy and the mysteries of Eleusis."

Knowledge of the brain is one of the greatest of all revolutions. The brain is that part of the human being, that extraordinary organ, whereby matter is capable of thinking for itself.

The human brain contains between 30 and 60 billion, perhaps even 100 billion, cells. Each contains extensions that ramify so as to constitute thousands of separate branches. These branches make contact with the identical extremities of thousands of other cells, and these junctions are called synapses.

The synapses are not fixed. They form and dissolve in a mysterious dance that constantly changes the shape, length, and extent of the active circuits and thus the associations between groups of cells belonging to different zones, each having its own delicate specialization. The number of possible combinations in a brain is greater than the number of atoms in the entire universe. No mathematical model is capable of taking account of such complexity. No program can predict the changes that may take place from one moment to the next due to the influence of a mental movement, the perception of a modification of the external world.

The human brain is the most complex structure in the known universe.

Cerebral Asymmetry: The Functions of the Brain

Schematically, it could be said that cerebral asymmetry—that is to say, the existence of separate functions based on the two hemispheres of the brain, which are integrated, though not completely, in the overall performance of the brain—could be translated by the following data.

The information processed verbally is handled by the left brain, and that which is processed visually is handled by the right brain. (This point is of extreme importance when using the "archaeographical" method to reveal the images behind the shapes of lettering.)

Music is processed separately, memorized, and understood by the right brain. If rhythm and tempo are perceived by the left brain, the melody, tone, and resonance are perceived by the right brain.

To summarize, the left brain is the analytical and logical side of the brain, the side of intelligence or *bina:*

> *Inter legere:* to choose between, to discern. But this etymology is inadequate to cover the extent of the concept. There is also a sense of linking, calculating, evaluating, anticipating, guessing. An ability to design models of reality, without losing sight of the fact that these are only models, is also part of the equation. But intelligence is also the ability to attribute its real weight to each of the elements which constitutes an external or internal reality and to be able to conceive of complex and dynamic interactions in space and time between these elements. All of this is translated in the word "understand"—take together—and this contains a strong element of mystery, since understanding a situation is still very different from understanding a human being.
> (Lucien Israël, *Cerveau droit,* 37)

In other words, the left-hand side is responsible for language, analysis, verbal memory, the numeric aspects of arithmetic, the logical dissection of problems. The right-hand side must perceive and understand emotions and visual and spatial concepts; it handles information in a comprehensive, inclusive manner, and its knowledge is more intuitive than analytical. This hemisphere was long neglected, but it plays an important role in our presence in the world, in ways that complement those of the left hemisphere. An attempt must still be made to understand how the two brains cooperate in the normal individual to achieve integrated behavior.

It would be wrong to believe that the left brain alone is what makes us different from the higher animals. Remember that the metaphor, the symbol, intuition, and imagination are all functions of the right brain in *Homo sapiens.*

"Finally, who is in charge here?" is the question asked by Sally Springer and Georg Deutsch, the authors of *Left Brain, Right Brain.* Studies show that while it is usually the hemisphere that specializes in a type of processing or response that takes charge of a cognitive or memory task in the normal individual, that is not always the case. It depends on the particular history of the person.

> The mechanism of this unicity is not known. Nothing more can be said about it at present. Much remains to be done in order to understand the integrated functioning of the hemispheres which, in any case, involve the most complex problems of human consciousness. But it has been realized that this integrated functionality has precisely the role of combining the two different experiences,

two approaches to the external and internal reality, two visions of the same individual story. That is the innovation of Sperry's revelation and his school, who have made it possible to have a different perception of the cultures and civilizations which man has built on his planet.

Lucien Israël notes that for Roger Sperry the "separate" right brain, considered outside its association with the left, perceives, thinks, learns, memorizes, reasons, makes choices, produces acts of will, and expresses emotions. But for Sperry, the integration creates an entity that is quantitatively and qualitatively greater than the sum of the two parts. On the basis of this dichotomy, it ought to be possible to briefly survey the roles of the right brain and left brain on the basis of the civilizations, and especially to compare the complex cultures and civilizations of East and West.

Clearly this diagrammatic summary (which has been borrowed from Lucien Israël) ought not to mask the complexity of the subject and the multiple considerations involved, both on the epistemiological and the philosophical levels. However, a large part of our current thinking concerning "whatability" is based on this distinction between the halves of the brain and consists of a sort of repair, a *tikkun,* of the forgetfulness of the right brain, the forgetting of *khokhma.* Whatability is a rehabilitation of the categories handled by the right brain, an invitation to return to wisdom, to an ethical and pedagogical perspective, and to construct the possibility of a future in which the human psyche achieves a better balance.

What do we know today of ourselves? Very little. However, it is clear that the right brain is an active brain. Half of our relationship with the world has been neglected, or at least underestimated, hitherto by most of the intellectuals of the Western world.

If Heidegger could write that the history of the human being was a forgetting of the human being it could be said that the history of Western metaphysics since Plato is a forgetting of the contribution of the right-hand side of the brain, the *khokhma.* It is a sort of anesthesia of the right brain, to the benefit of the hyperactivation of the left.

This note is a mere glimpse, a train of thought that the author leaves to the experts. These remarks may well be a path that leads nowhere.

20

The Dialectic of Opening and Closing
Khessed, Din, and *Tiferet*

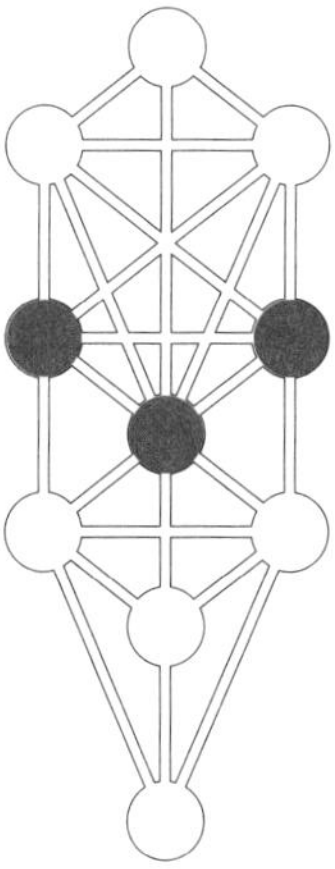

. . . the mystery of evil, the only one in which God does not make us believe but makes us think.
—Marie Noël, quoted by Sylvie Germain in *Etty Hillesum*

One should not be surprised if an unfathomable crime in some way calls for inexhaustible meditation.
—Vladimir Jankélévitch, *Le Pardon*

Good and Evil: The Ethical Approach

The balance and harmony of the world rest on the three pillars of *din, khessed* and *tiferet.* These three *sefirot* also invite an ethical reflection on the question of good and evil, as well as the more general question of open and closed structures. We shall thus pursue our interpretation on the basis of new perspectives.

These three *sefirot* are also arranged in the *segol* formation.

The Kabbalah proposes a totally original concept of good and evil. Everything that tends to be in harmony, in the musical sense of the term, with the dynamic and the creative forces that animate living things is "good." Everything that is opposed to the vibration of the creative force of the breath of life is "evil." Of course, such "evil" cannot be understood in the usual sense of the word; it does not resemble the evil from which our world suffers—in fact the contrary. This is the "evil" that consists in rejecting the reality of an imperfect world, that is to say, the very possibility of reaching perfection and the freedom thus implemented.

Liberty is the good and positive foundation of reality, it provides the strength that makes it possible to progress toward perfection and constantly animates dynamism and aspiration. Necessity or destiny, on the other hand, limits and curbs this freedom of spirit, since it subjects it to the restrictions of natural laws. The evil in our world lies in everything that diminishes the rhythm of perfecting and developing, both in nature and the material world as in the world of the spirit. Everything that stultifies and weakens the spontaneity of free will, through habits, mechanical repetition, spiritual inhibitions, and a passivity of the intelligence, is an open door to what could be called the domain of evil.

The Dialectic of the Perfect and the Imperfect

They asked Rabbi Levi Isaac of Berditchev: "Why is the first page number missing in all the tractates of the Babylonian Talmud? Why does each begin with the second?"
He replied: "However much a man may learn, he should always remember that he has not even gotten to the first page."
—Martin Buber, *Tales of the Hasidim*

It is a surprising paradox.

There is thus "absolute good" at the divine source, which is the perfection of all perfection. As it is perfection, no change is desirable, so there is no dynamic. But for creatures, this absolute good represents an "evil" because perfection excludes all creation and all freedom. "The very root of evil is hidden in the depths of absolute good and it is the act of denying the miracle and the possible" (The Master of Lights *[Baal Ha-Orot]*, quoted by Yosef Ben Shlomo, *Shirat Ha-Hayyim*).

For man, good resides in the gap between the perfection of God and the transgression of this perfection through the creation of the world. This creation is a break in the immanence of perfection. Any creation is less perfect than the source of all perfection.

The being of the world thus conjugates with "imperfect" and "unexpected"!

The imperfect reality of the world outside God is logically in opposition to His perfection. But for man, it is this imperfection that becomes his entry into perfection, within the meaning of the very kabbalist formula devised by André Neher: "The perfection of man is his perfectibility."

The Kabbalah and Art

There is an idea here that is encountered in the world of art. Art is the perfection of untrue forms.The greatest artistic perfection must be imperfect, and it is then infinite in its effect.

A perfect circle, a true vertical, are pure, ideal "objectities" that in their mathematical infallibility, which is devoid of conflict, can never assume the uncertainty of the secret or invented shapes, which turns even the most rigorous artist into someone who, in the words of Dante, has the rectitude of art and a hand that trembles.

When Robert Delaunay paints his "circular shapes," the circle is born from the displacement—transgression and transcendence—of all the disparate shapes, which deviate from their own continuity, which are imperfect, and which refuse to "turn in a circle." Art is the perfection of imprecise shapes. They are not balanced within themselves, unlike mathematical figures, whose structure expresses the constancy of a particular law.

An artistic form, whether dotted, linear, flat, or three-dimensional, is a meeting place, self-propelling, with antagonistic tensions, opening and closing, which constitutes the energetics of space, in breadth and depth.

It is not a finite and completed structure. It is form that is being formed.

A work of art is not a form in matter; it is that which passes through matter at each side, offering it its rhythm and energy.*

The Circle and the Straight Line: Necessity and Freedom

To represent the two states—the perfect and the imperfect—the Kabbalah, especially the Lurianic Kabbalah, offers the images of the circle and the straight line. The circle symbolizes the need for enclosure within its laws, the enclosure that prevents the advance of freedom. The straight line, which extends forward endlessly and without limitation, symbolizes freedom or the essence of reality in development. Man, who usually only perceives the outward aspect of such phenomena, only encounters the circle and the straight line. But these two principles actually apply to all reality.

On the one hand, certain forms of necessity are at work even within the world of the spirit; on the other, the freedom of "the straight line" also exists within natural law. In the words of the Master of Lights *(Baal Ha-Orot),* "Even in the 'circles,' that is to say in the laws necessary for existence, in the very heart of their regularity and firmness, in their immutable nature, whatever it is to which they apply, the 'straight line' continues to operate. For even in the abyss of obscurity which leaves its mark on the most inflexible links of necessity and causality, the light of liberty shines secretly and gives the strength of hope of redemption, whatever the situation of enslavement" (quoted by Y. Ben Shlomo, *op. cit.*, 55 ff.).

The Kabbalah uses two key terms to define the closed situation of the circle and the openness of the straight line leading to infinity: *din* and *khessed.*

* On this theme, see Henri Maldiney, *Regard, parole, espace* and *L'Art, l'éclair de l'être.*

Wassily Kandinsky, *On Points*, 1928.
Kandinsky's painting is based on the theory of point-line-plane shapes, a theory present in the texts of the Kabbalah, which formulate a geometric approach to the Hebrew alphabet.

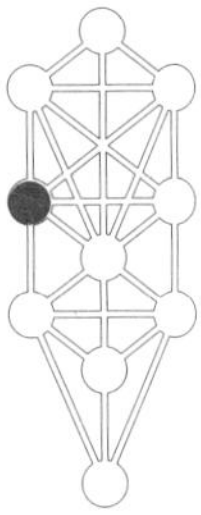

Din, or the Need for the Structuring of Forms

> ***Having a system is something that is fatal for the mind; not having one is also fatal, hence the necessity to maintain both requirements while at the same time losing them.***
> —F. Schlegel

The *din* is literally the "law," "judgment," in the ritual sense of what must be done and what must not be done. It also means judgment in the legal sense, a judgment pronounced by a judge that may lead to anything, even capital punishment. The *din* is the fact that things are a particular way and no other. The *din* is all the immutable laws of physics that make things able to repeat themselves and make the world go round. These are the laws of universal gravitation, the implacable logic of cause and effect.

The *din* ensures that the world will continue to exist. The laws of the *din* ensure that the universe will be maintained in its substance, subsistence, and persistence. The *din* basically permits the organization of the physical, the organic, and the social. It is rigor and justice. It is organization as opposed to anarchy.

The laws of the *din* are necessary laws, since without them there would be no landmarks and no possible shape or form. The *din* is the limitation of things. It is also the strict finiteness of the world, man, and things, the passage and the enclosure of the infinite in the finite.

To clarify this, the Kabbalah provides an image. In graphic terms, the *din* is a point or period—the absolute point; the absolute determinant, timeless and spaceless. The *din* is a closed configuration, the result of a movement of singularization. It makes living things possible, since it gives form to things.

Yet the absolute *din* that does not contain the opening offered to it by *khessed* is a movement that withdraws from the place of creation and life: "This is the history of its own heaviness, its own extinction and its own death. The memory of light in the thought of the *din* grows dim, because it only contained light when it began and has none left for the future. Light of Beginning which constantly returns unchanged through the eternal cycle of the laws of nature" (Y. Ben Shlomo, *op. cit.*).

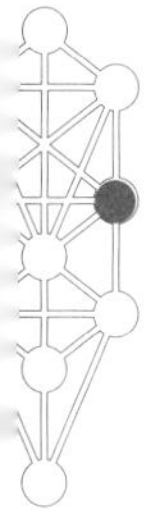

Khessed, or Creative Freedom

Khessed is the opening of closed forms. It is movement, the dynamic moment of shapes, the tensions that lie at the heart of existence. Unlike the point or the circle, which are the symbols of the *din*, the straight line, by its tension, is the most simple indicator of the possibility of infinite movement. *Khessed* is born from movement or, more exactly, from the abolition of sovereign rest that is enclosed upon itself, that of the point. There is a leap here from the static to the dynamic. The straight line is the exact opposite of the original element—the point.

Khessed is the dynamic of that which exists, which is open, the breath of life, exhalation in the act that permits the very existence of everything to open. The breath of life *(khessed)* universalizes that which the form *(din)* particularizes. *Khessed* is encountered in every gesture of giving and loving, the reaching out to another person. *Khessed* is goodness, the concrete gesture of goodness intended for another person. It is also desire, the insatiable desire for the infinite.

In man, the image of God, the human being is broken and smashed by the desire that runs through him. All desire is a desire for another—not only the desire of someone for someone or something, but the desire to be different, the desire to emerge from a definitive definition of self. In the dimension of *khessed*, man not only tends to be "better" or "more," he desires above all to be other.

Khessed is animated by the dynamic will of the being who seeks to go beyond the pure necessity of the physical laws of the world to attain the metaphysic of light and creative freedom.

Tiferet, or Harmony

If it is possible, as has just been done for teaching purposes, to differentiate between *din* and *khessed*, it is rare to encounter them in real life in their separate, absolute states. The Midrash Rabba on Genesis, a text of the Kabbalah about which much commentary has been written, teaches, "In the beginning, God thought of creating the world on the basis of *din* alone. He saw that world could not survive, so he also added *khessed*."

This means that a world that is only natural and physical, without openness and respiration, without renewal and creativity, could not survive. A perfectly structured world, from which dreaming and imagination were missing, would not be viable.

Another text of the Midrash Rabba teaches, "In the beginning, God thought of creating the world on the basis of *khessed* alone. He saw that world could not survive, so he also added *din*."

This means that, in the reverse situation, that a world that was merely an expansion of light, love, poetry, and imagination could not survive, since no stable form would exist in which to put beings and things. The world is the balanced meeting, the harmony of *din* and *khessed*, and this harmony is called *tiferet*.

In any finite reality, one must distinguish between that which is necessity *(din)* and that which is will *(khessed)*. And since all reality, except that of God, is finite, everything that exists in this world is based on necessity (*din*) and the foundation of freedom *(khessed)*.

Tiferet is the balance between the closed *(din)* and the open *(khessed)*. It unites the vital breath and the limited structure of beings and things. This articulation of the infinite breath of life in specified forms is called rhythm. Nor is it simply life; it is the pulse, the rhythm of life.

21

Mastery and Beauty, Politics, and Aesthetics
Netsakh and *Hod*

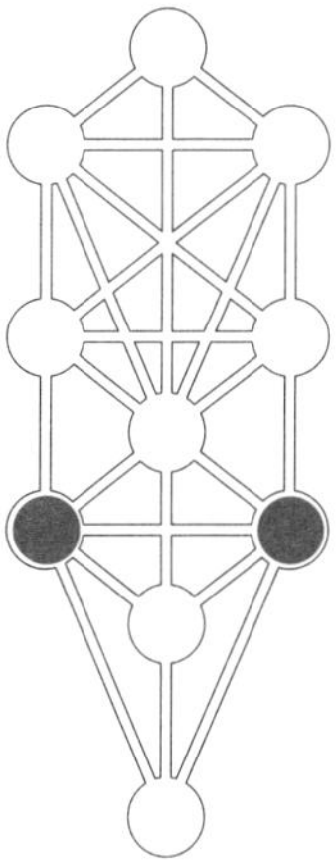

It is forbidden to despair.
—Rabbi Nachman of Breslov

The two *sefirot netsakh* and *hod* form a diptych in the shape of the vowel *tsereh:*

● ●

Politics, Economics, Morality

Netsakh, in Hebrew, means "victory," in the sense of mastery of something. It also means "eternity."

Man is constructed on a the model of the sefirot and pursues his personal structuring by acquiring mastery in various fields.

Having accepted being totally within what he is doing *(keter)* and organizing his mind according to the *khokhma-bina-da'at* triad, after modeling his record as a human being in the world on the *khessed-din-tiferet* triad, man turns to matter and the concrete aspects of the world, which must be organized in such a way as to make the world most effectively viable and for the greatest number of people.

That is the organization of the City. It is the need for politics, economics, and the control of urges. The typological character of this *sefira* is Joseph. The Bible recalls how, having resisted the temptation of the Potiphar's wife (mistress of passions), he became the (political) viceroy of Egypt, whose economy he reorganized.

A kabbalist cannot be allowed to follow the contemplative life; he must become involved in the concrete realities of the world.

Hod, Aesthetics, and Ethics
The Kabbalist Is Essentially an Artist

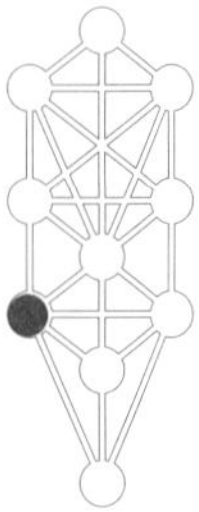

The concrete organization of the world that the *sefira* of *netsakh* invites us to contemplate ought not to allow us to believe that only technical pragmatism is important and that men need merely satisfy their physical needs for the world to be in harmony. There is another fundamental dimension—aesthetics. Beauty is part of the harmony of the world!

Man is both an artist and a work of art.

In the Hebrew Bible, the word *oman*, "artist," only appears once, in verse 2 of chapter 7 of the Song of Songs, in the following context:

> How lovely are your feet
> in sandals,
> O daughter of nobles!
> Your rounded thighs are like jewels
> The work of an artist's hand.

The work of the artist is in the roundness of the thighs, but also and primarily in the beauty of her steps in sandals. Art is in the walk, in the metaphysics of what is to come, "the metaphysics of the shoe" and of the path.

A work of art is an opening, a window of the world onto its most essential future. It is setting in motion, the path, the journey.

It is the path that opens up the way, setting in motion the dynamism of a being always evolving, always ready for the journey, always in search of something new, "extending toward," the eroticism of the swaying walk, the eroticism of the woman, the curve of whose thighs is a sign of the child she is carrying, of the opening to time into time.

An opening onto tomorrow. . . .

Living Is Being Born at Every Moment

If *keter* stresses the dimension of the present, this is not a negation of the other dimensions of time. For the Kabbalah, the three tenses must be fully embraced, and this is the very meaning of the tetragrammaton, whose etymological meaning is "past," "present," and "future."

Rabbi Nachman of Breslov taught, "It is forbidden to be old." What does this phrase mean? Rabbi Nachman wanted us to be capable of retaining a state of childhood in all that is constructive in relation to the dimension of the future.

What is so wonderful in the child and the adolescent is their ability to say: "When I grow up, I . . ." I want to be, I want to do. . . .

This extraordinary little phrase contains all the power of a dream, of expectation, of impatience, of the time to come. This magical little phrase has all the power of a formidable word: hope. A child is carried along by hope; its time is virtually messianic.

Better still, a child does not hope—it is hope itself.

Hope is knowing that everything is always open, that the future is a present that life offers us, that one can always be transformed, change direction, invent new routes without being confined in the role of "adults" into which we have shut ourselves or in which others have imprisoned us.

Erich Fromm, in *Zen Buddhism and Psychoanalysis*, says, "Living is being born at every moment."

The Principle of Hope

We are now no doubt better able to understand what Rabbi Nachman of Breslov meant. One must never lose the power of hope; one must never stop growing up. One must always be able to say," "When I grow up, I . . ."

This touches upon a new definition of old age. A person is old when he has lost hope. A person is old when instead of seeing hope as a door opening onto the future, he sees it opening onto the past. Old age is a nostalgia for hope. It is when one does not have the strength to say, "Tomorrow." Childhood is desire, anguish, tears, and laughter; it is above all dreaming, the sacred dream of growing up.

The *sefira* of *hod* is a prohibition on stealing the dream and the power of childhood, which we have all borne one day and which we may not have sufficiently preserved. The *sefira* of *hod* is knowing how to retain hope, the dream; telling oneself that tomorrow will always be possible, even if tomorrow never comes. "Never despair," Rabbi Nachman of Breslov would repeat incessantly; carry within you this power of childhood! Hope to make birth and rebirth possible, all of which is enshrined in the single Hebrew word: *tiqva.*

22

Foundation and the Kingdom: Receiving, Transmitting, Giving
Yessod and *Malkhut*

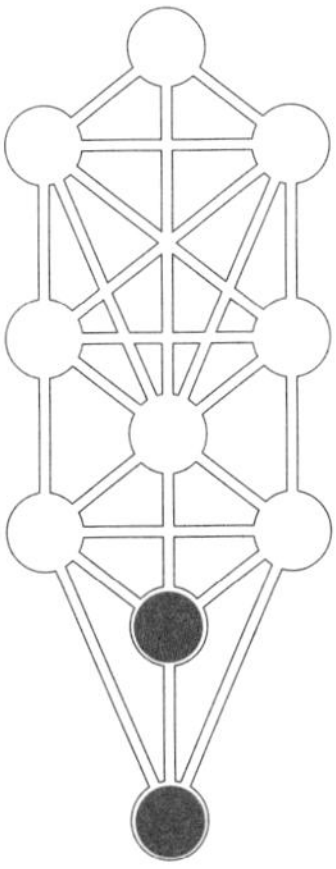

The study of the Torah is the theological foundation of Judaism.
—Haïm Brezis, *Un Mathématicien juif*

Yessod, or "Foundation": The Question of Transmission

The last two *sefirot* are arranged in a diptych that takes the form of the short "e" or silent vowel, *shevah:*

:

It is the basic ground plan of the Kabbalah in miniature.

It is giving and receiving, as well as masculine and feminine. *Yessod* gives, and *malkhut* receives.

This chapter completes what has been explained earlier concerning the basic ground plan of the Kabbalah.

light of infinity *(or en-sof)*
⇩
receipt of the light *(qabbala)*

The light of infinity has been "filtered" through the eight *sefirot* and can now be received and perfect the *qabbala* or "receipt."

The *yessod* is the aspect of "transmission" and "giving" of the elements acquired in the higher *sefirot.* It is not enough to receive it, it must also be transmitted.

On the Tablets of Stone

We already showed that the originality of Sinai was the revelation of a text. But not just any text! It was a text engraved on tablets of stone.

Why stone?

In Hebrew, the tablets of stone are called *lookhot avanim. Even* means "stone." If the word *even* is divided in two, it reads *av* and *ben,* "father" and "child." The word for stone thus means the genealogical link that unites father and child; that is to say, the bond between the generations. Giving the Torah on tablets of stone thus means that the fundamental importance of its transcription is not the stone, a static material, but the dynamic generational link of its transmission.

The Power of Transmission

Archaeological and historical discoveries have brought to light numerous similarities between the Torah and legislative and narrative texts from the same region and period. Examples are the texts found at Ras-Shamra and the famous Codex of Hammurabi.

Without any recourse to apologetics, it should be noted however that

Study and transmission: from generation to generation.
(Prischenfried, *L'Étude du Talmud.*)

the difference between the Torah and these texts is that the former came down as a whole and has been constantly enriched, while the latter are only vestiges, the ruins of a thought process and a civilization, the remains offered by archaeology and history.

These remarks indicate the fundamental idea of the power of the Bible text, which lies not merely in its contents but in its ability to be transmitted by a people from generation to generation. They key word in the Bible text may be the word *transmission.* It is no accident that Moses is called *Moshe rabbenu,* “Moses, our master.” It is in the very meaning of the word *ivri,* “Hebrew,” from the root *laavor,* “to pass,” “pass on,” “transmit”!

The Ten Commandments are known in Hebrew as *aseret ha-dibrot,* “the ten sets of words,” and they are the laws of speech and its transmission. The Bible stresses this aspect on several occasions. It does so by recalling that the words of the Torah had been written down on tablets of stone. When the people of Israel crossed the Jordan to enter the Promised Land, God commanded Moses to take large stones, cover them with lime, and engrave the whole of the Torah on them.

This basic idea runs right through kabbalistic thought, in the form of *yessod* and *malkhut,* representing man and woman, man and his neighbor, parents and children, the master and the disciple, and so on. But how can they be transmitted, how can they be given in a fair, balanced, and harmonious way?

Etymologically speaking, Kabbalah means “the act of receiving.” There is an art in knowing how to receive the light of infinity. It is also an art to know how to give. The gift and the receipt are totally linked to the Kabbalah. But there are different ways of giving. These ideas are present in the articulation of *yessod* and *malkhut.*

Malkhut: Adam Qadmon

If the *sefira* of *yessod* really constitutes the ability to “just give,” *malkhut* represents a pause in the Kabbalah, the completion of the act of receiving, the translation of the *sefirot* into the world of reality and the period of history.

We have dwelt at length on the ten fundamental modes or behaviors of human beings that, if performed to perfection, raise man to the status of the *adam qadmon;* this means not merely "primordial man," as it is usually translated, but "man who is constituted in that which is essential." The ten *sefirot* are thus represented among numerous kabbalists in the shape of a man. Such a man may then receive the perfect light of infinity and enter into the circle of initiates.

Breakage in the Process of Giving and Receiving

Let us return for a moment to one of the important phases of creation. We have evoked the three fundamental moments that constitute the triad of *tsimtsum-shevira-tikkun.* In "Travels of a Spark," p. 191, we produced a cosmogonic interpretation of the triad. We offer here an anthropological, existentialist interpretation.

What happens after the *tsimtsum* ?

The light penetrates the void in the form of energy-light and becomes matter in the form of ten receptacles, the *sefirot,* which are designed to receive and hold the light. Each *sefira* is simultaneous masculine and feminine: feminine in what it receives, and masculine when it gives. Light from the luminous ray reaches the first *sefira,* which, once filled, transmits the surplus light to the next *sefira.*

If a *sefira* receives light and is filled by it but fails to transmit it to the following *sefirot,* since the energy of the light contained in the *sefira* is stronger than that of the receptacle, the receptacle will explode. This is the phenomenon, already mentioned, which the Kabbalah calls the "breaking of the vessels."

Life: Receiving and Giving

What is the existential, concrete meaning of this great allegory of the world used by the Kabbalah?

It has been shown that the river is an important image for the Kabbalah. It is used again in order to explain the meaning of the breaking of the vessels.

Commentators suggest we look at the map of Israel. As can be seen below, the Mediterranean is on the left, and the River Jordan on the right, flowing from north to south, into Lake Tiberias, also known as the Sea of Galilee. It flows out of the lake southward, into another body of water that is usually known as the Salt Sea in Hebrew, but in English is called the Dead Sea. The kabbalists asked themselves, Why is it called the Dead Sea? What is the definition of something that is dead? The answer is extraordinarily simple but extremely significant. Lake Tiberias (the name comes from that of the Roman Emperor Tiberius), known in Hebrew as Kineret, is the lake of life, since it receives the Jordan, fills with its waters, and releases it farther on. It receives, and it gives.

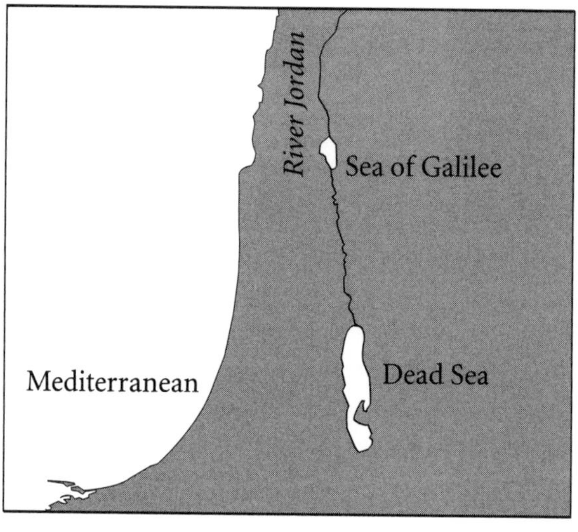

The masters observed that *kineret* has two meanings. *Kinor* means a harp (in biblical Hebrew), and the lake is shaped like that instrument. It can also be read *keter nun*, the "crown on the letter *nun*" or "of the fiftieth level," the highest in the kabbalistic hierarchy. Giving-receiving is the *keter-nun,* the highest level of life. The Dead Sea or Yam Ha-Mavet (the name is sometimes used in Hebrew), on the other hand, receives the Jordan, "takes"

its water, but gives nothing back. That is the very concrete definition of death: that which is capable of receiving, but not of giving back. And receiving without giving back is exactly what is involved in the "breaking of the vessels."

Sharing Bread

This idea of receiving-giving can be found in every aspect of life, especially in the ritual of eating. For the kabbalists, the ritual of the meal is a fundamental one. Eating is drawing on one's strength and implementing the dynamic of the sparks of holiness; it is a kabbalistic rite that consists in performing the *tikkun,* that is to say, the repair of the broken vessels. The *tikkun* is performed by washing the hands and sharing bread.

The purification of the hands and the blessing during the meal are part of the same ritual, which is as follows: before breaking and eating bread, one washes one's hands in a bowl (not directly under the faucet.) Water is poured into the bowl, and this is then poured over the hands from a smaller receptacle (just as Lake Tiberias is filled with the waters of the Jordan in order to subsequently give them back); thus the hands are purified.

This ritual is called *netilat yadayim.* It teaches that purity is an ethical concept that translates itself into "receiving-giving"—that is, sharing! According to tradition, before one can eat, one must first ensure that the domestic animals have received food, then bread must be broken, even if one is eating alone. This is an extraordinary example of an ethical symbol imported into everyday life, meaning: I cannot begin to eat without performing this ritual, which means that I am ready to share my bread with someone else.

Sharing the Dream

Parents dream of the child they would like to conceive, the mother dreams of the child to come which she carries inside herself, the child dreams of the day in which it will see the light, and if they do not dream together, life will not come into the world.

—Leonardo da Vinci, reported by J. Salomé in *Dis, Papa, l'amour c'est quoi?*

The word *lekhem,* "bread," is written in Hebrew with the three letters *lamed-het-mem.* The bread must be dipped in salt, *melakh,* a word that is written with the same letters as *lekhem* but in a different combination. The same three letters, *lamed-khet-mem,* are also those of the word *khalom,* "dream" *(het-lamed-mem).* Eating is sharing a dream!

23

The Symbol of the Tree in the Kabbalah

Rabbi Nachman said: "Why are the words of the Torah compared to a tree (Proverbs 3:18)? Just as a shrub can set fire to a great tree, so novice students can stimulate the minds of the great masters."
—Talmud Taanit, 7a

For man is the tree of the field
—Deuteronomy 20:19

The ground plan of the Kabbalah uses the same metaphors on many occasions, which thus become special images. This applies to Jacob's ladder as well as, perhaps more fundamentally, to the tree.

The "Great Tree"

The divine powers grow within creation like a tree, irrigated with the waters of absolute wisdom. The tree of the *sefira* within which God has planted his strength is also a tree of the worlds and, to some extent, the tree of true life. The root is situated in the topmost *sefirot*; the trunk covers the middle area and the compensating forces; the branches and twigs extending from it contain the extreme possibilities of divine activity.

All these elements taken together stress the principal aspect in which this structure is depicted in the Kabbalah, i.e., growth from top to bottom. The primordial light that manifests itself and offers a face thus takes the form of a tree of light, *ilana ravreva* or "great tree."

The ten *sefirot* constitute the mystical tree of God or the tree of divine power. Each of them represents a branch of which the common root is situated in the *en-sof*, the infinity of the primordial light, unknown and unknowable. But the *en-sof* is not only the hidden root of all roots but also the sap of the tree. Each branch represents an attribute that does not have an independent existence but is there by virtue of the *en-sof*, the source of all life. This tree of God is the infrastructure of the whole universe; it grows through creation and extends its branches in all their ramifications. Everything that has ever been created and that exists in the world exists only for the reason that something of the power of the *sefirot* inhabits it and operates in it.

The "Small Tree"

As its name indicates, the Tree of Life speaks of the living world and of man, who is at the heart of life. In the Kabbalah, man is called the "small tree," *ilana zuta* in Aramaic. As it says in Deuteronomy 20:19, "ki ha-adam ets hasadeh." This teaches that man is also the place in the ten *sefirot* through which light and energy must pass in order for life to be transmitted to the heart of man and beyond him in the process of multiple creations and begettings.

The Blessing

The meeting of the *sefirot* of the great tree and the ten *sefirot* of the little tree produces that which the Kabbalah calls the "graft" or "blessing." To be blessed is to have succeeded in connecting the ten internal *sefirot* with the ten cosmic *sefirot*, thus making it possible for the energy of the living being to circulate and bring all that is necessary for perfect harmony and equilibrium.*

* See Rabbi Menahem Nahum of Chernobyl, *Meor Enayim al hatora, parasha lekh-lekha.*

Danihel

The Importance of the Tree in the Kabbalah

In his book *Wisdom of the Kabbalah,* the Chief Rabbi of France, Alexandre Safran, a modern scholar of the Kabbalah, develops a long meditation on the tree, of which the outlines are reproduced here.

The tree is one of the most important symbols of the Kabbalah. Some of the masters call it the "friend of man." It symbolizes life; it is the "tree of life." It incarnates life in the widest sense, embracing animate and inanimate objects. The model for respect for all beings, for every living thing, is the respect that we owe to the tree, which personifies God Himself, the Creator and His creative forces—the tree of the *sefirot.* That is why, of all the elements of this nature that are unjustly called "inanimate," the tree is the one of greatest interest to the Torah, the sages, and the kabbalists. The latter are preoccupied with the protection of all of nature, being resolutely opposed to its deterioration, its mindless exploitation, but they seek to protect the tree with particular force. And they do so not only in peacetime but also under exceptional circumstances such as those created by war.

The Bible itself says it clearly: "When in your war against a city you have to besiege it for a long time in order to capture it, you must not destroy (*lo tashkhit*) its trees, wielding the ax against them. It is they that feed you, you shall thus not cut them down; for man is the tree of the fields" (Deuteronomy 20:19).

Man Is the Tree of the Fields

The Kabbalah pays special attention to the tree due to the similarities it discerns between the tree and man. It sees not only a resemblance, but a real relationship between the crown of the plant world, the tree, and the crown of the animal world, man. This relationship between the representatives of the two worlds as friends is expressed through their appearance and their vocation. Both "stand upright," both "bear fruit," and both offer their protection to all those that need it. The tree stands tall and looks toward the skies; man stands upright before God, raises his eyes to the heights. The tree nourishes and comforts man with its fruits; man, and especially the *tsadiq,* the just man, helps and fortifies his peers through his fruits, which are his good deeds, for the Bible says, "There is fruit for the just [and] the fruit of the just is a tree of life." Through its shade, the tree protects man from fire and sun; man, and especially the *tsadiq,* protects his followers, his contemporaries, his generation.

Man Lives with the Tree

The kabbalists emphasize the care that we should lavish on the tree and the responsibility we have for its life. Rabbi Yehuda He-Khassid (twelfth–thirteenth centuries), "the pious," strictly forbade the cutting down of fruit trees and even advised strongly against cutting down sterile trees *(ilanei serak),* except in cases of grave necessity for man.

The kabbalist talks to the tree. With his lips, he speaks to it; with his ears, he listens to the rustling of its foliage; with his eyes, he follows the flexible lines of its body. He "blesses" it; he includes it in his prayers. He rejoices with it when it grows; he suffers with it when it dies. Rabbi Nachman of Breslov teaches that "there are moments when voices cross the world from one end to the other, without anyone being aware of it; it is at the moment when a fruit tree is cut down and at the moment when the soul leaves the human body."

The New Year of the Trees

The tree and man have a common element of destiny. Man feels this, and that is why he demonstrates his attachment to the tree. He expresses it in celebration, because apart from the New Year for man, *rosh-hashana lashanim* (literally, "the head of the year for the years"), there is a New Year for the trees ("head of the year for the trees"), *rosh-hashana lailanot.*

Rosh-hashana lailanot enjoys great favor with kabbalists, who have written a *tikkun,* a special ritual prayer, for it and ordained that on this day fifteen varieties of fruits should be eaten, especially fruits from the Land of Israel (15 being the value of one of the names of God, which is written Yod-Heh).

The Tree and the Resurrection of the Dead

The "New Year of man" and the "New Year of the tree" can be distinguished from each other by the season in which they are celebrated. The first is in the fall and the second in the spring. The fall reminds man of his finiteness and the limited span of his life; the spring offers him the "rebirth" of the tree, the renewal of life. Thus, on the one hand, man is made conscious of the fact that he is mortal, and on the other, the tree, by reviving, is a sign for man that his death may not be final.

In fact, after each of these "deaths," which are repeated (as is every other phenomenon in the history of nature), the tree once again proves its "resurrection"; it announces it by returning to life, and being always the same. Thus the presence of the tree, on the physical level, is an indicator of man's future on the physical and metaphysical levels. In his faith, in his certainty, the kabbalist sees, with his spiritual eyes, now, this very day, the future resurrection of the dead. This resurrection of the dead is heralded by the resurrection of the tree. The kabbalist awakens to the true future. The present, everyday miracle of the re-creation of the whole of nature, which was dead yesterday, heralds the miracle of tomorrow, the revival of the dead. The life and resurrection of the tree are thus the experience of life and the resurrection of man.

Like the tree, which, having passed through the winter, renews itself, man renews himself, flourishes, after having lived through wintry, harsh, and dark periods; he changes, while remaining the same.

Man resembles the tree on the level of his natural existence, and on the level of his spiritual, historical life he is linked to the Torah, which is also itself comparable to a tree, since in the Bible it is "the tree of life for those who attach themselves thereto." In fact, the "Torah of life" was given to Israel to ensure its life, its endurance, because it is the work of the Eternal, the expression of His will. Thus man lives in the shade of He who is the "Source of Life," the "Great Tree"—God.

The Tree, God, the Angel, and Food

Two different words in Hebrew mean "tree," *ets* and *ilan*. The first is used in the language of the Bible, the second in the oral literature of the Midrash and the Kabbalah. The word *ilan* comes from the Aramaic *ilana* and has the numerical value 91.

Ilan is written *aleph-yod-lamed-nun*

אילן

1 + 10 + 30 + 50

91

As will be explained later, the numerical value of words, known as gematria, makes it possible to change one object into another, a person into something else and back again. Gematria is the "philosophers' stone of the kabbalist." Thus tree *(ilan)* is the equivalent of the word *malakh,* "angel," which also has a value of 91 in gematria.

Malakh is written *mem-lamed-aleph-kaf*

מלאך

40 + 30 + 1 + 20

91

Here we discover one of the fundamental functions of the angel. The angel is he who brings the light of the *sefirot* into the world and to man, enabling them to grow and be connected with the source of life. The word *malakh*/"angel" is written using the same letters as the word *maakhal*/"food." This is easily understood on the basis of what has just been said.

The most surprising phenomenon is the meeting between the number 91 and the name of God. The ineffable name of God, the tetragrammaton YHVH, has an actual numerical value of 26. However, this unpronounceable name is usually replaced by the word *adonai,* "lord," whose numerical value is 65. The sum of the two names is 91, that is to say *ilan*—the tree again!

YHVH is written *yod-heh-vav-heh*		*Adonai* is written *aleph-dalet-nun-yod*
יהוה		אדני
10 + 5 + 6 + 5		1 + 4 + 50 + 10
26	+	65
	91	
	Ilan	

Part Five

The Horses of Fire

5

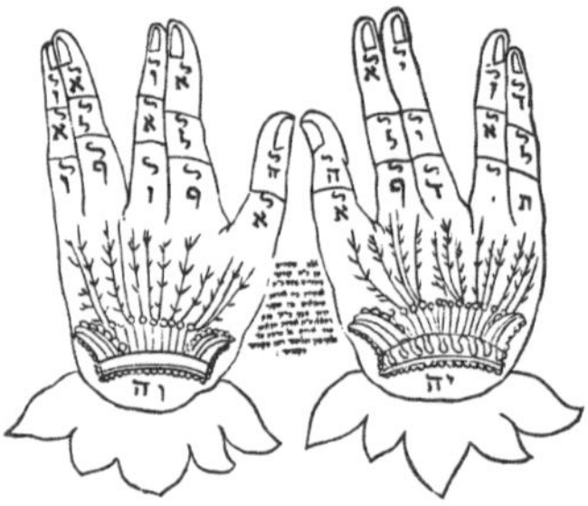

24

The Letters of Creation

Let us find the lost letter or the obliterated sign, let us recompose the dissonant scale and we shall gather strength in the spirit world.
—Gérard de Nerval

The Thirty-six Ways of "Energy-Vibration"

The "Book of Creation" begins with this famous passage: "By twenty-six marvelous ways of wisdom, God created the world through the three meanings of the root SFR: the written book, the number, and the told tale.

"Thirty-six marvelous ways of wisdom: the ten *sefirot* and the twenty-six letters of the alphabet."

When the Kabbalah is presented as "the experience that makes it possible to receive the light of infinity," one might ask oneself what difference there is between the Kabbalah and all the other mysticisms, since all of them speak of energy, vibration, and light. This is an important question because it makes it possible to better discern the peculiarity and specificity of the Kabbalah. Or to put it more forcefully, what is it that makes the Kabbalah more than a mere translation of that which we encounter in other mystical or spiritual trends that highlight the importance of our attachment to infinity?

We have shown that the light of infinity *(or en-sof)* passed in a special way through the decade of fundamental elements, the *sefirot.* However, the Kabbalah has another path along which the energies of the higher world can travel in order to feed the lower worlds. This path consists of the letters of the Hebrew alphabet and the text of the Torah.

The Hebrew language is the "holy language" *(lashon haqodesh)* because the Hebrew letters possess an extraordinary creative force, an energy that makes them the primordial tools of Creation. In the beginning of the creation of heaven and earth, God said: "Let there be light!" And there was light! There is a mystery of the letters of Creation, as regards their shapes, their meanings, and their numerical values. One of the major preoccupations of the Kabbalah is to unravel these secrets.

A midrash teaches:

> Before the creation of the world, the letters, the 22 letters already existed; but they remained mysterious and secret, hidden in the depths of divine mysteries. When God took the decision to create, the letters began to move like 22 princesses in a royal procession, advancing one after the other toward the heavenly throne. But they presented themselves in the reverse order to that of the alphabet; so that it was Tav, the last letter, which made its entrance first and was the first to present its petition:

ת

> —Master of the world, of grace, use me in order to perform your creation. Am I not the letter that completes the word which is engraved upon your scepter: the word "truth" (in Hebrew: emet)?

אמת

> —You are indeed worthy, replied the Holy One, Blessed be He. But it is not fitting that I use you in order to create the world, because you are destined to be marked upon the foreheads of the faithful who have obeyed the law from Aleph to Tav, and also because you form the last letter of the word for "death" (mavet). For these reasons, it is not fitting for me to use you for the purpose of the creation of the world.
>
> So the letter Tav withdrew. . . . What could it reply?
>
> Then it was the turn of the letter Shin. She presented herself and laid claim to the fact that she constituted the initial letter of the Divine Name (Shaddai).

ש

—It is fitting to use the initial of the holy name Shaddai for the creation of the world.

שדי

—Indeed, replied the Holy One, Blessed be He, you are worthy, you are good, and you are true. But the forgers will use you to swear the most terrible lies, by associating you with the letters Qof and Resh, to form the word "lie" (sheqer). . . .

And the letter Shin withdrew, while its companions, the letters Qof and Resh, did not even dare present themselves.

ק ר

All the other letters thus filed past, in turn, each claiming rights and qualities which made them especially suited to be the special tool with which the world would be created. And, each time, the Holy One, Blessed be He, replied by using an irrefutable argument which confounded all their pretentions.

Finally, there came the turn of the next-to-last letter, the letter Bet.

ב

—Master of the Universe, may it please You to make use of me in the creation of the world, because I am the initial of the word which is used to bless you—Blessed be He (Barukh).

ברוך

And the Holy One, Blessed be He—finally—agreed:

—Indeed, I shall use you in order to inaugurate the creation of the world and you will thus be at the basis of the whole "work of creation."

And what about the letter Aleph, the very last, that is to say the very first, what happened to it?

It stayed where it was, without presenting itself.

—Aleph, Aleph, why have you not presented yourself to me like the others?

And Aleph replied:

—Master of the Universe, seeing all the letters present themselves to you to no avail, why should I present myself also? Then when I saw that you had already granted the letter Bet this precious gift, I understood that it did not behoove the

King of Heaven to take back the gift that he had given to one of his servants in order to gratify another.

The Holy One, Blessed be He, then cried:

—O Aleph, Aleph, although I shall use the letter Bet for the creation of the world, you shall be the first of all the letters and I shall have no unity but in you; you shall be at the root of all calculations and all the actions performed in the world, and nowhere shall there be unity, unless it is in the letter Aleph!
(Zohar, translation quoted by Renée de Tryon-Montalembert)

25

Abracadabra: The Power of Words

Human society, the world, the whole of man is in the alphabet. . . . The alphabet is a well-spring.
—Victor Hugo

The Golem

According to the position of the moon, it should have been nearly midnight, the hour for which we waited. But my master wanted to hear the dogs barking because, as the Kabbalah teaches, Rabbi Eliezer says: "The night is divided into three parts. At the end of the first part, the donkey begins to bray; in the middle of the second part the dogs bark; and at the beginning of the last, the babe suckles at the breast of its mother and the wife chats to her husband."

At the place in which we found ourselves, the river flowed more slowly, the bank was broad, and the slope was gentle.

By the light of the moon, which was perfectly round on this fifteenth day of the first month of spring, I distinctly saw my master sitting and swaying, his eyes closed, facing the East.

He had spent all of the early part of the evening in meditation, prayer, and immersion. He had also asked me to prepare myself. The night was cold.

As soon as the dogs began to bark, he rose calmly and solemnly. His tall shadow was silhouetted on the ground. In places, the snow was still quite thick. With his stick, he began to trace a drawing on the ground. Gradually, the shape of a man appeared. He had begun at the head, then drew the neck, the arms. . . .

As soon as he was halfway between the head and the feet, at the level of the umbilicus, he stopped. He held out large buckets to me and said to me: "Go to the river. Into the bucket you hold in your right hand, you must pour 248 measures using this goblet. Into the bucket you hold in your left hand, you must pour 365 measures."

When I returned with the 613 measures, my master had just carefully drawn in the feet. He took the container with his right hand and poured water over each of the limbs of the man of earth that he had made. He repeated the operation with his left hand. Then he asked me to stand on the feet of the shape. He placed himself in front, behind the head, and lit a candle.

He asked me to repeat meticulously all the words, and even all the sounds that he would pronounce, even if I did not understand the meaning, and to concentrate on the vibrations of the words that came out of my mouth.

He pronounced different vocalized variations of the Name and the 231 combinations of the alphabet, which I repeated after him.

Then he rose, walked around the effigy seven times, and then started to do so all over again, after having turned over the earth from which the human form had been made. When he had finished the last round of the second cycle, the earth began to tremble. My master covered the earth with his prayer shawl, which he had worn throughout the operation, and made a sign to me to go away.

I withdrew a little way and saw the creature with a human form emerging from the earth. Seized with an irresistible anguish, I fell to the ground, inanimate.

Abracadabra . . .

This story combines versions of a very ancient Jewish legend that crops up in all the texts, at every period, and in every place.

Some versions of this legend have become particularly famous, virtually "official," notably that of the sixteenth-century rabbi of Prague, the High Rabbi Loeb, better known in Hebrew literature by the acronym the Maharal of Prague.

This creature of water and clay, of fire and breath, is the Golem. The face of the Golem varies. Some have termed it a monster, others an automaton, a powerful hero, the defender of the poor, the weak, and the humble. Whether a docile servant or a rebel, it is the central character of tragedies, accidents, and realistic, and often surrealist, adventures.

Yet the Golem represents a single theme, namely, the reassurance that there is a solution, a way out, even when one is on the verge of disaster. A powerful breath of hope emanates from the Golem, one that is almost messianic.

But if the Golem fascinates, it is no doubt for the most fundamental reason. It is because through it man feels himself filled with a creative power. Man is no longer merely a craftsman or artist; he becomes a creator, a life-giver.* By fashioning the Golem, man puts himself in the same situation as God creating the first man, replacing the breath of God by the power of the vibration of the letters of the Hebrew alphabet.

This power and this energy of the letters are at the center of the Kabbalah and are found in the popular "magic word":

abrakadabra

which in Aramaic means: "He has created as he has spoken," that is to say, according to the power of the word. In fact, in biblical and kabbalistic Hebrew the expression would be:

abrakaamra

The verb in this expression is *omer,* the creative "word," and not *daber,* the organizing "speech."

* The reader who is interested in the subject of the Golem is referred to the encyclopedic work by Moshe Idel, *The Golem,* and to the section about it by Gershom Scholem in *Kabbalah.*

An Eyewitness Account of the Golem

One day, when I was still a student, I asked a great professor who was a historian of the Kabbalah :

—Do you believe in it?

He looked at me in surprise.

—Believe in what?

—In the Golem, I ventured in a timid and troubled voice.

He turned to me, smiling gravely.

—I do not know, he said, but I want to tell you a story that was told to me in Bologna in 1945 by a Holocaust survivor, a native of Prague. This is what he told me:

"The Golem never died and even during the war, he came out of hiding to protect the synagogue. When the Germans occupied Prague, they decided to destroy the Altneuschul, the very ancient synagogue. They were on the point of doing so when, suddenly, in the silence of the synagogue, giant steps were heard tramping over the roof. They saw the shadow of a gigantic hand which fell from the window to the floor. . . .

"Terrified, the Germans threw down their tools and ran away in a panic.

"I know that everything has a rational explanation. The synagogue is so old that the slightest shock, such as steps or a thunderclap, produces an echo which can be heard for a long time. And the window panes are old, the squares of glass are distorted and create shadows which produce strange shapes on the floor. A bird's foot could make the shadow of a gigantic hand as it fell on the floor. . . .

"And yet . . .

"And yet, there might be something in it."

(Reported by Moshe Idel in *The Golem*)

26

In the Beginning There Was the Point...

The Creation of the World and Alphabet

In the kabbalistic and Hasidic tradition, the matter of which the world is made rests upon the structure of the Hebrew alphabet. Hebrew is the geography (the writing of Earth) and the geometry (measurement of Earth) of that which has been created.

We shall now show how the divine name YHVH is constructed in the same geometrical way using the very structured logic of the deployment of the point in the plane, and subsequently in space. This is one of the lesser-known aspects of gematria.

In the Beginning There Was the Point...

For kabbalists, in the beginning, after the contraction of the divine, the *tsimtsum*, and the first emanation of light, there was the *beriya*. This word literally means "creation," the transition from absolute nothingness to a state of being, the transition from *ayin* to *yesh*, to produce the raw material of the universe, which in biblical Hebrew is called *tohu* and in midrashic Hebrew is called *even shetiya*, "foundation stone." In philosophical Hebrew, which is based on Greek, this raw material is called *heyuli,* meaning "hyletic matter."

This raw material, the infinitesimal element in matter, had a specific shape, the point.

Creation—*beriya*—designates the birth of this point of matter, which was perceived in antiquity as something that cannot be reduced to an even smaller element and was thus called "atom" (that is to say, "unsplittable").

If one were to use physics as a metaphor to describe the creation of the world, one would explain this point of matter as being the smallest particle of matter that will ever be discovered.

So, in the beginning, there was the point. . . .

It was the transition from nonbeing to a visible being, the threshold, the infinitesimal boundary, the emergence of being. The point should be perceived not as being something static but as the dynamic and balanced result of a set of contradictory forces, the forces of retention and of concentration, and the forces of expansion.

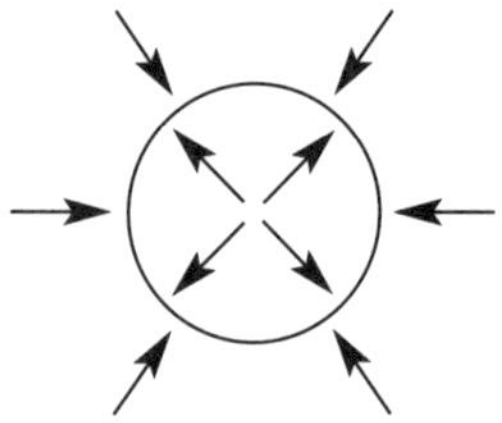

The Metamorphoses of the Point

The second phase of creation for the kabbalists is called *yetsira:* "formation." These are the infinite metamorphoses of the point in relation to the various forces that now come into play. For the kabbalistic masters, the first transfiguration of the point was a vertical line, the birth of which can be explained in several different ways:

- An internal force within the point became stronger than an external force, which made it possible for the point to expand:

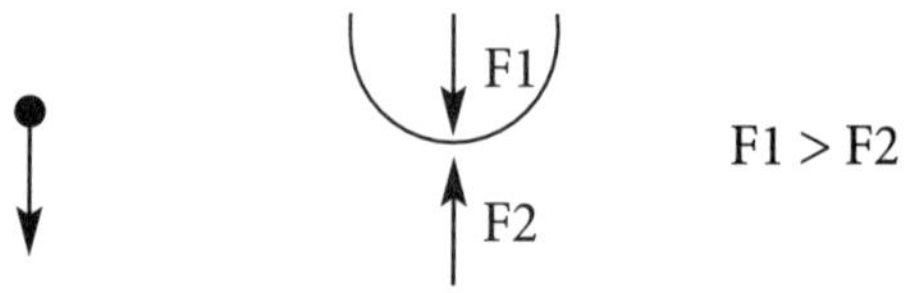

- An F1 force, which had previously been balanced with an F2 force, disappeared for various reasons, and the point was thus able to extend:

- The definition of the line was considered to be a displacement of the point. The line would thus be the result of a "struggle" between the forces of the point and other forces that succeeded in moving it (in this case, superior forces that came from on high):

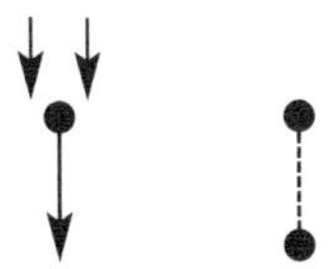

Within the framework of this third hypothesis, one or two forces could intervene, affecting the shape of the line:

- The shape produced by a single force acting in a constant manner on the point is a line that continues indefinitely in the same direction, that is to say, a straight line. Movement results from the fact that a shape has suppressed the concentric tension of the point so as to displace it indefinitely in one constant direction.
- In the second case, the linear shape results from the joint action of two forces. This situation may be doubly reinforced, depending on whether the intervention of the two forces was simultaneous or successive. (Simultaneous action produces a curved line, and successive action produces an angular or broken.)

    The angle of the curve depends on the amount of power exercised laterally in relation to the force that, acting alone on the point, produces a straight line. In the same way, the length of each of the segments of a broken line is dependent upon the time during which the forces were in operation, while the nature of the angle that would drastically alter the trajectory is an effect of intensity of the force that comes into play when the first force is interrupted.

Point, Line, Plane

After this vertical line a horizontal line was born and attached to it, and thus the plane was born.

Thus the following came into being:

- the point
- the (vertical) line
- the plane

For kabbalists, these three basic geometric shapes are the basis of the Hebrew alphabet. All the letters are constructed on the basis of a combination of the point, the line, and the plane, of which the archetypes are three letters of the alphabet: *yod, vav, dalet.*

Thus, the letter *yod* is a point, the letter *vav* is a straight line, and the letter *dalet* is a plane.

Consequently, *aleph,* the first letter of the alphabet, is the "first composite letter." It consists of the three letters *yod-vav-dalet,* the line of the *vav* being inclined to the left (remember that Hebrew is read from right to left).

The letters were subsequently stylized, becoming more rounded or angular, depending on the various traditions.

א

27

Knights and Kabbalists

A work dies to be completed.
—Paul Valéry

Silence is the highest form of thought, and it is by developing a trace that is silent to the day that we shall find our place in the absolute that surrounds us.
—Christian Bobin, *Le Huitième Jour*

The Horses of Fire

The path of infinity passes through a very special material, namely the book and the letters of the Torah, that is, primarily the twenty-two letters of the Hebrew alphabet, which are the basic receptacles.

A passage from the Tikkunei Zohar uses a wonderful expression whereby the letters of the Torah are likened to "horses of fire." The Master of the Lights, Baal Ha-Orot, comments on this:

> There are cases in which man cannot attain depth of thought merely through the path of his own mind. The solution is to increase his creative power by linking it to the letters of the Torah which will enable him to rise so much higher, and to do so faster and more surely than if he merely uses his own strength.
>
> There is the foot-soldier who marches through the texts and thoughts of the Torah using only his own strength and who does not help himself to advance by using the letters of the Torah.

There is the man who does not have the strength to march and who advances upon the letters of the Torah, even in areas in which he could simply walk as a pedestrian of meaning.

There is also the man who walks forward wherever he can and is assisted by the letters of the Torah, not just in cases of weakness but like a knight who mounts his horse in order to honor the meaning he is in the process of exploring. (*Orot Ha-Torah*, chap. 5)

Letters, Light, and Energy

To penetrate the world of Hebraic thought, one must know the material in which it is formulated.

It is quite impossible to understand anything about Hebraic thought, and the texts of the Kabbalah in particular, if one does not understand that the world did not predate the language, but words were formed in it and by it. The dynamic of the worlds coexists with the dynamic of language. A constant exchange of forces runs between the two processes. The whole cycle of the future depends on this exchange, which is in constant operation.

After the first great *tsimtsum* that took place in the universe, the light of the *en-sof* returned in the form of a ray of light; this is the phase of the second *tsimtsum*. But here, the light of the ray was still too bright to be received by living things. The ray of light-energy thus underwent another *tsimtsum* (which could be called the third *tsimtsum*) in order to be first accepted into the matter that is at the frontier of matter and energy: the letter *aleph*.

The *Aleph*

The *aleph* is a letter that is visible but silent, pure visibility. It is the only letter that is not pronounced at all. It is not even a consonant in the strictest sense of the word because it has no sound or resonance on the ear. It enables the beauty of silence to emerge, which is the nucleus of any speech, the audible void around which the possibility of speech revolves.

When a kabbalist composes or listens to music, he is listening, first of all, for the silent song of the *aleph*.

The letter *aleph.* Calligraphy by Franck Lalou who stresses the dynamism of this letter which looks like a man walking and which receives the light of infinity (*or en-sof*).

Writing music, for the Kabbalah, means wanting the silence to be heard. In reality, the lyrics and notes are there to accentuate the silence.

The kabbalist must therefore first create the silence, model it, modulate it, and try to give it a place in the world so that he can hear it vibrate. The notes that will make it resonate must therefore be sought first. Musical notes are a sounding board for the melody of the *aleph.*

Between earth and sky, there is a ladder. Silence is at the top of this ladder. Everything that we write or say is an intermediate degree in an attempt to attain the silent whiteness of the Saphir.

Elijah, one of the greatest prophets of Israel, experienced it in an extraordinary revelation, which the Bible relates in these terms (Book of Kings I, 29: 11–13):

> And lo, the Lord passed by. There was a great and mighty wind, splitting mountains and shattering rocks by the power of the Lord; but the Lord was not in the wind. After the wind—an earthquake; but the Lord was not in the earthquake. After the earthquake—fire, but the Lord was not in the fire. And after the fire, a thin voice of stillness *[qol demama daqa]*. When Elijah heard it, he wrapped his mantle about his face and went out and stood in the entrance of the cave.

The *aleph* is the highest degree of clarity, which no word can express nor explore. For how can one speak of that which, by its very nature, cannot be expressed in words? Of course, there are certain expressions to express a void that designate, in uncertainty and anxiety, the possibility of a meaning to be found and to be given to this absolute, defined in the sense that is the light of infinity.

The kabbalist restrains himself from excessive verbosity. He wants to write words that will be organically inserted into silence, that do not seek to dominate silence . . . silence that will always be more difficult to represent than the ease of finding words.

The *aleph* is the symbol of energy.*

* On this point, see *Mysteries of the Alphabet*, by this author (New York: Abbeville Press, 1999).

Letters and *sefirot* inside a set of boxes, like a Chinese puzzle. Diagram created by Rabbi Moses Cordovero in *Assis Rimonim* ("Pomegranate Juice"), commentaries on the *Pardess Rimonim* ("Pomegranate Orchard"), Sixth Gate (rev. ed.; Jerusalem. 1962).

Black Fire on White Fire: An Approach to the Theory of the Husks

Lettering for the Kabbalah is "black fire on white fire"; it is considered to be like a husk or shell. This is what the Kabbalah calls a *qlipa* (*qlipot* in the plural). The function of the *qlipa* is to screen and protect man from being blinded by the too powerful light of the *en-sof.*

Since the light of the *aleph* is too bright—it could not be seen without blinding the person receiving it—it "clothes itself" in another "husk," namely, the letter *bet,* the second letter of the alphabet. Light thus travels along its path by successively wrapping itself in the twenty-two letters of the alphabet. Thus, light wraps itself first of all in the *aleph,* which wraps itself in the *bet,* which wraps itself in the *gimmel,* and so on.

The second letter thus contains another letter; the third letter contains two letters, the *aleph* and the *bet;* and so on, right up to the twenty-second letter, which thus contains the twenty-one preceding letters. The farther down the alphabet one goes, the more screens there are against the light of infinity. That is why the masters of the Kabbalah explained that when one gets to the last letter of the Hebrew alphabet, the *tav,* the light is so weak that it is barely perceptible.

Using this theory, new meaning could be given to gematria, the system of numerology, using the numerical values of the letters. The numerical value of a letter, and consequently that of a word, is that of the number of *qlipot,* husks or envelopes, which protect the light contained in the letter.

Thus, if the letter *aleph* has a value of 1, it is because it only has one envelope or husk.

The letter *mem* has a numerical value of 40, which means that there are forty envelopes or husks around the core of light at the heart of the letter.

The higher the numerical value of a letter, the harder it is to attain its core of light.

The Text of the Kabbalah and the Metaphor of Fire

The metaphor of fire is omnipresent in the texts of the Kabbalah, especially in relation to the text of its various components. Thus, as has been said, letters are called "horses of fire," words "chariots of fire," and the entire text "black fire on white fire."

It is interesting to note that, for the Talmud, the definition of a book can only be understood on the basis of the critical and extreme situation of a fire endangering the existence of books.*

* These themes were developed at length by the author in *Le Livre brûlé* and the first part of *C'est pour cela que l'on aime les libellules.*

The first revelation of the Name of God to Moses came during the incident of the Burning Bush. God said: "I shall be what I shall be" *(Ehyeh asher ehyeh)*. Here is a calligraphic representation of this phrase in letters of fire.

Text and the Musical Metaphor

Another important metaphor that ought to be known to appreciate the full meaning of the text is that of music. The words are like a melody. The context, which gives a different meaning to the same words every time they are read, is like the harmony. The repetition and structure of the text are its rhythm.

Melody, harmony, and rhythm make the text into a musical partition that ought to be heard in all its shades of meaning. It very often happens that the reader is satisfied merely with the melody. No doubt the sounds of the text are very beautiful, but if this method alone is adopted, the text does not reveal itself in all its depth.

The rhythm may be that of a word that appears several times in the same text, or a figure repeated several times like a chorus or refrain, such as the figure 7, which symbolizes the rhythm of time for the whole of the text of the Bible.

28

A Description of the Twenty-two Letters of the Hebrew Alphabet

The Kabbalah: A Mysticism of Letters

How did God proceed to create the world? The author of the *Sefer Yetsira* explains that the universe was created through the intermediary of the ten *sefirot,* the special powers or modes that the Divinity inscribes in the worlds. He uses the twenty-two letters of the alphabet to do so, thus creating thirty-two wonderful voices of wisdom, or thirty-two basic instruments.

Understanding the creation of the world means knowing the mysteries of the alphabet. The Hebrew alphabet uses three basic shapes. The kabbalists have played on the shape, the meaning, and the numerical value of letters simultaneously.

We will present various kinds of script here, and then some examples will be given of kabbalistic analyses based on these letters.

The Assyrian or "Holy" Script and the Cursive Script

The first script, in importance and in usage, was that which we know today and which is used both in printing and in writing the liturgy of the sacred scrolls is known as the *ktav ashuri*, "the Assyrian script."

אבגדהוזזחחטיכךלמםנןסעפףצץקרשת

This is the script that is usually the subject of the kabbalistic commentaries and analyses. Each letter is interpreted on the basis of its shape, numerical value, and the image on which it is based, which is preserved in the actual name of the letter.

For example, the *aleph* takes the shape of a man walking. It can be broken down into two *yods* and a *vav*, and its numerical value is thus either 1 or 26.

The second type of script is cursive script. This is the script that is used to write quickly by hand and for nonliturgical texts.

אבגדהוזחטיכךלמםנןסעפףצץקרשת

This script is derived from a more ancient script known as Protosinaitic.

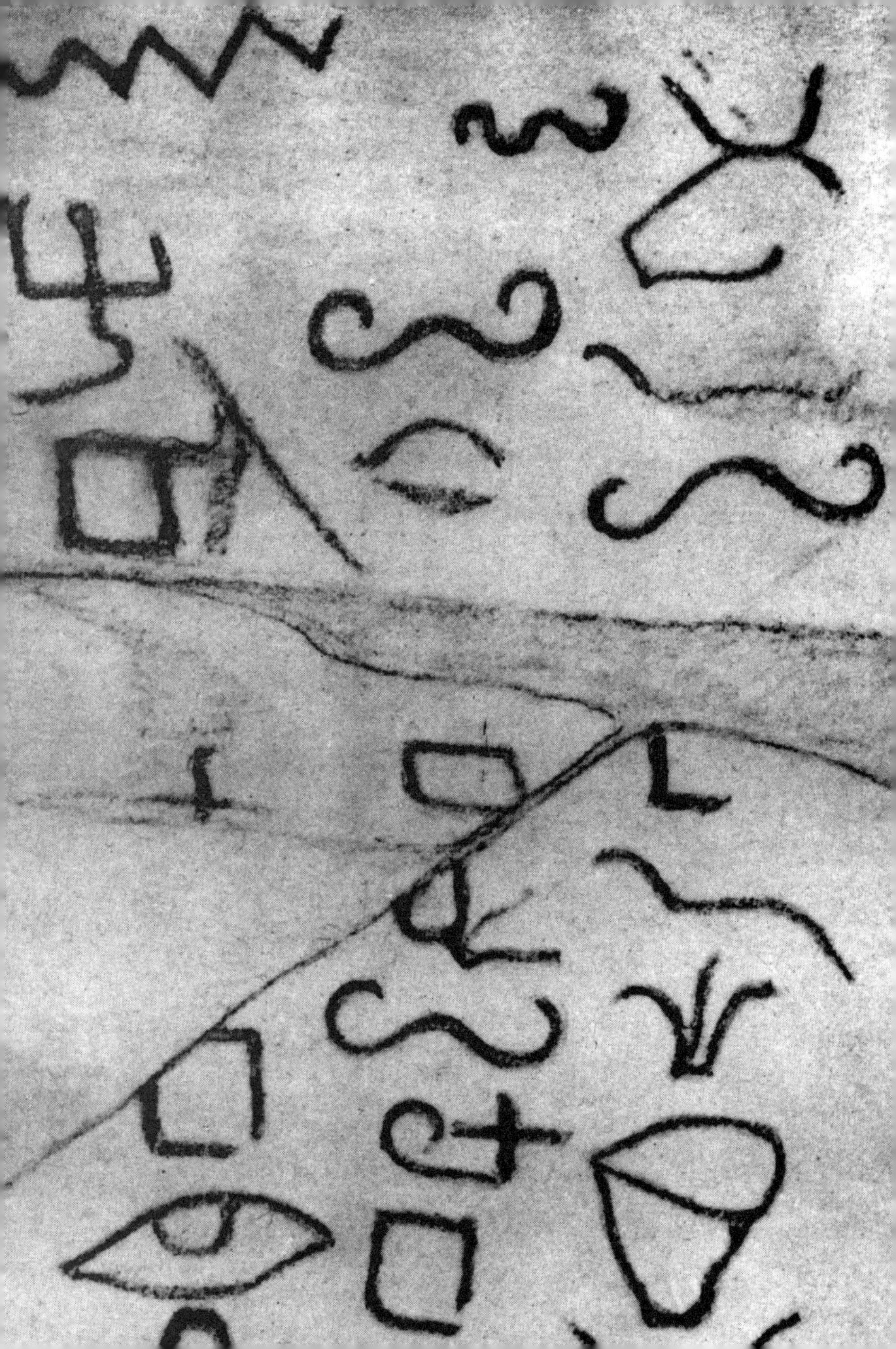

Protosinaitic Script

The third and oldest script is the Protosinaitic script. This dates from the period when letters consisted of images (originally, about 3,500 years ago, when that which was to become our alphabet was born, the letters were actually images or pictures). The simplification of this writing produced what is known as *ktav ivri,* "Hebrew writing." The kabbalists, who considered Hebrew to be a holy language, often refer to the image of the letter, either in its present form or in the form that is retained in its memory due to the name of the letter. The analysis is always conducted on several levels, and all the interpretations are complementary.

This earliest alphabet was discovered in 1904–5 by a British archaeologist by the name of W. F. Petrie, during the excavations at Serabit-El-Khadem, in the Sinai Desert, hence the name Protosinaitic. Based on Egyptian hieroglyphics, it was used to write down a Semitic language, no doubt that of the Hebrew workers or slaves then to be found in Egypt, since the period corresponds to that of the end of Hebrew slavery in Egypt, the Exodus from Egypt, and the revelation on Mount Sinai.

Protosinaitic consists of pictograms (drawings), which represent consonants. It is from this alphabet that all of the following scripts developed: Canaanite script, which became known as Phoenician script in its Greek version, Aramaic script, Paleohebrew and Hebrew, Nabbatean, Greek, and Arabic, right down to our modern European alphabets, which we acquired via the Etruscan and Latin alphabets.*

* See Ouaknin, *Mysteries of the Alphabet.*

29

Archaeography

Thinking is always interpreting, that is to say explaining, developing, deciphering, translating a sign.
Translating, deciphering, developing are pure forms of creation. There is no greater number of explicit meanings than there are clear ideas. There are only meanings implied in the signs; and if thought has the power to explain a sign, to develop it in an Idea, it is because the Idea is already in the sign, in an enveloped and wrapped state, in the obscure state of that which forces one to think.
—Gilles Deleuze, *Proust et les signes*

The significance of the discovery of Protosinaitic and the link between letter and image is that it shows that there is a memory of the underlying image inherent in each letter, and thus in each word. The return to this image is called "archaeography," and it makes it possible to produce new analyses of a Western language such as French, English, German, Italian, and so on.

Archaeography is the word that the author has created to designate the analysis and interpretation of words, not only on the basis of their etymology but also on the basis of the original graphic shape of the letters of the alphabet.

This is a return to the "picture-shape" of the letters of the alphabet, which we encountered in Protosinaitic. The Protosinaitic alphabet is right at the edge of the image and the letter, somewhere between the pictogram and the alphabetic sign.

Archaeography does not reject etymology, but supplements it through a dialogue and a dialectic that involve play between the eye and the ear, in which the "eye hears" and the "ear sees" very well what is involved. Archaeography is a sort of commentary on the enigmatic verse in the Bible: "And all the people saw the voices" (*Vekhol haam roim et haqolot*; Exodus 20:19).

The vision of the voices, the understanding of speech through looking, may have been the pictographic shape that has embedded itself in the memory of each of the letters of the alphabet. Each letter possesses a graphic or pictorial memory, and everyone possesses a corresponding graphic unconscious.

This aspect of the memory of the image, in the letter and in man, opens the way to research into hidden images and archaeographic interpretation.

The names of the Hebrew letters retain a memory of the image that the letter conveyed in the Protosinaitic script. Thus the *aleph* means "ox" or "bull"; the *bet,* "house"; the *gimmel,* "camel"; and so on. The Kabbalah uses the meaning of these letters in its commentaries referring to the name of the letter relating to the image.

The following table, which shows which letter corresponds to which image or images, will help to reveal the images and hidden meanings in Hebrew words or names and those contained in any Western language (the figure shown at the end of each explanation of a letter is the numerical value).

***Aleph* / A**: head of an ox or bull: Strength, force, energy, human being, possibility, beginning, teaching; numerical value **1** or **1,000.**

***Bet* / B**: house: Introversion, welcoming, couple, intimacy, family, shelter, the celestial vault; **2.**

***Gimmel* / C**: camel (dromedary): Extroversion, taking beyond oneself, doing good, weaning, ripening, releasing oneself, rendering good for good; **3.**

Dalet / D: door and opening: Female breast, female sex, descent, abundance, pouring, spreading, entering, leaving, extracting; **4.**

Heh / E: breath: Cry, man praying, inhaling, expression, sign of the feminine gender, of direction and of a question, emptying of breath and of energy; **5.**

Vav / F, U, V, W: hook, nail: Coordination, channel, conduit, finger, the phallus, desire for a relationship, coitus; **6.**

Zayin / G, Z: arrow, weapon: Relationship with others, war, conflict, face-to-face, revolution, fracture, breakage, distance, logic of contradiction, crossing, inappropriateness, questioning, time, cycle, multiplicity, moral laws; **7.**

Khet / Kh: barrier: Closure, protective rampart, present time, sin if one remains enclosed, enclosing; **8.**

Tet / T: This letter has no meaning in Hebrew and is not found in Protosinaitic. It passed into Greek as the *theta*, but is not present in Latin. It is one of the two "t" sounds, which are now identical but may once have had a different sound, like the hard "d" and "t" in Arabic; consistent with its apparent foreignness, it is usually used to indicate the "t" sound in a word that has been introduced into Hebrew from another language; **9.**

Yod / I, J, Y: hand: Taking, giving, exchanging, showing, counting, multiplicity, structuring, unity, benediction; **10.**

Kaf / K: palm of the hand: Hollow, receiving, taking, giving, trade, kiss, time, covering, blessing; **20.**

Lamed / L: spur: The spur of desire, to cause to advance, to motivate, studying, teaching, overtaking, exceeding, height, to create oneself, to invent oneself, to exceed oneself; **30.**

Mem / M: water: Movement, dynamism, path, identity in movement, questioning one's identity, questioning the origin; **40.**

Nun / N: fish: The hidden, the intimate, the feminine, place of concealment, fetus in the amniotic fluid, life, birth to come, child, grandchild, descendancy, multiplicity, abundance, benediction; **50.**

Samekh **/ X:** tree with branches (pine or cedar of Lebanon): Skeleton, roof-beam, infrastructure, ladder, stick for supporting and upholding, fishbone; **60.**

Ayin **/ O:** eye: Seeing, looking, appearing, disappearing, visible-invisible, source, threshold, passage, consulting, discovering, multiplicity, international meeting, translation, foreign languages; **70.**

Peh **/ P:** mouth: Speaking, eating, breathing, disengaging, exhaling, opening, sex, transmission of memory, story; **80.**

Tsadeh **/ Ts:** fishhook, anchor: This letter is rare in Protosinaitic script and did not pass into the Latin alphabet. Its equivalent existed in the alphabets of Greek dialects such as that of Thera and Corinth. It represents hooking, harpooning, anchoring, chasing, fishing, capturing, ambushing, seducing, preventing, restraining, target, objective; **90.**

Qof **/ Q:** cleaver: Separation, interruption, slicing, deciding, chilling, freezing, imitating, making a hole and considering the void, eye of the needle, delving into the depths; **100.**

Resh **/ R:** head: Beginning, being at the head, having a spirit of leadership, the extreme, intellectual dimension; **200.**

Shin **/ S:** tooth: Having an analytical mind, masticating, reducing, archery, sending, launching, reducing; **300.**

Tav **/ T:** sign: Mark, musical note, symbol, meeting, alliance, completing, indicating, end of an extreme process; last letter of the Hebrew alphabet; **400.**

30

The Combining of Letters
The *Tseruf*

The twenty-two letters, he has traced them, carved them, multiplied them, weighed them, and permutated them, he has shaped from them all creatures and everything that has been created.
And in what way has he multiplied them?
Aleph with all of them
all of them with Aleph.
Bet with all of them
all of them with Bet.
Gimmel with all of them
all of them with Gimmel. . . .
All of them move in a circle: thus they emerge from two hundred and thirty-one gates. All the words emerge under a single name.
—"Book of Creation"

Circulating the Energy

Beyond the shape and meaning of the letters of the alphabet, the Kabbalah is interested in their dynamics and their combinations.

The basic idea at the root of this momentum of language is the light of the infinite, which reaches man through the intermediary of the letters used as a "vehicle." Static letters provide a static light—or, to quote another metaphor, static letters are like stagnant water in a pool or pond, with all the negative consequences that this involves.

The kabbalist receives light and transmits it through a dynamic language. The energy that man receives takes shape within him and risks becoming a prisoner if it does not continue its journey. In this case, it produces a knot or node of energy that blocks the flow of divine cosmic current, and man no longer feels inhabited nor filled with light. The knots must therefore be untied; in kabbalistic tradition, this begins with the untying of the knots of language through a very important technique of making combinations of letters, called *tseruf.*

Tseruf became popular through the drawing of squares, said to be magical, in which words and their combinations of letters were placed. Certain words made sense, and others became pure sounds, which thus appeared to be magic words or passwords. *Amor* became *Roma*; *sator* became *rotas; Marie* became *aimer* ("to love")....

Tseruf and Divine Presence

Tseruf ("combination") is, in some texts, called *ma'asseh merkava* ("action of the celestial chariot"). This fundamental nomenclature teaches that the divine presence or *shekhina* is contained in the momentum of language through the intermediary of the infinity of combinations.

This may stress, as we have already done above, the extraordinary responsibility of man for the divine presence. It is man who, through his skill and his art of combining, will create or not create room for the s*hekhina.*

The *Tseruf* as the Essence of Language

The use of gematria or numerical values makes it easier to memorize the fundamental relationship between "combination" and "language." Remember that in Hebrew, numbers are represented by letters of the alphabet. Each word therefore has a numerical value derived from the sum of the figures and number represented by each letter, taken separately.

Thus, it will be seen that the words *tseruf* ("combination") and *lashon* ("tongue") have the same numerical value: 386.

Tseruf is written *tsadeh, yod, resh, vav, peh:*

צירוף

90 + 10 + 200 + 6 + 80

386

Lashon is written *lamed, shin, vav, nun:*

לשון

30 + 300 + 6 + 50

386

This numerical analogy between "combination" and "tongue" invites us to consider the fact that a tongue or language is the result of infinite combinations; that is, it is the dimension of internal dynamics that makes it into a language—not a formalized language that already exists in dictionaries and whose words are available to all, but as a tongue that is constituted and renews itself while renewing the being who reinvents it.

The Six Phases of *Tseruf*

The root of a Hebrew word generally consists of three letters. Analysis of the combinations consists in discovering and revealing all the possible combinations of these three letters. These number "n!"; i.e. the factorial number of the letters. Thus, a three-letter word would contain 3! combinations; i.e., 3 x 2 x 1 = 6 combinations. A four-letter word would have 4! combinations; i.e., 4 x 3 x 2 x 1 = 24 combinations.

The art of *tseruf* consists in deploying these combinations and discovering the internal and external logic. Internal logic means the articulation of a certain semantic logic between the various combinations. External logic implies seeking articulation with other words and other conceptual horizons relating to the meaning discovered in the new combination.

Let us take, for example, the word *tseruf* itself, and deploy its set of combinations. They will surely be very instructive as to the secrets and richness of the art of combining.

The word *tseruf* has the root Ts-R-F. This three-letter root can be written in six different combinations, which will be analyzed in the following order:

R-Ts-F;
R-F-Ts;
F-Ts-R;
F-R-Ts;
Ts-R-F;
Ts-F-R.

We shall try to discover the meaning of each of these combinations.

The Law of Succession, or *Retsef*

The first internal logic in the world is that of the succession of letters of which the word is constructed, which enables it to mean what it does.

The law of succession is called *retsef: resh-tsadeh-peh.* This root means "the act of being in continuity on the same level in such a way that one can walk without stumbling," hence the more traditional meaning of this root: "paving, laying down slabs or flooring, to grant succession, continuity, continuation". The root can also be broken down into *rats-peh,* which means "running mouth," speech that is continuous, without stammering or hesitation. As often happens in Hebrew, the same root may mean one thing and its opposite; *ratsaf* thus also means "breaking, crushing," that is to say reducing and "breaking" the rhythm of continuity. A third meaning of *retsef* is "burning coal."

The first meaning, "flooring, paving, a row of stones set side-by-side," is also understood in the metaphorical sense, which was highlighted in respect of the word *stone* as "letter." The *retsef* is thus a series of stone-letters, and thus a "word" or a "house." The word *retsef* subsequently took on the meaning of "covering, sheathing, laminating."

But *retsef* is first and foremost a logical sequence in time, a succession of events, of musical sounds. The concept of continuity has given the meaning of pursuit, pursuing someone with one's love, "assiduity."

In summary, a word always has a prime meaning that is conferred upon it by the law of the sequencing of letters, a law that in Hebrew is called *retsef:* it is the first phase of the art of making combinations.

Zero Degree of Meaning, or *Rafats*

The second phase of the combination is provided by the permutation of the third and second letters of the word *retsef,* which becomes *refets* or *rafats:*

R-Ts-F → R-F-Ts

This combination produces a word of which there is no trace in the dictionary: *rafats.*

Man at Point Zero

Rafats is meaningless!

A fundamental event in the logic of the production of meaning through the combining process, as one of the semantic possibilities, is a pause, a silence to continue to discover other words within words and beyond words. The second phase is thus one of "zero degree of meaning," a pre-semantic moment in which the interpreter, artist, or hermeneut must wander off into the desert or leave on a solo voyage across the infinite ocean. At a certain moment, he will encounter "the line, the zero parallel: it is a unique moment, a special point, a sacred zone through which passage symbolizes a decisive initiation. It is an imaginary line, a geographical point zero, but by its very nullity, representing this degree zero to which man could be said to tend, through the need to attain an ideal landmark, from which, free of himself, of his prejudices, his myths, and his gods, he could return with a changed attitude and a positive new approach" (Maurice Blanchot, *The Space of Literature*).

Silence

> ***Silence is the highest form of thought and we develop this mute attention against the day when we shall find our place in the absolute that surrounds us (...)***
> —Christian Bobin

"Man at point zero" is a fundamental experience of language—the experience of language as silence. But perhaps a lot of words are needed to express the silence and make it heard. . . .

The *rafats* is a new level of language that silence has produced. It is the poetry of silence, more silent than pure silence, for being silent is not always the best way of being silent. In fact, being silent is very often significant; that is, silence still belongs to the sphere of the senses. Silence is thus extremely noisy and loses its mission of obliterating sense, its vocation of undoing work, its path of "idleness."

Furthermore, in order to reach point zero, one needs to understand that there is such a thing as non-spoken speech, "speech which takes the place of speech and is used for the purpose of resembling it but speech which, in doing so, disarms speech and disarms anyone who abandons himself to it" (Blanchot, *Space of Literature*).

This silence of words that speak in order to say nothing is perhaps the very essence of literature. Language belongs and does not belong to literature. It belongs to it because words are needed in order to enter the world of speech, but at the same time, it does not belong to it, because it is in silence that language most obviously abandons its nature of providing meaning.

To say that language is silence (the second phase of *tseruf*) is thus not to revel in the paradox but rather "to clearly show the paradoxical nature of literature which says something while saying nothing which, in being produced, deafens to an insistence on meaningful discourse" (Blanchot, *Space of Literature*).

The Angel of Oblivion

Throw your heaviness into the depths!
Man Forgets Man, forget!
Divine is the art of forgetting.
Do you want to fly,
do you want to feel at home in the heights
throw the heaviest part of yourself into the sea!
Here is the sea, throw yourself into the sea
Divine is the art of forgetting!
—Friedrich Nietzsche

We read in the Talmud (tractate Nidda, 31a):

> Rabbi Simlai teaches:
>
> "What does an embryo resemble in its mother's belly? It is like a folded document. Its hands are on its temples, its elbows against its legs and its heels against its buttocks. Its head rests between its knees, its mouth is closed, its umbilicus open. It eats what its mother eats and drinks what she drinks. It does not produce excrement; if it did, it would kill its mother. As soon as it emerges into the open air, the organs open that were closed and those that were closed open. If it were not so, the child could not live, even for a moment. A lamp burns above the head [of the embryo], and it contemplates the world from one extremity to the other, as it is said: 'When His lamp shone over my head, and His light guided me in the darkness' [Job 29:3]. Do not be surprised at this: behold, a person may have a dream which takes place in Spain although he is here in this very spot. There is nowhere better for man to stay, for it is said: 'O that I were in months gone by, In the days when God watched over me' [ibid., 2].
>
> "What is the period which [is counted] in months, but not in years? It is pregnancy! The whole of the Torah is taught [to the embryo], for it is said 'Then he instructed me and said to me: may your heart retain my words; keep my commandments and you shall live' [Pr. iv: 4], and also 'When God's company graced my tent' [Job xxix: 4]. What is the purpose of this last quotation? It is because you might believe that it refers only to the prophet, but listen: 'When God's company graced my tent.' This means: as soon as the child is born, an angel comes to him and strikes him on the mouth, thus making him forget the whole of the Torah."

There is thus an angel of oblivion who allows the child to "learn," and not merely to "re-remember," as is the case in the Platonic myth of reminiscence.

In order to learn, one must begin by forgetting. That is what Moses taught in his own way when he broke the Tablets of the Law, a gesture of which God himself approved, saying to him "Yishar kokhekha" ["Bravo!"]. You have done well to break them because sometimes the abolition of the Law is its implementation. The commentary could be made: "If you had not broken them, oblivion would have been forgotten!"

The Last Two Phases of *Tseruf*

Words are like birds; why keep them shut away in cages?
—Rabbi Nachman of Breslov

After the *retsef* and the *rafats,* the dynamic life within the word supplies the word of the power to say something else. The Hebrew word for this "supplication" is *patsar.* Meaning is thus "breached"; this is the stage of *parats* or *perets.* The word is ripe for a new "combination" or *tseruf;* the meaning is released and flies away, as the *tsipor,* "bird."

To summarize, the six phases of the combination are:

· *retsef:* sequencing
· *rafats:* zero degree of meaning
· *patsar:* supplication
· *parats:* breached
· *tseruf:* a combination
· *tsipor:* bird.

The Master of *Tseruf*: Rabbi Abraham Abulafia

One of the greatest masters of *tseruf* was Rabbi Abraham Abulafia (1240–1291). Abulafia understood *tseruf* ("combination") to mean the science of association and permutation of the Hebrew letters.

The technique was revived by Hasidim in the Rhineland, who developed Abulafia's system and pushed it to its extremes as well as providing a mystical justification for it. In fact, prior to the advent of Abulafia, *tseruf* was a technique used by scholars to delve into the secrets of the law. The three classic devices of gematria (the calculation of numerical values), *notarikon*

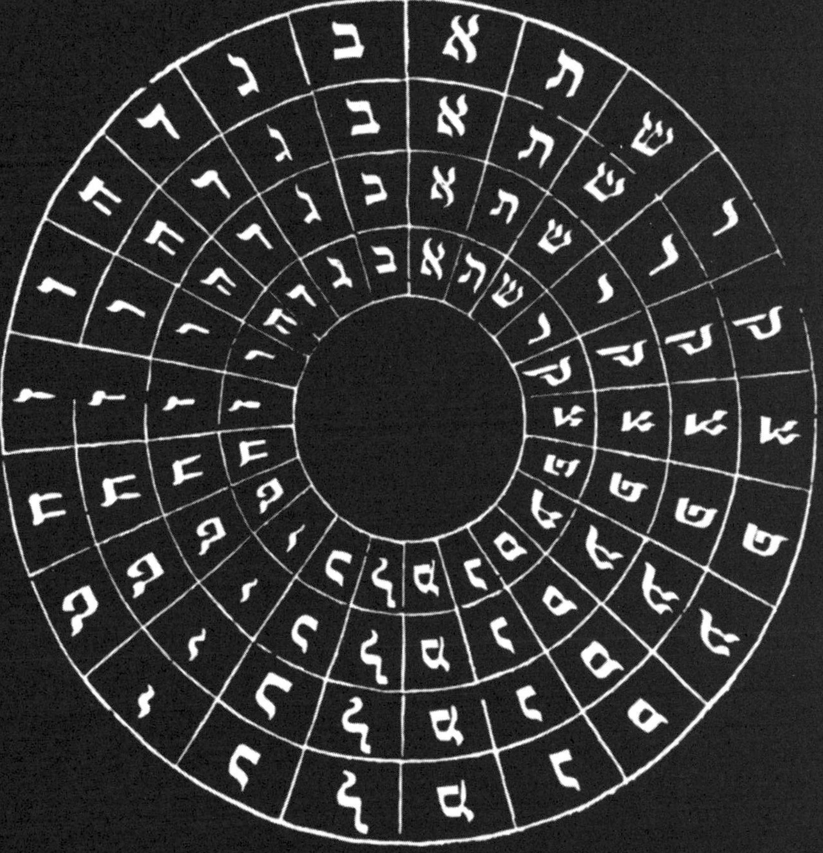

The circle of *tseruf.* The mystic is turning the alphabets in a circle and enters into a state of ecstasy. Diagram from the *Pardess Rimonim* ("Pomegranate Orchard") by Rabbi Moses Cordovero, Thirtieth Gate of Part II (new ed,. Jerusalem, 1962).

(analyses of the first letters of a word and anagrams), and *temura* (replacing a letter by one or more other letters) were the main methods used. Through Abulafia, they became part of a wider system of channeled meditation in which the subject of the meditation was no longer exclusively the Holy Scriptures, but writings in general. The meditation was used in three strata—pronunciation *(mivta)*, writing *(mikhtav)*, and thought *(machshava)*—to match the threefold distinction made by the *Sefer Yetsira (sipoor, sefer, sefar)*.

As regards the *mikhtav*, Abulafia did not confine himself to studying the combinations of the letters within words and their permutations according to their numerical values; he studied the shapes of the letters themselves. "Many of the later kabbalists, and especially the Christian kabbalists, were extremely enthusiastic about this science of *tseruf* which they regarded as the kabbalistic procedure par excellence, but too often they isolated it from Abulafia's philosophy in general, which was judged to be too daring, so much so that, deprived of its mystical foundation and in the hands of these false disciples *tseruf* became a wonderfully operational plaything, but to no purpose" (Moshe Idel, *The Mystical Experience in Abraham Abulafia*).

The influence of Abulafia is still so strong today, no doubt thanks to the scholarship of Moshe Idel, that it can even be found in the skin of a hero of modern literature, *Foucault's Pendulum* by Umberto Eco. Abulafia—Abu to its friends—is the name given to a computer that enables its owner to launch himself into the delights of *tseruf*, while quoting extracts from the *Sefer Yetsira* and other major kabbalistic works.

Kabbalah: a literary game that is a serious introduction, though a lighthearted one, to the magical world of the art of combinations.

The Theory of Untying the Knots

For Abulafia, *tseruf* was a means to an end—a method, not the very nature of mystical scholarship itself. Abulafia believed that the human soul lived in this material world in a state of captivity. More specifically, as Gershom Scholem explains, he thought that the light of the infinite, which is the very vitality of the soul, is a prisoner held captive in the closed structure of matter.

Through *tseruf,* as well as by means of other contemplative techniques, Abulafia claimed to be able to release the captive soul and the light of infinity from its chains of matter. Hindered by the emotions imposed upon it by the body and the material world, and having been taught to live in the world below, the soul is no longer capable of recognizing the One from whom it issued. For Abulafia, the aim of a mystical experience is the deliverance of such a soul. All his writings are designed to show the way in which this can perceive the divine—and reach it. In other words, he seeks to know how the light can regain its source or be connected to it.

Abulafia uses the image of the knot that must be undone and not cut; that is, on the path leading to ecstasy and prophetic vision he seeks not to remove or obliterate the physical ego but to sublimate it.

For the soul to rise above the concrete world, it must be possible to meditate in an absolute, that is to say an abstract, manner. The abstraction, the absolute object, is for Abulafia the Hebrew alphabet. It is an object because it is visible and palpable; it is abstract because it is the expression of the fundamental spiritual reality. *Tseruf* is in fact only part of the preparation of the disciple for ecstasy, only one of the scales that the soul must perform in searching for Oneness before attaining the level of absolute contemplation.

Untying the knots requires a long and exacting transformation of the ego. The divine life in man must be liberated to enable the human being to participate in the divine, and this can only be done gradually, due to the demands of everyday life.

Abulafia, the founder of modern Jewish meditation, thus proposes a series of positions and breathing exercises to be used before practicing *tseruf.*

A Musical Metaphor

Far from being a jumble of letters, figures, words, *tseruf* is a progressive technique that enables a disciple to release his soul in a state of controlled ecstasy which he is able to regulate constantly:

Abulafia despises the irrational and to some extent unconscious forms of ecstasy and accuses them of being dangerous follies. For him, the practice of tseruf is a sort of musical composition. Just as a composer combines the notes of the scale according to fixed rules and not anarchically, so the mystic combines letters, by following a strict pattern. And just as the talented musician is inspired to produce melodious tunes, so the inspired mystic finds the melody and original harmony of the Great Name—and by listening to these chants of a new type, the soul feels itself uplifted toward God."
(Idel, *Abraham Abulafia*)

The Technique of the "Leaps": *Kfitsa* and *Dillug*

Before practicing *tseruf*, or at the same time, the disciple will perform his first meditations by associations of ideas. Abulafia, who was always concerned with controlling the development of the inner self, defined the method that the soul should use to jump from one area of associations to the next. It is this skill at skipping or leaping *(dillug)* or bounding *(kfitsa)* that enables the disciple to make successive leaps from one sphere to another, each time expanding his field of consciousness—right up to the divine. *Dillug* and *tseruf* open the way to the ecstatic vision.

During this engineered and controlled ecstasy, the soul should be in contact with the divinity. The kabbalist is then said to be in *devequt* with God—union without fusion. Through his knowledge and love, the kabbalist becomes a sort of prophet. That which Abulafia calls "ecstasy" is, in fact, prophetic vision in the sense in which Maimonides and the Jewish philosophers of the Middle Ages understood it.

We have dwelt at length on the Kabbalah of Abulafia because it had such an impact on other kabbalists; a large number of his intuitions were later repeated in the new Kabbalah, the Hasidism of the Baal Shem Tov, and, as will be seen below, the philosophy of the Baal Shem Tov's descendant, Rabbi Nachman of Breslov.*

* To learn more about Abulafia, the reader is directed to read *L'Expérience mystique d'Abraham Aboulafia*, by Moshe Idel; as well as Gershom Scholem, *Major Trends in Jewish Mysticism*, 134 ff., and Guy Casaril, *Rabbi Siméon Bar Yochaï et la Cabbale.*

31

The Kabbalah and Healing

The Channels of Energy

The Kabbalah's mission is to channel human existence into physical, psychological, and spiritual well-being, while stressing the close interrelationship between the physical and psychological.

For the Kabbalah, disease is the result of a blockage in the circulation of vital energy, the capacity to receive the light of infinity. A sick person is a person who is blocked, obstructed, chained, "corked." The Kabbalah speaks of channels, *tsinorot,* through which man is linked to infinity. When these channels are blocked or obstructed, when they become tangled or knotted, the Kabbalah speaks of "obstruction of the channels" (*stimat hatsinorot*).

Healing therefore consists in unraveling the knots that block the circulation of the "vital influx" *(shefa, shin-peh-ayin).*

שפע

Note that if this word is not written in the order of the three letters *shin-peh-ayin,* and two letters are transposed, it becomes the word *pesha, peh-shin-ayin,* which means "sin."

For the Kabbalah, sin is not primarily moral but existential. Sin is the very fact of not being open to the possibility of receiving the light of the *en-sof.*

The Kabbalah seeks to expose the knots that block the flow of light and unravel them, essentially by making language move.

In the kabbalistic and Hasidic tradition, the influx of energy-light tends to concentrate in the Hebrew alphabet, and more especially in the letters of the Holy Name. The momentum of language is thus the central kabbalistic technique for achieving balance and good health. The kabbalistic technique of well-being is linked to the fulfillment of harmony through the intermediate worlds of the ten *sefirot,* a harmony created by the correct use of the letters and figures, which give man access to the intermediate worlds.

One of the essential aspects of Jewish worship is to place the momentum of language in the context of reality to remind man, the reader of the signs of the world, that he exists only as part of the momentum of being.

The Joy in the Heart of the Kabbalah

The Kabbalah is an advocate for a joyful and happy existence. Through the Kabbalah, sadness disappears; the ethic is all for a renewal of thought and action through joy. Rabbi Nachman of Breslov formulates this categorical imperative thus: "Mitsva gedolah lihyot besimkha tamid" ("It is a great mitzvah [obligation] to always be in joy"). "Sadness is the exile of the divine presence" was another of his sayings. "But when man performs an action with joy, he opens himself to the future miracle, he spreads the sparks of holiness which had been kept prisoner in the closed beings. When joy seizes the body of man, he raises his hands as well as his feet. He thus cannot prevent himself from dancing."

Joy has such an important place in the Kabbalah that it governs disease and healing. As far as Rabbi Nachman, for example, is concerned, there is only one reason for all illness: sadness. It is a great mitzvah to always be joyful, to gather one's own strength and distance oneself from sadness and bitterness with all one's power and might. All the diseases that attack man are the result of the deterioration of joy, a deterioration which itself comes from a distortion of the "deep melody" *(nigun)* of the ten "vital pulses" *(defaqim).*

When joy and song are harmed, people fall sick.

Joy is a great remedy. It is a question of finding within oneself a single positive point which can make one rejoice, and to cling to it.

Joy is the creation of a space in which speech can be expressed and exist.

Joy is linked to the capacity to express oneself, to say what one has to say, to break the chains of captivity, the circle of ready-made words and thoughts. Joy is the capacity of man to reinvent himself.

Joy is a dance, a ring dance that has the power to break open a link of the chains of captivity and inject new breath into life.

Kabbalah and Pleasure

In the kabbalistic tradition of the school of Abraham Abulafia, the ultimate aim of the Kabbalah is to attain levels of knowledge that are those of the prophetic experience. This experience can be acquired through a set of techniques of recitation and repetition of the holy names and the key words, linked to breathing and visualization techniques. For Abulafia, the prophetic experience ought to cause man to unite with the celestial powers and open the way to the immortality of the soul.

It is important to realize that, contrary to the numerous doctrines of mysticism that recommend asceticism to attain states of ecstasy, Abulafia believed that ascetic behavior was quite unnecessary in order to attain a prophetic state.

The Jewish Kabbalah does not contain a trace of that devaluation of matter and the body that can be found in Neoplatonic literature. There is no conflict between a sharpening of the intellect and the body.

Abulafia goes even farther, moving in a daring direction by using certain erotic and sexual images that are mere metaphors for the mystical relationship between man and the higher powers, images that emphasize the pleasure involved in the prophetic experience.

In many of his essays, however, Abulafia is careful to explain that enjoyment is to a certain extent the aim of prophetic experience. In his book, *The Light of the Intellect,* he writes, "The letter is like matter, and the vowel point is like the breath which gives this matter momentum; the understanding which functions and causes to function is like the intellect, and it is this which reacts upon breath and upon matter; and the pleasure which is drawn from this by he who has acceded to that which it was possible for him to attain constitutes the true purpose thereof."

In his book *The Treasure of Hidden Delights,* he adds, "You shall feel that a new breath will be added to you, that will awaken you and that will pass through your whole body, and it will cause you pleasure and you will have the impression that there falls upon you, from head to foot, the oil of a perfumed balm and you will feel a contentment and great joy, mixed with ecstatic joy and trembling which will fill you completely, body and soul."

Abulafia is thus ready to consider physical pleasure as a proper manner of expressing the feeling that accompanies the prophetic experience, as opposed to those authors who also use the metaphor of the union between man and woman but for whom the image of physical coupling is used as a metaphor to describe love of God.

The Kabbalah makes it possible to receive the energy of the light of infinity and thus to feel a happiness that translates itself primarily in concrete terms by the fact of being in good health.

Healing and the Name of God

In English, the word *therapy* mainly implies healing or providing a cure. The remedy and the physician or doctor are produced "after the event" to repair a break in the body, the spirit, or the soul. Greek has followed the Hebrew, however, and given therapy the extended meaning of a preventive and prospective attitude to sickness.

The Hebrew word *terupha* and the Greek word *terapeia* both mean much more than a mere cure. In Exodus 15:26, God actually presents himself as a healer: "And he said: if you listen to the voice of YHVH, your God diligently, doing what is upright in His sight, giving ear to His commandments and keeping all His laws, then I will not bring upon you any of the diseases that I brought upon the Egyptians, for I the Lord thy God am your healer."

Why does God need to claim to be a healer if He had not sent down any disease? The following interpretation has been offered: the physician is not merely a healer; he must ensure that man does not fall prey to any illness. In preventive medicine the doctor performs the role mainly of an instructor and teacher who teaches others how to take care of themselves.

The initial meaning of the word *healer* is "he cares for"; hence the meaning of servant and worshiper. He is the person who cares for and looks after something, such as the body. Hence the extended meaning, "he who cares for the sick."

The kabbalistic commentaries on this verse stress the use of the phrase "if you listen to the voice of YHVH," which they interpret literally as meaning, "If you understand the meaning of the tetragrammaton YHVH, you will be protected from sickness, and you will receive the light and energy of the infinite in the most perfect way possible."

Health means taking care of the tetragrammaton, taking care of the being. Taking care of the being means taking care of time, and how it fits into the temporality of existence, which extends between memory and hope, between that which we are, that which we have been, and that which we could become. Taking care of the being is taking care of time, and ensuring no dysfunction of temporality.

> This means that we must care particularly for that which is not sick and that which is not mortal within us. Thus, the therapist does not concentrate first and foremost on the sickness itself or on the patient, but on that which is beyond the reach of the sickness and beyond death in him. Philo puts it thus: taking care of being and not of my being or his being. Being is not a thing, but a Space, an Opening which must remain free. God is the freedom of man. Take care of this liberty, do not alienate it from anything or anyone, keep it alive and humble. Take care of man in that which escapes man. . . . The cure is something which is given to us as a bonus.
>
> (Jean-Yves Leloup, *Prendre soin de l'être*)

All of the techniques used in the Kabbalah have no purpose other than that of maintaining this openness and thus offering us the way of life.

32

How to Extract Meaning
The Book and the Void

We have already evoked the need for the void as a fundamental dimension for giving momentum to language in the *tseruf.* The idea will now be discussed in greater depth, showing that the void constitutes the meaning of words and is the foundation of the very possibility of existence.

Letters Cut into the Void

Tsimtsum . . .

In the beginning there was the void. . . .

The masters of the Talmud teach that the letters of the Ten Commandments were not written on stone but engraved, and not merely engraved, but cut right through the stone from one side to the other. It is thus exciting to realize that the substance of which the writing of the Law and the revelation consisted was a void!

The letters of the Ten Commandments were produced "in a void," as one might say "in marble" or "in wood." The actual substance of the writing is a nonsubstance.

Astonishing!

Rabbi Simeon Resh Lakish teaches, "The Torah given to Moses by the Holy One, Blessed be He, was a white fire engraved by a black fire; it was of fire, engraved by fire, given from fire, as it is said: 'Written with His right hand, a law of fire (*Esh-dat*) for them.' " Nachmanides comments on this text as follows:

> We have an authentic tradition whereby the whole of the Torah consists of the set of the names of God; or a single great name of God. Thus the words which we read could also be distributed in a completely different way. The Torah written in "black fire on white fire" signifies, in fact, that the text was written without any breaks between letters, an uninterrupted sequence from first to last. A text consisting of a single word or name, a sequence of letters which contains no legible word having any meaning in the language of men.
> (Gershom Scholem, *On the Kabbalah and Its Symbolism*)

From Sexual Circumcision to Textual Circumcision

Thus before being able to read, one must be able to compile the book. The reader is a true creator. Reading becomes an activity, a production. An infinity of books is thus constantly present in the Book. There is no history but histories.

The first task of the reader is to produce cuts, cutting a space or void between the letters to form words, between certain words to produce sentences, between certain sentences to close and open new paragraphs, and finally, between paragraphs to produce books.

This cesura, this introduction of the void into the body of the text, is an event that heralds the entry of meaning into the world. This is the inaugural cut that symbolically ties in with the moment when the male child is introduced into the community—the circumcision. It should therefore come as no surprise that the Hebrew word for "circumcision" is also the word for "word" *(mila)*.

The word is the result of a cut, a cut that is part of the way in which it makes its first linguistic appearance. Giving meaning on the basis of a word is first and foremost to circumcise the text, converting it from a text of letters to a text of words, the origin of whose meaning lies not in the letters but in the void, the white space between the letters, white space that Rabbi Levi Isaac of Berditchev called the "Torah of the Messiah." This cut or space converts the "Torah of God" (a text consisting entirely of letters) to the "Torah of men" (a text of words). It is a circumcision of the text, but also the circumcision of God revealing Himself as text.

The Four Books

There are consequently four books:

The Torah of God—*Torat Ha-Shem*—is a text consisting exclusively of letters. It is a single long word, or single name, which can have no possibility of containing meaning, for the infinite thus combines with the most crushing finiteness of non-sense. Words do not yet exist. There is no cut, no break, no punctuation, no rhythm, no white space. Letter after letter, the stream of writing flows between two signposts: the *bet,* the first letter of the Torah, and the *lamed,* the last letter of the Torah. This text is also called the *Torat Qadmon* ("originating Torah"). The originating Torah is "insensate": it does not offer the reader the option of a semantic perception.

The Torah of Moses—*Torat Moshe*—is the text with which we are familiar, which consists of words that Moses has produced through the introduction of the cut between the letters, the circumcision of language.

The Torah of Man—*Torat Ha-Adam*—consists in producing new words and new meanings by creating breaks or cuts in the words in different places. This stage of the book corresponds to the Talmud, the interpretation, which is called "reading by the bursts of brilliant light."

The Torah of the Messiah—*Torat Mashiakh*—is the text we shall read when we become capable of reading the white letters between the black ones.

The Fertile Void

This idea of a void between the letters, which constructs the meaning, is an idea found in other cultures, especially in the philosophy of Chinese art. Lao-tzu teaches in the eleventh chapter of the *Tao*:

> Although thirty rays converge on the hub
> It is the median void
> Which moves the chariot
> Clay is used to shape the vessels
> But it is upon the void inside them
> That their usage depends
> There is no room that is not pierced by door and window
> For it is again the void
> Which makes a home possible
> Being has its aptitudes
> Which are employed by the non-being.

The Japanese tradition also stresses this void, which is one of the fundamental elements of Japanese culture.

There is a famous garden in Kyoto, that of the Zen temple Ryoan-ji, which consists of fifteen rocks scattered over a sandy surface. Yet from whatever angle one looks at them, one can only see fourteen rocks at the same time. When the fifteenth is visible, the fourteenth disappears, and so on. The invisible rock expresses the hidden center. Everything that is essential is visible and hidden at the same time. Between the visible and the hidden there is an empty space. There is a word in Japanese for this empty space between two things; it is *ma*.

That is a surprising terminological coincidence when one realizes that in Hebrew the essence of everything, or "what," is also called the *ma*, indicating the essence and question "What?" and man. The *ma* is empty, as is the space between two atoms. Empty—and yet we know that this void is the expression of a powerful energy that links and bonds two atoms, just as the void of the universe links and contains the planets and the galaxy.

It becomes easier to understand why this void appears as the true reality of everything. Michel Random, a French expert on Japanese culture, remembers spending a whole day with the famous writer Yukio Mishima: "While he was taking me on a tour of his home, I noted with surprise that all of the furnishings were either modern or eighteenth-century French. 'Why do you not having anything Japanese in your home?' Mishima replied with a laugh: 'Here only the invisible is Japanese.' "

The Tree and the Serpent, the Body and the Void

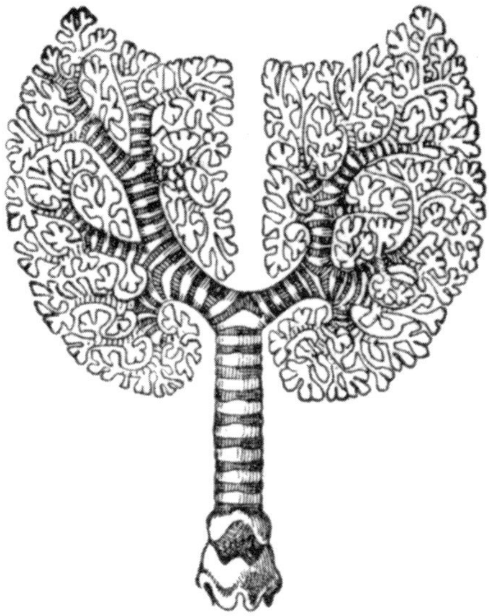

Can one live without a void?

Let us conduct an interesting experiment.

To live, man needs a nutritional and respiratory input of energy. This input of energy reaches the body and passes into it via the respiratory and alimentary canals, the trachea and the bronchiae, as well as through the mouth and esophagus. These are empty conduits.

What would happen if they were not kept empty?

What would happen if liquid plaster were poured into the trachea and the bronchiae?

What shape would one find if one opened this filled body? That of a tree in reverse. It is for this reason that the term "bronchial tree" is used. And if the mouth and esophagus were filled, would one not find the image of a serpent, its head and body?

One could advance the following theory: The images of the serpent and the tree that are at the center of the symbolism and the original sin in the Book of Genesis find their origin in a very specific consciousness that sin is the act of not respecting the internal void within man, not respecting the heart of the being, the "nothing" at the ontological core of existence.

No doubt this is the meaning of the words that Rabbi Levi Isaac of Berditchev repeats and comments upon throughout his works, especially in the *Parashat Mishpatim:* "Everyone has a duty to look at their nothingness and to respect it"*(Kol ekhad ve'ekhad tsarikh lehistakel al ayin shelo oolekhabed oto").*

33

Astrology and the Kabbalah

If each letter represents an image, each letter also has a corresponding time, first and foremost the twelve months of the year. It is important to realize that the calendar kept by the Kabbalah, the Jewish calendar, is both lunar and solar. The start of each month, which is called *rosh khodesh* (literally "the head of the month"), is defined by the new moon. The full moon always corresponds exactly to the fifteenth of the month. There are months of twenty-nine and thirty days.

The first month of the year begins with the spring. The Bible has no names for the months, which are designated simply by the terms "first month," "second month," and so on. It was only later, after the Babylonian exile, that the Jews imported names for the months, names that were of Babylonian origin. The following table shows how the Hebrew months correspond to the calendar used in the West:

Nissan: March–April	*Tishri:* September–October
Iyar: April–May	*Kheshvan:* October–November
Sivan: May–June	*Kislev:* November–December
Tamuz: June–July	*Tevet:* December–January
Av: July–August	*Shevat:* January–February
Elul: August–September	*Adar:* February–March

Since the Hebrew calendar is both lunar and solar, to catch up with the sun cycle, in some years there are thirteen months. These are said to be "pregnant" or "embolismic" *(meooberet).* This thirteenth month is called Adar II *(Adar sheni),* and it follows the last month, which becomes Adar I *(Adar rishon).*

Kabbalistic astrology uses the Hebrew alphabet to relay the internal energy of each month. Its twenty-two letters are the tools between the concrete and the spiritual worlds, which are used to link them together.

Astrology and Freedom of Choice

There is a very important expression in the Talmud and the Kabbalah, "En Mazal le'Yisrael" ("Israel is not subject to the influence of the stars"). The stars do not determine anything. Despite the wheel of fate, we have an almost limitless degree of freedom of choice. The horoscope contains constraints, restrictions, and blinkers that prevent us from feeling free or becoming free. These constraints and restrictions represent a certain level of existence, but we can overcome them and thus gain access to a higher level of consciousness.

This access is only gained through a higher form of meditation and by living a more spiritual life. Only then can we become masters of our destiny—which appears at first to be so restrictive—and be free of it. Then we can finally go beyond and change our star charts.

When an individual is born on a particular day, the kabbalist has no difficulty in reading the report of his psychological profile. More importantly, by following this chart, the individual can acquaint himself with its initial plan, create another, and thus escape from being locked into a situation of predestination.

Astrology is important in the Kabbalah because it teaches us that we can overcome the first givens of our chart. The horoscope must never be allowed to affect freedom of choice. The words *star* and later *destiny* are both translated as *mazal* in Hebrew—"that which flows, which lets pass." The word is also used to designate astrological signs. What is the link between the two meanings?

Rabbinical calendar, at the beginning of a Bible
drawn in 1300 by Joshua Ben Abraham Ben Gaon.

The constellations are channels of energy; they are filters of the light. In fact, they receive energy from infinity, obstructing part of the life force but allowing another part to flow through. The role of kabbalistic astrology is not to calculate horoscopes nor even to predict the future, but to understand the weight of the influences we have to deal with every month, and consequently to protect us from the negative aspects present in the universe.

It is learning in order to understand and escape the dangers.

Kabbalistic astrology follows the dictum, "Know thyself," so we do not fall passively into the trap of our natural inclinations. There are no bad signs or unlucky moments. In every case, man can find good and transform evil into good.

Stars and Disasters: Escaping One's Fate

Being free is not at all doing what one wants to but wanting what one can.
—Jean-Paul Sartre

Freedom is not the freedom to succeed but the freedom to undertake. Undertake with resolve; a freedom to plan, that is always in the planning stage; a creative freedom.
–Jean-Paul Sartre

The text of the Bible and the commentaries of the Talmud teach that Abraham entered into history in the very moment at which he closed the gates of destiny.

> He said: "Lord God, Adonai-Elohim, what will you give me? Seeing that I shall die childless, and the one in charge of my household is Eliezer, a son of Damascus. . . . Since you have granted me no offspring, my steward shall be my heir!" The word of the Lord came to him in reply "That one shall not be your heir; none but your very own issue shall be your heir."
>
> And he took him outside and said, "Look toward heaven and count the stars, if you are able to count them." . . . So shall your offspring be."
> (Genesis 15:2–5)

Rashi offers the following commentary about this last verse:

"He took him outside." This means in the literal sense that He took him out of his tent in order to show him the stars. The Midrash interprets the sentence to mean that God was telling him, "Leave! Leave your astrology, leave your destiny. It is true that Abraham was destined to be childless but Abraham would have a child. It is also true that Sarah, your wife, was destined to be childless, but Sarah would have a child. I shall change your names to change your stars, to change your fate."

Leave your fate! Leave your astrology!

The Talmud comments on the story, using the expression "ayn mazal le-Yisrael,"meaning literally, "Israel is not subject to the influence of the stars"!

"Israel," in biblical terminology, refers to anyone who, like the patriarch Jacob, became Israel after his struggle with the Angel (Genesis 32). Jacob fought; although victorious, he was left with a limp. "Acquiring a limp" was part of his victory. But the struggle has never ended. Jacob's fight with the angel is first and foremost just that—overcoming, in human existence, the angelism of a history written with ease. It is the rejection of a history that is already mapped out in advance, like a destiny.

"There are no stars for Israel" means that man must not submit himself to astrological destiny, to astrological determinism, or to determinism of any kind. Submission to the stars *(astres)* is a "disaster" *(désastre)*, according to the play on words devised by Maurice Blanchot in *L'Ecriture du désastre.*

The history of a people in general and the individual in particular lies precisely in the fact of "not being destined." The action of men, their deeds, and their words have produced all the possible ruptures, upheavals, and shifts in the course of history. Fate does not precede history, it follows it.

A man who does not wrench himself away from his fate is, in the terminology used by the Czech philosopher Jan Patocka, a "prehistoric" man.

"Prehistory" is not a period or an era but an attitude to the world. Being "prehistoric" is the failure to rebel, when man accepts the world passively, in the naive evidence of an unquestioning simplicity. The "prehistoric" man is the man of the "star signs," whose destiny has been carved out for him, who slavishly hangs upon the words of astrologers and fortunetellers.

But even the prehistoric attitude is not definitive. Man is capable of reversing the situation at any time; the questioning, historic man can make his entrance at any moment. He must then adopt an attitude of rejection and begin to question fate. He abandons the violence of ready-made thoughts and situations in which he is anonymous, overwhelmed by the mass of the "one" in which he was spoken of without ever having access to himself. The puppet theater is replaced by a theater of live actors in which "man conjugates with the unexpected."

The relationship of the Kabbalah with astrology is one of the abandonment of the astrologic and the prehistoric. The kabbalist becomes the creator of the question; he agrees to bear fruit and become the creative freedom and the planning stage. To do so, he has to abandon the world of "star-disaster."

Astrology and the Tetragrammaton

As was stressed in the basic ground plan, the tetragrammaton is the most important intermediary, synthesizing all the others and thus combining and including all of them within itself. It is, at one and the same time, the *sefirot,* Jacob's ladder, the columns of the Temple, the three columns on which the world rests, the letters of the alphabet, the numbers, and more. Everything takes place through the tetragrammaton; all the energy from on high passes through the structure of the tetragrammaton to reach the human being and give him life and the breath of existence.

The tetragrammaton consists of four parts (Y-H-V-H), while the year is divided into two parts. The first six months, from Aries to Virgo, are male; these months are linked with the desire to give and correspond to the first two letters of the tetragrammaton: YH. The last six months, from Libra to Pisces, are female; these months represent the *kelim,* the receptacles, which they receive, and correspond to the letters VH of the tetragrammaton.

Each of the twelve months also corresponds to a different combination of the tetragrammaton. In fact, there is a sign of the zodiac for each month, one letter of the alphabet, one part of the body, and a combination of four letters of the tetragrammaton. Kabbalistic astrology analyzes this set of data not to foretell the future or a person's fate but to understand how a person can become free and escape his or her predestination.*

ה	Aries	March	♈
ו	Taurus	April	♉
ז	Gemini	May	♊
ח	Cancer	June	♋
ט	Leo	July	♌
י	Virgo	August	♍
ל	Libra	September	♎
נ	Scorpio	October	♏
ס	Sagittarius	November	♐
ע	Capricorn	December	♑
צ	Aquarius	January	♒
ק	Pisces	February	♓

Table of Correspondence

* The reader is referred to the book by Jacques Halbronn, *Le Monde juif et l'astrologie,* and should also consult the following works: Rav Matitiahu Glazerson, *Les Secrets de l'astrologie hébraïque*; and Saadya Gaon, *Commentary on the Sefer Yetsira.*

Part Six

Gematria

The Art of Making Figures Speak

6

Aleph	א	a	1
Bet *or vet*	ב	b	2
Gimmel	ג	c	3
Dalet	ד	d	4
Heh	ה	e	5
Vav	ו	f, u, v, w	6
Zayin	ז	g, z	7
Khet	ח	kh	8
Tet	ט	t	9
Yod	י	i, j, y	10
Kaf *or khaf*	כ	k	20
Lamed	ל	l	30
Mem	מ	m	40
Nun	נ	n	50
Samekh	ס	x	60
Ayin	ע	o	70
Peh *or pheh*	פ	p	80
Tsadeh	צ	*ts*	90
Qof	ק	q	100
Resh	ר	r	200
Shin *or sin*	ש	sh *or s*	300
Tav	ת	t	400
final Kaf	ך	k	500
final Mem	ם	m	600
final Nun	ן	n	700
final Peh	ף	p	800
final Tsadeh	ץ	*ts*	900

34

Numbers and Letters
Gematria and Numerology

Gematria: The Numerical Value of Language

Gematria, the calculation of the numerical value of Hebrew letters and words, is one of the thirty-two rules of hermeneutics recorded by Rabbi Yossi Ha-Galili at the end of the tractate Berakhot of the Talmud. Gematria is the twenty-ninth of the thirty-two rules, a *halakha le-Moshe mi-Sinai*—a rule transmitted to Moses from Sinai, and thus an integral part of Oral Law.

Hebrew alphabetic numeration is based on the decimal system. It uses all twenty-two letters of the Hebrew alphabet, plus the five final letters, by associating them with figures in the following order:

- the first nine letters represent the nine simple numbers, from 1 through 9
- the next nine represent the tens, from 10 through 90
- the next four represent the first four hundreds—100, 200, 300, 400
- the five final letters represent 500, 600, 700, 800, and 900

There are thus three levels, each containing nine elements:

- units: 1, 2, 3, 4, 5, 6, 7, 8, 9
- tens: 10, 20, 30, 40, 50, 60, 70, 80, 90
- hundreds: 100, 200, 300, 400, 500, 600, 700, 800, 900.

It should be noted that in Hebrew, the letters *kaf, mem, nun, samekh, peh,* and *tsadeh* are written differently when they occur at the end of a word. They are then said to be "final" and have a different numerical value. The final *kaf* represents 500; the final *mem*, 600; the final *nun*, 700; the final *peh*, 800; the final *tsadeh*, 900. However, the majority of kabbalists do not abide by this rule, which is used for practical purposes in Talmudic and modern Hebrew, as in representing the Hebrew date and in the page numbering of this book, and give the final letters the same numerical value as they have when used in their nonfinal shape.

Anyone wanting to use the numerological system of gematria to work out numbers of words in the Latin alphabet must ensure that the Hebrew letters chosen correspond to the correct letters in the Latin alphabet. The table on the preceding page shows the corresponding Hebrew and Latin letters, with their numerical values.

For example, the numerical value of the first name, Heloise:

חהלעישה

H+E+L+O+I+S+E

8 + 5 + 30 + 70 + 10 + 300 + 5

428

35

The Various Methods of Gematria
Playing with Figures and Letters

Mystique and Mystification: A Preliminary Remark

Hebrew writing consists of twenty-two letters, all of them consonants. Each letter represents both a letter and a number. Each association of letters may become a word and a number. The Hebrew language thus contains a set of very serious "plays" on figures and letters that make it possible to produce an infinite number of interpretations and new perspectives. These "games" with figures and letters are known as gematria, a Greek term related to the English word *geometry* ("measure of the earth").

Gematria is one of the most popular aspects of the Kabbalah, but the Kabbalah cannot be reduced merely to gematria. Every kabbalist worth his salt masters the secrets of gematria, but when all is said and done, an excellent Gematrist is nothing more than an excellent mathematician! It is often in this very realm of the Kabbalah that the difference is played out between mystique and mystification. . . .

At the end of this section the meaning of gematria will be discussed, but first it is worth knowing how this "sacred mathematics" works. Numerous methods of gematria are used. Here are the rules by which it operates and some examples to help the reader understand how it is used.

Simple Gematria

Simple gematria is the most frequently used. It is a straight translation of words into figures and numbers on the basis of the table on page 334.

First example:

The word *herayon,* which means "pregnancy of a woman," has a numerical value of 271.

הריון

H + R + Y + U + N

5 + 200 + 10 + 6 + 50

271

This happens to be exactly the number of days of a woman's pregnancy (nine months, each lasting 30.11111 days, gives 271 days).

The Kabbalah (Nidda 38a and b) teaches:

> Shmuel said: "A woman can only go into labor two hundred and seventy-one, two hundred and seventy-two, or two hundred and seventy-three days after conception"; he was following the opinion of the pious men of old. We are taught in fact that the pious men of old only had sexual relations with their wives on the fourth day of the week, in order to avoid defiling the Sabbath (which would fall 271, 272, or 273 days later).
>
> "Only on the fourth day?"
>
> "Let us say: after the fourth day of the week."
>
> Mar Zutra asked: "What were their arguments?"
>
> "And it is written: 'The Lord let her conceive . . .' [*herayon*] (Ruth 4:13)"

Thus the numerical value of *herayon* is 271.

Here is a second example:

The word *adam* is written ADM and has a gematria of 45. This number is written using two letters, *mem* and *heh,* producing *ma,* "What?"

אדם	מה
aleph-dalet-mem	*mem-heh*
A + D + M	M + E
1 + 4 + 40	40 + 5
45	45

A third, and even more surprising, example:

In Hebrew, "father" is *av.*

Mother in Hebrew is *em,* which is written *aleph-mem.* The same word can also be given a different vowel, producing *im,* which means "if."

Father, *av,* has a numerical value of 3 (*aleph* = 1; *bet* = 2), whereas mother, *em,* offers a gematria of 41 (*aleph* = 1; *mem* = 40).

father		**mother**
av		*em*
אב		אם
aleph-bet		*aleph-mem*
1 + 2		1 + 40
3	+	41
	44	
	child	
	yeled	
	ילד	
	yod-lamed-dalet	
	10 + 30 + 4	

This extraordinary mathematical result shows that a combination of the words *av* and *em,* "father" and "mother," translates numerically into the number 44, the precise numerical value of the word *yeled,* child: father + mother = child.

Rabbi Isaac Luria completes this gematria with another remark concerning a sexual encounter. For the Kabbalah, this is the union between the twenty-two Hebrew letters of the alphabet donated by the father and the twenty-two donated by the mother. The encounter between the maternal alphabet and the paternal alphabet gives birth to a child.

This is also "confirmed" by the gematria. The gematria or numerical value of the word *yeled* is: *yod* (= 10) + *lamed* (= 30) + *dalet* (= 4), making a total of 44, which is the sum of the two parental alphabets!

In this example, gematria invites us to consider the following idea. Saying that "father" and "mother," each in their own way, possess the twenty-two letters of the Hebrew alphabet is expressing the fundamental relationship between language and fertility; it is stressing the fact that "making" a child is first and foremost a dialogue and that the human being anchors the possibility of his existence in the linguistic potential unleashed in speech.

Simple Expanded Gematria

The second category of gematria retains the same numerical values of the letters but separates each word into its individual letters and calculates the sum of the word on this basis. In such a case, the maximum number of letters needed to produce the word are used.

Take, for example, the letter *yod,* the tenth letter of the alphabet; it can be written as a "y," in its simple form, or as "yod," the expanded form. In English, for example, the letter "h" is the simple form and "aitch" the expanded form.

First example:

Take the word *yeled.* In simple gematria, it has been shown to possess a numerical value of 44. If the letters are broken down individually, they produce the following result:

י *yod* is written *yod-vav-dalet* (10 + 6 + 4 = 20);
ל *lamed* is written *lamed-mem-dalet* (30 + 40 + 4 = 74);
ד *dalet* is written *dalet-lamed-tav* (4 + 30 + 400 = 434).

This gives a total of 528, which is the simple expanded gematria of *yeled.*

Second example:

In simple gematria, the tetragrammaton YHVH has a numerical value of 26 (10 + 5 + 6 + 5). In simple expanded gematria, the Name is written

י *yod* (*yod-vav-dalet* = 10 + 6 + 4 = 20);
ה *heh* (*heh-aleph* = 5 + 1 = 6);
ו *vav* (*vav-aleph-vav* = 6 + 1 + 6 = 13);
ה *heh* (*heh-aleph* = 5 + 1 = 6).

The total is thus 20 + 6 + 13 + 6 = 45.

The tetragrammaton in its expanded form produces 45, or *shem ma.**

* This type of expanded reading is used in the Kabbalah mainly in relation to the names of God.

The Little Gematria

The little gematria uses the same numerical values as the standard gematria but only takes account of numbers in units.

Thus, for example, 10 and 100 become 1, just as 20 and 200 are 2, 30 and 300 are 3, and so on.

Example:

It has been shown that the word *herayon,* "pregnancy," has a numerical value of:

הריון

H + R + Y + U + N

5 + 200 + 10 + 6 + 50

271

In little gematria, this produces:

5 + 2 + 1 + 6 + 5

19

19 itself becomes 10 + 9

which produces 1 + 9

10

which produces 1

The same result, based on 271, is obtained by adding up the figures. The sum of (2 + 7 + 1) equals 10, which is thus equal to 1.

Cumulative Dynamic Gematria *(Ribooa)*

"Cumulative dynamic gematria" takes into account the fact that a word is a letter-by-letter construct based on various successive stages, each of which has a meaning in itself. It involves seeing the word and the world not as what they are but in their various constituent parts.

Since the demonstration of this form of gematria was originally produced using the names of God, especially those names that consist of four letters, this cumulative dynamic gematria is called *ribooa,* "quadrature" or "squaring" (from the root *arba,* "four").

First example:

Let us take an example in English:

The word *child* can be written all in one piece, "child," or each stage can be stressed, by writing each letter, then adding the next on the next line. The result is:

C
CH
CHI
CHIL
CHILD

The same example is used in Hebrew from the word *yeled* ("child"), which is written using the *ribooa:*

Y
YL
YLD

The gematria would thus be:

10
10 + 30 = 40
10 + 30 + 4 = 44
Total = 94

It should be noted that in the little gematria, 9 and 4 produce 13, a number that corresponds to the age at which boys become men, the bar mitzvah.

Second example:

Let us take the Holy Name Ehyeh, "I shall be," the expression through which God revealed himself to Moses in the incident of the Burning Bush.

אהיה

We have four letters, *aleph-heh-yod-heh,* which produce the following cumulative dynamic gematria:

aleph	1
aleph-heh	1 + 5 = 6
aleph-heh-yod	1 + 5 + 10 = 16
aleph-heh-yod-heh	1 + 5 + 10 + 5 = 21
	Total = 44

It can thus be said that the cumulative dynamic gematria of Ehyeh is 44.

This number is not new to us, since it corresponds to the simple gematria for "child," *yeled.*

This is a good example of the attraction of gematria. After having demonstrated the relationship between "I shall be" and "child," one must ask oneself what this similarity means. This is where the interpreter comes onto the scene, and we pass from what might be called the objective dimension of gematria to its purely subjective dimension. Anyone can and may produce a personal interpretation.

Third example:

It is written thus in the Book of Deuteronomy (27:2–8):

> Moses and the elders of Israel charged the people . . . : You shall set up large stones. Coat them with plaster and inscribe upon them all the words of the Torah. . . . Upon crossing the Jordan, you shall set up these stones. . . . And on these stones you shall inscribe every word of the Torah, explain them well.

The expression "explain them well" is *ba'er hetev* in Hebrew. The Talmud comments in tractate Sota (32a), "*ba'er hetev,* this means in seventy languages."

How does the Talmud deduce from the expression *ba'er hetev* that "explain them well," means translating them into seventy languages? The Vilna Gaon comments in *Liqootei Hagra,* "If we make a *ribooa* of *hetev,* we in fact obtain 70!" *Hetev* is written, *he-yod-tet-bet:*

היטב

thus producing:

he	5
he-yod	5 + 10 = 15
he-yod-tet	5 + 10 + 9 = 24
he-yod-tet-bet	5 + 10 + 9 + 2 = 26
	Total = 70

The simple gematria of *hetev* is 26:

he-yod-tet-bet

making 5 + 10 + 9 + 2.

The difference between simple gematria (26) and cumulative dynamic gematria or *ribooa* (70) is 44 (70 – 26).

Seventy is an important number in the Kabbalah, one which we have already encountered in the basic ground plan. It is the number for *sod*, "secret."

One could comment: in order to pass from "well-*hetev*-26" to "secret-*sod*-70," the dimension of 44 (the child, *yeled*) must be maintained, since he is always excited about new things and has that extraordinary glow that was mentioned in the short commentary concerning *tiqva*, "hope."

It is the custom on the Festival of Lights (Hanukkah) to light an eight-branched candelabra in memory of the victory of the Maccabeans over the Greeks in the year 166 B.C.E. An additional light is kindled each evening, on the principle that holiness must be increased, not diminished. On the first night, one light is lit; on the second, two; on the third, three, and so on until all eight are lit on the eighth night.

The total number of candles lit over the eight days is thirty-six.

$$1 + 2 + 3 + 4 + 5 + 6 + 7 + 8$$

This number corresponds to the hidden light of the thirty-six hidden just men on whom the fate of the world depends.*

Some commentaries note that in fact, each evening the number of candles lit corresponds to the day, but there is an extra one that is used to light the others and that burns beside them. This light is called the *shamash* ("servant"). There are thus thirty-six lights in all, plus the eight *shamashim*, which makes a total of forty-four lights.

The number forty-four crops up again!

Differential Gematria

Differential gematria consists in calculating the numerical value that exists between two letters.**

* See André Schwarz-Bart, *The Last of the Just*.

** We would like to acknowledge the assistance of Laurent Picard, who initiated us into this form of gematria, which is his *khidush* (innovation).

To make it clearer, let us take the example of a two-letter Hebrew word.

We could use the word *shem,* "name," which consists of the letters *shin* and *mem,* whose numerical values are 300 and 40 respectively. Differential gematria consists in understanding what unites the two letters *shin* and *mem*. The meaning of a name is not the addition of two letter—such as *shin* + *mem*—but the movement, the direction that leads from the *shin* to the *mem,* the direction that we discovered in the indications provided in their numerical values:

shin → *mem*

300 → 40

260

In order to pass from the *shin* to the *mem,* from 300 to 40, one must go via 260, which is thus the differential gematria in this instance.

Gematria in Alphabetical Order (Gematria *Siduri*)

Although it is used only infrequently, this gematria consists of giving letters a value related to their position in the alphabet. Thus, *aleph* is 1, and *kaf* is 11, not 20 as in standard gematria. The values of the letters are from 1 through 22 (or from 1 through 27 if the final letters are counted as well).

Example:

Take the same word *yeled,* "child," which is written Y-L-D. In classic gematria it has a value of 44. In gematria according to alphabetical order, the following is obtained—

Y = 10

L = 12

D = 4

—making a total of 26. The kabbalists drew fascinating conclusions since when calculated using simple Gematria for the tetragrammaton the answer is also 26, a number for which we offer an interpretation in the chapters devoted to the names of God.

The Gematria of Permutation (*AT-BaCh*)

According to the Midrash Tana'im, a table of equivalents was revealed to Moses on Mount Sinai, in which the first letter of the alphabet, the *aleph,* is interchangeable with the last letter, the *tav;* the second, the *bet,* is interchangeable with the second-last, the *shin,* and so on. These permutations were called the *At-BaCh,* the initials of the first four letters used in these permutations. The result is the following table:

aleph → *tav*
bet → *shin*
gimmel → *resh*
dalet → *qof*
heh → *tsadeh*
vav → *peh*
zayin → *ayin*
khet → *samekh*
tet → *nun*
yod → *mem*
kaf → *lamed*

For example: The word *bereshit,* the first word in the Hebrew Bible, becomes *shagabama.* This last word has no meaning, but it provides another gematria that could lead to some important considerations.

It should be noted that for the mystic, that a word does not mean anything is a gateway to the possibility of detaching it from its ties with the world and thus attaining higher levels of consciousness. It is a way of creating a void and awaiting the *ayin,* "the nothing." It is thus a meditation procedure identical to that of the *tseruf,* which suddenly reveals a word that means nothing. There are numerous cases, however, in which the word that appears through the permutation of *At-BaCh* does indeed have a meaning.

Gematria of Permutation (*El-BaM*)

The Midrash Tana'im reproduces another table of equivalents, which it also claims was revealed on Sinai. The principle is identical to the previous permutation system, but the *aleph* is coupled with the *lamed*, and the *bet* with the *mem*, hence the expression *El-BaM.*

This produces the following table:

aleph → *lamed*
bet → *mem*
gimmel → *nun*
dalet → *samekh*
heh → *ayin*
vav → *peh*
zayin → *tsadeh*
khet → *qof*
tet → *resh*
yod → *shin*
kaf → *tav*

So *At-BaCh* and *El-BaM* are merely two variations of the same idea.

The twenty-two-letter alphabet is divided into two segments of eleven letters each. The first eleven letters, from *aleph* through *kaf*, are written vertically; then the second eleven letters are cut, once starting at the end, from *tav* through *lamed*, and once in the natural order of the alphabet from *lamed* through *tav.*

The commentators have also remarked that the internal movement of the alphabet is in the dimension of *khessed* (grace and ontological entropy) when the letters are in alphabetical order, and in the dimension of *din* (rigor and structure of the being) when deployed in reverse alphabetical order.

The majority of words combine *khessed* and *din*, and in numerous cases they establish a balance between the two dimensions.

Examples:

AV, "father," is written *aleph-bet* (the letters being in alphabetical order).

SaV, "grandfather," is written *samekh-bet* (the letters are in the reverse order, because *samekh* comes after *bet*).

Note that the part that changes in the *tseruf* is not only the meaning but the division between *din* and *khessed*, that is to say, the ontological balance of the word.

Gematria by Jumping a Level in the Alphabetical Structure *(AYaQ BaKhaR)*

We saw at the beginning of this section that the letters were divided into three levels:

- the units: 9 letters;
- the tens: 9 letters;
- the hundreds: 9 letters with the final letters.

Thus, for example, that which corresponds to the *aleph* is the *yod* on the second level and the *qof* on the third level. Similarly, the *bet* becomes *kaf* on the second level and *resh* on the third level.

Through this rule, revealed on Sinai, it is possible to switch the letters within a word to the second or third level, which would produce different words and numerical values. This permutation system is called *AYaQ BaKhaR,* for the initials of the first letters in each of the three levels:

aleph → *yod* → *qof* = *AYQ* (pronounced "*ayaQ*")
bet → *kaf* → *resh* = *BKR* (pronounced "*baKhaR*")

The *Kollel:* Adding to the Usual Value

A 1 is often added to the numerical value of a word or phrase. This method is called "gematria *im hakollel*"—"gematria with inclusion." According to Rabbi Eizik Haver, a disciple of the Vilna Gaon, this addition is explainable by the fact that the root of a word is closely linked to its higher source.

Example: The numerical value of *berit,* "pact," is 612 (2 + 200 + 10 + 400), which, added to its supreme source, 1, produces 613, the number of the commandments in the Torah.

According to the commentators, justification for using the *kollel* can be found in the Torah itself, in (Genesis 48:5), where it is written, "Ephraim and Menashe shall be mine no less than Reuben and Simeon." The verse thus produces the equation:

Ephraim and *Menashe* = *Reuben* and *Simeon*

confirmed in the gematria of names. But this equation only becomes correct if one adds the *kollel*, the "+ 1".

$$(331 + 395) = (259 + 466) + 1$$

There is a variation of the *kollel* that consists in adding the number of letters to the word, if one is using gematria on a word, or the number of words, if one is using gematria on an expression.

Examples:

Khalom, "dream," has a numerical value of 78
(with the *kollel* : + 1 = 79).
Khalom tov, "good dream," has a numerical value of 78 + 17 = 95
(with the *kollel* : + 2 = 97).

Notarikon

Notarikon is not true gematria. The method does not necessarily involve figures. It is the science of acronyms (making the initials of a group of words into a word).

Examples in common English usage include:

In mathematics and economics, *notarikons* are used frequently: GDP: gross domestic product; SCD: smallest common denominator; QED: *Quod erat demonstrandum*, Latin for thus it has been shown.

Associations also frequently use *notarikon*, as in: FDA: Food and Drug Administration; UN: United Nations; NATO: North Atlantic Treaty Organization; AP: Associated Press; SEC: Securities and Exchange Commission.

There are even examples in such expressions as the word *posh*, which is an acronym for "port out, starboard home," referring to the favored shady side for a stateroom on ships sailing between England and India.

This play on words is an important reading method for kabbalists, who take account of the initials or the last letters of words.

Examples in Hebrew:

The three final letters of the first three words of the Bible—*bereshiT barA elohiM* ("In the beginning, God created . . .")—create the word *emet* ("truth").

אמת

In the expression *lekhem min hashamayim*, "bread from the skies," used to designate the manna that God sent down to the Children of Israel during their forty-year wanderings in the desert, the initials of the Hebrew words produce *LaMaH*, which means, "Why?"

On the other hand, a word can become an expression. That is the case in the example of the month of Elul, the month that precedes the Jewish New Year, which is written *aleph-lamed-vav-lamed*. The initials of this month read as an acronym produce *Ani Ledodi Vedodi Li* ("I am my beloved's and he is mine," from the Song of Songs). The name of God, ShaDaI, that is written on the parchment inside the *mezzuzot* that Jews fix to the doorposts of their houses, reads as the *notarikon* of *Shomer Daltot Israel*, "guardian of the doors of Israel."

In fact *notarikon* depends on the powers of the imagination of the interpreter, which enables him to discover acronyms in biblical verses or groups of words, or even to construct a *notarikon* from a group of words or verses.

Temura

Temura derives from the Hebrew word *lehamir* and means "permutation."

It is a form of *tseruf* that is both more flexible and more complex, because one can take a word and break it down into two, then produce a permutation of some of these letters but not the others, and so on. This is what is called "reading in bursts."

Example:

The word *khokhma,* "wisdom," becomes *koakh-ma,* "force of what?"

The word *bereshit,* "in the beginning," becomes *berit esh,* "pact of fire," or *bara shit,* "he created six."

The "Nut Garden"

The initials of the words *gematria, notarikon,* and *temura* form the word *gnt,* which is pronounced "*ginat*" and means "the garden of. . . ." This has produced several plays on words among the kabbalists, as well as titles of kabbalistic works, such as the *Ginat Egoz* ("The Nut Garden," by Rabbi Joseph Gikatillia, a reference to the Song of Songs).

The walnut is a kabbalistic symbol, since it has a thick husk or shell *(qlipa),* and the fruit inside is shaped like a brain with its two hemispheres. Furthermore, the word *egoz* has a numerical value of 17, which is also that of the word *tov,* "good."*

Nut is also, therefore, a form of homage coded in the second degree to the author of the Zohar, Rabbi Moses Shem Tov of Leon.

The gematria of *tov* must have been well known in Spain from the thirteenth through the seventeenth centuries. Cervantes himself alludes to it in *Don Quixote,* when he calls the Dulcinea of Toboso "the Dulcinea of Tov," a "seventeen-letter name," to use his own expression.

Gematria: A Way of Releasing Energies

Gematria is not a game of figures and letters but a method of opening up, of interpretation, and of momentum for the thought processes. It is a brilliant instrument for interpreting and expanding texts, breaking the husks that conceal the inner light of words and thus entwining with the infinite light of which they are the source.

It is important to stress that the reader should pay less attention to the

* As regards the secret of the walnut, see the article by Josef Dan in *Jewish Studies,* no. 17 (1966): 73.

size of the numbers than to the letters, which are combined through the numerical equivalents, whose juxtaposition always has great philosophical significance. It is from this rapprochement that the meaning emerges; this is a process of deep thought and contemplation.

Gematria is a way of opening up to something else, a pretext, a springboard, a passage; it is not enough to devise equations and show equalities. The meaning is not in the original word nor in the word arrived at, but somewhere between the two.

Gematria is a starting point for thought; it is not thought itself. It is not a translation but a proposition, an invitation to wander down an unknown path. Gematria makes it possible to go "beyond the verse."

The role of gematria is to extract a word from the primary meaning given to it by letters; thus the word enters into a dynamic that makes it tend toward infinity. The book is the site of an explosion. The word is no longer perceived as an isolated entity but in a complete set of relationships; this then produces a sliding of infinity itself into the closed wording.

The transition from a "word-in-letters" to a "number-in-figures" that returns, in its turn, to a word formed of letters, and so on, introduces us to knowledge that is no longer a totality but a process of expansion and dynamism. Gematria should not be reduced to a mere technique, it must be the starting point for a train of thought. Gematria is a technique of mysticism.

By permutating the letters of which a word consists, by seeking their numerical values, by changing, substituting, transposing, combining, splitting letters and words, the kabbalist is drawn into an extended meditation that leads him into the heart of the energy that resides within the letters.

There is an energy in letters and between the letters. The act of "reading in bursts" releases an energy received by the kabbalist, who uses it for himself and to transmit to those around him.

6

36

The Secret of Perfect Numbers and Friendly Numbers
Pythagoras and the Kabbalah

Mathematicians love to build bridges.
—Barry Mazur

So do kabbalists.
—Kafka might have added

The Baal Ha-Orot, the Master of Lights, taught that *khidush,* that is novelties for the mind and intellectual discoveries, often result from interdisciplinary encounters. This is particularly true of mathematics and the Kabbalah.

"The value of bridges in mathematics is considerable," writes the mathematician Barry Mazur;

> They make it possible for groups of mathematicians living on distant islands to exchange ideas and explore the creations of others. For mathematics are islands of knowledge in an ocean of ignorance. For example, there is an island of geometrists, who study contours and shapes, there is an island of probabilists, on which mathematicians study risks and probabilities.
>
> These islands can be counted by the dozen and each has its own language that is incomprehensible to the inhabitants of the others. The language of geometry is very different to that of probability, and the jargon of differential calculus is impenetrable for those who are only concerned with statistics.
>
> (Quoted in Simon Singh, *Fermat's Last Theorem*)

The same is true of the Kabbalah. Kabbalists are obliged to build bridges between the various fields of their own discipline, as well as with other disciplines that may appear to the uninitiated to be foreign to it. According to a teaching by Rav Léon Yehuda Askenazi (known as Manitou), there was once an important meeting between kabbalists and the school of Pythagoras. Pythagoras had learned the secrets of the organization of the world from the masters of the Kabbalah, and passed them on in turn to his school, known as the Fraternity of Pythagoras. It would appear that the influences were in fact mutual, and that the researches of the Pythagoreans had a reciprocal influence on the schools of kabbalism. We shall briefly mention Pythagoras and his school in order to show the importance of certain meeting points between the two schools.*

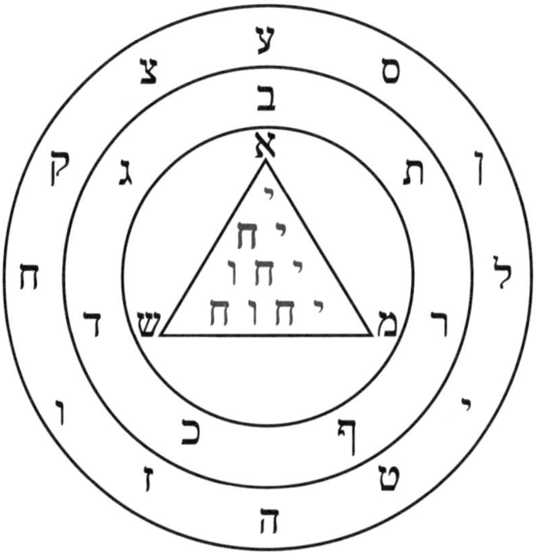

The Tetragramnon as a *ribooa* inside three circles which demonstrate the level of the letters according to the *Sefer Yetsira*: the three mother letters, the seven double letters, and the twelve single letters. This *ribooa* is based on the Pythagorean tetractys (1 + 2 + 3 + 4 = 10).

* We would like to thank Lazare Kaplan for telling us about *Fermat's Last Theorem* by Simon Singh, which has opened up many new horizons in the field of mathematics and made it possible to formulate a few important *khidushim.* We recommend the reader to another extremely instructive book which is a serious mathematical work, containing a wealth of information and anecdotes, the *Théorème du Perroquet* by Denis Guedj. The biography Pythagoras used here is based on Singh's version.

Everything Is Number

Pythagoras of Samos exercised a huge influence over mathematics. His character is shrouded in mystery. There is no firsthand information about his life and work, and since he is shrouded in myth and legend, historians have difficulty in distinguishing fact from fiction.

Pythagoras acquired his mathematical knowledge in the course of his journeys. It is claimed that he got as far as India and Brittany, but it is much more likely that he collected some of his techniques and mathematical tools from the Egyptians and Babylonians.

The fact that Babylonia was one of the greatest sites of the development of the Kabbalah at the time is of crucial importance. This was in the sixth century B.C.E., exactly the era of the writings of the prophet Ezekiel, a Hebrew prophet who had been exiled to Babylonia, and was one of the first great mystics of the *merkava.*

The Egyptians and the Babylonians had gone beyond the limits of elementary arithmetic and were capable of performing complex operations that enabled them to devise sophisticated accounting systems and build architectural structures of great quality. Of course, they considered mathematics simply as a useful instrument for resolving practical problems; thus their reasons for researching some of the elementary rules of geometry were to re-establish the boundaries of the fields that were flooded during the annual rising of the Nile.

The word *geometry* itself signifies "measure of the earth." The word is found in the Kabbalah in the form of gematria, which, as has been shown previously, means anything that is related to numbers and geometric figures.

After twenty years of traveling, Pythagoras had learned all the mathematical rules of the known world. He went back to his home in Samos, on the Aegean Sea, with the intention of founding a school dedicated to philosophy, and especially to the rules of mathematics that he had discovered. He hoped to find numerous recruits with open minds who would help him to develop new, radical philosophies, but in his absence the tyrant Polycrates had changed the island. Once liberal, it had become intolerant and reactionary. Polycrates invited Pythagoras to his court, but the philosopher understood that this was a ruse destined to reduce him to silence, and he declined the offer. He left the city and went to live in a remote cave, where he could meditate without interruption.

The parallel with Rabbi Simeon Bar Yokhai is striking. Rabbi Simeon also had to flee the political authorities and also took refuge in a cave where he compiled his famous commentary that would later become the key text of kabbalistic thought—the Zohar.

Pythagoras found isolation difficult to bear and finally offered money to a boy to become his student. This pupil was also called Pythagoras. Pythagoras the master paid Pythagoras the student three obols per lesson. The master realized that after a few weeks the repugnance the boy had felt for knowledge had been replaced by enthusiasm. To gauge how successful he had been, Pythagoras pretended that he could no longer afford to pay his student and that the lessons must therefore end, at which point the boy offered to pay for his education rather than interrupt it. The student had become a disciple.

But the philosopher-mathematician was forced to flee from the island, along with his mother and his single disciple. Pythagoras set sail for southern Italy, which was then a Greek colony called Magna Graecia. He settled in Croton. There he was lucky enough to find the ideal patron, Milo, the richest man in the city and one of the strongest men known to history.

The reputation of Pythagoras, the "sage of Samos," had already spread throughout Greece, but that of Milo was even greater. He was a man of Herculean strength who had been crowned a record twelve times in the Olympic and Pythian Games. But apart from being an athlete, Milo studied and encouraged philosophy and mathematics. He reorganized his house so as to be able to offer Pythagoras enough space to be able to run a school. That is how the most creative mind and the most powerful body came together.

The Pythagorean Fraternity

From the security of his new headquarters, Pythagoras founded the Fraternity, a group of six hundred disciples who were not only capable of understanding his teaching but also able to take full advantage of the new ideas. Each disciple who joined the Fraternity had to donate all his possessions to a common pool; anyone who left it would receive double what he had put in on his arrival, and a stele was erected to his memory.

The Pythagorean Fraternity was an egalitarian institution, which included numerous sisters. Pythagoras' favorite students was Milo's own daughter, the beautiful Theano, and despite the difference in their ages, Pythagoras eventually married her.

Shortly after founding the Fraternity, Pythagoras invented the word *philosopher*, thus indicating the purpose of his school—to seek to discover the secrets of nature.

Pythagoras and Kabbalistic Circles

There are numerous parallels between the Pythagorean Fraternity and kabbalistic circles, especially the dimension of secrecy, but there is another fundamental difference that will be explained.

Many people were aware of the aims of Pythagoras, but nobody outside of the Fraternity was aware of the extent or the details of his success; each member of the school had to swear never to reveal any of his mathematical discoveries. It was known, however, that Pythagoras had established an ethic that would change the course of mathematics.

The Fraternity was a religious community, and one of the idols it worshiped was Number. Its members presumed that in understanding the relationships between numbers, they could discover the spiritual secrets of the universe and come closer to the gods. In this they were both close to and distant from the Kabbalah—close, because for the kabbalists numbers are also tools to be used to attain the most perfect understanding of the world—and thus accede to the worlds above and come closer to the light of infinity, the source of all worlds—but also very distant, for never in the Kabbalah is Number deified or confused with a god or idol. As far as the Kabbalah is concerned, the number remains a tool, a medium, an intermediary world, a sign.

The Search for the "Perfect Number"

The Fraternity were particularly interested in studying arithmetical numbers (1, 2, 3 . . .) and their fractions. Arithmetical numbers are also called whole numbers, and fractions are known in mathematical terminology as rational numbers; that is, proportional relationships between whole numbers. From the infinity of numbers, the Fraternity sought those that had a particular significance, of which a few of the most interesting were called "perfect" numbers.

According to Pythagoras, numerical perfection depended on the divisors of a number, some numbers dividing perfectly into an original number. The question of divisors is contained in the Kabbalah in reference to the founding action of the creation of the world—division. According to the text of Genesis, God created the world by dividing and separating it—the sky from the earth, light from darkness, day from night, the waters above from the waters below, the cosmos from chaos, the seas from the continents, and so on.

Pythagoras divided numbers into three categories:

- perfect numbers
- excessive numbers
- imperfect numbers.

When the sum of the divisors is larger than the number itself, such a number is termed an "excessive." Thus, since the divisors of 12 are 1, 2, 3, 4, and 6, 12 is an "excessive number," because the sum of its divisors is 16.

On the other hand, when the sum of the numbers of a divisor is less than the number itself, it is called an "imperfect" number. Thus, 10 is an "imperfect number" because the sum of its divisors (1, 2, and 5) is only 8.

The most significant and the rarest numbers are those whose divisors actually add up to the same number. Thus the number six 6, whose divisors are 1, 2, and 3, is a perfect number: $1 + 2 + 3 = 6$.

Perfect numbers are rare; between 0 and 1,000, there are only three—6, 28, and 496. (The fourth is 8,128, the fifth 33,550,336, and the sixth 8,589,869,056.)

The Mystery of the Figure 6

There is no shadow of a doubt that the kabbalistic tradition not only knew but also used perfect numbers, and this has been true since the most ancient times. The patriarchs of the Bible knew them, but the most significant proof of the fact lies in the formulation of the biblical text.

The eleventh chapter of *Tikkunei Zohar* teaches, "What is the meaning of the word 'bereshit,' the first word in the Book of Genesis? The literal translation is 'in the beginning,' but the kabbalistic tradition breaks down the word bereshit into two words 'bara shit,' that is to say 'he created six.' For the kabbalists, the beginning, the genesis of the universe, was inaugurated by the creation of 'six.'"

The actual structure of the text stresses this concept because the first word of the Bible (which means "he created six") consists of six letters. It can perhaps be understood, therefore, that the whole Jewish structure of time is based on the existence of the perfect number, 6. The world was created in six days. Then came the Sabbath. The slave had to work for six years, and he was freed in the seventh. Jews are allowed to till the soil for six days, but on the seventh the land rests, a process called *shemita.* The world was created for six thousand years, the seventh millennium will be the messianic age, and so on.

Even the Christian commentators and theologians observed the phenomenon of the perfection of numbers. There is evidence in the remarks of Saint Augustine in *The City of God,* in which he says, "although He was capable of creating the world in an instant, [God] decided to spend six days doing so in order to reflect the perfection of the universe." Furthermore, Saint Augustine claimed that 6 was not a perfect number because God had chosen it but rather because perfection is inherent in the nature of the universe: "Six is a perfect number in itself and not because God created everything in six days; the opposite, rather, is true; God created all things in six days because the number is perfect, and it would remain perfect even if the work of six days had never happened."

The Wisdom of the Number 28

Commentators have noted that the first verse of Genesis consists of exactly twenty-eight letters, 28 being the second perfect number. The book of the Zohar emphasizes this structure of the first verse in the expression *kaf-het atvan de ma'asse bereshit,* "the 28 letters of the creation of the beginning."

בְּרֵאשִׁית בָּרָא אֱלֹהִים אֵת הַשָּׁמַיִם וְאֵת הָאָרֶץ

"In the beginning, God created the heaven and the earth"

The number 28 is dwelt upon extensively in other texts. Note that in Hebrew, the number is written *kaf-khet,* which when read as a word, means "strength."

The word *khokhma,* "wisdom," is read as *koakh-ma,* an expression that can mean "strength of what?"—the "force of questioning," or "what is the strength of 28 ?"—as if the question surrounding the number 28 was a special form of wisdom in itself.

Rashi, the great commentator, is certain of the answer to the question when he devotes his first commentary on Genesis to an evocation of this "force-28." He quotes verse 6 of Psalm 111: "The power [*koakh*] of his works he reveals to his people" *(Koakh ma'assav higid le'amo).*

The kabbalists have noted that the number of phalanges on each hand is fourteen.

This number is written in Hebrew	10 + 4,
i.e.	*yod-dalet,*
which reads as the word	*yad,* "hand," יד

The word *hand* is thus the result of the articulation between the body, figures, and letters. The anatomical structure of the organ (fourteen phalanges) evokes a number (14) that can be converted into letters and words *(yod-dalet = yad).*

Rabbi Nachman of Breslov explains, on the basis of these remarks, the importance of clapping the hands during prayer. The two hands together (14 + 14) indeed produce the sum of 28.

This number is written in Hebrew	20 + 8,
i.e.	*kaf-het,*
thus forming the word	*koakh, "strength" or* "force"

כח

This "force" is that which enabled the world to pass from nothingness to a state of being.

Note that if 28 is multiplied by 20 (the first component of 28), the result is 560, which reads as *yifat,* "splendor," a synonym for the word *zohar.*

20 x 28 = 560 = splendor

If 28 is multiplied by 8, which is the second component, the result is 224, which represents the numerical value of the word *derekh,* "path."

8 x 28 = 224 = path

The number 28 is a perfect number that refers to the "dynamic of splendor" or "shining path": *derekh hazohar.*

It should also be noted that the word *ahava,* "love", has a dynamic gematria that is also equal to 28. In fact, in Hebrew, *ahava* is written using the letters *aleph-heh-bet-heh,* which in cumulative dynamic gematria produces:

אהבה

aleph	1
aleph-heh	1 + 5 = 6
aleph-heh-bet	1 + 5 + 2 = 8
aleph-heh-bet-heh	1 + 5 + 2 + 5 = 13
	Total = 28

The Twenty-eight Times of the World

Another text, apart from the first verse of the Torah, gives an indication of the importance of the number 28. This is a famous group of verses from Ecclesiastes *(Qohelet)*. Chapter 3 begins:

> To everything there is a season.
> And a time for every purpose under heaven.
> A time to be born, and a time to die.
> A time to plant and a time to pluck up that which is planted.
> A time to kill and a time to heal.
> A time to break down and a time to build up.
> A time to weep and a time to laugh.
> A time to mourn and a time to dance.
> A time to cast away stones and a time to gather stones together.
> A time to embrace and a time to refrain from embracing.
> A time to seek and a time to lose.
> A time to keep and a time to cast away.
> A time to rend and a time to sew.
> A time to keep silence and a time to speak.
> A time to love and a time to hate.
> A time of war and a time of peace.

All existence is summarized in twenty-eight lines—the twenty-eight fundamental times that break life down into its most essential parts. The Hebrew version of the text clearly brings out the structure of 28, highlighting it by using a type of arrangement of text on the page that is called *shira,* meaning "poetry" or "song,"which is extremely rare in the Bible.

ג

לַכֹּל זְמָן וְעֵת לְכָל־חֵפֶץ תַּחַת הַשָּׁמָיִם׃ א

עֵת לָלֶדֶת וְעֵת לָמוּת 2
עֵת לָטַעַת וְעֵת לַעֲקוֹר נָטוּעַ׃
עֵת לַהֲרוֹג וְעֵת לִרְפּוֹא 3
עֵת לִפְרוֹץ וְעֵת לִבְנוֹת׃
עֵת לִבְכּוֹת וְעֵת לִשְׂחוֹק 4
עֵת סְפוֹד וְעֵת רְקוֹד׃
עֵת לְהַשְׁלִיךְ אֲבָנִים וְעֵת כְּנוֹס אֲבָנִים ה
עֵת לַחֲבוֹק וְעֵת לִרְחֹק מֵחַבֵּק׃
עֵת לְבַקֵּשׁ וְעֵת לְאַבֵּד 6
עֵת לִשְׁמוֹר וְעֵת לְהַשְׁלִיךְ׃
עֵת לִקְרוֹעַ וְעֵת לִתְפּוֹר 7
עֵת לַחֲשׁוֹת וְעֵת לְדַבֵּר׃
עֵת לֶאֱהֹב וְעֵת לִשְׂנֹא 8
עֵת מִלְחָמָה וְעֵת שָׁלוֹם׃

מַה־יִּתְרוֹן הָעוֹשֶׂה בַּאֲשֶׁר הוּא עָמֵל׃ רָאִיתִי אֶת־הָעִנְיָן 9 י
אֲשֶׁר נָתַן אֱלֹהִים לִבְנֵי הָאָדָם לַעֲנוֹת בּוֹ׃ אֶת־הַכֹּל 11
עָשָׂה יָפֶה בְעִתּוֹ גַּם אֶת־הָעֹלָם נָתַן בְּלִבָּם מִבְּלִי אֲשֶׁר
לֹא־יִמְצָא הָאָדָם אֶת־הַמַּעֲשֶׂה אֲשֶׁר־עָשָׂה הָאֱלֹהִים מֵרֹאשׁ
וְעַד־סוֹף׃ יָדַעְתִּי כִּי אֵין טוֹב בָּם כִּי אִם־לִשְׂמוֹחַ וְלַעֲשׂוֹת 12
טוֹב בְּחַיָּיו׃ וְגַם כָּל־הָאָדָם שֶׁיֹּאכַל וְשָׁתָה וְרָאָה טוֹב 13
בְּכָל־עֲמָלוֹ מַתַּת אֱלֹהִים הִיא׃ יָדַעְתִּי כִּי כָּל־אֲשֶׁר יַעֲשֶׂה 14
הָאֱלֹהִים הוּא יִהְיֶה לְעוֹלָם עָלָיו אֵין לְהוֹסִיף וּמִמֶּנּוּ אֵין
לִגְרֹעַ וְהָאֱלֹהִים עָשָׂה שֶׁיִּרְאוּ מִלְּפָנָיו׃ מַה־שֶּׁהָיָה כְּבָר טו
הוּא וַאֲשֶׁר לִהְיוֹת כְּבָר הָיָה וְהָאֱלֹהִים יְבַקֵּשׁ אֶת־נִרְדָּף׃
וְעוֹד רָאִיתִי תַּחַת הַשָּׁמֶשׁ מְקוֹם הַמִּשְׁפָּט שָׁמָּה הָרֶשַׁע 16
וּמְקוֹם הַצֶּדֶק שָׁמָּה הָרָשַׁע׃ אָמַרְתִּי אֲנִי בְּלִבִּי אֶת־הַצַּדִּיק 17

ואת־

Chapter III of *Ecclesiastes*, which deals with the structure of time, arranged in two columns of fourteen lines each.

The "Friendly Numbers"

220 284

A derivative of this contemplation of numbers and their relationship to their divisors bring us to another category of numbers with surprising properties, one that is also employed in the text of the Bible and its kabbalistic commentaries. These are "friendly numbers," which are closely related to those perfect numbers that so captivated Pythagoras.

The friendly numbers consist of pairs of numbers of which each is the sum of the divisors of the other. The Pythagorians made the extraordinary discovery that 220 and 284 were friendly numbers. That is because the divi-

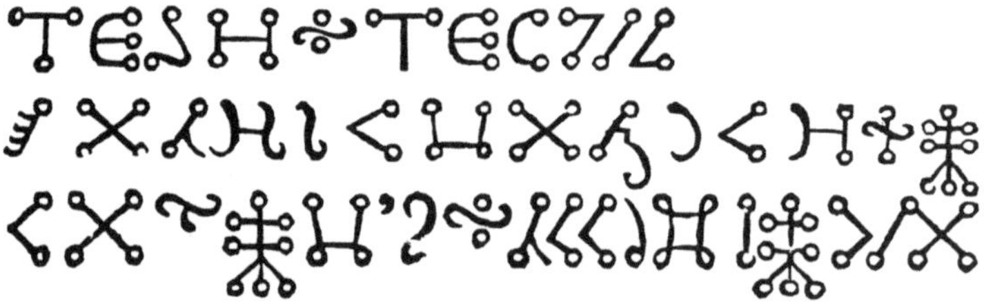

Kabbalistic amulet for love and friendship,
written in so-called "magic" letters used especially for amulets.

sors of 220 are 1, 2, 4, 5, 10, 11, 20, 22, 44, 55, and 110, whose sum is 284; in any case, the divisors of 284 are 1, 2, 4, 71, and 142, whose sum is 220. So the pair 220 and 284 is considered to be symbolic of friendship.

In his book *My Best Mathematical and Logic Puzzles,* Martin Gardner mentions that in the Middle Ages, talismen were inscribed with these numbers, which were claimed to attract love. An Arab numerologist records the custom of engraving 220 on one fruit and 284 on another, eating one, and giving the other to the object of affection, as a sort of mathematical aphrodisiac.

New friendly numbers were not discovered until 1636, when Fermat discovered the pair constituted by 17,296 and 18,416. Descartes was to discover a third pair (9,363,584 and 9,437,056), and Leonhard Euler made a list of as many as sixty-two pairs of friendly numbers. Strangely, all these eminent mathematicians ignored the lower numbers, but in 1866, at the age of sixteen, Niccolo Paganini discovered the pair 1,184 and 1,210.

The "Social" Number

In the twentieth century, mathematicians extended the idea of friendly numbers and began searching for so-called social numbers, sets of three or more numbers that form closed sequences.

For example, a comparative examination of 12,496, 14,288, 15,472, 14,536, and 14,264 will show that the sum of the divisors of the first number forms the second, the sum of the divisors of the second forms the third, the sum of the divisors of the third forms the fourth, that of the fourth forms the fifth, and the sum of the divisors of the fifth forms the first. The longest social sequence discovered hitherto consists of twenty-eight numbers, of which the first is 14,316.*

Let us return to the pair 220 and 284, considered to be symbolic of friendship. The Bible uses one of these numbers in a context in which it is clearly used in this symbolic association. When the patriarch Jacob is pursued by his brother Esau, who wants to kill him, he decides to welcome him and attempt a reconciliation. But he nevertheless prepares for war, in case Esau rejects this. Furthermore, he begins to pray and sends his brother magnificent presents to put him in a positive frame of mind. These presents consist of successive flocks of sheep and goats. And indeed, the first two flocks that he sends consist of precisely two hundred and twenty-two heads (Genesis 32:14).

* This is the information conveyed by Simon Singh in his book *Fermat's Last Theorem*. The reader will have noted in passing the presence of the number 28.

Where the verses do not give exact numbers, they are created in the commentaries by using sets of figures and letters. When numbers are mentioned explicitly in the text, they read "*darshenu*": "Interpret them for us!"

What is the significance of the numbers 200 and 20?

How were they chosen?

What secrets do they contain?

The only plausible answer is that Jacob was aware of the tradition of the pairs of friendly numbers 220 and 284.

Tenderness and the Bed of Love

The numbers 220 and 284 seem to belong to a tradition of which the patriarchs were already aware. But what do they mean over and above their purely numerical aspect?

The number 220 is written *resh-kaf* in Hebrew, which is pronounced *rakh* and means "tender."

רך

The number 284 is written *resh-peh-dalet* and is pronounced *rapad;* the root means "to prepare a mattress," "to prepare a bed of love."

רפד

This root can be found in the *Song of Songs* (2:5).

Sustain me when I am faint.
Prepare a bed for me in the apple orchard
for I am sick with love.

Thus, the sending of the message "220—tenderness" invites the reply "284—the bed of love has been prepared."

Playing the "tenderness card" can sometimes be fraught with danger!

37

God and Pi (π)

The Forces that Uphold the Possibility of the Universe

The question asked of kabbalists is whether, after the original void has been put in place, it is possible to maintain this void.

When faced with the problem of infinity that has contracted to make room for the world, Rabbi Isaac Luria did not merely describe the withdrawal of infinity but went further, asking himself what forces were at work in Creation that would make infinity retract, remain at the edge of the void, and not invade it again. In a word, what forces maintain the void and, conversely, uphold the world and allow it to continue to exist?

The Name of Shaddai

A kabbalist is not merely someone who looks at the world, but someone who asks himself how the world manages to do what it does. When one learns how to look at the world, one learns that it is not a static object but in perpetual movement, constantly changing. In other words, the kabbalist sees the world not as a disjointed succession of unrelated objects but as the very movement of the genesis of the world, in which conflicting forces are at work. The Kabbalah interrogates the world in genesis, in the process of being, not a world that has been set down at random, whose elements are disparate.

Rabbi Isaac Luria imagined a force that came from out of the void, as if the cosmic void contained a voice that said and repeated infinitely: "That is enough! Do not come!" In Hebrew, this force has been given the name of Shaddai, which means "that is enough," an abbreviation of "he who has told the world that that is enough."

It is also the name of God, which designates the force that prohibits the infinite from reoccupying the void it has left. Shaddai is the name of God the self-limiting. It is the name of limitation, and thus of *din,* the purpose of which is to make possible creation and thus to balance *khessed.* To summarize the theory of *tsimtsum,* the space occupied by the world is created by an emptying or withdrawing of the infinite and by a force that maintains the light of the infinite at the periphery. This force is called Shaddai.

ש ד י

Consequently, someone endowed with *khessed* tempered by *din* is called a *khassid.* In effect, the limitation is marked by the word *dai,* meaning "enough." Furthermore, in the word *hassid,* one can read the word *khessed,* as well as the word *dai,* thanks to the letter *yod* that has been added. The ritual winding of the *tefilin,* the phylacteries worn for prayer on the head and right arm, are a way of writing *Shaddai* on the body using various knots that make the shapes of the letters *shin-dalet-yod.*

The Mystery of the Circle and of Pi (π)

To return to the question of Shaddai and the internal forces within the universe that prevent infinity from reoccupying the empty space, we need to try and explore further the secret of the void, from which the world and man was created, and whose importance we have just explained.

At a lecture given at the Alliance Israélite Universelle in 1996, which marked a significant event in the history of Jewish thought and which was called "The Circle and the Straight Line, Transcendence and Immanence,"

Léon Askenazi (known as Manitou), one of the greatest Jewish educators and thinkers of the twentieth century, opened up new perspectives on this particular question.

After explaining the *tsimtsum* and the meaning of the name Shaddai, a force used to protect the empty space, Léon Askenazi explained, "What is so extraordinary, is that the Greeks foresaw the existence of this mystery which permits the world to exist, within whose protection the world exists." What did he mean? What do the Greeks have to do with the theory of *tsimtsum*? In fact, the Greeks proposed an explanation of the world to humanity that was based on mathematics and geometry. In studying the properties of the circle, they came close to intuitively understanding the void of the universe that upholds the earth of men.

In fact, if the problem is studied from the mathematical point of view, the void in a circle, the space inside it (the possibility that the circle has an area), is constituted by a certain relationship between a straight line and a circle.

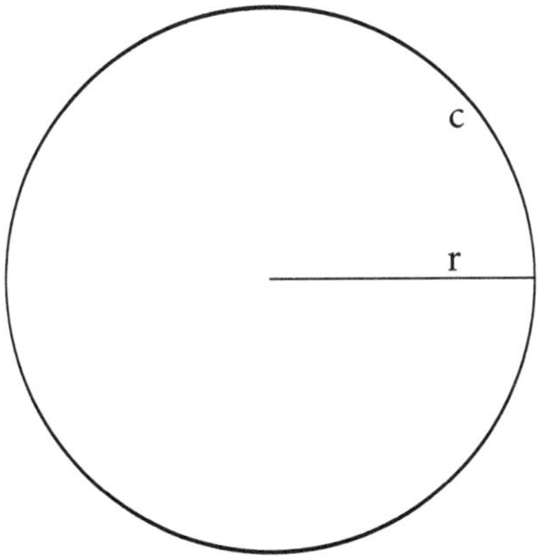

$$\pi = \frac{c}{2r}$$

The "mystery" is in the relationship between the straight line and the circle.

It is defined by pi (π), a transcendental or infinite number, a number whose exact value can never be ascertained, one that escapes any attempt at a "definition" or enclosure within fixed, static measurements, but whose approximate value is 3.14 (and whose rational value is 22/7). Pi (π) as a number is a window on infinity.

Pi (π) and the Name of Shaddai

The Greek mathematicians, especially Archimedes, attempted to use science to resolve the problem of the circle (or limitations permitted by the world) and the radius (or diameter) that retains the void around its center. That is how they found the value represented by pi (π). The metaphysical speculations of the masters of the Kabbalah thus combine with the calculations of the Greek mathematicians.

One of them, Rabbi Joseph Gikatillia, affirmed that "the circle is constructed on the basis of the name of Shaddai," which, as has been explained, is the force that maintains the limit between infinity and void at the core of infinity. He refers specifically to the episode that ends the story of the Garden of Eden: an angel stood at the gate and brandished a sword with which he traced the circle of the universe.

What is the link between *Shaddai* and the formula that describes the relationship between a circle and a straight line? As has been shown several times, there is a correspondence between Hebrew letters and numbers, one which is called gematria. Like all words, the name of Shaddai possesses a numerical value. It is the sum of the three letters of the word *Shaddai* in Hebrew:

shin-dalet-yod
300 + 4 + 10
314

If we perform "Hebraic" (or "algebraic") mathematics, the respective numerical value of the letters of Shaddai *(shin, dalet,* and *yod)* are 300, 4, and 10. The gematria of the name thus amounts to the sum of the letters, i.e. 314. Whether it is an astonishing coincidence, a brilliant intuition, or even another revelation of the mysteries of the universe, 314 represents the approximate value, multiplied by 100, of pi (π), the transcendental, infinite number! This number is precisely the relationship of forces that makes it possible to place limits on the physical world, limits that exist through the word *Shaddai* at the metaphysical level. Its rational value (22/7) relates to the link between the 22 letters of the Hebrew alphabet and the number seven, the primary meaning of which is in the biblical concept of the rhythm of time—the first appearance of 7 in the Bible is in the seven days of Creation.

Numbers and the Harmony of the World: The Image of a River

The kabbalists used various metaphors to explain their ideas; life and existence were likened to the flow or current of a river. The image of the river is also used by the prophets, especially Ezekiel, as well as among certain philosophers such Heracleitus or poets such as Hölderlin. These authors seem to have a "fluvial metaphysic."

Einstein was one of the first people to become interested in the phenomenon of meanders from the physical point of view. He postulated that rivers tend to increase the number of meanders because the slightest curve will cause the current to flow faster on the outer shore, which will accentuate erosion and the meander. The more the meander is accentuated, the faster the current will flow at the outer shore, and the faster it flows, the greater the amount of erosion, and so on. There is a natural phenomenon that curbs the chaos, however: when carried as far as it can go, the meander causes the river to turn back on itself, short-circuiting itself. The river then takes the shortest route, cutting off the meander.

Professor Hans-Hendrik Stolum, an earth sciences expert at Cambridge University, England, has calculated the relationship between the length of rivers from source to mouth and their true length as the crow flies. He made an extraordinary discovery. Although the ratio varies from one river to the next, the average value is slightly higher than three; that is, the actual length is more or less three times the direct distance. In fact, the ratio is almost 3.14, the approximate value of pi (π). The balance between the opposing forces at work in the rivers is an average of π between the true length of the river and the direct distance from source to mouth, a ratio found most often in rivers that flow slowly across plains with a gentle slope, as in Brazil or the Siberian tundra.

In other words, the following hypothesis might be considered: the ratio that exists between a tendency to entropy, deployment, and expansion on the one hand—that which the Kabbalah would term *khessed*—and the tendency toward order and restriction, on the other—that which the Kabbalah would term *din*—is in the order of π. The relationship between chaos and the cosmos tends to have the value of π, i.e. 3.14 or, in kabbalistic language, Shaddai. It's worth thinking about.

Part Seven

The Names of God

7

יהוה

38

God Is the Text
The Mystical Meaning of Study in the Kabbalah

God is the axiom par excellence.
—Haïm Brezis, *Un Mathématicien juif*

Who Is God?

It may be one of the peculiarities of Judaism that the first question it asks is not, Who is God? but, In what way did He reveal himself? or, Does He still reveal himself to men?

For Judaism, the question of God is the question of the revelation of God. Seeking to understand God is seeking to understand the specific manner, the original way, in which the infinite enters into contact with the finite, through which the Divinity has tried to reveal Himself to men. This remark is fundamental, for it makes it possible from the outset to distinguish between the various ways of tackling the problem of God and the meaning of religion in each of the religious traditions that have arisen and spread throughout the history and geography of man. The nature of Revelation is intrinsic to the understanding of the nature of the divinity, whether singular or plural.

As Maurice Blanchot put it so well: "If there is a world in which, while seeking truth and the rules of life, one encounters not the world but a book, then it is in Judaism, that at the beginning of everything, the power of words and exegesis is affirmed, in which everything begins from a text and everything comes back to it, a single book in which a prodigious sequence of books unfolds, a library that is not only universal but which takes the place of the universe and which is even more vast and more enigmatic than the universe."

The Revelation Is the Revelation of a Text

After his first words to Abraham, God reveals himself successively to Isaac, Jacob, and Moses, each time in a special way. The first three revelations are revelations made to an individual, but the fourth, the Revelation on Mount Sinai, is made to a group through Moses.

The Revelation on Mount Sinai, the collective revelation of God to the Jewish people, is of a very special nature. If one rereads the text of Exodus describing this exceptional moment, one notices—it is well known but worth stressing—that God is only a voice addressing the people from the mountaintop through Moses; God remains withdrawn, invisible; his only incarnation is his voice, his words that engrave themselves upon the Tablets of the Law.

The text is surprising because it speaks of a vision of voices: "And all the people saw the voices" (Exodus 20:15). This verse is explained by the commentators as a vision of the text given and revealed upon Sinai.

The Revelation is first and foremost the revelation of a text; this is the revolution contained in the Bible story. And the first and basic relationship with God is a relationship with this text of the Law. Jewish mysticism radicalizes this, though, in the following formula: "Qudesho berikh hoo ve torato ehad hoo" ("The Holy One, Blessed be He, and His Torah are one"). God is the Text!

It is through this text that man learns to know God.

God is first and foremost the Creator of Heaven and Earth and the whole universe, and man was the last creature to be created by Him, arriving on the sixth day, as the culmination of this Creation.

Elohim, YHVH, and Adonai

In this story, it is God who brings order to the world. Everything has its proper place, which must be respected so that the balance of the world is maintained. This organization applies for things and for living creatures. It is the Law of the world, physical and metaphysical, mathematical and ethical. God the Creator is thus both an organizing force in the world and the force that upholds the worlds. This God is called Elohim in the biblical text, which opens with this famous sentence: "In the beginning, Elohim created the heavens and the earth."

We could ask the question, "Who is God?" The question is asked here in English, but it could also be asked in other languages, in which "God" would be replaced by "Dieu," "Got," "Zeus," and so on. But these terms cannot express the special way in which Judaism speaks to God. In fact, Judaism has many ways of saying the name of the Divinity, and they are not equivalents of each other.

The study of the various names of God is one of the central preoccupations of the Kabbalah, which, as has been shown in previous chapters, studies the shapes of letters, the numerical values of each word and each name, and the special forces concealed within these words and names. Even if God is unique, He reveals himself to man in many different ways. In fact, God reveals himself through ten names.

The Ten Names of God

The kabbalistic tradition reveals ten names for God, some more frequently used and better known than others. Each of these names corresponds to a particular *sefira.*

יהוה

- YHVH: This name is never spoken. It is the ineffable Name, or *shem ha-mefurash.* It is also called *shem havaya.* The name is also said to be on the order of *midat ha-khessed* or *midat ha-rakhamim.* It thus appears in a context in which God manifests himself in his attribute of generosity or compassion and mercy. It has the simple numerical value of 26.

אדני

- Adny: This name, pronounced "*adonai,*" is the voiced form of the previous name. It is called the *shem adnut* or *shem adny*, and must never be pronounced in vain. It has a simple numerical value of 65.

יה

- Yah: The name derived from the tetragrammaton. It is found in *halleluyah,* "praise God." Of its two letters, one is masculine (the *yod*), the other feminine (the *heh*), representing the combined force of the couple, the worlds above and the worlds below, the heavens and the earth. It has a simple numerical value of 15.

אל

- El: This word means God, but it also means "toward." It is often used in conjunction with another divine name or as an adjective or complement, as in "the House of God," (Bet-El), "God on high" (El-Elyon), and so on. It has a simple numerical value of 31.

אלוה

- Eloha: This name is derived from the previous one; it is a construct of El to which the last two letters of the tetragrammaton, *vav-heh,* have been added. It has a simple numerical value of 42. (This name seems to be alluded to in the permutation called *El-BaM,* which was discussed earlier. *BaM* also has a numerical value of 42.)

אלהים

- Elohim: The God of Creation. This is one of the most often used names in the Bible and expresses the forces of nature. It is another derivative of the name El, with the addition of two more letters of the tetragrammaton, *yod-heh,* plus the letter *mem,* which makes it look like a masculine plural. It is in the same mode as *din* and is used when God manifests his rigor or the laws of nature. It has a simple numerical value of 86.

אהיה

- Ehyeh: This name of God, which has been discussed previously, is used for the first time when God appears to Moses at the Burning Bush. It has a simple numerical value of 21.

שדי

- Shaddai: An important name that governs the balance of the forces of nature between order and disorder. It is also at work in the *tsimtsum,* the withdrawal of the divine, and has been much commented upon and compared with Pythagorean preoccupations. The root of the word is *shad,* "female breast." It has a simple numerical value of 314, which has caused a number of kabbalists to compare it to pi (π).

אל-שדי

- El-Shaddai: A derivation of the previous name. It is read aloud as *Ha-Shem,* "the Name." It has a simple numerical value of 345.

צבאות

- Tseva'ot: Translated by the expression "Lord of Hosts" (*tsava* means "army"). This literal translation is confusing, as it conjures up the image of a militaristic God. The army referred to, in kabbalistic terms, is in fact the army of angels from the celestial spheres, who are organized into various camps and legions. *Tseva'ot* can also be translated as "army of letters" *(tseva-ot).* This would be the word for the manifestation of the divine in written form. It has a simple numerical value of 499.

The Name, the Book, and the Incarnation

As has been said, there is God-Elohim, God-YHVH, the four-consonant name that is never spoken, the Ineffable Name that some incorrectly write as Yahweh or Jehovah, incorrectly because such a transcription is in itself an attack upon the infinity of God. When the tetragrammaton YHVH appears in a text, it is read *Adonai,* "Lord," or *Ha-Shem,* "the Name." The name of Shaddai, the self-limitation of God, was necessary for the purpose of the creation of the world and in order to be able to continue to be present in it. It is the theory of *tsimtsum* that has been discussed at length above.

The infinity of God is self-limiting. He created the world and became its guest in a finite form. For the Kabbalah, this passage from the infinite to the finite occurs through the text.

To understand the importance of this idea, it could be compared to the incarnation of God in Christianity. For Christians, the infinite deity also becomes finite through the body of Christ. For kabbalists, the incarnation is produced in the body of the Text.

Study Is the Theological Foundation of Judaism

This statement indicates the importance of reading and study in Judaism. It has been said, "God is the text." This means that the most radical manifestation of the divinity is through the text, the Book, and the letters of the alphabet.

The transition from the infinite to the finite, the possibility of the finite to exist on the basis of infinity, the *tsimtsum,* the contraction of God, pose an important theological problem. If God allows himself to be finite, does he still remain the infinite Godhead?

This is a problem that kabbalists and Talmudists have been aware of, and it must be answered; if God is finite, a God of this world, he becomes an idol. And if God is enshrined in the Book, there is the risk of "textolatry"! In that case, the text must be given its status of infinity; all the means must be used to give it an infinite meaning. This is what the kabbalists and Talmudists succeeded in doing.

The "Text-God" must be accorded its status of infinity; in other words, every means must be used to give it an infinite meaning. These means consist of all the rules of interpretation that have been explained in the previous chapters, and especially gematria, *tseruf,* and so on. The need to interpret the text as the liberation of the divine is one of the fundamental meanings of all the work of kabbalists and Talmudists. Everything else is merely an analysis of the methods of achieving this aim and the levels of interpretation. The Talmud is not a way of better understanding the Bible text or better understanding God, since that would be to misappropriate God and enclose the infinite. Rather, it is a means of interpreting the text in such a way that the words it contains—and this is what it is unique about it—can be interpreted in a plurality of ways.

And it is this plurality which becomes freedom—of God and men!

The question of the relationship to the text is not merely that of reading but of interpretation. Interpreting is discovering meaning but not truth—not revealing a secret, but revealing that a secret exists. It is for this reason that the masters of the Kabbalah have always sought a language that simultaneously reveals and hides. It is for this reason that the most appropriate style they have found is that of poetry.

An interpretation does not reveal one true meaning of a text, but there is such a thing as a true interpretation of a text. Truth does not mean the appropriateness in relation to certain prior existing meanings, but resides in being "open to." . . .

Reading is unknotting, unraveling, deconstructing the set of predeterminations and prior enclosures of the world. When reading unknots, unravels, when it opens up the mind to a different perspective of the text, when interpreting a text means not attaching a meaning to it but attempting to evaluate how many meanings it has, what its dynamic is—that is truth!

The Talmud and the Kabbalah are the set of interpretations that the commentators have given to the text of the Revelation, from the time of Moses to the present day. The text of the Revelation explodes through the effect of interpretation. It is what we call "reading in bursts."

The masters of the Talmud and the Kabbalah emphasize one fundamental idea: that the Jewish people are not the "People of the Book" but the "People of the Interpretation of the Book," to use a formula favored by Armand Abécassis. Unlike Descartes, the Talmudist and the kabbalist do not say, "I think, therefore I am," but "I read, I interpret, I think, I criticize, I oppose, I listen, I write, I question, I reply, I quote, I tell, I name, I discuss, I interpolate, I pray, I think, I learn, I teach, I live, therefore I am."

Reading is an essential activity for a Jew, since through reading he can reject all the determinisms of the senses that set him in the mold of a certain determination of being. Reading is a philosophical as well as a political gesture, a referendum in which the reader has no choice other than yes or no, to accept or to reject. Reading is a political gesture, since freedom of interpretation is also an existential freedom.

The Text Is a Great Name of God: The Tetragrammaton Is Its Essence

For kabbalists, the letters of the Hebrew alphabet are a royal road to the sacred source within us. They make it possible to ascend to transcendence.

The nucleus of the Hebrew language is expressed in the various names of God, and essentially through the tetragrammaton YHVH, from which all the other nouns and words flow. In relation to the basic ground plan of the Kabbalah, the names of God are in the intermediary world and make it possible for the light of the infinite to pass to the *kelim,* the vessels that are man and the cosmos as a whole. In the context of this chapter, the following fundamental idea can be stated; that the text of the Torah is the Great and Divine Name, and the tetragrammaton YHVH is at its core.

Names of God and Meditation

All of the kabbalistic teachings stress the essential role of the names of God in order to attain the mystical state. The name of God is used as a means of attaining the propehtic state. In this respect, certain kabbalists recall the case of Abraham, of whom the Bible says, he "invoked the Lord by name" (Genesis 12:8).

Rabbi Pinhas Ben Yair asked, "Why do people pray without having their prayers answered? Because they do not know how to use the Explicit Name *[Shem ha-meforash].*" The "knowledge of the name of God" is none other than its usage. Other passages allude to the power of God's name. Thus the psalmist sings, "*They invoke chariots, they invoke horses, but we invoke the name of the Lord our God*" (Psalms 20:8). Far from indicating a particular prayer, this verse should also be taken to mean exactly what it says.

Another extract from the same psalm confirms this point of view by introducing a new concept: "May we rejoice *[ranen]* in Your Salvation, arrayed by standards in the name of our God, may the Lord fulfil your every wish" (Psalms 20:6). The word *ranen* refers to a method of meditation that includes the name of God. And again we find a similar concept in the following verse: "All of the nations have beset me, by the name of the Lord I shall surely cut them down" (Psalms 118:10).

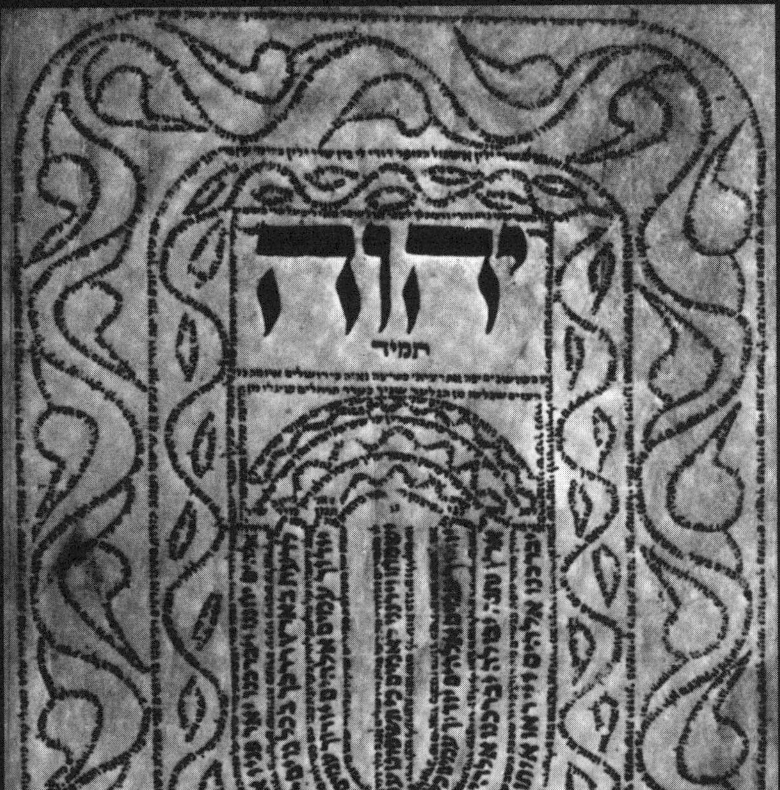

The seven-branched candelabra inscribed with the letters of Psalm 67, surmounted by the inscription: "The tetragrammaton is always before my eyes." This illustration in a prayerbook or on the walls of a synagogue, is an aid to meditation and concentration on the permanent presence of God.

The Four Numerical Deployments of the Tetragrammaton

The Kabbalah teaches that there is a name that contains seventy-two letters. It is constructed from a set of three verses of the Book of Exodus (14:19–21) which consist of seventy-two letters. This research into the number 72 is because it is the numerical value of the word *khessed*, "loving-kindness" or "goodness," one of the *sefirot*.

In certain texts of the Kabbalah the tetragrammaton is written in the form of twenty-four little spheres, each bearing a three-pointed crown, which produces 24 x 3 = 72. There are also four numerical deployments of the tetragrammaton with the values of 45, 52, 63, and 72.

The Tetragrammaton: An Unpronounceable Name

The name YHVH is purely visible, four consonants without a vowel, making it ineffable, a name made to be hidden, on which is never spoken. The name withdraws at the same time as it gives. This essential paradox affirms a relationship with God that cannot be reduced to a consciousness that theorizes, defines, or combines. Through this withdrawal into silence, the Revelation preserves the transcendence of that which it manifests.

The absence of vowels that makes the name unpronounceable creates an unbridgeable distance, removing the possibility of taking God for an object.

The tetragrammaton is like a hole in language, from which language itself derives meaning. It is a name that is written so as not to be pronounced according to its own letters, but to be commented upon, translated into other letters and other names. The name YHVH offers the unthinkable.

All the interpretations that will be provided in the following chapters are mere outlines, orientations on which to ponder, and "secrets" should be understood as: "We reveal that a secret exists"; in no case do we reveal the "secret" itself.

Seeing the four-letter name is to be engulfed in the nothingness of the senses, to penetrate into an annihilation of consciousness, to experience a vacuum, a void, the infinite. . . .

39

The Secrets of the Tetragrammaton
The Geometrical Approach

It has been shown that the basic shapes of the Hebrew letters are written geometrically as "point-line-plane."

These statements make it possible to have a better understanding of the secrets of the geometry of the tetragrammaton. The tetragrammaton consists of four consonants without vowels: *yod-heh-vav-heh: YHVH.*

יהוה

Where does this name come from?

According to Rabbi Ishaya Horowitz, it is the result of the history of the primordial point and its metamorphoses.

As has been shown, the "point-*yod*" becomes the "line-*vav*" and the "plane-*dalet*." These three graphic shapes themselves produce the letter *yod* when written as broken down into its components:

The Cave of Makhpela: The Letter *Heh* in the Tetragrammaton

The tetragrammaton is written *yod-heh-vav-heh;* the letter *heh* thus appears twice. However, according to Rabbi Isaac Luria, the two *hehs* are two different letters because they consist of different elements.

He calls this doubling of the *heh* "The Cave of Makhpela," since the word *makhpela* literally means "doubling of the *heh*," and the Cave of Makhpela is the burial place of Abraham and Sarah. In fact, the shape of the *heh* can be written in two ways:

- a *dalet* and a *vav*:

- or a *dalet* and a *yod*:

The Tetragrammaton is thus created from a double usage of the *yod*, consisting of the elements *yod-vav-dalet:*

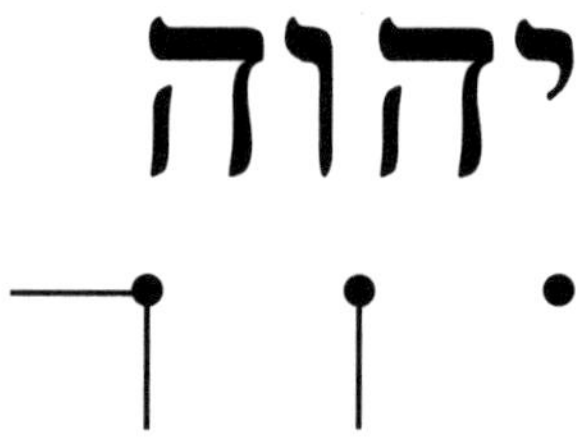

in order for the first stage to become *yod-dalet-vav* = the first *heh*;

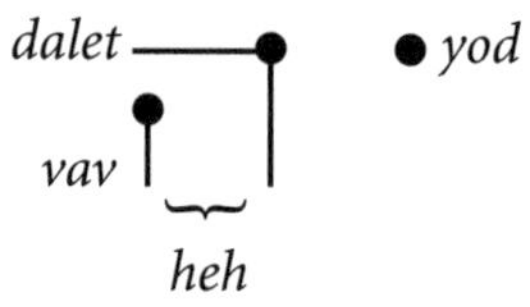

and in order for the second stage to become *vav-dalet-yod* = the second *heh.*

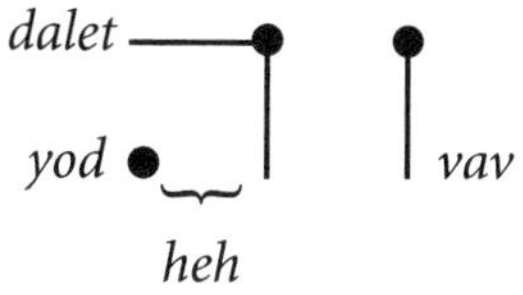

The tetragrammaton thus turns into an explosion of the point *(yod)* into two points that are arranged in space as a mirror image: *yod-dalet-vav/ vav-dalet-yod.*

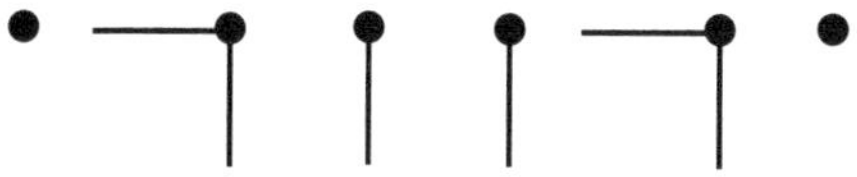

The tetragrammaton is the movement of a point that returns to the point.

The Name withdraws at the same time that it is given. This is an essential paradox that affirms a relationship with God that is irreducible to knowledge. By thus retreating into silence, the Revelation retains the transcendence of that which is manifested.

The tetragrammaton refers to nothing other than itself; in this it is unlike a proper name, which refers to the person who bears it. It does not refer to any other reality that might be God.

We have tried to tackle the Name through its graphic, an enterprise fraught with ambiguity and risk. Spatializing the name of God, giving it a tangible, visible form and thus one that might be spoken, as do those who pronounce it "Yahweh" or "Jehovah," might lead to the construction of an idol, not of stone but of words.

An analysis of the graphics of the name ought thus to make it easier to understand its construction as a deconstruction based on the point. In fact, as we have said: "The point returns to the point."

The name is a meditation on nothingness that becomes a being, and which returns to nothingness. It is entry into movement and an infinity of time.

40

The Secrets of the Tetragrammaton
The Mathematical Approach

The Kabbalah considers that man constructs and renews the meaning of the original text.
—Haïm Brezis, *Un Mathématicien juif*

The Enigma of the Number 26

One of the questions that arises is that of the specificity of the gematria of the tetragrammaton.

The tetragrammaton *yod-heh-vav-heh* has a simple gematria of 26:

יהוה
yod-heh-vav-heh
10 + 5 + 6 + 5
26

Why 26?

To reinforce the question, according to some writers, meditation on the alphabet and the names of God consists in always having in mind the tetragrammaton and its numerical value of 26, finding this numerical structure in all the other letters and, if possible, in everything in nature.

As far as the Kabbalah is concerned, all the letters are derived from the tetragrammaton, and the inner structure of some of them relates directly to the Name. This applies particularly to the *aleph*, א, which consists of two *yods* and a *vav* that, when combined, produce a numerical value of 26. The same applies to the *lamed*, ל, *tet*, ט, and *qof*, ק, which are based on the letters *kaf* and *vav*.

Fermat: A Revolutionary Mathematical Discovery

We have mentioned several times the bridge that exists between mathematics and the Kabbalah. Even apart from the subject of gematria, the meeting between Pythagoras and the kabbalists, and their mutual interest in perfect numbers, many other similarities may be uncovered in the future if kabbalists continue to pursue this interdisciplinary research.

The book by Simon Singh entitled *Fermat's Last Theorem* includes a clear and easily comprehensible explanation of perfect numbers, friendly numbers, and social numbers, but it also tells the stories of the lives of the various mathematicians, each more enthralling than the last.

One of these heroes was Pierre de Fermat, the greatest French mathematician of the eighteenth century, who merely noted in the margin of his exercise book:

$x^n + y^n = z$, *impossible if* $n > 2$.
I have found a wonderful solution,
but do not have room here to develop it.

This theorem, accompanied by the original remark, would for the next three hundred and fifty years become the Holy Grail of the world of mathematics, as the most formidable minds throughout the centuries and throughout the nations attempted to solve the equation.

Leonhard Euler, an eighteenth-century genius, had to admit defeat. In the nineteenth century, Sophie Germain assumed the identity of a man in order to pursue studies that hitherto had been forbidden to women. Evariste Galois, on the eve of his death, jotted down a theory on a few sheets of paper that would revolutionize science. Yutaka Taniyama committed suicide from despair, while Paul Wolfskehl found the enigma to be a reason for living.

In 1993, a young Englishman named Andrew Wiles, who was a professor at Princeton University, spent seven years of lonely research and several months of doubt, but was finally able to settle the fate of this extraordinary conundrum and present it to an astonished scientific community.

If this passage shows the importance and seriousness of Fermat's research, what retains our attention here is neither his last theorem nor the discovery of a new pair of friendly numbers, which alone would have turned him into a celebrity, but another of his discoveries, which seems at first glance to be a mere mathematical curiosity and yet which has the power to revolutionize kabbalistic thought.

Fermat noted that 26 lies between two numbers, one a square ($25 = 5^2$), the other a cube ($27 = 3^3$). He then sought other numbers that were positioned between a square and a cube, but he could find none, and he asked himself whether 26 was, in fact, unique. Several days of intense effort enabled him to construct a complex reasoning, showed that it was: "The number 26 is a number that is unique in the whole mathematic universe." Fermat announced this unique property to the scientific community, then challenged anyone to disprove it. He admitted that he had proved it, but it amused him to wonder whether anyone else had sufficient imagination to do the same. Despite the simplicity of the statement, the proof is incredibly difficult, and Fermat took particular delight in challenging the British mathematicians Wallis and Digby, who admitted defeat.

The gauntlet had been thrown down to the kabbalists. How could this discovery be translated in terms of gematria, and beyond it, in mystical terms?

That there was a uniqueness about the number 26 was something of which the kabbalists were acutely aware, but what was the importance of the position of the number between 25 and 27, between a square and a cube?

From a geometrical point of view, a square is an area, and a cube is a volume. Perhaps 26 was a dimension other than an area and a volume; more specifically, a dimension that made it possible to pass from an area to a volume!

According to mathematicians, powers show different stages of development of matter in space:

- the point is written as 0
- the line is written as 1
- the plane is written as 2
- the volume is written as 3.

The number 26 would thus be a fourth dimension, enabling the transition from the second dimension to the third. It could not refer to time, since the time dimension is also necessary to pass from 0 through 1, and from 1 through 2.

A kabbalist could possibly be defined as someone who one day notes in one of the books of the Kabbalah that he is currently reading or writing, in relation to a unique property of the tetragrammaton, "Cuius rei demonstrationem mirabilem sane detexi hanc marginis exiguitas non caperet" ("I have a truly wonderful demonstration for this proposition, which this margin is too narrow to contain"). This was the marginal note that Fermat wrote in the Latin version of *Arithmetica* by Diophantes of Alexandria (c. 250 B.C.E.). The specialty of this Greek mathematician living in Egypt lay in problems whose solutions consisted of whole numbers, problems that are today defined as diophantine equations. He spent his life in Alexandria collecting known problems and inventing new ones, which he collected in a treatise entitled *Arithmetica*. Of the thirteen books of the original treatise, only six survived into the Middle Ages, and these inspired the mathematicians of the Renaissance and Pierre de Fermat. The other seven books were lost in dramatic circumstances.*

Another problem to contemplate. . . .

* See Simon Singh, *Fermat's Last Theorem.*

41

The Secrets of the Tetragrammaton
The Dynamic Approach

The sages are greater than the prophets in everything, for the prophets are sometimes inspired, sometimes not, whereas the holy spirit never leaves the sages even for a brief moment . . . . Those who devote themselves to the study of the Torah hold themselves Above, in a place called Torah that is the foundation of all faith. The prophets hold themselves in a lower place, Below. Happy are those who devote themselves to the study of the Torah for they are at the highest level and exceed all others.
—Zohar II, 6b, and III, 35a

The Ineffable Tetragrammaton and the Concept of Time

There are grounds for asking the exact meaning of this enigmatic name, which for Jewish thought is the very heart of existence.

The tetragrammaton is the Supreme Being, but it is first and foremost a word consisting of four consonants without vowels, a pure image of which nothing can be seen, a pure silence of which nothing can be heard, unless it is the very silence itself at the deepest depths of language, silence as the foundation of language. However, the masters of the Kabbalah teach that these four consonant-letters tell us something vital. When combined, they are written *hvh, hyh, yhh,* meaning "the present" *(hoveh),* the past *(hayah),* and the future *(yeheh).* The tetragrammaton is not the name of God, but an opening onto the three dimensions of time. The Supreme Being is time!

In other words, the tetragrammaton YHVH can be translated as:

to be,

to have been,

to be going to be.

The name of God thus marks the precise balance of time; it could be translated by the expression "the being of time," the balanced potentiality of the three tenses, past, present, and future.

The masters of the Kabbalah ask a question in this regard, whose consequences would appear to us to be revolutionary as to the perception of language and its link to reality. Of course the tetragrammaton names time, but it is just one word among many others in the language, except that it has the special attribute of being unpronounceable, the Ineffable. But it does not indicate in any way its privileged position of containing an evocation of time and temporalization.

There are grounds for questioning the exact meaning of the enigmatic YHVH that is called the tetragrammaton. First of all, these four letters offer a *tseruf,* a possible combination of the letters used to write the word *havaya,* "existence." The tetragrammaton is, for Jewish thought, the very heart of existence.

The Name of God, Time, and the Dynamic of Language

Although the four letters of the tetragrammaton can describe the three time frames, the tetragrammaton-Name itself is a present in the concrete existence of the written word. It has been "foiled" in what is said, "coagulated" in the present of its enunciation—a static word that is incapable of the dynamic reality that it enunciates!

In order to emerge from this contradiction and render adequate, or at least more adequate, the name and the time frames to which they refer, the masters of the Kabbalah have invented a reading system that gives the word a physical dynamic and symbolically prevents it from remaining imprisoned in its enunciation and inscription.

This dynamic consists in reading a word not only in its present existence as a word—from its visible letters—but also to reveal the past and future letters of the word, and analyze the dynamic of the transition from one level to the next. As an illustration, take the English word *time.* As a written word, these letters indicate only its present tense. The "past-of-the-word" is constituted from the letters that precede "time" in the succession of the letters of the alphabet. Thus, the past of the word *time* is *shld.* The dynamization of *shld* according to the rules of succession of the alphabet produces the word *time:*

S H L D
⇩ ⇩ ⇩ ⇩
T I M E

Shld is the symbolic past of *time.* Similarly, the future is indicated by the letters that follow the letters in the word *time,* namely *ujnf:*

T I M E
⇩ ⇩ ⇩ ⇩
U J N F

This reading discloses and reveals the existence of the hidden in each perception; it is the phenomenology of chiaroscuro, a respect for the shade and silence present in every manifestation, but more often obscured. It is not a matter of revealing the hidden, but of revealing the very fact that something has been hidden.

Phenograms and Genograms

Jewish tradition contains a large and rich body of research into linguistics, which takes account of words within words, words beneath words, words above words. The same work has been done in the numerical perception of the language, which causes the unheard meanings to resound.

Contemporary linguistics has revealed the existence of a "subtext" and introduces a distinction between the "phenotext" and the "genotext." Initially, we intend using this terminology by reapplying it to letters or "grams," specifically "phenograms" and "genograms."

A phenogram is a word whose letters are visible and can be read, letters that are present in written or spoken form. A genogram represents invisible letters in the present tense of the word, which precede or follow the word, which construct and conduct the visible word, either projecting it forward or taking it backward.

Hypograms and Metagrams

For greater clarity, we suggest refining the terminology and using the term *hypogram* to describe the letters that precede those of a word and *metagram* those that follow them, using the sequence of letters of the alphabet.

Example:

Take the Hebrew word *em,* "mother" (two letters, *aleph-mem*).

The metagram constituted by these two letters and which follows them in the order of the alphabet is *b, n—bet-nun.* These two letters form the word *ben,* "son" or "child."

EM
⇩
BN

Its hypogram consists of the two letters that precede it: in this case, *tl,* which form the word *tel,* "mound or small hill."

TL
⇩
EM

If the Hebrew language demonstrates a proximity between the words *har,* "mountain," and *isha hara,* "pregnant woman," a linguistic proximity resulting from the resemblance of shapes, it is not impossible to consider the *tel*-hill in an analogy of shape with the pregnant woman. In such a case a semantic logic accompanies the play and movement of the letters in their alphabetical sequence.

תל

tel (hill, belly of a pregnant woman)

⇩

אם

em (mother)

⇩

בן

ben (child, son)

The Metagram and the Hypogram of the Tetragrammaton

The hypogram of the tetragrammaton YHVH is written TDHD:

T	D	H	D
⇩	⇩	⇩	⇩
Y	H	V	H

and its metagram is written KVZV:

Y	H	V	H
⇩	⇩	⇩	⇩
K	V	Z	V

KVZV is pronounced *kuzu.* It is striking that this Name of God is to be found in the ritual of the mezuzah.

Kuzu in the Ritual of the Mezuzah

The mezuzah is a piece of parchment on which the first two paragraphs of the Shema are written (Deuteronomy 6:4–9 and 11:13–21). The parchment is rolled up and placed inside a little box made of wood, metal, or other material. The mezuzah must be fixed to a doorpost, to the right of the entrance, and one-third of the way down from the top of the door, measured from the lintel. If the door is too high, the mezuzah must be within reach of the hand.

Before fixing the mezuzah, the following blessing is said: "Blessed art Thou, O Lord God, King of the Universe, who has sanctified us by Thy commandments and commanded us to fix a mezuzah."

In the Shema, the word *mezuzah* also has the meaning of "doorpost." Fixing a mezuzah on all the doors of a home, with the exception of those rooms in which one does not live, is a positive commandment *(mitsvat asseh),* because it is written in Deuteronomy (7:9), "You shall write them upon the doorposts of your house and upon your gates."

A mezuzah is only fixed to a permanent dwelling. According to the Zohar, the word *mezuzot* (the plural of *mezuzah*) can be broken down into two words, *zaz mavet,* an imperative form that means "may death move, go away, may death depart." The Talmud tells the following story:

> A man called Artaban sent Rabbi Yehuda the Prince a gemstone of great value. To thank him, Rabbi Yehuda the Prince sent him a mezuzah. Artaban was surprised by the gift: "I sent you a gemstone and you thank me with a little piece of parchment!" Rabbi Yehuda answered that the parchment was more valuable than any gemstone.
>
> Artaban did not reply, but thought to himself that Rabbi Yehuda was talking himself out of his predicament with a few fine words.
>
> A few years later, Artaban's daughter fell ill. All the doctors attended one after another at her bedside, but in vain. Artaban remembered the words of Rabbi Yehuda the Prince. He fixed the mezuzah to the door of his daughter's bedroom . . . and she recovered!

The structure of the mezuzah may help us to better understand the significance of this ritual. The back of the parchment bears the words *kuzu bemukhsaz kuzu.* What is this obscure phrase that, even in Hebrew, appears to be meaningless?

The secret of the phrase *kuzu bemukhsaz kuzu* is revealed through a knowledge of metagrams and hypograms. Written on the back of a parchment, these kabbalistic words are metagrams of the formula "the Lord our God" in the Jewish confession of faith: "Hear O Israel, the Lord (*YHVH*) our God (*elohenu*) the Lord (*YHVH*) is One." The mezuzah is the ritual that enacts this idea, so essential to a language in pure movement, a man in movement.

When placed on the doorpost of a house, the mezuzah reminds a man who has traveled a long way that the journey must not end, that man must continue to reinvent himself.

But the mezuzah, which is a sign of momentum, also indicates the way in which this momentum should be achieved. It is the momentum of language, of which the example is *kuzu.*

Man, a being who uses language, accedes to living time through living language, the language of study and interpretation. Refusing dead meanings and single meaning, he reopens words to their multiple and expanded meanings, thus escaping any enclosure, any lassitude, to invent himself, to live and be reborn at each and every moment. The rite of the *mezuzah* is a perpetual invitation to travel.

In fact, every Talmudic text opens with the statement of being on the way, even when the expression is not formulated explicitly. The Kabbalah, the Midrash, and the tales of the Hasidim are all written in a traveling spirit, about men who think as they walk along and ponder the truth during their wanderings.

This is certainly the meaning of the verse: "You shall speak of them . . . when you are on your way" (Deuteronomy 6:7). Everything depends on being on the way. We are closer to the place we seek when we are in the process of getting there than when we are convinced that we have arrived, and have merely to settle in.

Taking the road, being on the way . . .

A Play on the Ego

Rabbi Tsvi Elimelekh of Dynov, author of *Bnei Issakhar*, suggested that it would be interesting to investigate the numerical value of the hypogram and metagram of the tetragrammaton.

Y H V H

⇩

T D H D

9 + 4 + 5 + 4

Hypogram = 22

⇧

K V Z V

20 + 6 + 7 + 6

Metagram = 39

"Twenty-two" is written with two letters, *kaf-bet,* and does not mean anything in Hebrew. It thus relates to a structure of the figure 22. For the

Hebrew-speaking reader, this refers first and foremost to the law of laws, the twenty-two-letter alphabet.

"Thirty-nine" in Hebrew is written using two letters, *lamed-tet,* and can be written *lat* or *tal.* The kabbalists read it as *tal,* "dew," and offer the following reading rule: each time the word appears in the Bible or commentaries, we are in the presence of the metagram of YHVH; that is, the tetragrammaton in movement.

The sum of the hypogram and the metagram is 61 (22 + 39). This number can be the numerical value of a large number of words or expressions. Rabbi Tsvi Elimelekh suggests the word *ani:*

aleph, nun, yod

1 + 50 + 10

61

Ani means "I," the expression of the subjectivity of the human being in his freedom and creativity.

What is the meaning of the equivalence between "I" and the number 61?

It should probably be interpreted as follows: being a human being, someone who says "I," means not presence in itself but the dynamic of an existence that integrates memory (hypogram) at the same time as projection and anticipation (metagram). The subject is not the ego (present), but the connection of the "having been" with the "having to be."

The kabbalist knows how to correctly link memory and hope, roots and the fruits to come.

42

The Secrets of the Tetragrammaton
The Practical Approach

One of the strongest ideas in Judaism is that of the deed or action. For this reason, for example, the practice of Judaism is rich in physical movement. It is often more original in its expressive nature than in that which it intends to express, though the latter is nevertheless extremely profound.

This could be considered as the fundamental difference between East and West. For the Oriental, the deed is the decisive link between man and God; for the Westerner, the link is faith. This split is thrown into unique relief in Jewish practice. None of the books of the Bible make much mention of faith; they say much more about actions. Each action, however humble and apparently insignificant, is in some way directed toward the divine. A good deed makes it possible to receive a share of the light of infinity.

The Ritual Is an Extraordinary Laboratory of Ideas

This preeminence of ritual over representation in society, which is constantly reaffirmed, has never interfered with extensive, prolific intellectual creativity, despite a widespread misconception to the contrary, a creativity with a long and impressive history.

The ritual is an extraordinary laboratory of ideas. It plays the role of research on the first level and is behind a huge religious literature. The Kabbalah has its own way of relating the *aggadah*—literally, "legend"—the stories or underlying philosophy of the rituals.

The Book of the Zohar, one of whose sections is called Midrash Ha-Ne'elam ("Analysis of the Invisible Worlds"), can be read as a linear biblical commentary on the narrative and prescriptive texts. It tries to show how each law and each precept have not only a philosophical but also a mystical basis.

Ritual and the Untying of Knots

The Hebrew word for "knot" is *qesher,* a variation of the word for "lie," *sheqer. Lehatir* means both "untie" and "permit, authorize." The key expressions of Jewish law, the *halakha,* are *mootar* and *assoor,* "permitted" and "forbidden," which can also be understood as "untied" and "attached." In kabbalistic terms, that which is permitted is that which unties and permits the passage of the influx of light; that which is forbidden is that which creates a knot and prevents the release and passage of energy through the channels.

It can thus be understood that numerous aspects of Jewish ritual consist of attempting to break out of these restrictive structures. Examples are the festival of Passover, which marks the liberation from slavery, and the festival of Tabernacles (Sukkot), which commemorates the time spent in the desert (living in temporary huts to bring out the group identity for safety reasons). Ritual is thus a manner of attaining harmony with the dynamic vibrations of the influx of energy and letting it circulate within the human being. Anything that hinders this circulation of energy creates a knot or knots that must be untied.

The Mystical Stakes in Ritual

By taking a particular action, man moves closer to the Creator and provides the conditions he needs to receive the energy of the *en-sof.* This rapprochement is called *devekut,* "cleaving to God."

Some kabbalists believe this is achieved by man ascending to God. Others believe it is done by allowing the divine presence or *shekhina* to descend. In both cases, it is is a matter of reuniting that which had been separated, a separation symbolized by the exile of the *shekhina,* whose return must be permitted.

According to Talmudic and midrashic thought, one of the fundamental results of keeping the commandments is that the divine presence comes down and dwells among the Jewish people. This ability to dwell among them is a basic characteristic of the *shekhina.*

> The divine presence deserted Paradise after Adam's sin and continued to ascend toward heaven due to the subsequent sinning of successive generations. The ten ascensions of the *shekhina* and its withdrawal far from the world required positive human activity to cause it to descend again into this world. There is a midrash which describes its descent in ten stages, a descent which began with the actions of Abraham and culminated with the building of the Temple by Solomon, to which the *shekhina* eventually returned, adopting its original state, and which it was able to inhabit down here. . . . The quintessence of the *mitzvot* ("commandments") and the good deeds performed by someone in this world is to prepare his soul and arrange great and good things on high, so as to bring down upon it the influx of light from the higher emanation.
> (Charles Mopsik, *Les Grands Textes de la kabbale*)

For Moses of Leon, man must become a throne upon which a higher throne rests. Man is thus capable of causing the divine effusion to fall upon him.

The Name and the Rite

Numerous ritual objects are designed so as to incorporate the tetragrammaton or other names as part of the material. Jewish ritual is defined as this incorporation. It is possible to show that all Jewish rituals operate in this way. A few classic examples:

The *talit,* the shawl worn for prayer, has ritual fringes at each corner. The fringe is called the *tsitsit,* and each consists of eight cords, knotted in such a way as to write the tetragrammaton. One of the cords is first rolled around ten times (the letter *yod*), then five times (the letter *heh*), then six times (the letter *vav*), then five times again (the letter *heh*). This makes twenty-six turns in all. In another tradition, the number of turns is 39, corresponding to *kuzu.*

The phylacteries or *tefilin,* leather boxes worn by men during prayer on weekdays, are inscribed with the name Shaddai, as is the mezuzah, the little piece of parchment placed at the entrance to houses.

The *sukka,* the hut or booth in which Jews live during the Festival of Tabernacles (Sukkot), is written *samekh-vav-kaf-heh.* The letters *kaf-vav* add up to 26, the numerical value of the tetragrammaton, and the *samekh-heh* to 65, which corresponds to the numerical value of the name Adonai. The sum of the two names contained in the word *sukka* is 91. This is also the numerical value of the word *malakh,* "angel."

A Fundamental Symbol: The Act of Love

In the Temple, the *shekhina* resided between two cherubim to teach that the relationship between human beings is the source of the descent of the divine influx into the world. The Kabbalah considers the relationship between man and woman to be the most important one, that which enables the *shekhina* to descend. The Kabbalah perceives a fundamental inversion of images and metaphors. God is made in the image of man, and the relationship between God and the world of men is in the image of the human couple and all the varieties of dual relationships—man-woman,parent-children, master-disciple, and so on. However it is the conjugal, or rather love, relationship that is the favorite metaphor, as the Bible shows in the Song of Songs.

Love, as has been shown in the basic ground plan, is the primary value on which the world rests. This reunion of the beloved and the betrothed is a refrain that runs through kabbalistic literature and is translated at the cosmic level by the reunion of man with the Creator, as a successful experiment performed by the Kabbalah.

This mystical union is called the "*yihud* of the Holy One, Blessed be He and and his *shekhina.*" Thus, prior to any ritual action, the kabbalists pronounce the words "Leshem yihud qudsha berikh hu ooshekhinta" ("For the purpose of the union of the Holy One, Blessed be He, and His *shekhina*").

43

The Secrets of the Tetragrammaton
The Ethical Approach

A Short Metaphysic of the Hand

We shall not take sides in the debate that pits Anaxagoras against Aristotle, nor give priority to the hand over the mind or the mind over the hand. We shall merely point out the existence of the important dialectic that can be found in numerous languages between "taking" and "understanding."

Aristotle, in criticizing Anaxagoras, said, "It is not because man has hands that he is the most intelligent of beings, but because he is the most intelligent of beings that he has hands."

The hand takes, and the mind understands. The hand is captured, and the spirit, through concepts, grasps meaning, takes it in, and understands, so that the words used in philosophical language to convey this act reveal the concreteness of the association. In German, for instance, *Begriff* means "concept," and *begreifen* means "to grasp" or "to understand" intellectually, from the root *greifen,* "to grasp," a term that hints at the brutal action of grasping.

The Stoics used a well-known image to symbolize wise knowledge: "Apart from the sage, no one knows anything." This was demonstrated by

Zenon when he extended his hand, fingers outstretched: "This is the representation," he said, then he folded his hands over slightly: "This is assent." Then he closed his hand completely, making a fist, and said that this was comprehension. This is why he gave understanding the name *kataiepsis*, which had never been used before. Then he brought his left hand down over his closed fist and grasped it firmly, saying that this was "the knowledge that no one possesses except the sage" (reported in Cicero, *First Academics*, Book II, XLVII: 145).

A master of the Talmud, however, began his first lesson by making the following gesture: he brought his left hand over the closed fist of his right hand and grasped it firmly, saying that this was the wisdom of the fool, who thought he knew and who thought that he had captured the world within the mesh of his net; the vicious pride of the small mind, which thinks that it can tame the infinite.

His second lesson consisted in releasing the right fist from the left hand before gradually extending his fingers like the opening of a flower, claiming that this was the way that intelligence flourishes; then he opened his hand entirely, fingers wide apart and open to the possibility of a meeting.

This is the hand made for caresses, he said. It is the hand of the sage who knows that he knows nothing, but who knows the value of the meeting and the gift. Then he crossed his hands and said, "This is the bird of freedom."

Indian dance contains the gesture used by the talmudic master. The lotus bud inaugurates the still hesitant thought; then it opens; the spirit is released and discovers the color of a sky that beckons to infinity.

A spirit opens up, making the graceful movement of transcendence.

The flower becomes a bird.

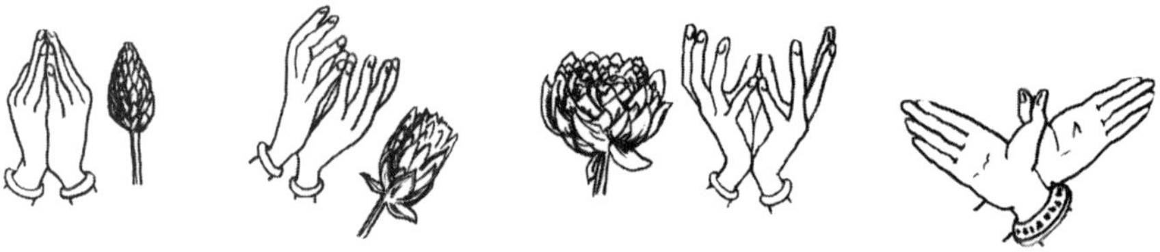

Anatomy and Language

For kabbalists, the closed fist—the hand that seizes or holds—is associated with the letter *yod,* which in fact means "hand."

The open hand, which is mainly represented as the five fingers, is associated with the letter *heh,* which is also the figure 5.

The kabbalists also note that the hand has fourteen phalanges, a number that in Hebrew is written 10 + 4—*yod-dalet*—which forms the word *yad,* "hand." The word for "hand" is thus the result and the connection between the human body, figures, and letters. The anatomical structure of the organ (fourteen phalanges) produces a figure (14) that becomes letters and a word (*yod-dalet* = *yad*).

Rabbi Nachman of Breslov used this discourse on the hand to explain the importance of clapping one's hands during prayer. The two hands combined produce the sum of 14 + 14 = 28, a number that in Hebrew is written *kaf-het,* producing the word *koakh,* which means "strength" or "force."

This force is that which has made it possible to pass from the world of nothingness to that of being. There is an allusion to this through the structure of the first verse of the Torah, which consists of exactly twenty-eight letters, which are called *kaf-khet atvan de ma'asseh bereshit,* "the 28 letters of creation and the action of beginning."

Hand and Time

The importance of the phalanges in early antiquity, in Mesopotamia and Egypt, can be found in the art of arithmetic. Each phalange corresponds to a number from 1 through 12. The thumb is used for counting. One can count up to twelve on one hand, and on the other one can memorize the series of twelves counted, from once to five times. Each finger thus represents one dozen.

The hand with its five fingers constitutes a base of 60, which, like 12, is used as the basis of numerous activities in everyday life, the most important being the clock and the division and scansion of time:

12 hours of day 12 hours of night
60 seconds = 1 minute 60 minutes = 1 hour.

The Talmudic and kabbalistic traditions are very much aware of this method of calculation, which is no doubt inherited from Babylonian culture. There is evidence of this in such Talmudic expressions as "dream is one-sixtieth of prophecy," "sleep is one-sixtieth of death," "visiting the sick removes one sixtieth of the sickness," or "one measure of the forbidden in certain situations is cancelled out by sixty measures of the permitted."

The Priestly Benediction

Here again is an example of the priestly benediction, when the priests extend their hands to the public, saying:

> May the Lord bless you and keep you
> May the Lord make his face to shine upon you and be gracious unto you
> May the Lord lift up his countenance upon you
> And grant you peace.

This blessing in Hebrew contains exactly sixty letters—as if it consisted in bestowing sixty packages, sixty sparks of time, upon the human being, as if the blessing was designed to restore to man the dynamic of time, of strength, and a will to construct the future.

As if it were a curse no longer to have the strength to reinvent oneself, which is renewal and freedom; as if the curse were to cause time to become static, "always here and now," an ineffectual, imprisoned, and violent present.

The Hand and the Tetragrammaton

The masters analyzed the tetragrammaton as the completion of the basic ground plan, which was translated into the actions of "giving-receiving."

The hand that takes an object and encloses it, grasps it in closed hands, describes the letter *yod,* whose actual meaning is "hand." But taking an object is not offering it. The hand must also be open, a sign of wanting to give. This intention is translated into the opening of the hand, into expansion. These are the five fingers of the open hand, the letter *heh.*

But here again, intention is not enough.

The gesture of opening must be extended by a movement of the arm, which extends toward the other. The extended arm is thus in the shape of the letter *vav.* In this diagram, the hand that will receive opens in turn and produces the shape of a second letter, the *heh.*

Yod: closed hand (taken)

Heh: open hand (intention of giving)

Vav: extended hand (movement toward another)

Heh: open hand (receiving)

The tetragrammaton is written each time there is an exchange, each time man remembers that being means sharing.

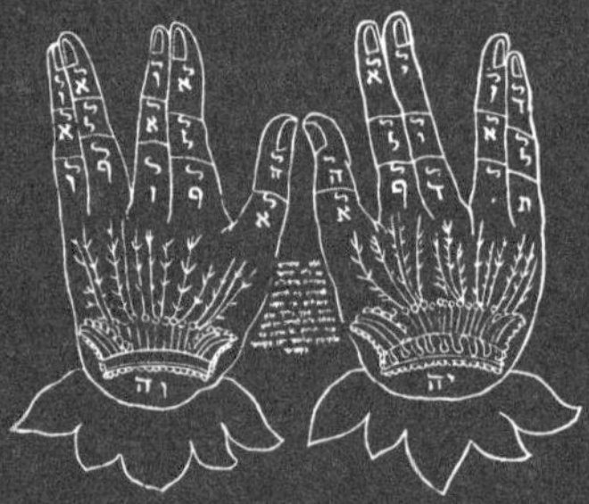

As a Conclusion
If You Want To, You Can

We have now reached the end of our walk through the universe of the Kabbalah. What we have discovered is merely a tiny part of this immense universe. We hope that we have not merely passed through the Kabbalah, but that it has also passed through us. We may be more enlightened, more exalted, and more confident of man's capacity to become better.

We have opened the path; the edifice that we sought to present is far from complete, but we wanted to begin with what we considered to be the fundamentals.

A book is a hand extended for the purpose of the dialogue that we hope to pursue with the readers.

Rabbi Tarfon taught, "You are not required to complete the work, but nor are you at liberty to abandon it" (Avot 2, 16).

Words are life, life is words! But are we yet able to speak? Do we yet know how to hear, to see the words that open the gates to the future for us, the gates of our soul, the gates of a smile, the miracle of a face, a meeting?

Perhaps time has come as a retort to speech, as a retort to traveling words, to words that circulate the joy of being, in the lightness and freshness of a dawn that brings renewed hope of an even higher, freer day. . . .

Let us go, let us walk, let us advance "in the swirl of the swell of wandering words" (Paul Celan).

Words, the right words, in their essence, are the bursting forth of the already-there. They stammer that not everything is static, enclosed in the death of the instant, an orphan without descendants. Somewhere there exists a force that makes it possible to begin, to begin again. History is more powerful than destiny!

Words, the right words, are poetry. . . .

In this book that I have called the Kabbalah.

It is a burst of reading and a burst of time. It teaches that we have a creative force within us, a force of invention and innovation.

A force for receiving the light.

A force for offering it as well.

If you want to, you can.
Son of man, look!
Contemplate the light of the Presence that resides in all existence!
Contemplate the joyful life force of the upper worlds!
See how it descends and impregnates every package of life which you perceive
with your eyes of the flesh and your mind's eye.
Contemplate the wonders of Creation and the Source of all life,
the rhythm by which each creature lives.
Learn to know yourself.
Learn to know the world, your world.
Discover the logic of your heart and the feelings of your reason!
Experience the vibrations of the Source of life which is in your very depths and
above you and all around you.
The love which burns in you, let it rise to your powerful root,
extend it to all the souls of all the worlds.
Look at the lights . . .
Look inside the lights . . .
Rise and rise upward
for you possess a powerful force.
You have the wings of wind,
the noble wings of the eagle. . . .
Do not deny them for fear that they will deny you.
Seek them and immediately they will find you.
(Baal Ha-Orot, The Master of the Lights, *Orot Ha-Qodesh*, I: 64)

Do not be content with "good"! Seek rather to express "goodness."
Be generous, offer your light.

Nothing is written of the way.

It is we who trace them and invent them as we advance.

The Kabbalah teaches us that the flower opens like the wings of a bird.

A master walks along the path.

He shows a flower to his disciple saying:

—You are a bird.

—But I do not have wings! replies the disciple.

—Words are your wings, speak, fly away! Cross space and time, break the chains of a history that does not belong to you and that does not have the right to weigh you down and hold you back. Break through the horizon and find the precious moment of creative tearing asunder, where suddenly things take on a different aspect in an unknown landscape.

Remember that although they have to die, men are not born to die but to innovate, to open themselves up to birth and rebirth. Since you have been born, you are condemned, you are condemned to be free. . . .

Do not forget it!

You possess within you the force to dominate evil, always.

If you fall, pick yourself up!

Never despair.

If you cannot achieve your aim today, you will be able to do so tomorrow, for great is the force of hope.

Now, go! Alone.

Go and discover the world.

If one day you are in distress, call upon my name, and I shall come to help you.

Go! I give you my blessing.

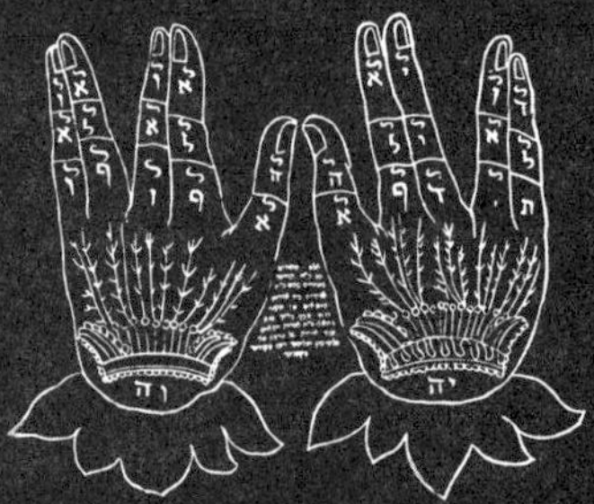

Bibliography

Abécassis, Armand. *Les Temps du partage.* 2 volumes. Paris: Albin Michel, 1993.
Abelson, J. *Jewish Mysticism.* New York: Hermon Press, 1969.
Amado-Lévy-Valensi, Éliane. *La Poétique du Zohar.* Paris: Éditions de l'Éclat, 1996.
Askenazi, Léon (known as Manitou). "Le Cercle et la Droite, transcendance et immanence." *Pardès,* no. 23 (1995).
———. *La Parole et l'ecrit.* Paris: Albin Michel, 1999.
Altmann, Alexander. "A Note on the Rabbinical Doctrine of Creation." *Journal of Jewish Studies* 7 (1956).
Atlan, Henri. *Les Etincelles du hasard.* Paris: Editions Le Seuil, 1999.
Baal Shem Tov. *Shivkhei Ha-Besht* (In praise of the Baal Shem Tov). 2 vols. New York and Jerusalem: A. Weinstock Editor, 1983.
Bakan, David. *Sigmund Freud and the Jewish Mystical Tradition.* Boston: Beacon Press, 1958.
Banon, David. *La Lecture infinie.* Paris: Le Seuil, 1987.
Ben Ish Hai (Rabbi Yossef Hayyim of Baghdad). *The Halakhot of Ben Ish Hai.* Jerusalem: Yeshivat Hevrat Ahavat Shalom, 1989.
Ben Shlomo, Yosef. *Shirat Ha-Hayyim: Poetry of Being.* Translated by Shmuel Himelstein. Tel Aviv: MOD Books, c. 1990.
Béresniak, Daniel. *La Kabbale vivante.* Paris: Trédaniel, 1995.
Berg, Philip S. *The Kabbalistic Connection.* Jerusalem: Kabbalah Research Center, 1983.
Bergson, Henri. *The Creative Mind.* New York: Greenwood Press, 1968
Bible, the. *The Holy Scriptures of the Old Testament.* Bilingual version. London: British and Foreign Bible Society, 1961.
———. *Tanakh: A New Translation of the Holy Scriptures.* Philadelphia: Jewish Publication Society of America, 1985.
Bilski, Emily D. *Golem!* New York: Jewish Museum, 1988.
Blanchot, Maurice. *The Space of Literature.* Lincoln: University of Nebraska Press, 1982.
Bobin, Christian. *L'Homme qui marche.* Cognac: Le Temps Qu'il Fait, 1995.
———. *Le Huitième Jour.* Paris: Lettres Vives, 1986.
———. *Lettres d'or.* Montpellier: Fata Morgana, 1987.
———. *La Vie passante.* Montpellier: Fata Morgana, 1990.
Bokser, Ben-Zion. *From the World of the Cabbalah: The Philosophy of Rabbi Judah Loew of Prague.* New York: Philosophical Libray, 1954.
Brezis, Haïm. *Un Mathématicien juif.* Interviews with Jacques Vauthier. Paris: Beauchesne, 1999.
Buber, Martin. *I and Thou.* Translated by Walter Kaufmann. New York: Scribner, 1970.
———. *Tales of the Hasidim: The Early Masters.* Translated by Olga Marx. London: Thames and Hudson, 1961.
———. *Ten Rungs: Hasidic Sayings.* Secaucus, New Jersey: Carol Publishing Group, 1995.
———. *The Way of Man: The Teachings of Hasidism.* Lyle Stewart, 1995
Casaril, Guy. *Rabbi Siméon Bar Yochaï et la Cabbale.* Paris: Le Seuil, 1964.
Chang, Chung-Yuan. *Creativity and Taoism.* New York: Harper & Row, 1970.
Cohen, Rabbi David Hacohen (called Ha-Nazir). *The Voice of Prophecy: The Hebrew Logic of Listening.* Jerusalem: Mossad Harav Kook, 1978.
Dan, Josef. *The Christian Kabbalah: Jewish Books and their Christian Interpreters.* Jerusalem: Josef Dan, 1998.
Danby, Herbert, trans. *The Mishnah.* Oxford: Oxford University Press, 1933
Deleuze, Gilles. *Differénce et répétition.* Paris: PUF, 1964.

———. *Proust and Signs.* London: Athlone Press, 1933.
Derrida, Jacques. *Adieu to Emmanuel Levinas.* Meridian, Calif.: Stamford University Press, 1999.
———. *Margins of Philosophy.* Chicago: University of Chicago Press, 1982.
Dolto, Françoise. *Dominique: Analysis of an Adolescent.* London: Souvenir Press, 1984.
———. *L'Image inconsciente du corps.* Paris: Le Seuil, 1984.
Eco, Umberto. *Foucault's Pendulum.* San Diego: Harcourt Brace Jovanovich, 1974.
Egli, René. *Le Principe LoL²A: La Perfection du monde.* Paris: Editions d'Olt, 1997.
Elstein, Yoav. *Ekstaza veha-hasipur ha-hassidi* (Ecstasy and the history of Hasidism). Ramat-Gan: Bar-Ilan University, 1998.
Epstein, Perle. *Kabbalah: The Way of the Jewish Mystic.* Boston and London: Shambhala, 1988
Foglio, Hélène. *Yoga, son et prière.* Paris: Le Courrier du livre, 1982.
Franck, Adolphe. *The Kabbalah; or, The Religious Philosophy of the Hebrews.* New Hyde Park, New York: University Books, 1967.
Fromm, Erich. *The Art of Loving.* New York: Bentham, 1956.
———. *Psychoanalysis and Religion.* New Haven, Conn.: Yale University Press, 1950.
Fromm, Erich, et al. *Zen Buddhism and Psychoanalysis.* New York: Harper, c. 1960.
Ganzfried, Rabbi Shlomo. *Kitzur Shukhhan Arukh, Code of Jewish Law.* New York: Hebrew Publishing Company, 1927.
Gaon, Vilna (Elijah ben Solomon). *Likutei Hagra* (Collection of the teachings of the Vilna Gaon de Vilna). With commentary by Rabbi Eizik Haver. 2 vols. Warsaw, 1889.
Gardner, Martin. *Wheels, Life and Other Mathematical Amusements,* New York: Freeman, 1983.
Gikatillia, Rabbi Joseph. *Gates of Light* (Sha'arei Orah). New York: HarperCollins, 1994.
———. *Ginat Egoz* (The nut garden). Jerusalem: Attia Editions, 1990.
Glazerson, Matitiahou. *La Secrets de l'astrologie hébraïque.* Paris: Edistar, 1993.
Goetschel, Roland. *Meir ibn Gabbay: Le discours de la kabbale espagnole.* Leuven: Peeters, 1981.
Gold, Robert. *Dieu et le nombre pi.* Jerusalem: Editions Otniel Bnai Kenane, 1997.
Green, Arthur. *Tormented Master: A Life of Rabbi Nahman of Breslav.* Birmingham: University of Alabama, 1976.
Greenbaum, Avraham. *Rabbi Nahman's Tikkun.* Jerusalem: Breslov Institute, 1984
Gruenwald, Ithamar. *Apocalyptic and Merkavah Mysticism.* Leiden: E. J. Brill, 1980.
———. "The Beginnings of Jewish Mysticism in Europe." *Jerusalem Studies in Jewish Thought* 6, nos. 3–4 (1986): 15–54.
———. "Jewish Mysticism in Transition: from the *Sefer Yetsira* to the *Sefer Ha-Bahir.*" *Jerusalem Studies in Jewish Thought* 6, nos. 3–4 (1986) 15–54.
Guedj, Denis. *Le Théorème du perroquet.* Paris: Le Seuil, 1999.
Halamish, Moshe. "The Place of the Ari as Legislator." In *Fourth Congress of Jewish Mysticism,* edited by R. Elior and Y. Liebes, 259–85. Jerusalem: Bar-Ilan Ilan, 1992.
Halbronn, Jacques. *Le Monde juif et l'astrologie.* Milan: Archè de Toth, 1985.
Halevy, Z'ev ben Shimon (known as Warren Kenton). *Adam and the Kabbalistic Tree.* London: Gateway Books, 1985.
———. *Kabbalah and Exodus.* Bath: Gateway Books, 1988.
———. *Symbols of Judaism.* With M.-A. Ouaknin. New York: Assouline Publishing, 2000.
Heidegger, Martin. *What Is Called Thinking?* New York: Harper & Row, 1968.
Henry, Michel. *La Barbarie.* Paris: Grasset, 1987.
Heschel, Abraham Joshua. *God in Search of Man.* New York: Farrar, Straus, Giroux, 1955
———. *A Passion for Truth.* New York: Farrar, Straus, Giroux, 1973
———. *Tora min Ha-Shamayim* (Theology of Ancient Judaism). 2 vols. London and New York: Soncino, 1965.
Heschel, Abraham Joshua, and Samuel H. Dresner. *The Circle of the Baal Shem Tov: Studies in Hassidism.* Chicago: University of Chicago Press, 1985.

Hoffman, Edward. *Mystique juive et psychologie moderne.* Paris: Dervy, 1988.
Idel, Moshe. "Infinities of Torah in Kabbalah." In *Midrash and Literature,* edited by G. Hartman and S. Budick, 141–57. New Haven, Conn.: Yale University Press, 1986.
———. *Le Golem.* Paris: Éditions du Cerf, 1992.
———. *Kabbalah: New Perspectives.* New Haven, Conn.: Yale University Press, 1988.
———. *Language, Torah, and Hermeneutics in Abraham Abulafia.* Albany: State University of New York Press, 1988.
———. *The Mystical Experience in Abraham Abulafia.* Albany: State University of New York Press, 1958.
———. "The World of Angels in Human Form." In *Studies in Jewish Mysticism and Ethical Literature Presented to Isaïah Tishby,* edited by J. Dan and J. Hacker, 1–66. Jerusalem, 1986.
Ifrah, Georges. *The Universal History of Numbers.* London: Harvill, 1998.
Israël, Lucien. *Cerveau droit, cerveau gauche: cultures et civilisations.* Paris: Plon, 1994.
Jabès, Edmond. *Aely.* Paris: Gallimard, 1972
———. *The Book of Questions.* Middletown, N.Y.: Wesleyan University Press, 1983.
Jacobson, Yoram. *Hasidic Thought.* Tel Aviv: MOD Press, 1998
Jankelevitch, Vladimir. *Le Pardon.* Paris: Aubier Montaigne, 1967
Judah Ben Samuel (Rabbi Yehuda He-Hassid). *The Book of the Pious* (*Sefer Hassidim*). Northvasle, New Jersey: Jason Aronson, 1997.
Kafka, Franz. *Complete Stories.* Edited by Nahum Glatzer. New York: Schocken Books, 1988.
Kahndissepz, Gaetan. *L'Escapade.* Translated from the Spanish by Nadège Spatszi-Kahn. Paris: Imprimerie Impériale, 1863; revised edition, reviewed and corrected by M.-A. Ouaknin, Jerusalem: Editions Clin d'œil, Zag and IFSROM, 1999.
Kaplan, Aryeh. *Meditation and Bible.* York, Maine: Samuel Weiser, 1978.
———. *Meditation and Kabbalah,* York, Maine: Samuel Weiser, 1989.
Katz, Jacob. *Halakha ve-Qabala* (Halakha and Kabbalah). Jerusalem, 1984.
Kook, Rabbi Abraham Isaac. *Hadarav* (Spiritual diary). Jerusalem: Re'ut, 1998.
———. *Mussar Avikha, Midot Rehaya* (Ethics of your father). Jerusalem: Mossad Harav Kook, 1985.
———. *Orot* (Lights). Jerusalem: Mossad Harav Kook, 1990.
———. *Orot Haqodesh* (Lights of sanctity). 4 vols. 2nd ed. Jerusalem: Mossad Harav Kook, 1969.
———. *Orot Hareaya* (The lights of vision). Jerusalem: Mossad Harav Kook, 1985.
———. *Orot Hateshuva* (The lights of return). Jerusalem: Mossad Harav Kook, 1985.
———. *Orot Ha Tora* (The lights of the Torah). Jerusalem: Mossad Harav Kook, 1985.
———. *Rosh Milin* (A mystical work on the Hebrew alphabet). Jerusalem: Mossad Harav Kook, 1985.
Leibovitz, Néhama. *Commentaries on the Book of Exodus.* 13th ed. Jerusalem: Jewish Agency, 1992.
Leloup, Jean-Yves. *Prendre soin de l'être.* Paris: Albin Michel, 1999.
Levi Isaac of Berditchev, Rabbi. *Quedouchat Lévi* (La Sainteté de Lévi). Jerusalem, 1958.
Levinas, Emmanuel. *Beyond the Verse.* London: Athlone Press, 1994.
———. *Collected Philosophical Papers* Dordrecht: Lancaster, Nijhoff, 1994.
———. *In the Time of Nations.* London: Athlone Press, 1994.
———. *Proper Names.* London: Athlone Press, 1996.
Liebes, Yehuda. "New Orientations into Research of the Kabbalah." *Pe'amim,* no. 35 (1992).
———. *The Sin of Elisha: The Four Who Entered Paradise and the Nature of Talmudic Mysticism,* Jerusalem: Hebrew University of Jerusalem, 1986.
Luria (or Louria), Isaac Rabbi (called the Ari or Arizal). *Complete Works.* Edited by Rabbi Hayyim Vital. Jerusalem: Yeshivat Kof Yehuda, 1988.
Maimonides, Moses. *Guide for the Perplexed.* Translated by Salomon Munk. Lagrasse: Verdier, 1979.
Maldiney, Henri. *L'Art, l'éclair de l'être.* Seyssel: Editions Comp'Act, 1994.
———. *Regard, parole, espace.* Lausanne: L'Âge d'homme, 1994.
Menahem Nahum of Chernobyl, Rabbi. *Meor Enayim al hatora, paracha lekh-lekha* (The light of the eyes). 2 vols. New York: Shikun Skvera, 1997.

Menahem Nahum of Chernobyl and Arthur Green. *Upright Practices: The Light of the Eyes.* New York: Paulist Press, 1982.
Mopsik, Charles. *Le Livre hébreu d'Enoch.* Lagrasse: Verdier, 1989.
———. *Les Grand Textes de la kabbale: les rites qui font Dieu.* Verdier: Lagrasse, 1998.
Munk, Elie. *Ascent to Harmony.* New York: Feldheim, 1987.
Musaph-Andriesse, R. C. *From Torah to Kabbalah.* London: SCM Press, 1981.
Nachman of Breslov, Rabbi. *The Empty Chair.* Woodstock, N.Y.: Jewish Lights, 1994.
———. *Liqutei Moharan* (Collected teachings of Rabbi Nachman). Translated by Moshe Mykoff. Jerusalem: Breslov Research Institute, 1990.
———. *Sipurei Maasiyot* (Tales). 1810; new ed., Jerusalem: Breslov Research Institute, 1999.
Nachmanides. *Perush al Ha-Tora* (Commentaries on the Torah). Jerusalem: Mossad Harav Kook, 1978.
Nathan of Nemirov, Rabbi. *Liqutei Halakhot* (Anthology of laws). Commentaries on Hebrew law on the basis of the mystical teaching of Rabbi Nachman of Breslov. 3 vols. Jerusalem: Editions Braslav, 1978.
———. *Liqutei Tefilot* (Anthology of prayers). Jerusalem: Braslov Publishing, 1977.
Neher, André. *Exile of the Word: From the Silence of the Bible to the Silence of Auschwitz,* Philadelphia: Jewish Publication Society of America, 1980.
———. *Le Puits de l'exil.* Paris: Editions du Cerf, 1992.
Ouaknin, Jacques. *De générations en générations, être juif.* Paris: Editions Bibliophane, 1989.
———. *Le Livre et la vie.* Paris: Belles Lettres, 1994.
Ouaknin, Marc-Alain. *Bibliothérapie: Lire, c'est guérir.* Paris: Le Seuil, 1994.
———. *C'est pour cela qu'on aime les libellules.* Paris: Calmann-Lévy, c. 1998.
———. *Le Colloque des anges.* Fata Morgana, Montpellier: 1995.
———. *Concerto pour quatre consonnes sans voyelle.* Paris: Balland, 1991.
———. *Les Dix Commandements.* Paris: Le Seuil, 1999.
———. *Lire aux éclats, éloge de la caresse.* Paris: Points-Seuil, 1994.
———. *Le Livre brûlé.* Paris: Lieu commun, 1986.
———. *Le Livre des prénoms bibliques et hébraïques.* Paris: Albin-Michel, 1997.
———. *The Mysteries of the Alphabet.* New York: Abbeville Press, 1999.
———. *La Plus Belle Histoire de Dieu.* Paris: Le Seuil, 1997.
———. *Tsimtsoum: Introduction à la méditation hébraïque.* Paris: Albin Michel, 1992.
Pirqei de Rabbi Eliézer. Translated by M.-A. Ouaknin and Eric Smilévitch. Lagrasse: Verdier, 1983.
———. English translation. New York: Sepher-Hermon Press, 1981.
Rabinowicz, Harry M. *The World of Hasidism.* Hartford, Conn.: Hartmore House, 1970
Reichelberg, Ruth. *Don Quichotte ou le roman d'un juif masqué.* Paris: Points-Seuil, 1999.
Ricœur, Paul. *The Conflict of Interpretations.* Evanston: Northwestern University Press, 1974.
Rosenzweig, Franz. *L'Etoile de la rédemption.* Translated by A. Derczanski and J.-L. Schlegel. Paris: Le Seuil, 1982.
Rubinstein, Aryeh. *Hasidism,* New York and Paris: Leon Amiel, 1975.
Safran Alexandre. *The Kabbalah,* New York: Feldheim, 1975.
———. *Wisdom of the Kabbalah.* New York: Feldheim, 1991.
Schâfer, Peter. *Synopse zur Hekhalot Literatur.* Tübingen: J.C.B. Mohr, 1981.
Schneerson, Rabbi Menahem Mendel. *On the Essence of Chassidus.* Paris: Tora et Communication, 1990.
Schneour Zalman of Lyadi, Rabbi (called Baal Ha-Tanya). *Likouté Amram, Tanya.* New York: Lyubavitch Foundation, 1980.
Scholem, Gershom. *Jewish Gnosticism, Merkabah Mysticism, and Talmudic Tradition.* New York: Jewish Theological Seminary Press, 1965.
———. *Kabbalah: A Definitive History of the Evolution, Ideas, Leading Figures, and Extraordinary Influence of Jewish Mysticism.* Meridian, Calif.: Stamford University Press, 1974.
———. *Major Trends in Jewish Mysticism.* Foreword by Robert Alter. New York: Schocken Books, 1995.
———. *Le Messianisme juif.* Paris: Calmann-Lévy, 1974.

———. *La Mystique juive, les thèmes fondamentaux*. Paris: Éditions du Cerf, 1985.
———. *On the Kabbalah and Its Symbolism*. Translated by Ralph Manheim. New York: Schocken Books, 1965.
———. *Sabbatai Sevi: The Mystical Messiah*. London: Routledge & Kegan Paul, 1973.
———. *Zohar, the Book of Splendor: Basic Readings from the Kabbalah*. London: Rider and Company, 1977.
Schwarz-Bart, André. *The Last of the Just*. Woodstock, New York: Overlook Press, 1959.
Sefer Habahir: The Book of Clarity. Bilingual edition. Translated by Aryeh Kaplan. Maine: Samuel Wieser, 1989.
Sefer Yetsira: The Book of Creation. Bilingual edition. Translated by Aryeh Kaplan. Maine: Samuel Wieser, 1990.
Shestov, Lev. *Athènes et Jérusalem*. Paris: Vrin, 1959.
Singh, Simon. *Fermat's Last Theorem*. London: Fourth Estate, 1998.
Spinoza, Baruch. *Collected Works*. Translated by Edwin Curley. Princeton, N.J.: Princeton University Press, 1985.
Springer, Sally, and Georg Deutsch. *Left Brain, Right Brain*. New York: Freeman, 1989.
Steinsaltz, Adin. *In the Beginning, Discourses on Chassidic Thought*. New York: Jason Aronson, 1992.
———. *The Thirteen Petaled Rose*. Translated by Yehuda Hanegbi. London: Basic Books, 1985.
———. *The Talmud: The Steinsaltz Edition, with Rashi's Commentary*. New York: Aramaic Random House, 1989.
Tishby, Isaiah. *The Wisdom of the Zohar* (with Fischel Lachower). Translated by David Goldstei. London: Littman Library of Jewish Civilisation, 1989.
Tryon-Montalembert, Renée de. *La Cabbale et la tradition judaïque*. In collaboration with Kurt Hruby. Paris: Retz, 1975.
Tsadoq Hacohen of Lublin, Rabbi. *Kol kitvei* (Complete works). Bnei Brak: Yahadut Publications, 1967–73.
Urbach, Ephraim. *The Sages: Their Concepts and Beliefs*. Translated by Israel Abrahams. Jerusalem: Yad Latalmud, 1987.
Vajda, Georges. *Le Commentaire d'Ezra de Gérone sur le Cantique des Cantiques*. Paris: Aubier, 1969.
———. *Recherches sur la philosophie et la kabbale dans la pensée juive du Moyen Âge*. Paris: Ecole des Hautes Etudes en Sciences Sociales, 1962.
Vigée, Claude. *Dans le silence de l'aleph*. Paris: Albin Michel, 1992.
———. *L'Extase et l'errance*. Paris: Grasset, 1982.
———. *La Faille du regard*. Paris: Flammarion, 1988.
———. *Le Parfum et la cendre*. Paris: Grasset, 1984.
Volozhyn, Rabbi Hayyim of. *Nefesh Ha-hayyim*. Translated by Benjamin Gros. Lagrasse: Verdier, 1986.
Vuillard, Paul. *La Kabbale juive*. Paris: Nourry, 1923.
Weiss Joseph. *Mekhqarim be-Hassidut Braslav* (Studies on Breslov hasidism). Jerusalem: Mossad Bialik, 1974.
Werblowsky, R. J. Zwi. *Joseph Caro, Lawyer and Mystic*. Philadelphia, 1977.
Wiesel, Elie. *Célébration hassidique*. Paris: Le Seuil, 1975.
———. *Contre la mélancolie*. Paris: Le Seuil, 1982.
———. *Le Golem*. Paris-Monaco: Editions Bibliophane-Editions du Rocher, 1999.
———. *Sages and Dreamers*. New York: Summit Books, 1972.
Zarader. Marlène. *La Dette impensée: Heidegger et l'héritage hébraïque*. Paris: Le Seuil, 1990.
Zohar. 24 vols. Commentary by Rav Ashlag, called Hassufam. Jerusalem: Mossad Harav Kook Publications, 1988. See also Scholem, G.

Acknowledgments

The time taken to taken to write a book does not always follow the logic of calendars. Sometimes night becomes day, day becomes night, vacations are taken up with study, and one's availability for our nearest and dearest may sometimes not be all that it ought to be.

Thanks are due to Dory, a wonderful companion, devoted mother, indefatigable first listener and reader whose advice was always relevant and illuminated the paths of thought and writing.

Thanks are also due to Gaddiel-Yonathan (brave soldier of the "890th," *be-hatslaha*!), Sivane-Mikhal, Shamgar-Maor, and Nin-Gal who by their kindness, comprehension, and smiles have recorded their bubbling presence all through the pages of the book.

This book, like the others, owes much to the teachings and advice of my father, Chief Rabbi Jacques Ouaknin, as well as to the encouragement, attention and enthusiasm of my mother Eliane-Sophie. May they both find the same joy that I experience in being able to render them this modest homage.

During my numerous stays in Paris, the warm Sabbath family welcome of Paulette and Marc Hirsch and their children enabled me to find a warm and friendly atmosphere that was conducive to study. Thank you for this art of hospitality.

I should also like to acknowledge my debt of friendship to Myriam and Sabine Pfeffer, as well as Mercedes and Paul Garboua, who for many years, during my stays in Paris, offered me a wonderfully warm reception, which enabled me to be available for study, teaching, and discussion.

The final editing of this book was done in conditions of calm and tranquility, thanks to the warm and friendly hospitality of Isabelle Rousseau, Jacques Aucomte, and little Nour (with the charming foot). May they find here the expression of our deep friendship and warm gratitude! Thanks also to Mariette Bazett, an important link in this chain of friendship, whose remarks and wise criticisms of an initial version of the present work made it possible to do some fruitful rewriting.

This book is the fruit and the product of research which I originally began about 15 years ago, based on research which has appeared in "preparatory" forms of the book in various articles and in my previous works. The material in this book has also been used for various teaching purposes in lectures, seminars, and in the courses I have given at the Department of Comparative Literature of Bar-Ilan University, Israel at the ALEPH Center, the Centre de Recherche et d'Etudes juives (Paris), the Association des amis de l'Aliyah des jeunes, Paris, the Cercle d'étude de l'avenue Bugeaud (Paris), and the Saturday morning and Saturday evening study circle of the Yedidia Community, in Jerusalem.

The ideas developed in this book would never have seen the light of day without the enthusiasm and talent of several "good fairies" (I apologize for having used the same expression in *C'est pour cela que l'on aime les libellules*) whom I should particularly like to thank, namely Monique Sander, Hélène Attali, and Mary Kaplan. My thanks also to Lazare Kaplan (not forgetting Antoine), Claudine Hazout, M. Hayyim Abbou, Elyette Yllouz-Dany, and all those, too numerous to mention, who discreetly but efficiently did all they could to ensure that our meetings of friendship and study should take place under the most favorable conditions.

Over these last few months, at intervals of a few weeks, two close friends and fellow students died suddenly and prematurely, one in Paris, the other in Jerusalem. I therefore evoke the memory of Lydia Messas and Elie Sagroun. May their memory be a blessing!

One is never alone when one writes, even if one sits in solitude over the desk. A book is a thrilling adventure shared by a large number of people whose hospitality, presence, and willingness to listen, as well as their questions and objections, make it possible to think and write. As the Talmud teaches, "I have learned a lot from my masters, and even more from my fellow students, but I have learned the most from those I taught."

Thanks to all the students and companions *(haverim)* whom I taught on courses, lectures, and seminars in Paris, as well as to my colleagues, students, and listeners of Department of Comparative Literature at Bar-Ilan University, who welcomed indulgently, with understanding and friendship, the hesitant and often clumsy beginnings of these reflections and meditations. Week after week, year after year, their vigilant criticism and commentaries opened new paths in study and interpretation and constructed the paths to the Kabbalah with me.

In particular, I would like to thank Ruth Reichelberg, who always encouraged me in my research and gave me much valuable advice, and Professor Gideon Shunami, head of the department, who guided me along the sometimes difficult paths of pedagogy. I also thank Aliza Aldema, the department's administrator.

I should also like to offer warmest thanks to my student and assistant Yifat Diamant, who offered me a key to the understanding of the writings of Rav Kook and mysticism in general.

I should also like to warmly thank Rav Menahem Brod of Kfar Habad, who generously gave of his time to help me penetrate the hidden secrets of *Hassidut Habad.* Thanks also to Rav Barukh Blizinski, the Rosh Yeshiva at Kfar Habad, who brought us together, and to Hayyim Liss.

May Mindy and Hayyim Korenberg find the expression of my warmest friendship here and my thanks for their hospitality and their passion for the same field of study.

I also acknowledge the contributions of Franck Lalou and Laziz Hamani, and thank them for having used their arts to embellish the book and make it beautiful.

This book is also an example of teamwork, from a team which shares the same passion for books and for thought.

I thank all of the team at Editions Assouline and very especially Julie David and Eléonore Therond, who guided me in producing the final copy and images for this text. I thank them for their kindness, expertise, and constant availability in dealing with the poetic overenthusiasm of the author.

Thanks are also due to Valérie Solvit, who, through her bridge-building art enables books to come to life, to travel and open up to the benevolent gaze of readers and critics.

Thanks again to Martine Assouline, my editor, so patient and talented, who always smilingly, in friendship but in firmness, was able to see this work through to its conclusion.

And finally, finally *(akharon, akharon khaviv),* my friendliest greetings and thanks to Prosper Assouline, without whom none of this would have happened!

Index

Cover: Diagram of the *sefirot.*
Pages 25, 345, 409 : © Photo Laziz Hamani/Editions Assouline.
Pages 36, 107, 247 : © Alinari-Giraudon, Paris.
Page 257 : © S. Oppenheim, Londons/D.R.
Page 287 : © Calligraphie Frank Lalou.
Where illustrations are not credited, the source cannot be identified.

The quotations used in this book are extracted from works mentioned in the bibliography. Where the work in question was originally written in French or Hebrew, the translation is that of the translator of this book, unless there is a specific mention to the contrary.

Graphic design: Éléonore Therond
English text design: Misha Beletsky
French text editor: Josiane Attucci
English editor: Susan Costello
Production editor: Ashley Benning
English translation: Josephine Bacon
Production manager: Louise Kurtz

The text of this book was set in Minion. Printed and bound in USA.

First Edition
10 9 8 7 6 5 4 3 2 1

Library of Congress Cataloging-in-Publication Data

Ouaknin, Marc-Alain
[Mystères de la kabbale. English]
Mysteries of the kabbalah / Marc-Alain Ouaknin.
p. cm.
Includes bibliographical references.
ISBN 0-7892-0654-4 (alk. paper)
1. Cabala—History. I. Title.

BM526 .O93 2000
296.1'6—dc21 00-03228